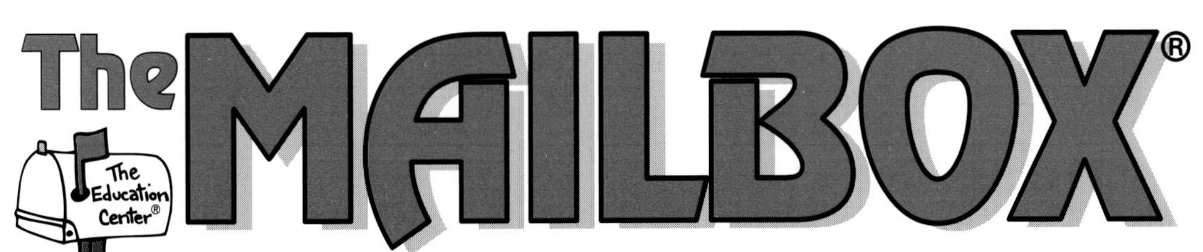

The Idea Magazine For Teachers®

KINDERGARTEN

2002–2003

YEARBOOK

Leanne Stratton, Managing Editor, *The Mailbox* Magazine
Deborah G. Swider, Managing Editor, *The Mailbox* Yearbook

The Education Center, Inc.
Greensboro, North Carolina

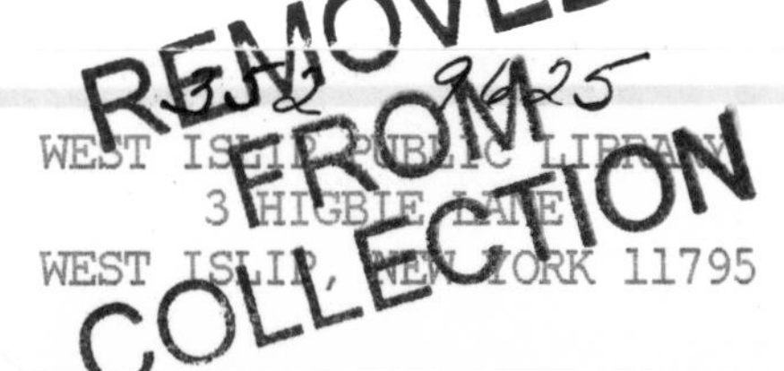

The Mailbox® 2002–2003 Kindergarten Yearbook

MANAGING EDITOR: Leanne Stratton
EDITOR AT LARGE: Diane Badden
STAFF EDITOR: Kimberly A. Brugger
COPY EDITORS: Tazmen Carlisle, Karen Brewer Grossman, Amy Kirtley-Hill, Karen L. Mayworth, Kristy Parton, Debbie Shoffner, Cathy Edwards Simrell
ART DEPARTMENT: Pam Crane, Nick Greenwood, Clevell Harris, Rebecca Saunders (SENIOR ARTISTS); Theresa Lewis Goode, Ivy L. Koonce, Sheila Krill, Clint Moore, Greg D. Rieves, Barry Slate, Donna K. Teal
THE MAILBOX® COMPANION.COM: Jennifer Tipton Bennett (DESIGNER/ARTIST); Stuart Smith (PRODUCTION ARTIST), Karen White (INTERNET COORDINATOR); Paul Fleetwood, Xiaoyun Wu (SYSTEMS)
COVER ARTIST: Lois Axeman
FOUNDING EDITOR IN CHIEF: Margaret Michel
PUBLISHER: The Education Center, Inc.
CHAIRMAN, CEO: Stephen Knight Pond
EXECUTIVE DIRECTORS: Katharine P. S. Brower (MAGAZINE PUBLISHING); Joseph C. Bucci (PRESIDENT, THE MAILBOX BOOK COMPANY™); James R. Martin (FINANCE AND OPERATIONS)
CURRICULUM DIRECTOR: Karen P. Shelton
EDITORIAL PLANNING: Kimberley Bruck (MANAGER); Debra Liverman, Sharon Murphy, Susan Walker (TEAM LEADERS)
EDITORIAL AND FREELANCE MANAGEMENT: Karen A. Brudnak; Hope Rodgers (EDITORIAL ASSISTANT)
EDITORIAL PRODUCTION: Lisa K. Pitts (TRAFFIC MANAGER); Lynette Dickerson (TYPE SYSTEMS); Mark Rainey (TYPESETTER)
LIBRARIAN: Dorothy C. McKinney
PREPRESS: Rhonda Ramsey (MANAGER)
MARKETING: Stephen Levy
MARKETING SERVICES: Lori Z. Henry (MANAGER); Vickie Corbett (ASSISTANT MANAGER); Georgia B. Davis, Troy Lawrence, Leslie Miller

ISBN 1-56234-551-6
ISSN 1088-5528

Printed in the United States of America.

The Education Center, Inc.
P.O. Box 9753
Greensboro, NC 27429-0753

Contents

All Together Now

All Together Now

Who's in the Spotlight?

Social Skills, Language

Help your new kindergartners get acquainted with the help of this flashy activity! Have students stand in a circle. Invite one child to stand in the center of the circle and hold a flashlight. Instruct youngsters to say the chant below while the child in the center spins slowly, flashing the light on the students in the circle. At the end of the chant, have her stand still and name the child who is "in the spotlight." Then have the identified child take her place in the center of the circle and hold the light for the next round.

Round and round the flashlight twirls,
Shining on the boys and girls.
Will it stop on you or me?
One more spin and we will see!
I see...

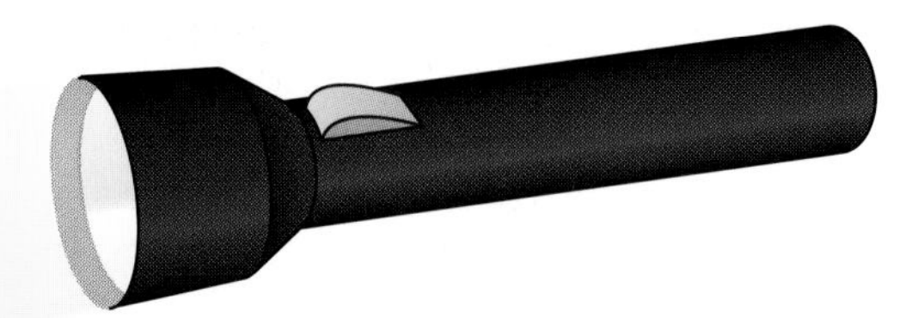

Karen Pasiuk
Old Saybrook, CT

Summer Memories

Language

Say farewell to summer by packing summer memories in a suitcase! Then help each youngster create a record of his summer vacation to share with the class. In advance, make a class set of the suitcase pattern on page 18. Pack a small suitcase with items that represent some of your summer activities, such as a bathing suit, shells, a beach ball, and vacation photos. At circle time, unpack the suitcase and tell your students about your summer vacation. Then give each student a copy of the suitcase pattern. Have him draw pictures on it to illustrate some of his summer memories. Then, after each child has had a chance to "unpack" his suitcase for the group, invite him to cut out the pattern and glue it in his journal. Good-bye, summer. Hello, kindergarten!

Jenny Drake—Gr. K, Southampton Academy, Courtland, VA

We Are Alike; We Are Different

Social Skills, Multiculturalism

Try this poster project to help emphasize to your little ones that all people are unique and special, but share many similarities too. In advance, take a head-and-shoulders photo of each child in your class. After discussing which characteristics people share and what things make each person unique, invite youngsters to look through magazines and cut out various pictures of people. Then label a sheet of poster board as shown. Have students take turns gluing the photos and picture cutouts onto the poster to make a collage.

Jennifer Weimann—Gr. K
Wollaston Child Care Center, Quincy, MA

The Missing Gingerbread Men

School Orientation

Help your new kindergartners get to know their school by conducting a hunt for some missing gingerbread men—with this fun twist. Prepare the dough for gingerbread cookies ahead of time; then let little ones help you roll it out and cut out the cookies. Take the cookies to your school kitchen along the way to a special class, such as P.E. or music. While your students are in their special class, bake the cookies, put them on a plate, and place the plate at the final stop of your planned tour. Put the empty pan back in the oven. Then, after their class, take the whole group to the kitchen to retrieve the cookies. Take the empty pan from the oven and say, "Oh no! The gingerbread men are missing!" Ask students to speculate about where the gingerbread men might have gone; then take youngsters on a tour of the school. They'll be thrilled to finally find the missing cookies at the last stop!

Andrea Marsh—Gr. K, Westside Elementary, Westmoreland, TN

Passport, Please

Social Studies

Introduce your students to a world of excitement when you do a once-a-month study of a foreign land! Gather youngsters on a magic carpet—a special area rug—and whisk them away to another country. Teach them how to say hello in the country's native language, allow them to taste a food from the region, do a related craft, and play a typical game. At each stop, have youngsters add a representative stamp or sticker to a passport. To make a passport, simply staple a few quarter sheets of paper together. Glue a child's photo onto the front and add her name. As you "visit" each country, write the country's name on a page and add a special stamp or sticker. Invite one child to be the passport checker for each country. Instruct him to stamp the date on each student's page. At the end of the year, each child will have a record of when and where she went on your marvelous magic carpet!

Rajean Shepherd—Four- and Five-Year-Olds
Kids First Preschool, North Platte, NE

B Is for Bubbles!

Phonemic Awareness

Spend some time in the sun blowing bubbles and building phonemic awareness! Seat youngsters in a circle on the grass outside. Have one child stand in the center of the circle. Blow some bubbles for the child to pop. As she pops each bubble, have her name a word that begins with the letter *B*. Vary the activity by choosing other letter sounds or by having students name colors, shapes, or classmates' names. Pop, pop, pop—the learning doesn't stop!

Millie Morris—Gr. K
Berkmar United Methodist Church, Lilburn, GA

All Together Now

Yeehaw!

Social Skills, Following Directions

Enhance a Wild West theme with this group game. Designate one child to be It. Divide the remainder of the group into threes. Have two children in each threesome hold hands to form a corral. Have the third child stand inside the corral and play the part of a little dogie, or calf, that's been rounded up! When the animals are in the corrals, have It give a starting signal by shouting, "Yeehaw!" Each little dogie then ducks out of her corral and runs to a new one. At the same time, It tries to run into one of the corrals. The little dogie left without a corral becomes It for the next round. Now that's some mighty fine fun!

Susan Bunyan—Gr. K, Linn Elementary School, Dodge City, KS

Part to Part

Language

Help youngsters learn the names for body parts with this fun partner activity. Pair up students and have the partners face one another. Call out a body part and have each student touch that body part to the same part on his partner. They'll soon be back-to-back, thumb-to-thumb, or knee-to-knee! Hee hee!

Melissa Lopez—Gr. K, Primitivo Garcia World Language School
Kansas City, MO

A Web of Spider Facts

Science

Studying spiders in October? Have little ones show off their arachnid knowledge while they weave this way cool web! Seat students in a circle. Give a ball of yarn to one child. Have him hold on to the end of the yarn and tell something he knows about spiders. Then have him continue to hold the end of the yarn as he tosses the ball to a child across the circle. Have the recipient state another spider fact, hold on to the yarn, and toss the ball to someone else. Continue until every child has had a turn and you'll have a supersized spiderweb!

Linda Ploch—Gr. K
Lutheran Church of the Cross Day School
St. Petersburg, FL

Moon Walk

Dramatic Play

Use your imagination and ignite those of your kindergartners with an imaginary trip to the moon! Using the style of the traditional rhyme "We're Going on a Bear Hunt," make up your own story about a visit to space. Have youngsters act out putting on space suits, climbing into a rocket ship, and blasting off to the moon! Be sure to make a soft landing, exit the ship, and take a walk on the surface. For a climax to the story, explore a moon cave and encounter a space creature; then quickly make your exit back to the rocket, doing the previous actions in reverse order. Ready? We're going on a moon walk.

Randalyn Larson—Gr. K, Memorial School, Jackson, MI

Thumbs Up for Colors!

Color Recognition

There are so many fun movement activities to help youngsters learn colors, but many require students to stand or move around the room. If you don't have the room or want a quieter version, try this tip! Give each child a colored Unifix cube to place on his thumb. When a game or song requires students with a certain color to stand up, have youngsters put their thumbs up instead!

Jodi L. Hanson—Gr. K, St. Helens Elementary School
Longview, WA

Sound Machine

Letter Recognition, Phonics

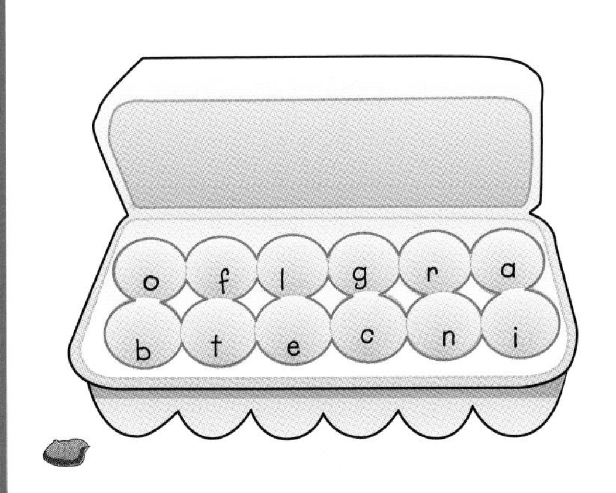

Make your own sound machine by recycling an empty egg carton! Randomly write 12 letters inside the cups of the egg carton. Then drop in a small pebble or a bingo chip. Have a child close the carton, turn it upside down, and shake it. Then have her turn it right side up and open it. Ask her to make the sound of the letter the pebble or chip has landed on.

Make this activity more of a challenge by transforming the sound machine into a spelling machine! Place three pebbles or bingo chips in the carton. Operate the machine the same way, but try to form a three-letter word with the three letters in the cups with pebbles.

Davena Cecil—Gr. K, St. Angela Merici School
Owensboro, KY

All Together Now

Hoop Groups

Social Skills, Language

Help your kindergartners discover what they have in common with this fun musical activity! Lay several Hula-Hoop toys on the floor and designate the number of students that may stand inside each one. Play music and have youngsters move around the hoops. When you stop the music, have each youngster step inside a hoop. Then have students in each hoop group talk to discover something they have in common, such as a food they like to eat, a color they are wearing, or a game they like to play. Then restart the music and have youngsters move again until it's time to form new hoop groups and find something else in common.

Millie Morris—Gr. K, Berkmar United Methodist School, Lilburn, GA

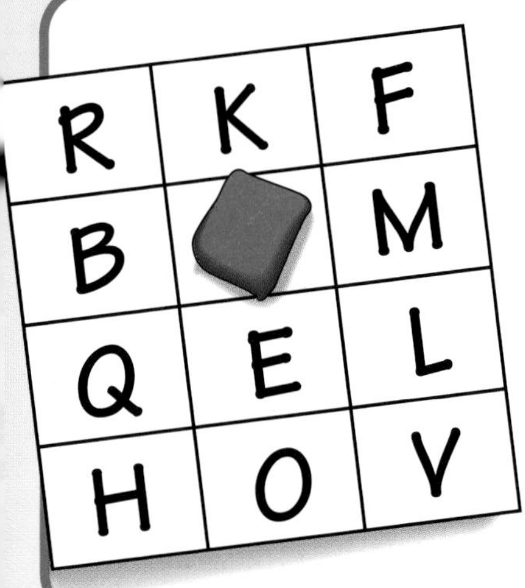

Toss 'n' Learn

Skill Review

Toss some fun into skill review with this idea! Make a number of review posters, each focused on a different skill area, such as letter identification, number identification, or beginning consonants. To make a poster, draw lines on a sheet of poster board to make a grid. Inside each space, write a letter or numeral for youngsters to identify or glue a clip art picture for rhyming or beginning sound review. Seat youngsters in a circle and place the poster on the floor in the center. Hand a beanbag to one child and ask her to toss it onto the poster. Have her identify the letter or number, or name a rhyming word or beginning consonant for the item shown in the picture. Then continue with the next child in the circle. Make plenty of posters, because your youngsters will want to keep tossing and learning!

Michelle Brown—Gr. K, Watervliet Elementary, Watervliet, NY

Skill-Packed Show-and-Tell

Basic Skills

Little ones love to show off their personal treasures during show-and-tell time. Squeeze extra learning into this traditional time by asking skill-based questions when a child shares an item. For example, if a child brings in a toy car, ask, "How many cars do you have in your collection? What letter is at the beginning of the word *car?* Can anyone name a word that rhymes with *car?*" What an easy way to slip in skills!

Millie Morris—Gr. K

Traveling Gingerbread Man

Social Studies

Spend the month of December learning about the travels of a runaway gingerbread man! First, compose a letter from the little old woman in this classic tale and enclose the recipe for a gingerbread man. Also include a warning to watch out, because he may get away! Have students help you follow the recipe and leave the cookie man in your cafeteria to bake. Then discover with your little ones that, of course, he's run away! (Place the cookie in the freezer for later use.) Make arrangements with friends far and wide to send postcards that tell how they've spotted the runaway cookie near their homes. Add a gingerbread-man sticker to your U.S. or world map to mark the origin of each card. Build a trap—a box decorated as a house—with candy inside and watch youngsters' excitement when they one day find the gingerbread man napping inside!

Linda Herman—Gr. K, Knights Elementary, Plant City, FL

Tic-Tac-Toe on the Floor

Logical Thinking

Make a tic-tac-toe grid on your carpet and invite your kindergartners to put their game-winning strategies to work! To make the grid, use the hook side of Velcro fastening strips. (They'll stick to the carpet without leaving sticky residue.) Cut paper plates into Xs and Os for a basic game, or use laminated die-cut shapes, such as evergreen trees and snowmen, to match the season. Who's ready for a game of tic-tac-toe?

Marie-Josee LeBlanc—Senior Kindergarten, Robeta Bondar Public School
Ottawa, Ontario, Canada

Winter Inside the Classroom

Language, Math

Kindergartners will enjoy playing in the "snow" inside your classroom! Bring out a super supply of cotton balls to serve as snowballs. Encourage youngsters to use the cotton balls to form letters, numbers, or shapes. Then invite them to have a friendly "snowball" fight by tossing the cotton balls at one another! Then hand out plastic shovels and have students shovel all the snow back into a container for use on another snowy day indoors!

Diane G. Williams—Gr. K, Seven Pines Elementary, Sandston, VA

Celebrating 100 Days

Math, Snack

To celebrate the 100th day of school, dress as if you were 100 years old! Use gray hair-coloring spray on your hair, walk with a cane, wear an old pair of glasses on your nose, and dress as a 100-year-old lady (or gentleman) might. Then show your kindergartners that 100-year-olds can still have plenty of energy by cooking up a snack in the shape of the number 100! Give each child a sausage link to represent the number 1. Then give her a precut (but not separated) mini bagel and have her ponder how she might make this one circle resemble the two zeros in the number 100. Soon someone will discover the trick of pulling the halves of the bagel apart, and each child's 100th Day snack will be complete!

Amy West—Gr. K, Olive Branch Elementary, Portsmouth, VA

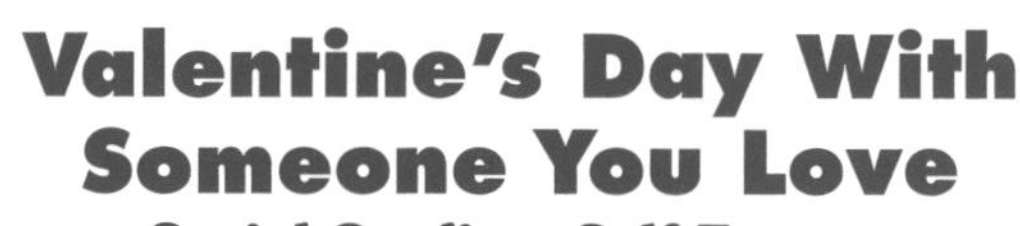

Valentine's Day With Someone You Love

Social Studies, Self-Esteem

You know how much your kindergartners enjoy your class Valentine's Day party each year. This year, make it even better by having each child invite a special loved one (perhaps a grandparent) to join the celebration! Have the visiting adults spend the day and join in on Valentine's Day crafts, snacks, and reading. Then invite students to open their valentines and have the adults help with reading them aloud. There's going to be a lot of love in your classroom!

Jo Vargo—Gr. K, H. C. Burgard School, Manheim, PA

The Caboose Is Loose!

Motor Skills, Following Directions

Every child will want to be last in line when you play this fun outdoor game! Have children line up one behind another. Have the child in front walk, run, skip, or do whatever action she chooses as the others follow and imitate her. At some point, shout, "The caboose is loose!" At this time, the last child in line—the caboose—becomes It and begins to chase everyone else as they scatter and try to avoid being tagged. The child who is tagged becomes the caboose for the next round of play, and the former caboose becomes the leader. What fun!

Kimberly Bush—Gr. K, Oakland Pre-K and Kindergarten, Oakland, NJ

Circle-Time Jar

Review

Help your students review concepts, skills, and songs they've learned throughout the year with the help of a simple jar! Each time you cover a new theme or skill with your class, jot down review questions or write down names of songs you've taught the class on individual slips of paper. Keep the slips of paper in your Circle-Time Jar, and continue to add to the jar throughout the school year. Each day at group time, pull out a slip (or two) and ask the question or announce the name of the song. Then invite students to answer or have everyone sing. Okay—who remembers the words to our Johnny Appleseed song?

Shannon Adams—Gr. K, Waxahachie Faith Family Academy
Waxahachie, TX

Who Took the Valentine From the Mailbox?

Language

Do your students like to play Who Stole the Cookie From the Cookie Jar? Then they'll love a seasonal interpretation of this favorite chant! Try playing Who Took the Valentine From the Mailbox? in February or Who Stole the Shamrock From the Leprechaun? in March. Make up your own variations for other months of the year!

Andrea Jeremiah—Gr. K, Moffett Public School, Moffett, OK

Letter Freeze

Phonics, Movement Skills

Put a phonics twist on a kindergarten favorite—freeze dance! Before you begin the music, say, "When the music stops, I want you to touch an object that begins with the letter *T*." Start the music and invite everyone to dance and move freely. Then stop the music and watch as everyone scurries to touch an object that begins with *T*. When all the children are "frozen" near their objects, give directions for the next pause in the music, such as "Next time, touch an object that begins with *R*." Then start the music again for more dancing and more letter-sound searching!

Kimberly Bush—Gr. K, Oakland Pre-K and Kindergarten, Oakland, NJ

All Together Now

Mystery Reader

Language

This name-oriented version of the traditional game Hangman helps students learn about vowels and consonants. To prepare, write "Mystery Reader" at the top of a board. Then make two columns labeled "Vowels" and "Consonants." Secretly choose a child to be the Mystery Reader, and write one blank for each letter in that student's name at the bottom of the board. Spelling that name is the purpose of the game!

To begin, have a student volunteer name a vowel and make its sound. Write the vowel in the "Vowels" column. Then students may ask if the letter is in the name of the Mystery Reader. If it is, write it in the proper blank. If not, cross it out. After listing and asking about all the vowels in the name, repeat the procedure with the consonants. When the Mystery Reader's name is revealed, have him help with choosing a book, reading a story, or using props during storytime.

Shannon Martin—Gr. K, Provena Fortin Villa, Bourbonnais, IL

Mystery Reader

Vowels: i, e, u

Consonants: g, p, t, l, k, r

P _ t r i _ k

A New Take on Attendance

Language, Thinking Skills

Squeeze learning into every portion of the school day—even attendance taking! Instead of having students respond to their names by saying, "Here" or "Present," ask them to respond by naming something in a particular category, such as a color, a shape, a vegetable, a type of weather, an animal, a book title, or any other thing that comes to mind. You might even have students choose the topics for attendance! Encourage each child to provide a unique answer when it's her turn. What an easy way to encourage thinking skills, listening, and speaking!

Melody Morris—Gr. K, Noel Elementary, Noel, MO

Star Pass

Language, Math

No one will want to pass up this fun activity! Seat students in a line, one student behind another. Give the first child in the line a cardboard star cutout. Then show him a flash card with a number or a letter to identify, a word to read, or a simple addition problem to solve. If the child answers correctly, he may pass the star to the child behind him. If he answers incorrectly, he gives the star to the child behind him and then moves to the back of the line for another turn later. When the star has made it all the way down the line, reward all your star students with gold star stickers!

Nancy Newberry—Gr. K, Cornerstone Academy, St. Louis, MO

Name That Noise!

Listening Skills, Logical Thinking

Here's a game that sounds like fun! In advance, record a variety of common sounds, such as a telephone ringing, a dog barking, a microwave beeping, and a clock ticking. Have youngsters listen to the tape and try to identify each sound they hear. As a follow-up, invite each of your noise detectives to record sounds at her own house and bring in the tape for the class to hear. Ready for another round of Name That Noise?

Rona Forman—Gr. K, The Mill Basin School, Brooklyn, NY

Duck, Duck, Guess

Thinking Skills

Play this new game similarly to the traditional Duck, Duck, Goose, but with a twist that will get your kindergartners thinking! Before seating everyone in a circle, put a small picture card necklace (see illustration) around each child's neck so that the card is in the back where the child can't see it. Play the game just like Duck, Duck, Goose until someone lands in the center of the circle. Then have the children in the circle give the child in the center clues about the picture on her card. When she guesses the picture, she may leave the center of the circle and be It for the next round of play.

Katie Morrow—Speech and Language
Watervliet Elementary, Watervliet, NY

Attribute Bugs

Sorting and Classifying

Help your kindergartners discover Venn diagrams with an activity that incorporates creativity and family involvement! Send each child home with a zippered plastic bag containing a few art supplies and a note asking parents to help their child create a bug. On half the notes ask for a bug *with* spots, and on the other half ask for a bug *without* spots. When everyone has brought in his creation, lay all the bugs on the floor outside of two plastic hoops. Ask students to sort the groups into the hoops by an attribute, such as spots/no spots. After a few rounds of sorting into distinct categories, give a sorting rule that allows for a bug to fit into *both* hoops. Someone will suggest overlapping the hoops, and your little ones will understand the purpose of a Venn diagram!

Kay Wisner—Gr. K, Alto Elementary, Alto, MI

All Together Now

Move and Read

Reading

Reinforce sight words with this musical activity that will also get little muscles moving! To prepare, make a supply of large cards labeled with sight words that you want your kindergartners to practice. Hang the cards high on your classroom walls or suspend them from your ceiling. Then play some music and ask students to hop, jump, dance, or stomp. When you stop the music, direct each child to stand under the sign closest to her. Ask a student volunteer to read the word on her sign. Then start the music again and give a new movement direction for more moving and reading fun!

Barbara Rochell—Gr. K, Waynesboro Elementary, Waynesboro, TN

The Letter Dance

Phonics

Here's a toe-tappin' tip for helping youngsters review letter sounds! Cut out large uppercase and lowercase versions of letters; then use clear Con-Tact paper to adhere the letters to your floor. Turn on some music and invite children to dance as they wish. Then stop the music and ask everyone to touch a foot to a letter on the floor. Ask a few volunteers to name words that begin or end with each letter. Then start the music again for more dancing. Stop again and repeat the activity, inviting other children to name words. Continue as student interest dictates; then try the activity again on a different day with different letters.

Lynne Christ—Gr. K, Galloway Kindergarten Charter School, Smithville, NJ

Lights, Camera, News!

Language, Social Studies

Increase career awareness and speaking skills with this fun twist on classroom jobs! Each day, stage a newscast in your classroom with one student as the anchorperson (to go over the calendar and events) and one as the meteorologist (to talk about the weather). Set up a table and chairs to serve as a news desk and post your calendar and weather information nearby on a wall. If desired, write out a simple fill-in-the-blank script for the students to memorize and recite each day, substituting the appropriate information. You might even videotape each child performing her job; then show the tape at the end of the year and invite each child to enjoy her turn in the spotlight!

Melinda Pitzer—Grs. K–1, Germantown Elementary, Germantown, IL

Tornado Words

Reading

You may have a reading whirlwind in your room when you try this tip for reviewing sight words! To prepare, write a sight word on each side of an index card. Make a large supply of these two-sided cards. Then use these cards for "tornado words." Show a child one side of a card and have him read the word; then twist it quickly around and have him say the word on the other side. Continue twisting the card back and forth, having the child read the two words faster and faster!

Diane Graham—Gr. K, Starry Elementary School, Marion, IA

End-of-the-Year Luau

Social Studies

Teach a bit about Hawaii as you help your kindergartners celebrate the end of the year. First, have each youngster make a paper lei. Die-cut a large supply of flowers (about 30 per child); then have students use a pencil point to punch a hole in the center of each cutout. Next, instruct students to string the flowers onto lengths of thick yarn. For a special Sand Snack, prepare a class-size batch of vanilla pudding. Then give each child a plastic bag with three vanilla cookies in it. Have each youngster crush her cookies. Then have her layer the pudding and crushed cookie sand into a snack cup. Add a few gummy fish for fun and serve with Hawaiian Punch drink! Play Hawaiian music and invite youngsters to try their hands (or hips) at hula dancing or the limbo!

Jennifer Neri—Gr. K, Rolling Hills Primary School, Dix Hills, NY

America the Beautiful

Language, Social Studies

Here's a perfectly patriotic idea for an Independence Day activity! After teaching youngsters the song "America the Beautiful," get them involved in making a class big book based on the song. Make a page for each phrase in the song's lyrics. Then have each child help illustrate one of the pages. For example, a child might draw or paint a sky scene for the words "Oh, beautiful, for spacious skies" or a mountain scene for "purple mountain's majesties." Ask each family to send in a special picture or photo they feel illustrates the beauty of our country. Attach the photo to the page that reads "America! America!" You're sure to get a unique and beautiful book!

Shelly L. Kidd-Hamlett—Gr. K, Helena Elementary, Timberlake, NC

Suitcase Pattern

Use with "Summer Memories" on page 6.

Arts & Crafts for Little Hands

Arts & Crafts for Little Hands

Snakes Alive!

Your youngsters will eagerly await the chance to wear these slithery creatures home! In advance, gather and straighten a wire coat hanger for each child. Cut a snake's tongue from red craft foam for each child. Help each youngster wrap newspaper around the wire and then secure the paper with tape. Form each snake, as shown, so the student will be able to wear it around the neck. Have each child dip newspaper strips in liquid starch and then wrap them around the snake. When the starch is dry, invite each student to paint his snake. After the paint dries, have each child attach sticky dots for eyes and glue a tongue to the mouth. S-s-super!

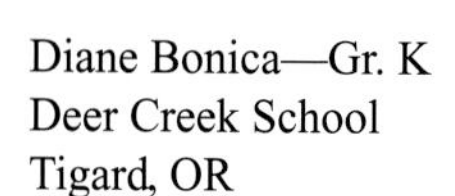

Diane Bonica—Gr. K
Deer Creek School
Tigard, OR

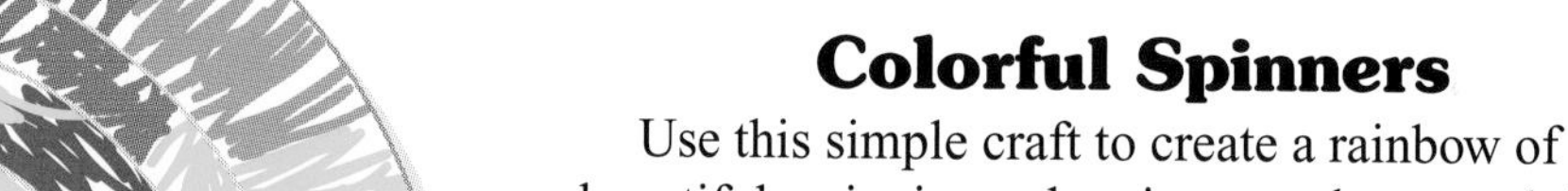

Colorful Spinners

Use this simple craft to create a rainbow of beautiful, spinning colors in your classroom! Give each child a paper plate and a supply of markers. Have her color the entire plate using a variety of colors. Then help each child push a brad through the center of the bottom of her plate and fasten it on top as shown. Now, encourage your little ones to spin, spin, spin their spinners!

Anne M. Cromwell-Gapp—Director
Connecticut Valley Child Care Center
Claremont, NH

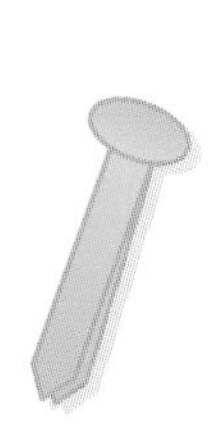

Johnny Appleseed Hats

Follow up a reading of *Johnny Appleseed Goes a-Planting* by Patsy Jensen by making these silvery hats. Provide each youngster with a 7" x 7" piece of tagboard, a 14-inch length of aluminum foil, and a 2½" x 8" piece of black construction paper. Cut a 1½-inch-wide strip of gray construction paper long enough to fit around each child's head and overlap slightly. Then guide each child through the steps below to complete his Johnny Appleseed hat. Hats off to you, Johnny Appleseed!

Directions:

1. Wrap the tagboard square with foil.
2. Cut the black paper into an oval shape to make a handle.
3. Staple the handle to the pot.
4. Staple the headband to the pot
5. Staple the headband to fit the child's head.

Robin Goddard—Gr. K
Mt. Vernon Elementary
St. Petersburg, FL

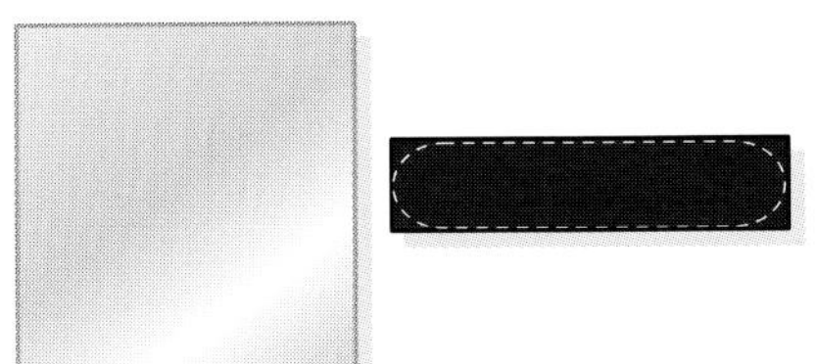

Apple Trees—One Foot Tall

These little apple trees make a big impression on all who see them! In advance, prepare a large container of warm, soapy water for easy cleanup. Have each child cut a treetop from green construction paper and then glue it to the top of a light blue sheet of construction paper as shown. Next, have her step in a shallow pan containing a thin layer of brown paint. To create a tree trunk, help each youngster position her foot on her paper and make a print. Then have her clean her foot with soapy water. Next, have her use a red bingo dauber to print apples on her tree. It's harvest time!

Diane Bonica—Gr. K
Deer Creek School
Tigard, OR

Arts & Crafts for Little Hands

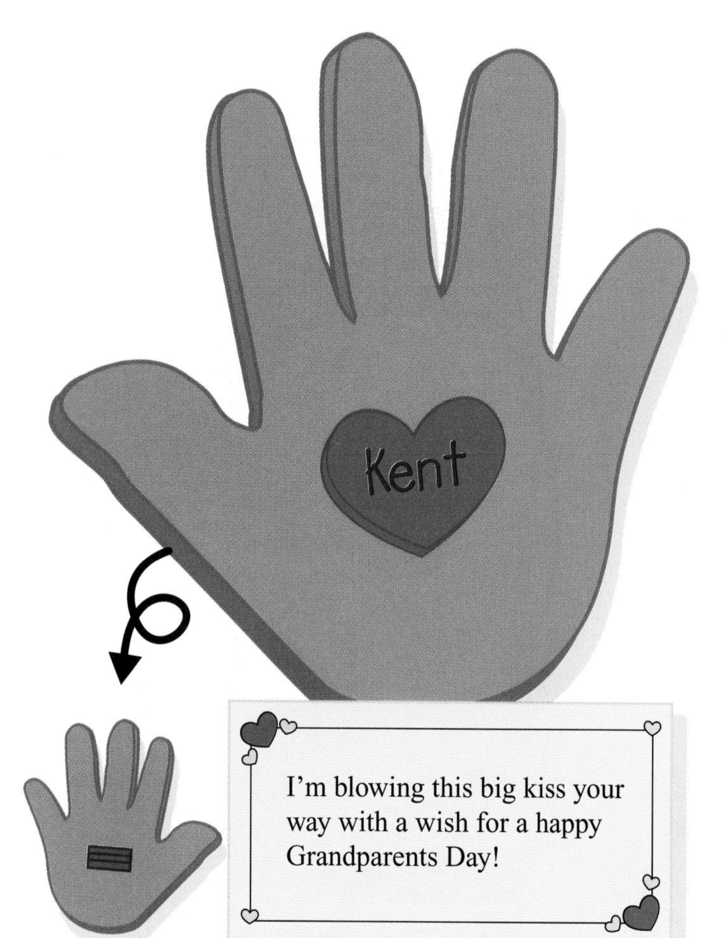

Grandparents Day Magnet

This sweet gift will remind grandparents that their grandchildren love them! To prepare, cut a 4" x 6" piece of flesh-toned craft foam in an appropriate color for each child. Cut 1½-inch hearts from red craft foam to make a class supply. Cut magnetic tape into one-inch pieces. Write the provided saying on paper and then photocopy it to make a class set. Have each youngster trace his hand on a piece of craft foam and then cut out the resulting shape. Use a permanent marker to write each child's name on a heart cutout. Instruct the child to attach a piece of magnetic tape to one side of the hand cutout and glue his heart to the center of the other side. If desired, have students make a magnet for each set of grandparents. Have your little ones present the magnets to their grandparents along with the printed notes. Happy Grandparents Day!

adapted from an idea by Susan Page—Gr. K
Thompsontown-Delaware Elementary
Thompsontown, PA

"Scent-sational" Painting

Your budding artists will be eager to complete these lovely smelling works of art! Have each youngster paint red flowers or hearts on a sheet of white construction paper. Before the paint dries, have the child sprinkle sugar-free strawberry gelatin powder on the wet paint. Then help her shake the excess from her paper. If desired, have each student add more details to her painting using a different color of paint. Then instruct her to sprinkle a different flavor of sugar-free gelatin over the newly painted area. Ahhh—art that's beautiful to the eyes and the nose!

Handy Bat

Put little hands to work creating this adorable bat! In advance, cut a bat body shape for each child from black construction paper. Have each youngster place both hands on a sheet of black construction paper as you trace around them. Cut out the hand shapes; then help the child glue the thumb of each cutout behind the bat body as shown. Next, have him make two white-paint thumbprint eyes and a thumbprint nose on the bat's face. Have him complete his bat by using a white crayon to draw a happy smile!

adapted from an idea by Deb Knott—Art
St. Anne's School
Wabasso, MN

Fall Hat

You won't "be-leaf" how cute these hats are! To make one, glue two 3" x 12" brown construction paper strips together end to end to make a headband. Label the front center of the headband "Happy Fall!" Next, staple three brown pipe cleaners to the front center of the headband; then add some masking tape over the staples on the back side to avoid scratching. Have each child select three real fall leaves and then tape one to the top of each pipe cleaner. Next, have each child bend the pipe cleaners in various directions to create a pleasing design. Fit each child's headband around his head and staple the ends in place.

Johanna Litts—Gr. K
North Central Elementary
Hermansville, MI

Arts & Crafts
for Little Hands

In a Pile of Leaves

What's the next best thing to rolling in a pile of real fall leaves? Making a picture of yourself doing just that! To prepare for this project, take your little ones on a nature walk and collect a good supply of small fall leaves. Press the leaves between the pages of a book to flatten them for several days. When the leaves are flat and dry, begin the project by gluing a flesh-toned paper circle to a piece of yellow construction paper for each child. Have each youngster decorate her circle to look like her. Then give her several dry leaves to glue around her face. Add the poem shown to each child's project.

Janette Shoemaker—Gr. K
Prairie View School
Oregon, WI

Chalk and Water Art

Here's an anytime art experience your kindergartners will love! First, fill a sink or large container with water. Have each child use a handheld pencil sharpener to sharpen sticks of colorful chalk into the water. Do *not* mix the chalk into the water—allow the chalkdust to float. You'll be able to see a swirling design form. Next, have a child lay a sheet of white construction paper on top of the water and press down very gently. Have him lift the paper off the water's surface and lay it design side up to dry. Can he see the swirl design on his paper? Cool!

Debbie Rowland

Scissors to Snowman

Snip your way to this snazzy snowman—he's easy to make! Fold up one long edge of a sheet of 9" x 12" white construction paper about $3\frac{1}{2}$ inches. Use scissors to cut slits about an inch apart along the fold, being careful not to cut all the way to the edge of the paper. Unfold the paper; then roll it from one short end to the other to create a tube. Glue the paper in place. Have each child use a black marker to add eyes and a mouth. Instruct him to glue on a nose cut from orange construction paper. Then have him cut a long strip of construction paper in any color and glue it around the neck of his snowman to form a scarf, allowing the ends to stick out. Finally, help each child thread a length of yarn through two holes punched in the top of the snowman. Tie the yarn into a loop, and hang the snowman to display.

Johanna Litts—Gr. K, North Central Elementary
Hermansville, MI

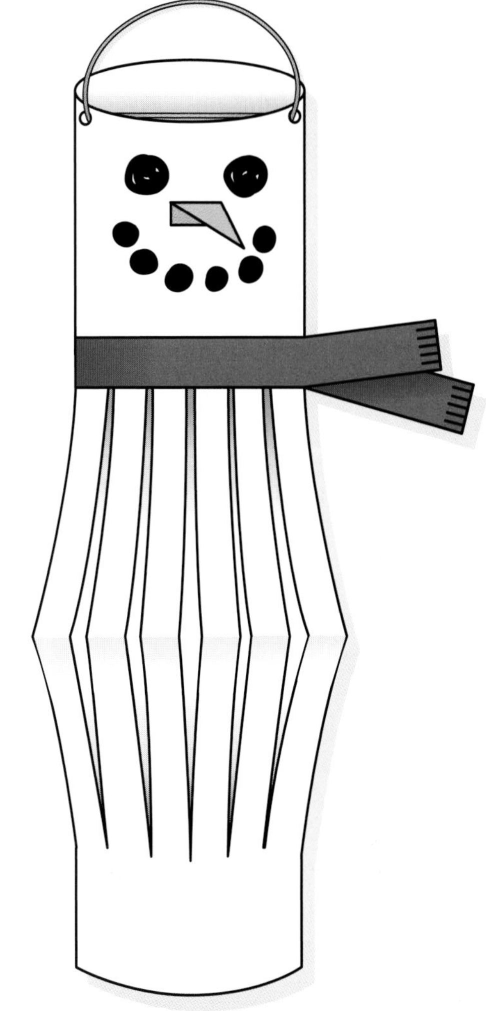

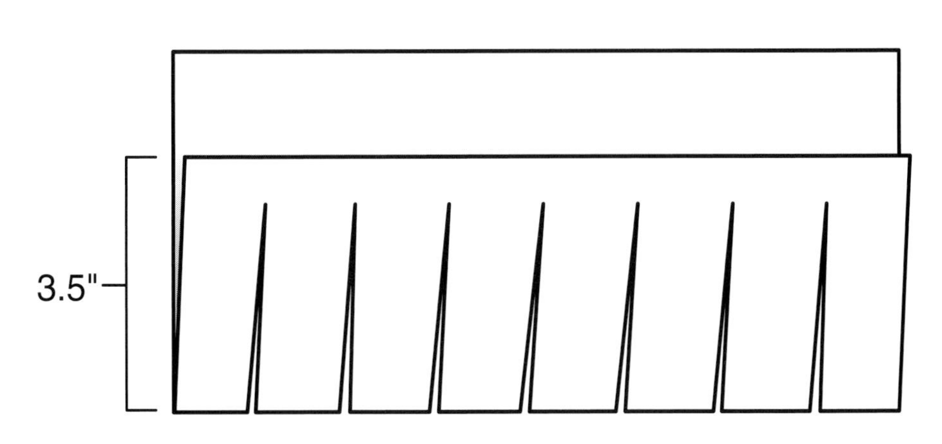

Shimmering Snowflake

A stencil makes this snowflake a cinch! To prepare, duplicate the snowflake stencil pattern on page 37 on tagboard. Cut out the outer circle; then laminate the stencil. Use an X-acto knife to carefully cut out the snowflake pattern in the center of the stencil.

Place the stencil in the center of an uncoated nine-inch paper plate. To ensure the stencil stays in place during use, use pushpins to attach the plate and stencil to a bulletin board within students' reach. Have each child select a bingo dauber and use it to dab color on the stencil to make a snowflake on her plate. Next, remove the plate and stencil from the wall. Invite the child to use glitter glue to add sparkly accents to her snowflake. Finally, punch a hole near the edge of the plate and add a loop of ribbon for hanging. Look, a beautiful blizzard has just blown into your classroom!

adapted from an idea by Kari Zimmerman—Gr. K, Juda School, Juda, WI

Nifty Nutcracker Hat

Your kindergartners will march right over to make this holiday headband! In advance, cut a class supply of thin white paper plates as shown, keeping the rim pieces. Also, for each child, trim an 8" x 8" square of blue construction paper to resemble the top of a nutcracker's hat as shown. To complete the project, have each child draw a nutcracker face and several curls of hair on the white paper plate. Staple the blue hat piece to the nutcracker's head. Then lay a rim piece across the bottom of the hat and cut the rim to fit. Staple the rim in place and have the child color it red. Instruct him to tape two bright craft feathers to the blue hat piece; then have him add a fancy gold-seal sticker. Attach the nutcracker face to a sentence-strip headband and staple the band to fit the child's head. This nutcracker is ready to wear!

Diane Gilliam
Virginia Beach, VA

Musical Paper Angel

This singing angel is la-la-la-lovely! Gather the materials listed below and then guide each child to follow the directions to complete her angel.

Materials (for one angel):
paper cup
sheet music paper (cut to fit around the cup)
tape
paper doily (cut in half)
Styrofoam ball
pink tissue paper squares
glue
markers
yarn
small bow

Directions:
1. Turn the paper cup upside down. Wrap the music paper around the cup and tape the edges in place.
2. Tape two doily halves to the back of the cup to create wings.
3. Glue the tissue paper squares onto the Styrofoam ball, covering it completely.
4. Use markers to draw eyes and a mouth on the Styrofoam ball.
5. Glue yarn to the ball to resemble the angel's hair.
6. Glue the head to the bottom of the cup.
7. Glue the bow below the head.

Carol Ann Bloom, State College, PA

Snowman Votive

Parents' eyes will light up when they see this cute holiday gift! To make a candleholder, paint a child's index finger with white acrylic craft paint. Have him press his finger onto the side of a clear or blue glass votive candleholder. Repeat the process two times, making a total of three fingerprint snowmen. When the paint is dry, have the child use fine-tip permanent markers to add eyes, a nose, a mouth, arms, and buttons to each snowman. Place a votive candle inside the holder and attach a copy of the poem shown, signed by the child.

Denise Fischer—Gr. K
William Bryant Elementary
Blue Springs, MO

Frosty Frame

Send home a photo in this merry frame! To make one, cut a 4" x 4" square of craft foam. Cut out the center of the square or, if desired, die-cut the center of the square with a holiday design, such as an evergreen tree. To decorate the frame, have a child paint a wooden ice-cream spoon with white tempera paint. Have her use glitter glue to add eyes, a nose, a mouth, and buttons to the spoon snowman. Then have her glue on a top hat cut from craft foam. Use hot glue to attach the finished snowman to one corner of the craft-foam frame. Glue or tape the child's photo to the back of the frame so that it shows through the opening. Then add strips of magnetic tape to the back, or punch a hole in the top and add a loop of ribbon for hanging. Too cute!

adapted from ideas by
Stacey Helders-Peran—Gr. K
Prince of Peace School
Milwaukee, WI

Kris Rangel—Gr. K
St. John's School
Glenwood City, WI

Arts & Crafts for Little Hands

Two Liters of Love!

Two-liter soda bottles make inexpensive and sturdy containers for valentines! To make a valentines holder, cut a clean, empty bottle at the top of the label; then remove the label completely. Hot-glue a wide decorative ribbon over the cut edge of the bottle to protect little fingers. Next, punch two holes on opposite sides of the bottle; then thread a ribbon through the holes and tie a knot at each end to make a handle. Now the bottle is ready for a child to decorate with heart-shaped sponges and tempera paint, paint pens, stickers, and glitter glue. Beautiful!

Kristy Helton
Open Arms Ministry
Vienna, MO

Hearts and Photos

These Valentine's Day keepsakes are sure to warm parents' hearts! To make one, paint a small wooden frame with pastel tempera paint. Next, use tacky craft glue to attach candy conversation hearts around the frame's opening. When the glue is dry, use school glue to paint over the candy hearts to seal them. When dry, put a picture of the child—sporting a pair of heart-shaped sunglasses—inside the frame!

Lynne Novak—Gr. K
St. Joseph School
Spruce Grove, Alberta, Canada

A Portrait of George

George Washington, that is! Have youngsters make these likenesses of the first president to celebrate Presidents' Day!

Materials for one:
head shape cut from skin-toned construction paper (approximately 6" x 6")
hat shape cut from blue construction paper (6" across the top)
6" strip of yellow construction paper
black and white construction paper scraps
7 cotton balls
red marker
semicircle cut from blue construction paper (7" on the straight side)
half a round 6" paper doily
glue
scissors

Directions:

1. Glue the hat shape onto the top of the head cutout.
2. Glue the six-inch yellow strip across the hat as shown; then trim the ends to follow the shape of the hat.
3. Cut two small white circles and two smaller black circles from the construction paper scraps. Glue them together to form two eyes; then glue the eyes to the face.
4. Use the marker to draw a nose and mouth.
5. Glue three cotton balls to each side of the face to make George's wig. Pull one cotton ball into two parts and glue these in place to make eyebrows.
6. Glue the doily atop the blue semicircle; then glue this in place below the chin.

Kathleen Rose—Gr. K, Park Falls Elementary, Park Falls, WI

Lincoln's Logs

Encourage your young artists to "build" these cabins in honor of Abraham Lincoln. Have each child glue eight wooden craft sticks to a sheet of white construction paper as shown. Give each child a door precut from brown construction paper, two windows precut from yellow construction paper, and a triangle roof precut from black construction paper. Have each child glue the paper shapes in place, adding details with crayons or markers to the windows, door, and scene as he wishes. Then invite him to finish his project by writing or dictating a sentence about Abe Lincoln at the top of his paper.

Robin Miller—Gr. K
Ganns-Middle Valley School
East Ridge, TN

Lucky Leprechaun Lid

These hats are a hoot! To make one, have each child glue a precut yellow construction paper buckle onto a strip of black construction paper. Help him wrap the black strip around a decorative green foil plant wrapper and glue it in place. Have him finish his leprechaun hat by gluing precut construction paper shamrocks all over it!

Deb Ernat—Gr. K
Holy Family School
Oglesby, IL

Dotted Rainbow

Gather bingo markers in all the colors of the rainbow for this dot-next-to-dot art project! On a sheet of white construction paper, have each child dab a purple bingo marker several times to form a small arch as shown. Then have her continue with blue, green, yellow, orange, and red bingo markers, making larger arches each time until she forms a full rainbow.

If you don't have bingo markers in every color, make smaller rainbows on half sheets of paper. Simply have a child dip a thumb into each color of paint and make thumbprints!

Leah Taylor—Gr. K
Maranatha Chapel School
San Diego, CA

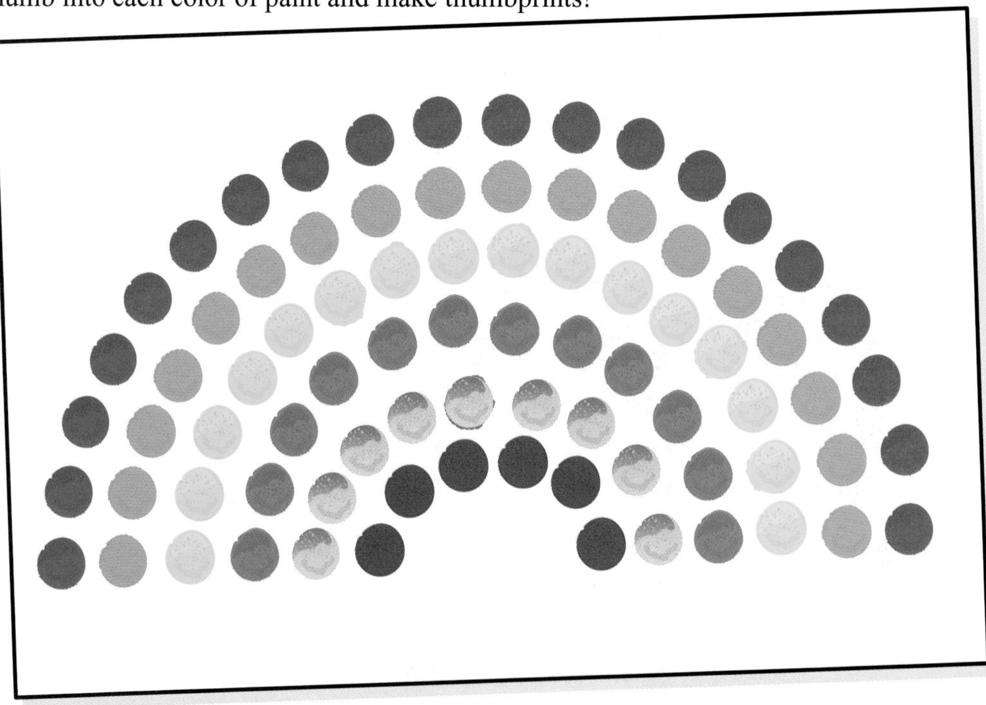

Arts & Crafts
for Little Hands

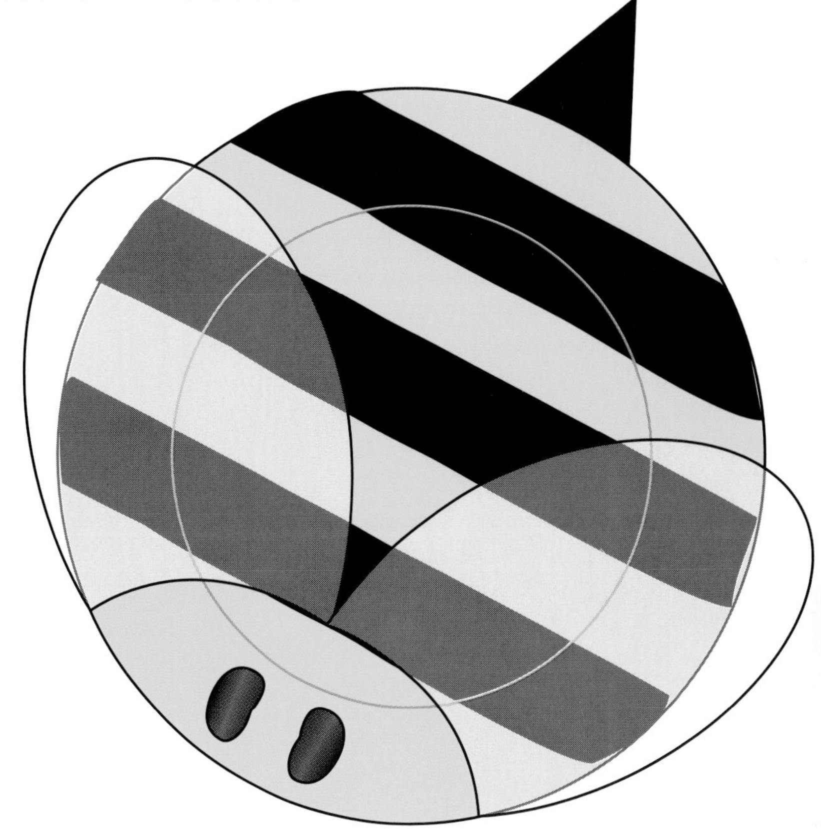

Bees to Behold!

Youngsters will make a beeline to create these cute critters! To make one, paint the back of a small paper plate bright yellow. When the yellow paint is dry, paint on black stripes, plus a curved line for the bee's head. When the black paint is dry, glue two waxed paper wings on top of the bee's body. Then glue a black construction paper stinger to the underside of the bee's body. Complete the bee by gluing on two black beans or plastic gems for eyes.

Leanne Gibbons—Grs. K and 1
Boston Public Schools
Mattapan, MA

Funny Bunny

These cute bunnies will be sure to step into your classroom! To begin, a child glues the rim of a white paper plate to the bottom half of a 12" x 18" sheet of dark construction paper. He glues on a pom-pom nose, pipe cleaner whiskers, and two big wiggle eyes. Next, have the child take off his shoes and socks. Paint the bottoms of both his feet with white tempera paint; then have him make two footprints above the paper plate. When the paint has dried, use a white crayon to make bunny-ear outlines around the footprints. Attach to each bunny a copy of the poem shown; then send the projects home for parents to enjoy!

Diane Bonica—Gr. K, Deer Creek School, Tigard, OR

Click Beetle

After sharing Eric Carle's story *The Very Clumsy Click Beetle,* invite your young artists to make click beetles of their own. For each child, cut a body-and-head shape (about ten inches long) from white oaktag. Cut a hole $1^{1}/_{2}$ inches in diameter near the center of the body. For the wings, cut an oval the same size as the beetle's body from white construction paper; then cut a slit through the center, stopping about an inch from one end. To complete the beetle, a child uses watercolors to paint the beetle's body black, the head blue, and the wings green or yellow. Hot-glue the lid of a baby food jar over the hole in the body; then staple the wings over the lid as shown. Have each child glue on green and black tissue paper circles to make the beetle's eyes. Then just have him press on the jar lid to hear his beetle click!

Lori Hosking, Milford Hill Learning Center
Milford, PA

Juice Can Maracas

Celebrate Cinco de Mayo and shake things up with these fun maracas! Ask parents to help you save frozen-juice cans and their lids. When you have a class supply, have each child decorate a $4^{1}/_{2}$" x 9" piece of white construction paper with colorful markers or scraps of tissue paper. Glue the paper around a can; then partially fill it with rice, dried beans, dried lentils, or pea gravel. Use colorful masking tape to attach the lid to the can. Then play the maracas to music with a Mexican beat!

Carla Houchin—Gr. K, Davis Elementary
College Place, WA

A Pin for Mom

Moms love jewelry, especially jewelry made by their children! So your students will be proud to present these wooden flower pins to their moms on Mother's Day. In advance, purchase a class supply of pin backs and small wooden shapes, such as hearts, along with a pretty flower stamp that will fit within the wooden shape. To make a pin, a child stamps the flower design onto the wooden shape and then colors it in with colored pencils. Spray or brush on a coat of clear acrylic sealer and allow it to dry thoroughly. If desired, have the child sand the edges of the wood a bit to give it an antique look. Then hot-glue a pin back in place and wrap the gift. This present is ready for giving!

Jennifer Bragg—Gr. K, Sunset Heights Elementary School, Nashua, NH

How "Tweet"!

These feathered friends are a perfect springtime project! First, have a child cut a zigzag line along the top of a brown or white paper lunch bag. Ask her to stuff some shredded newspaper into the bottom of the bag; then have her wrap a pipe cleaner around the bag about four inches from the top and twist it to hold the bag closed. Help her fold down the cut edge of the bag. Then have her paint the bag as she desires. Next, hot-glue a satin Christmas ball to the top of the bag (where the folded edge is). Have the child cut out a beak from orange construction paper and punch out two black paper dots for eyes. Hot-glue these to the bird's face; then hot-glue a craft feather to the back of the head so that it sticks up as shown. Have the child place the finished bird in a grapevine wreath nest.

Jane Conner—Gr. K, Falmouth Elementary School
Falmouth, VA

Arts & Crafts for Little Hands

Splendid Fish Stamps!

Dive into the book *Swimmy* by Leo Lionni with these fabulous fish prints! In advance, collect a class supply of figure eight–shaped foam packing pieces. Cut the end off of each packing piece as shown. Provide students with access to stamp pads with red and black ink. To begin the activity, read *Swimmy* aloud. Then give each child a 12" x 18" sheet of white construction paper and a packing peanut. Instruct the child to draw a large fish on his paper. Next, have him ink a packing piece with red ink and then print fish shapes on his illustration as shown. Instruct each child to use the same process to print his fish's eye with black ink. When the ink is dry, direct each child to cut out his fish and then glue it onto a 12" x 18" sheet of blue construction paper. If desired, invite him to draw or paint other ocean-related items around his fish. This project is sure to make a splash!

Kim MacMullett, Philadelphia, PA

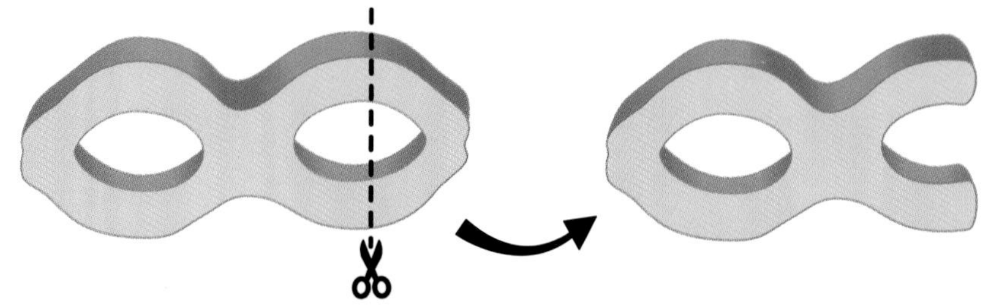

Star-Spangled Display

Use pasta to make this memorable flag display! In advance, create a supply of red rigatoni pasta by combining one box of rigatoni, one-eighth cup of red food coloring, and one-half cup of rubbing alcohol in a resealable plastic bag. Allow the pasta to sit for five minutes, turning the bag every minute to evenly coat the pasta. Lay the pasta on a brown paper bag and allow it to dry completely. Next, program a class supply of 8" x 10" white tagboard pieces with the American flag pattern as shown.

To begin the activity, give each child a piece of tagboard and 27 pieces of pasta. Instruct her to glue her pasta onto every other stripe on the flag as shown. Then give each child a 3" x 4" piece of blue construction paper and 13 silver star stickers. Explain to the class that the first American flag had 13 stars on it to represent the 13 colonies. Direct each child to place her star stickers onto her construction paper piece and then glue it in the upper left corner of the flag. Display the flags on a bulletin board with the title "Hooray for the Red, White, and Blue!"

Ann Schmidt—Gr. K, Lafayette Christian School, Lafayette, IN

A Fireworks Display!

Create an instant and safe fireworks extravaganza with this simple project! In advance, collect a class supply of empty film canisters; then make a hole in the lid of each one. Cut a large supply of 16-inch curling ribbon lengths in a variety of bright colors. To begin, instruct each child to paint a thin layer of glue on the sides and bottom of a film canister. Then have her lightly sprinkle glitter onto the wet glue. Assist her in pulling several lengths of curling ribbon through the hole in the lid. Knot the ribbons together under the lid. When the glue has dried, have each youngster place the lid on her canister. Take students outside to a large play area and encourage them to throw their fireworks into the air. Oooh! Ahhh!

Andrea Lovejoy—Five-Year-Olds
Park's Edge Preschool
Hales Corners, WI

Tropical Feathered Friend

Put little hands to work to create this perky parrot! To prepare, make a class set of tagboard copies of the parrot pattern on page 38. Cut a large supply of colorful tissue paper strips. Instruct each child to cut out his parrot pattern. Then have him color both sides of the parrot, adding an eye to the back side of the pattern. Instruct each youngster to cut on the dotted lines to create wing and tail-feather openings. Next, help each child thread tissue paper strips into the openings, as shown, to create wings and tail feathers. Finally, punch a hole near the top of the parrot and add a loop of yarn for hanging. Polly want a cracker?

Cindy Richey—Gr. K
Weber-Hardin Elementary
Mathis, TX

Hot-Air Balloons

Your little ones will be bursting to make these colorful hot-air balloons! To prepare, gather and clean a class supply of individual-serving milk cartons. Measure three inches up from the bottom of each carton; then cut off and discard the remaining portion. Gather the materials listed below and then guide each child to follow the directions to make her own hot-air balloon.

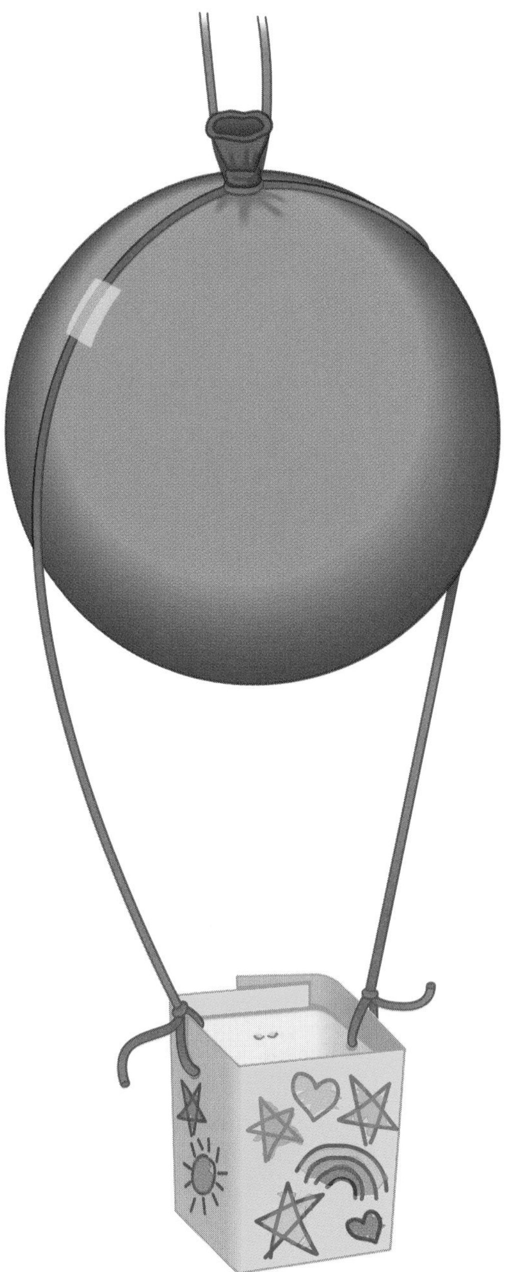

Materials for one hot-air balloon:
individual-serving milk carton (cleaned, dried, and trimmed)
3" x 11" construction paper strip
stickers, markers, and crayons
stapler
hole puncher
2 lengths of yarn
inflated balloon
tape

Directions:

1. Use stickers, markers, and crayons to decorate the construction paper strip.
2. Wrap the strip around the milk carton and staple it into place.
3. Hole-punch opposite sides of the milk carton.
4. Tie the middle of a yarn length to the stem of the balloon.
5. Tie the ends of the yarn to either side of the carton as shown. Tape the yarn in place.
6. Tie another length of yarn to the stem of the balloon and then hang to display.

Brenda Hume—Gr.K, Child Development
Sangaree Elementary
Summerville, SC

Lovable Ladybug Rocks

Your students will go buggy for these ladybug rock keepsakes! To prepare, gather a class supply of small, smooth stones. Have each child paint a stone with red acrylic paint. When the paint is dry, direct the child to use a black permanent marker to add details such as eyes, a shell dividing line, and spots. Have students take these cute critters home to share with their families.

Jeni Van Buer—Gr. K
Prince of Peace Academy
Clinton, IA

Snowflake Stencil Pattern

Use with "Shimmering Snowflake" on page 25.

Parrot Pattern

Use with "Tropical Feathered Friend" on page 35.

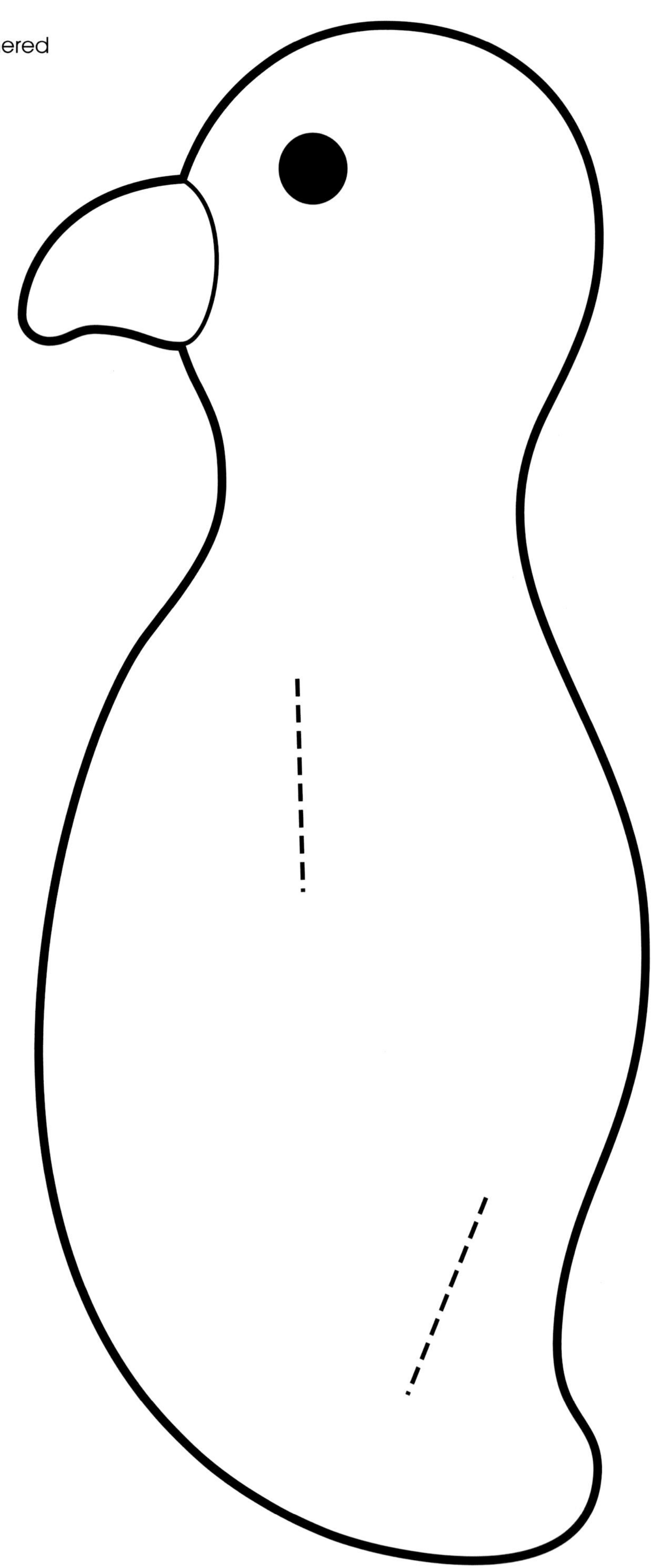

Book Features

A Beasty Story

Written by Bill Martin Jr. and Steven Kellogg
Illustrated by Steven Kellogg

Four adventurous mice set out on a colorful journey through the dark, dark wood and into a dark, dark house. Along the way they encounter many dark, dark colors that lead to a spooky surprise ending!

by Donna K. Battista

Light the Candles

Get your students in the mood to hear this tale by reading it by candlelight! In advance, have each child bring a small flashlight from home. Label each flashlight so it can be returned to its owner. To make a candle, tape a six-inch square of yellow tissue paper around the top of a flashlight; then twist the top edges together as shown. To make the candle glow, simply turn on the flashlight. Dim your classroom lights if possible and have each child hold a lit candle while you read the story. How's that for a spooky effect?

Flashy Learning

Your own flashlight will come in handy for this simple review activity. Turn off classroom lights and use a flashlight to shine light on different colors, numbers, or letters throughout the room. Invite students to call out the color, number, or letter featured in the spotlight.

Six Little Candles

Simple addition and subtraction practice takes place with this tasty activity. Provide each child with a napkin, six pretzel sticks (candles), and six red hots candies (flames). Have students use these manipulatives to calculate the answers to the problems you give them. For example, you could say, "Lily lit her candle and Willy lit his candle. How many candles were lit all together?" or "Six mice were carrying bright candles through a dark, dark house. All of a sudden, two candles went out. How many candles were still lit?" After several problems have been calculated, invite youngsters to eat their tasty candles!

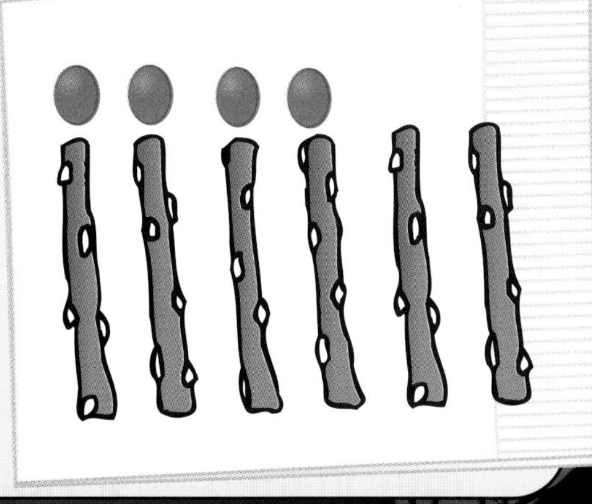

A Beasty Color Recount

A few squares of colorful paper are all you need to reinforce color recognition and listening skills. For each child, cut a set of three-inch construction paper squares, using the colors shown in the book. Give each youngster a set of squares and then reread the story. Each time a color is mentioned, have students hold up the corresponding paper square. After reading the story, ask questions such as "What color were the stairs?" or "Which color was mentioned after blue?" Have students respond by holding up the appropriate color.

A Moving Story!

Set up an obstacle course with simple props to help your youngsters retell the story. To set up the course, tape brown bulletin board paper to the outside of your classroom door to represent the house. Inside the classroom, place several red sponges in a row on the floor to resemble the stairs. Then use blue yarn to outline a large area on the floor to show the basement. Next, cover a small table with purple bulletin board paper to make the closet. Under the table place a green plastic soda bottle for the bottle and a box of white tissues for the beasties.

Invite small groups of students to complete the course, retelling the story as they go. Have students step through the doorway, over the sponges, into the square, and look under the table. After youngsters have looked at the green bottle, have them say "Boo," grab a tissue beasty from the box, and then complete the course in reverse to simulate the end of the story. Whew! What an adventure!

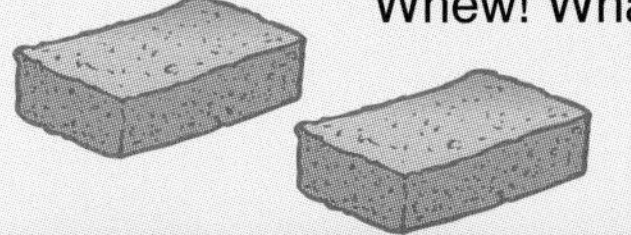

Rain

Written and Illustrated by Manya Stojic

This vibrantly illustrated story celebrates rain and its importance on the African plain. The land is hot and dry, but one by one the animals that live there sense that a welcome rainstorm is on the way. As the storm progresses, the happy animals enjoy its gifts. When dry times return, it's a sure bet that the animals will be sensitive to any rainstorm on the way!

by Lucia Kemp Henry

The Rain Is Coming

Before reading the story, have students tell you how they know when a rainstorm is coming. Next, show students the cover of the book and read the title. Ask the group to predict what the story line could be. Then read the story, pausing often for discussion. After reading the words "it rained and it rained and it rained," prompt students to predict what might happen to the dry African land. Once you've read the final page, encourage students to predict what could happen after the end of the story if the writer decided to continue the tale. Jot students' responses on a raindrop-shaped chart. Then wrap up the story session by having students share their ideas about the importance of rain and how it benefits not only animals, but people, too!

Alert Animals

Reinforce story vocabulary and the idea that each animal used a sense for detecting rain with this flannelboard activity. Photocopy the animal patterns on page 44 and prepare them for flannelboard use. Then sing the song below and display the animals on the flannelboard as they are mentioned. What a "sense-ible" song!

Rain Song
(sung to the tune of "London Bridge")

Porcupine smells precious rain,
Precious rain, precious rain.
Porcupine smells precious rain,
Smells rain coming.

Happy zebra sees the rain,
Sees the rain, sees the rain.
Happy zebra sees the rain,
Sees it coming!

Sing the song three more times, substituting "Happy baboon hears the rain," "Happy rhino feels the rain," and "Happy lion tastes the rain."

Experiencing Rain

Here's a great way to bring the delights of a rainstorm right into the classroom! To prepare, gather a rain-scented room deodorizer, a flashlight, a flexible metal cookie sheet, a clean spray bottle filled with water, and a class supply of small paper cups half-filled with cool water. Reread the section of the story that introduces how the animals use their senses to detect the storm. Then encourage your little ones to imagine that rain is approaching the classroom as they pass and sniff the rain-scented room deodorizer. Next, darken the room and turn the flashlight on and off to represent lightning. Wiggle the cookie sheet to mimic the sound of thunder. Then use the spray bottle to gently spritz each child with "rain." Finally, give each child a cup of water and have him taste the rain. Splish splash!

Dry Weather, Wet Weather

This wonderful weather-related tale makes it easy to teach your little ones about a wet-and-dry weather cycle. To prepare, cut a 4" x 8" cloud shape from gray construction paper. Make several copies of the animal patterns on page 44. Display the chart from "The Rain Is Coming" on page 42. Show students the last page of the book, prompting them to review their ideas about what could happen next. Lead students to conclude that a period of rain will probably follow the dry times, as the first part of the story illustrates. Then read the poem below to reinforce the idea that in some parts of the world, dry seasons and rainy seasons follow one another in a never-ending cycle. After reciting the poem, invite each child to choose an animal pattern, color it, and then cut it out. Have each child dictate to you why her animal needs rain. Write her response on a cloud cutout. Then have each child use her cloud and animal cutout in "Before-and-After Landscapes" on this page.

The sun is hot. The land gets dry.
There are no rain clouds in the sky.
Then rain clouds come and raindrops fall.
Now water's here for one and all.

The rainstorm goes. The sun comes out.
There is good water all about.
The land is wet. The water soaks in,
So grass and plants can grow again.

The sun is hot. The land gets dry.
There are no rain clouds in the sky.
Then rain clouds come and raindrops fall.
Now water's here for one and all!

Before-and-After Landscapes

The vivid landscape pictures in the story give a great sense of the differences in Africa's dry and wet seasons. Revisit the illustrations in the book and have students use descriptive words to compare the landscape *before* and *after* the rain. Then invite each child to draw and color his own before-and-after landscape on a large sheet of white construction paper. Instruct him to fold his paper in half and then unfold it. Have him illustrate the dry landscape on the left half of his paper and the rain-soaked landscape on the right. Instruct each child to glue his animal cutout to the center of the paper. Have him glue his cloud from "Dry Weather, Wet Weather" on this page, above the green scene. Instruct each child to add rain to his scene by cutting thin strips of blue construction paper and gluing them to the bottom of his cloud as shown. Post student projects on a wall end to end to sequence dry season and rainy season landscapes. The rain is coming!

The baboon needs the rain to get a cool drink.

The porcupine needs the rain to wash his pokey things.

Animal Patterns

Use with "Alert Animals" on page 42 and "Dry Weather, Wet Weather" and "Before-and-After Landscapes" on page 43.

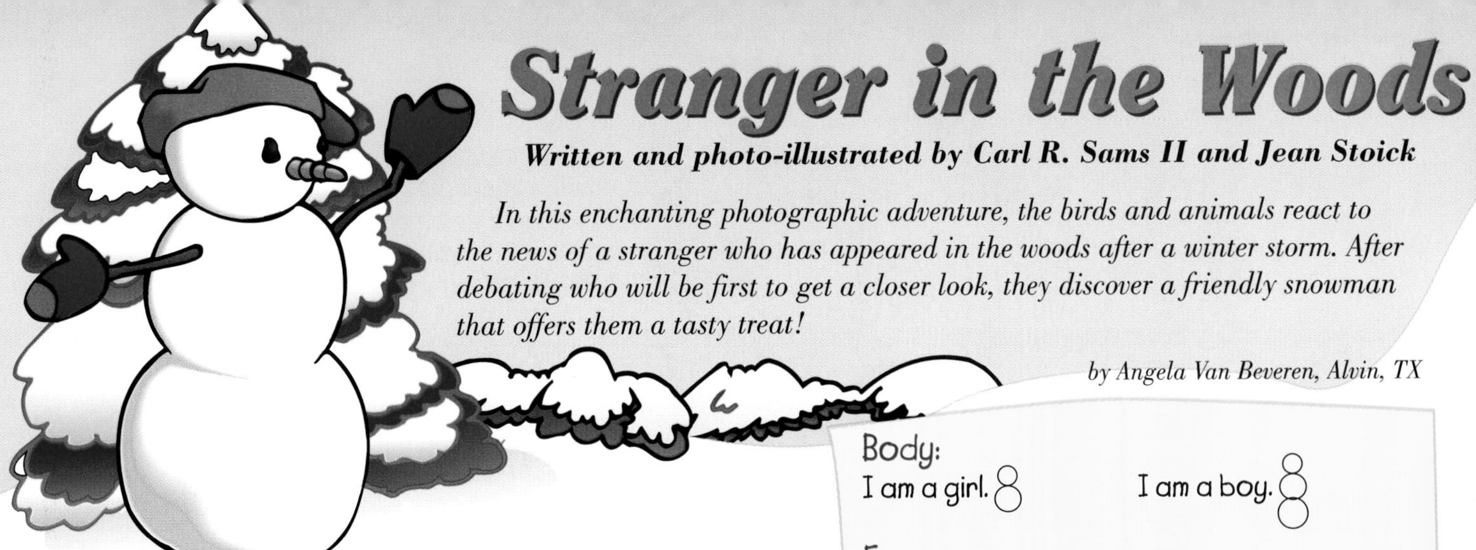

Stranger in the Woods

Written and photo-illustrated by Carl R. Sams II and Jean Stoick

In this enchanting photographic adventure, the birds and animals react to the news of a stranger who has appeared in the woods after a winter storm. After debating who will be first to get a closer look, they discover a friendly snowman that offers them a tasty treat!

by Angela Van Beveren, Alvin, TX

Body:
I am a girl.　　I am a boy.

Eyes:
I have blue eyes.
I have green eyes.
I have brown eyes.

Mouth:
Have you ever built a snowman?
Yes.
No.

Nose:
I like it when it's cold.
I like it when it's warm.

Hat:
I like to play outside in winter.
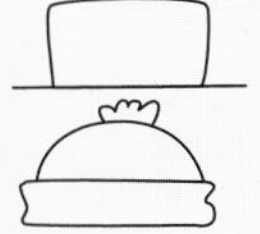
I like to play inside in winter.

I have this many people in my family.
(Glue on one button for each person.)

Symbolic Snowmen

Follow a reading of *Stranger in the Woods* with a snowman glyph activity that your young learners are sure to enjoy! Explain to each student that he will be creating a snowman that others can investigate to learn about the artist. Copy the legend on the right onto chart paper. Use the legend to help each student create his snowman glyph and help others understand what it tells. Provide each youngster with a piece of paper, crayons, glue, and several paper circles to serve as buttons. Read and explain each step of the legend and have students draw or glue accordingly. After the projects are complete, display the glyphs and the legend on a bulletin board titled "[Your name]'s Frosty Friends!"

Footprints in the Snow

Just as the animals from the story left footprints in the snow, so will your students with this simple center activity. To prepare, cut sheets of blue construction paper into 3" x 12" strips. Place the strips, a shallow pan containing a thin layer of white paint, and several plastic animals at a center. Invite each youngster to visit the center, select an animal, dip its feet into the paint, and then make prints on her strip. While students are at the center, play classical music and encourage them to stamp to the beat. After the paint has dried, use the strips to make a border for the bulletin board created in "Symbolic Snowmen" on this page. Now that's a nice trail of creativity!

Who's the Stranger?

Your little detectives will gain problem-solving practice in deduction with this easy game! Explain to students that there is a stranger in the class and that only you know who she is. To play, have all students begin by standing. Provide students with clues that are progressively more specific, having each child sit when a characteristic does not apply to her. For example, you could say, "The stranger is wearing red today." (Children not wearing red would sit down.) "The stranger has brown hair." (Children with hair color other than brown would sit down.) "The stranger is a girl." (All boys would sit down.) "The stranger has on shoes without laces." (Children with lace-up shoes would sit down.) "The stranger has an *a* in her name." Amy is the stranger! When the stranger has been identified, all students stand up and the game is repeated.

Snow Paint

The salt crystals in these paintings will create an icy image much to the delight of your little ones! Provide each child with a 9" x 12" sheet of blue construction paper, white paint, a paintbrush, and salt. Encourage each student to paint a snowy scene. Then, while the paint is still wet, have him sprinkle salt onto his picture. After the paintings have dried, have each child write a sentence about his scene. Then bind the pages to create a class book. The icy shimmer of this book will surely make it a class favorite and put warm smiles on your students' faces!

Feed the Birds

Feeding the birds and animals is great fun for the children in *Stranger in the Woods,* and with this fun bird feeder your little ones will share in that joy! In advance, gather a large snowman cookie cutter, a straw, yarn, peanut butter, birdseed, plastic knives, and a slice of bread for each child. Instruct each child to use the cookie cutter to cut out a snowman shape from her slice of bread. Then help each youngster use the straw to cut a hole in the snowman near the top. Tie a length of yarn through the hole to make a loop for hanging. Leave the snowmen out overnight to harden the bread a bit. Next, have each child spread peanut butter on her snowman and then sprinkle it with birdseed. Encourage each student to take her bird feeder home and hang it in a tree where she might secretly observe some feathered friends feasting on her snowman!

A Sparkly Snowfall

Turn your classroom into a winter wonderland with glitter glue and fishing line! Give each child a piece of waxed paper and a bottle of glitter glue. Instruct him to use the glue to draw a snowflake or snowman on his waxed paper. Allow the glue to dry. (This may take more than one day, depending on conditions in your area.) When the glue is completely dry, peel the figure off of the waxed paper and use a length of fishing line to hang it from the ceiling. What a cool creation!

Listen-and-Draw Snowmen

Strengthen listening skills with an activity that has youngsters drawing what they hear! Give each child a sheet of paper and crayons. Explain to students that you will read a story and they are to draw what they hear. Slowly read the story below, pausing periodically for students to complete each part of their pictures. After the pictures are finished, photocopy the story below to make a class set and give one copy to each child. Have her glue the story to her page. Encourage her to take her picture home and share it with her family. Now that's frosty fun!

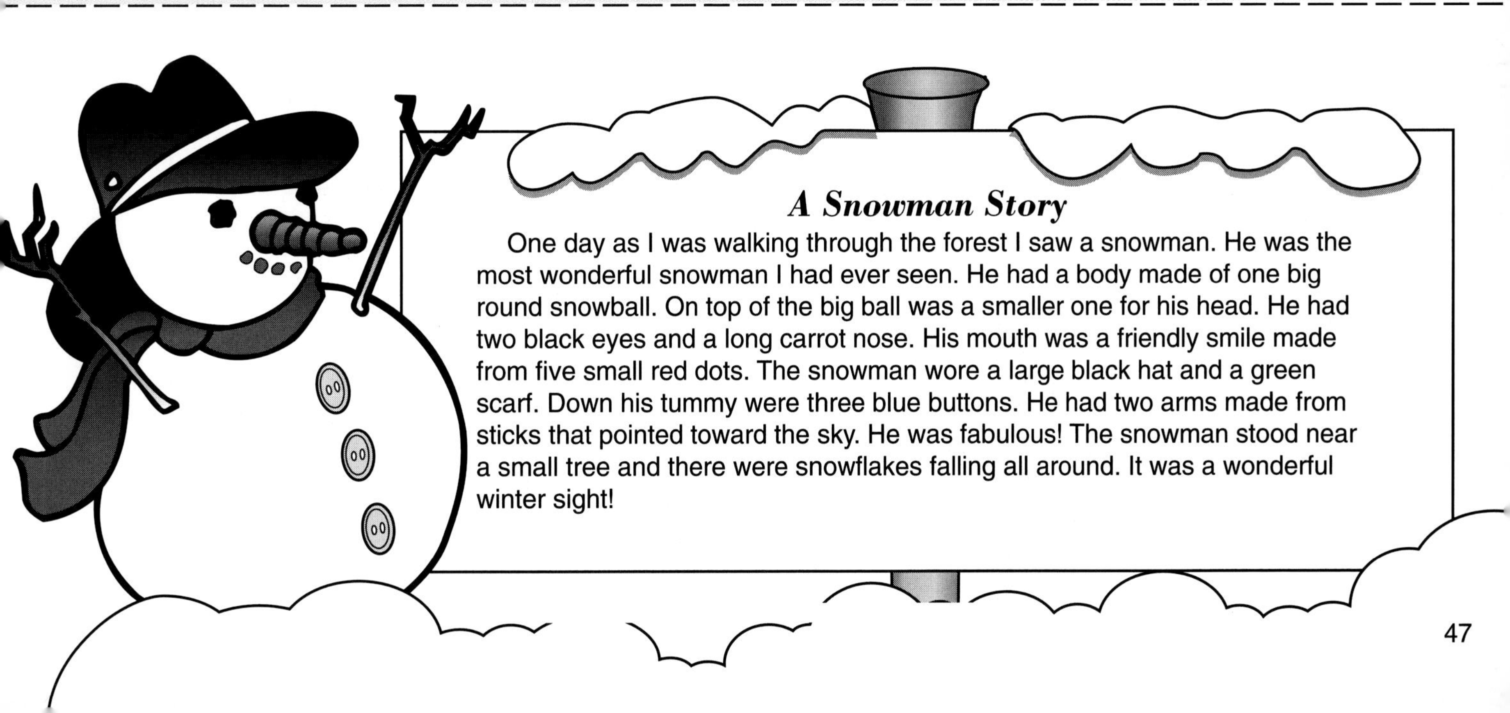

A Snowman Story

One day as I was walking through the forest I saw a snowman. He was the most wonderful snowman I had ever seen. He had a body made of one big round snowball. On top of the big ball was a smaller one for his head. He had two black eyes and a long carrot nose. His mouth was a friendly smile made from five small red dots. The snowman wore a large black hat and a green scarf. Down his tummy were three blue buttons. He had two arms made from sticks that pointed toward the sky. He was fabulous! The snowman stood near a small tree and there were snowflakes falling all around. It was a wonderful winter sight!

Piggies

Written by Don and Audrey Wood
Illustrated by Don Wood

The whimsical illustrations and playful text of Piggies *bring imaginary life to youngsters' fingers and thumbs. Use this book and the ideas in this unit to inspire your little ones to explore with their own little piggies!*

Perfect Pig Snouts

Your little ones will squeal with excitement when they wear these pig snouts! In advance, collect a class supply of clean Crystal Light drink mix tubs. To prepare, spray-paint the tubs pink. Hole-punch the opposite sides of each tub; then tie an 18-inch length of pink yarn through each hole. Give each child a prepared tub and have him use a permanent marker to draw nostrils on the bottom. Help each youngster tie the snout around his head. Have students wear the snouts while participating in the other activities in this unit. What cute little noses!

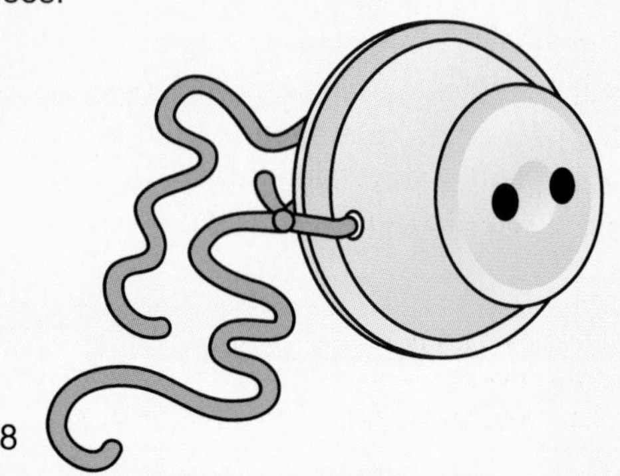

Ten Piggies

Your youngsters become piggies as they use props to act out the text in this book. Gather the props listed at right and position ten chairs in a line in front of the class. As you read through the book the first time, have students pay particular attention to the illustrations on each page, pausing briefly to talk about the props that each piggy has in the pictures. Then have ten volunteers hold the props and sit in the chairs, with those children representing the thumbs sitting in the end chairs and the others sitting in order toward the center of the row. Reread the book and instruct each pair of youngsters to stand and perform when mentioned in the story. Repeat the activity until all students have had a chance to participate. Your smart little piggies will like this idea!

Donna Battista—Transition Gr. 1
Parkview Elementary
Valparaiso, IN

Props

Two fat piggies
top hat
umbrella
basket with laundry

Two smart piggies
telescope
books
glasses

Two long piggies
basketball
wand

Two silly piggies
clown hat
jester's hat

Two wee piggies
teddy bear
balloon

Finger Play!

These piggy gloves will have your youngsters practicing skip-counting and more. Give each child a pair of clear plastic food-service gloves and ten sticky dots. Have him use a fine-tip marker to draw a pig face, as shown, on each sticker. Instruct him to apply one sticker to each glove fingertip. Have each youngster put on his gloves. Lead students to discuss the different ways the gloves could be used to skip-count. Invite ten children to stand in a line at the front of the room. Instruct them to wiggle their fingers accordingly as the class counts from 0 to 100 by fives and then tens. Repeat the activity until each child has had a chance to participate. Then challenge students to skip-count using the piggies of all of your students.

As another use, place pairs of gloves in your reading area and encourage students to wear them while retelling the story. Five, ten, 15, 20 piggies!

Donna Battista—Transition Gr. 1
Parkview Elementary
Valparaiso, IN

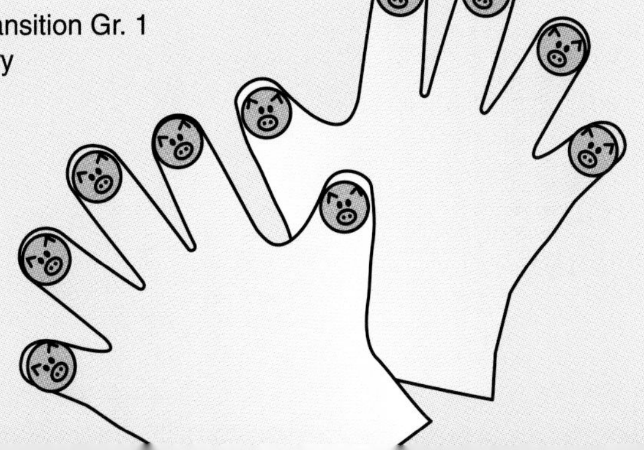

Pink Piggy Snack

Five ingredients is all you'll need to make this supercute and tasty snack. Gather the ingredients and supplies listed below and then guide each child through the directions to make her own Pink Piggy Snack! Yum!

Ingredients for one snack:
strawberry muffin
half a large marshmallow (snout)
strawberry cut in half (ears)
2 chocolate chips (eyes)
pink cake-decorating gel

Utensils and supplies:
paper plate for each child

Teacher preparation:
- Prepare muffins according to package directions.
- Cut marshmallows and strawberries in half.

Directions:
1. Put two ears on a muffin.
2. Add two eyes.
3. Add a snout and make nostrils with pink gel.

In the Tall, Tall Grass

Written and illustrated by Denise Fleming

This adventure begins with a small boy's discovery of a caterpillar as it makes its way through the tall grass. The reader is then treated to the caterpillar's view of the various creatures it encounters along the way. Lively language describes the movement and sounds that occur during this backyard tour, which concludes as the stars come out and the moon rises.

ideas by Angela Van Beveren, Alvin, TX

What's in the Tall, Tall Grass?

Writing, drawing

Your youngsters will enjoy the secrecy involved in this art activity as they make a scene for someone else to discover. Have students think about all the things that are hiding in the tall grass in the story, and then have them think about other things that they might find in the grass. Give each child two 9" x 12" sheets of construction paper, one green and one white. On the white paper, have each youngster draw and label things that can be found in the grass. Then instruct each child to fringe-cut her green paper to resemble grass, as shown, being careful not to cut all the way through to the edge. Next, have her glue her uncut edge of green paper to the bottom of her white paper. Then post the finished projects on a bulletin board titled "In the Tall, Tall Grass."

In Our Busy, Busy School

Writing, sequencing, rhyming

This class book will have your young authors pondering the events that occur in your school from morning to night. As a group, brainstorm a list of things that someone might see while taking a peek into the school at various times from early morning to night (lights coming on, children arriving, custodian cleaning, lights going off, etc.). Then select and sequence the events that you will include in your class book. Next, have students help you make a page for each event, patterning the text like that in *In the Tall, Tall, Grass* and using rhyming words when possible. Give each child or small group a page to illustrate. Laminate the completed pages for durability and bind them together; then title the book "In Our Busy, Busy School."

Name________________________________ Addition, reading color words

Math in the Tall, Tall Grass

Color the animals.
Write the problem.
Solve.

Color the birds green or blue.

_____ + _____ = _____

Color the bees orange or yellow.

_____ + _____ = _____

Color the ants brown or red.

_____ + _____ = _____

Color the snakes green or yellow.

_____ + _____ = _____

Color the frogs red or green.

_____ + _____ = _____

Color the bats black or purple.

_____ + _____ = _____

Color the beetles red or blue.

_____ + _____ = _____

Color the rabbits orange or brown.

_____ + _____ = _____

Note to the teacher: Use with *In the Tall, Tall Grass* on page 50.

When the Fly Flew In...

Written by Lisa Westberg Peters
Illustrated by Brad Sneed

This clever story follows the antics of a fly and some whimsical house pets as they unknowingly clean up a messy situation! It's sure to be a delight for any kindergarten listener!

by Donna K. Battista, Parkview Elementary, Valparaiso, IN

 Listening comprehension

"Fan-tastic" Comprehension

Following a reading of the book, check comprehension with this cool idea! To prepare, make a copy of the animal cards at the top of page 54 for each child. Give each child a copy of the animal cards and a six-inch paper plate. Have him color the cards and then cut them apart. Help each child fold his paper plate in fourths. Have him cut his plate along the fold lines. Instruct him to stack the pieces. Hole-punch near the point and attach a brad to create a fan. Have each youngster glue one animal card to each section of his fan. Then instruct students to use their fans to show answers to questions about the story, such as the following: Who dust-mopped the floor? Who ate the cookie crumbs? Who was dreaming? Who swept off a mountain of dirty clothes? Who cleaned up the cobwebs? You'll know at a glance which youngsters have comprehended the story.

 Understanding vocabulary
Movement 

On the Move

Your little ones will make the story come to life with this movement activity. To prepare game cards, program a set of index cards with nouns from the story, such as *cat, hamster, fly, dog, child,* and *mother.* Program another set of index cards with verbs from the story, such as *turned, streaked, flew, buzzed, flapped, swooped,* and *zagged.* Designate a starting and stopping point in the play area in your room. Instruct students to stand in a line at the starting point. Have the first child in line select one card from each set. Use the noun and verb listed on the cards to create a complete sentence, such as "The cat flew." Then have the child pretend to be a cat and fly across the play area. After each youngster has had a chance to participate, draw a card from each set and invite the entire class to move accordingly. Giggles are sure to be heard!

Finish

Start

Patterning
Problem solving

A Hamster's Snack

Your little nibblers will get some math practice and a snack with this yummy idea! To prepare, make a class set of the problem-solving mat on page 54. Next, stir together animal crackers, raisins, and popcorn to make a snack mix. Give each youngster a mat and a small cup of snack mix. Have him sort the mix by type and then present a variety of math tasks, such as making an ABC pattern using the snack mix or deciding of which snack type he has the most. Or pose math problems, such as "If the hamster ate two raisins and three pieces of popcorn, how many did he eat all together?" At the conclusion of the math activities, invite each child to nibble on his hamster's snack!

Sequencing

Sequencing a Story

When youngsters make these bookmarks, they'll be reminded of the story's sequence. In advance, make a class set of the mini animal cards on page 54. Cut construction paper into 2" x 9" strips to make a class supply. Give each child a copy of the animal cards and a paper strip. Have her color and then cut out the cards. Reread the story and have each student position the appropriate animal cards in sequence on her strip. Then check each student's work for accuracy. Next, have her glue her cards in place to complete her bookmark. Encourage each youngster to retell the story using the pictures on her bookmark as clues.

Playing a game
Singing a song

A Fly Flew in My Room

Make *When the Fly Flew In...* come to life by playing this chase game while singing this catchy song! Have students sit in a circle. Choose one child to be the fly and stand on the outside of the circle. As the song is sung, the fly walks around the circle until the lyrics say an animal chases him. The fly chooses a child to be the animal and the pair races around the circle one lap. The fly sits in the chosen child's place and the other child becomes the fly for the next verse. The first verse is repeated before each consecutive verse. At the end of the song, the fly sits with the rest of the group in the circle. Zzzz!

(sung to the tune of "The Farmer in the Dell")

A fly flew in my room.
A fly flew in my room.
Hey, look! See, there he goes.
A fly flew in my room!

A dog chased the fly.
A dog chased the fly.
Hey, look! See, there he goes.
A dog chased the fly!

A cat chased the fly.
A cat chased the fly.
Hey, look! See, there he goes.
A cat chased the fly!

A hamster chased the fly.
A hamster chased the fly.
Hey, look! See, there he goes.
A hamster chased the fly!

A parakeet chased the fly.
A parakeet chased the fly.
Hey, look! See, there he goes.
A parakeet chased the fly!

The fly said, "Goodbye."
The fly said, "Goodbye."
Hey, look! See, there he goes.
The fly said, "Goodbye."

Animal Cards

Use with "'Fan-tastic' Comprehension" on page 52.

Mini Animal Cards

Use with "Sequencing a Story" on page 53.

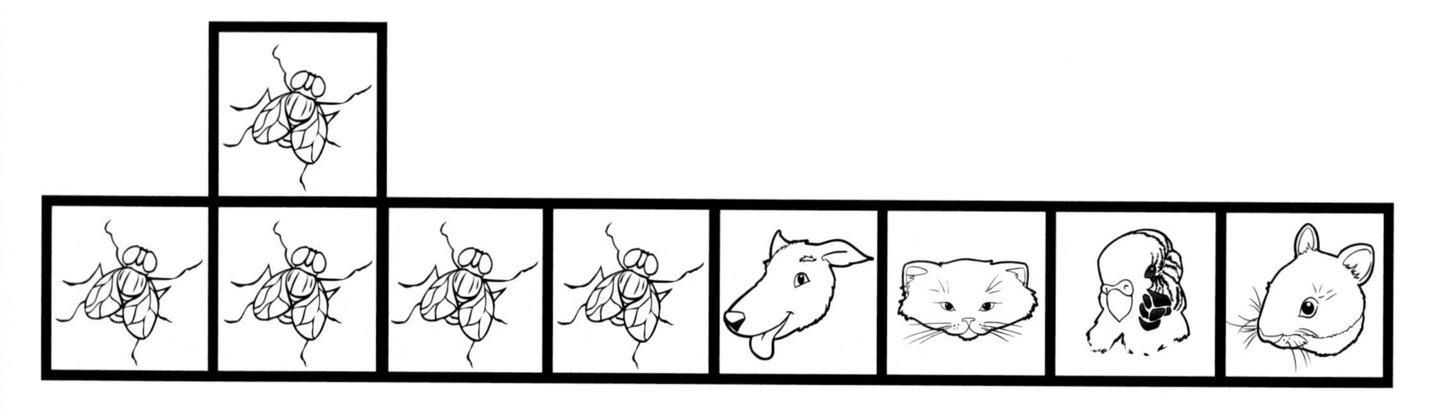

Problem-Solving Mat

Use with "A Hamster's Snack" on page 53.

BUILDING MATH SKILLS

Shape and color recognition

Shapes Freeze

Move right into shape and color recognition with this fun musical activity! To prepare, cut different shapes from various colors of construction paper to make a class set. Laminate the shapes; then tape them to the floor in a large circle. Turn on some lively music and have little ones step from shape to shape, moving around the circle until the music stops and you say, "Freeze!" Then ask questions, such as "Who is standing on the blue triangle?" and "Who is standing on the red oval?" After a few questions, restart the music and have students continue to play. Freeze!

Florence Paola—PreK and Kindergarten Special Needs
Jane Ryan Elementary
Trumbull, CT

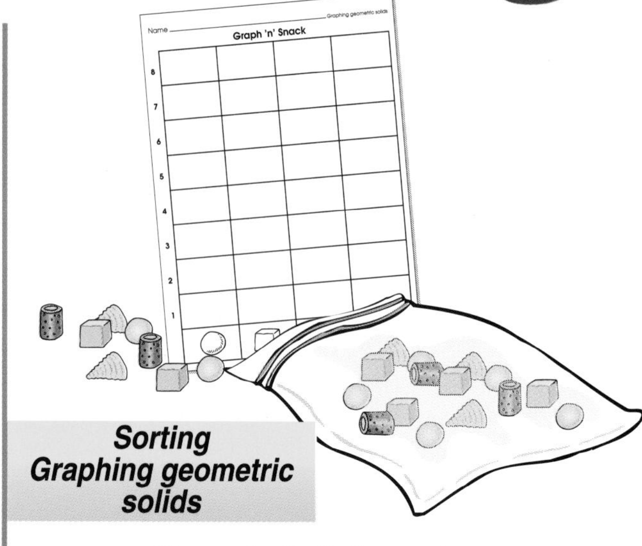

Sorting
Graphing geometric solids

Graph 'n' Snack

After teaching your kindergartners about spheres, cubes, cylinders, and cones, introduce some fun foods in these shapes for youngsters to sort, graph, and eat! Purchase or ask parents to donate cheese balls, cheese cubes, COMBOS snacks, and Bugles snacks. Mix all the snack foods together; then place a small cupful into a separate zippered plastic bag for each student. Give each child a bag and a copy of the graphing sheet on page 66. Have her sort the snacks by solid shape and then color a square on the graph to represent each one. After completing the activity, invite each child to munch her math manipulatives!

Kelly Borders—Gr. K
Vaughan Elementary
Powder Springs, GA

Identifying colors

A Colorful Mouse Book

After sharing *Mouse Paint* by Ellen Stoll Walsh, invite your youngsters to make their own mini mouse books to reinforce basic colors. To prepare, draw a simple mouse pattern and duplicate it onto gray construction paper to make two copies per student.

To make a booklet, each child cuts out his two gray mice to serve as front and back covers. Using one of the covers as a template, he traces and cuts out mice from eight different colors of construction paper. Help each youngster stack his pages between his covers; then hole-punch the stack as shown. Next, help him thread a pipe cleaner through all the holes and twist it to bind the book and form the mouse's tail. To get an idea of who can identify colors, invite each youngster to share his book with the class. What nice mice!

Kelly Dobias—Gr. K, Peifer Elementary, Schererville, IN

Math Skills

Counting
Comparing numbers

Football Math

Turn fall football fever into math mania with this morning activity! Have students decide on a team to track all season. Make a chart similar to the one shown. Use the chart to keep track of the scores for your team and its opponents. As you examine each game's score, use Unifix cubes to represent the numbers. Stack the cubes in groups of ten and count the total for each team. Compare the scores and determine which team had more points. Place a check mark next to the winning team. At the end of the season, count up the check marks for your team. Even if the players didn't come out on top, your students will!

Diane McHughes—Gr. K
Northside Elementary
Cairo, GA

Football Math

	Dallas √√√√√	Opponent √√√√
Sep. 18	39	8
Sep. 20	13	26
Oct. 4	37	16
Oct. 11	22	21
Oct. 18	10	6
Oct. 25	11	14
Nov. 2	3	43
Nov. 8	18	48
Nov. 15	43	16

Counting to 100

Piece by Piece to 100!

Here's a great activity to help little ones count the first 100 days of school! Before the start of school, buy a 100-piece jigsaw puzzle. Assemble the puzzle; then turn it over and number the pieces, beginning with the pieces on the outside edge. Then take the puzzle apart. Each day during calendar time, invite a student to add the next numbered piece to the puzzle. Periodically, have youngsters predict the finished image. Pop in the last piece on the 100th day of school—what an accomplishment!

Kim Lockley—Gr. K
Longfellow Elementary
Houston, TX

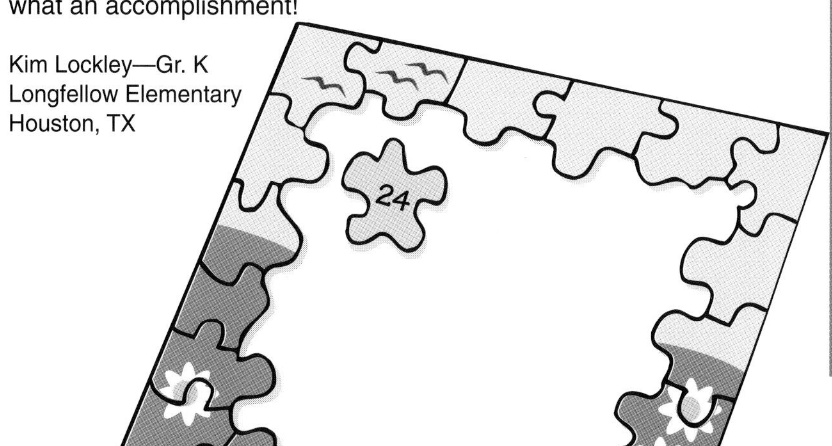

Numeral formation

Play Dough Digits

Help your kindergartners form numerals with the help of ever popular play dough! To prepare, make a set of flash cards with sticker sets representing the numerals you wish to have students practice. Then give each youngster a portion of play dough. Hold up a flash card and have youngsters quietly count the number of stickers on it. Then instruct each child to form her play dough into the corresponding numeral. At a glance, you'll know if any children are having trouble with reversals.

As a variation, make flash cards with number words instead of sticker sets.

Betsy Crosson—Gr. 1
Pleasant Elementary
Tulare, CA

Critical thinking

By the Slice

Want to build thinking skills? Have youngsters portion pepperoni slices for some paper-plate pizzas! In advance, draw lines on a small-group supply of thin white paper plates to divide each plate into six sections, as shown. Cut a large supply of brown or red construction paper circles (pepperoni slices). Give each child in a small group a paper-plate pizza and six, 12, or 18 paper pepperoni slices. Ask youngsters to top their pizzas so that each slice has an equal number of pepperoni slices.

Jill Beattie
Apple Place Nursery School
Chambersburg, PA

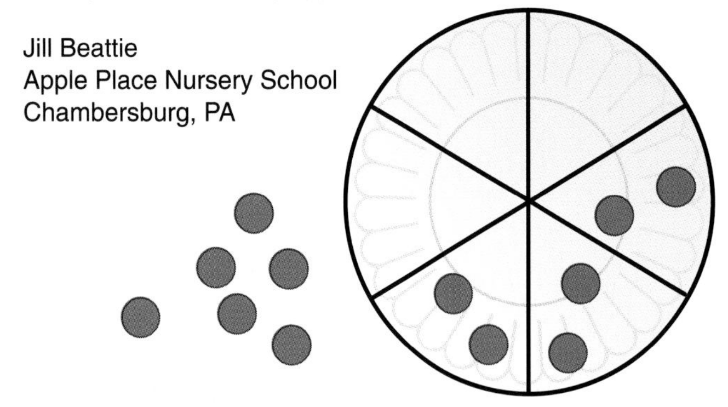

Counting

Jumping Beans

This activity, which mixes motor skills and math, will be a hit—you can count on it! To prepare, count out ten large, dried lima beans. Color one side of each bean with a permanent marker. Then put all ten beans in a plastic cup. Gather students in a circle and give the cup to one child. Have her shake the cup and spill the beans onto the floor in the center of the circle. Ask students to count the number of beans that land color side up. Then have them jump once for each colored bean. When the jumping's over, gather the beans. Then have the next child in the circle shake and spill for another round of Jumping Beans!

Linda Masternak Justice
Kansas City, MO

Number recognition
Number sequence

Take a Number!

Mix some math into your daily lineup routine. To prepare, write or type on a sheet of heavy paper the numbers from 1 to the number of students in your class. Laminate the numbers and cut them apart. Then attach a jewelry pin to the back of each one. Place all the number badges in a box or basket. Each day when your kindergartners arrive, have each child draw out a badge and wear it for the day. The number a child draws equals her spot in the line for the day. Besides reinforcing number recognition and sequencing, you can also introduce odd and even numbers by writing the numbers in two different colors!

Jacey Carn—Gr. K
Heathcote School
Essex, England

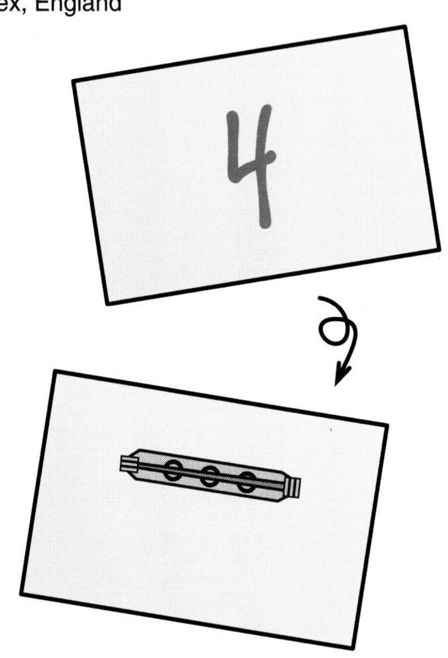

Math Skills

Shapes

Rubber Band Shapes

Help your students remember the distinction between a square and a rectangle with the help of a rubber band. Put a rubber band over your two thumbs and index fingers and stretch it to form a square. Then have the fingers "talk" as they explain that they are forming a square. Then have them play a game of tug-of-war—have the right hand pull to the right and the left hand pull to the left. Have the fingers realize they have just created a new shape—a rectangle!

Rebecca Bange—Gr. K
Little River Elementary
Orlando, FL

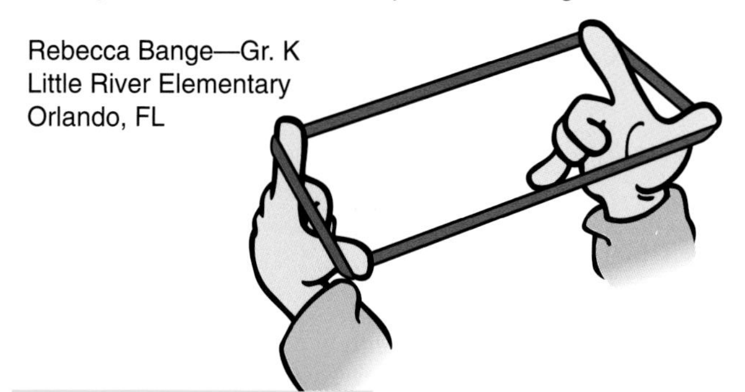

Odd and even numbers

Odd-and-Even Street

Teach the concept of odd and even numbers to your kindergartners with a real-world application—addresses! To begin, draw or paint a street on a long piece of bulletin board paper. Label one side of the street "Even" and the other "Odd." Attach the hook side of small pieces of self-adhesive Velcro tape along the street on each side, where houses would go. Next, invite youngsters to cut out and decorate houses. Program each child's house with a street number; then add the loop side of the Velcro tape to the back of each house. Invite each child to place her house cutout on the street, ordering the house numbers as you go, and placing the even and odd numbers on the appropriate sides. Finish up this activity by sending youngsters home to examine the numbers on their own houses and the addresses on their own streets.

Susan Potts—Gr. K
CASE Collaborative School
Concord, MA

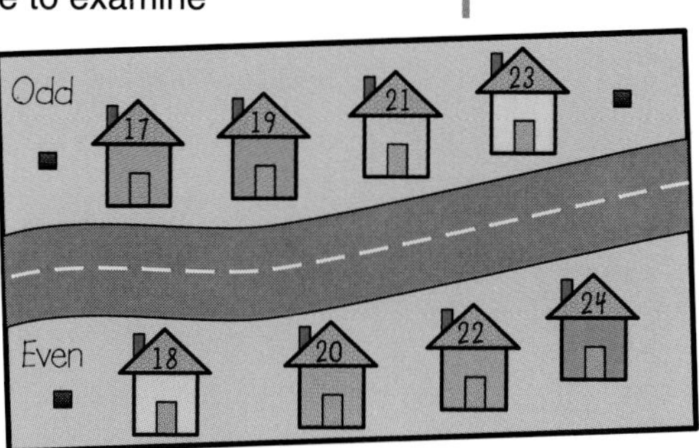

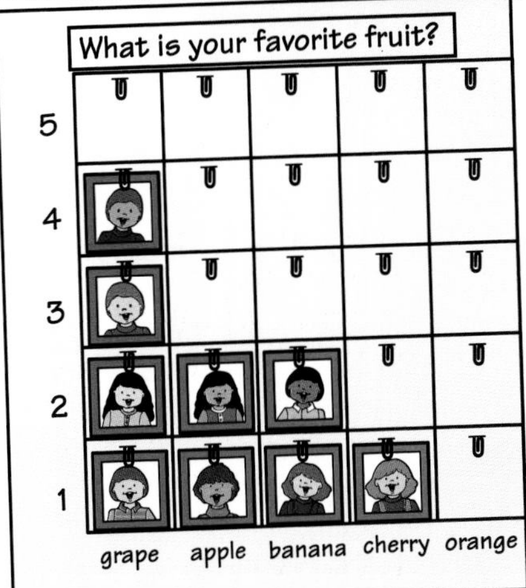

Graphing

"Photo-Graphing"

Daily graphing activities will be a snap when you use student photos as graph markers! To prepare, mount each child's school photo (or a reduced photocopy of a head-and-shoulders shot) on a separate square of tagboard; then laminate all the squares for durability. Next, create a large grid on poster board and laminate it too. For each graph, write a graphing question on a strip of paper and mount it near the grid.

To attach the photo squares to the grid, use an X-acto knife to cut a small slit at the top of each grid square. Slip a paper clip into each slit. Then students can simply tuck their photo cards under the clips to attach them to the grid.

Tarie Curtiss—Gr. K
Arthur Road Early Education Center
Solon, OH

Diane Nienkemper—Gr. K
St. Francis of Assisi School
St. Louis, MO

Identifying numbers
Counting

"Exer-dice"

Get kindergartners pumped up about learning higher numbers with this activity! Label each side of a cube-shaped gift box (stuffed with tissue) with any number from 11–19. Seat youngsters on the floor and toss the cube to a child. Have her identify the number that lands on top. Then have her choose an activity for the class to do, such as jumping jacks, clapping, or blinking. Have the number of repetitions match the number on the cube. Then instruct the child who chose the activity to toss the cube to someone else for another round.

Naomi Nussbaum, M.A.—Gr. K
Barnert Temple
Franklin Lakes, NJ

Skip-counting

Highlighted Hundred Chart

Assist your students in skip-counting by highlighting numbers on a hundred chart. Cover the 5s, 10s, or any other numbers you wish to focus on with colored plastic wrap or cellophane. Youngsters will see the appropriate numbers readily, and they may notice a pattern too!

Karen Alexander—Gr. K
Glenburn Elementary
Glenburn, ME

1	2	3	4	5	6	7	8	9	10
11	12	13	14	15	16	17	18	19	20
21	22	23	24	25	26	27	28	29	30
31	32	33	34	35	36	37	38	39	40
41	42	43	44	45	46	47	48	49	50
51	52	53	54	55	56	57	58	59	60
61	62	63	64	65	66	67	68	69	70
71	72	73	74	75	76	77	78	79	80
81	82	83	84	85	86	87	88	89	90
91	92	93	94	95	96	97	98	99	100

Non-standard measurement
Graphing

Amaryllis Excitement

Watch science and math skills bloom together with this seasonal project! At the beginning of December, purchase an inexpensive kit for forcing an amaryllis bulb. Plant the bulb with your students; then have a designated child record (draw) the bulb's progress each day. When the main stem begins to grow, measure its height each day with Unifix cubes. Then ask for predictions of when the plant will bloom. Graph the predictions and wait for the big day!

Beth Harkcom—Gr. K
William H. Blount Elementary
Wilmington, NC

Math Skills

1	2	3	4	5	6
John	12	13	14	Terry	16
21	22	23	Jane	25	26
31	32	33	34	Allen	36
			44	45	46

Number order

Hidden Numbers

Get every student involved in a daily math activity that reinforces number order. Each day, cover numbers on your hundred chart with small sticky notes, each one labeled with a student's name. Have each child tell what number she believes is hiding under her name. Then pull off the sticky note to see whether she is correct.

Karen Saner—Gr. K
Burns Elementary
Burns, KS

Problem solving

Fabric Math

Visit the fabric store for an inexpensive and fresh way to give youngsters a daily dose of math! Purchase small remnants or short lengths of fabric with large, repeating patterns that have lots of kid appeal. Mount each fabric piece on a sheet of poster board and display one a day for students to examine. Each day, ask a different question about the fabric piece, such as "How many dogs can you count on the fabric?" or "Add the red flowers and the blue flowers. What is the sum?" Have youngsters write their answers on individual slips of paper. Periodically change the fabric to keep the activity interesting. Seasonal fabrics are extra fun!

Nancy Newberry—Gr. K
Cornerstone Academy
St. Louis, MO

Counting numbers

Got It!

Roll the dice and see whether your youngsters enjoy this individual center activity, which reinforces counting and numbers! To prepare, make a supply of the number sheet on page 67. Place the copies and two dice in your math center. To play, a child rolls the dice. She counts the total number of dots showing on top and looks for the corresponding number on her copy of the reproducible. She says "Got it!" when she locates the number; then she colors its square. The child continues until she's colored every square on the sheet.

If desired, make the activity easier by supplying only one die, masking out the numbers on the reproducible, and reprogramming it with the numbers 1–6. To make the activity more difficult, supply three dice and reprogram the reproducible with the numbers 3–18.

Jennifer Brahos—Gr. K
Lewis and Clark Elementary
Mandan, ND

Sequencing numbers
Writing numbers

Pick a Card, Any Card

This deck of cards will help youngsters practice writing numerals in sequence. To make a card deck, simply label each of 20 index cards with a different number from 1 to 20. Then have a child pick a card. Have her write the number shown on the card on your board. Then instruct her to continue writing numbers in sequence to 20. (If a child draws the 20 card, invite her to write it on the board and then take another card from the deck.) Keep going until every child has had a turn to draw a card and write numbers.

Susan Bailey—Gr. K, Abercrombie Academy
Spring, TX

Understanding coin values

Give Me a Nickel!

Use the familiar gesture of a high five to help your kindergartners review coin values! Explain that for this partner activity, the number of fingers touching equals the number of cents in the coin's value. So if you call out, "Give me a nickel," partners should say, "Five cents!" and slap together one hand. If you call out, "Give me a quarter," partners should say, "25 cents!" and slap together both hands two times, followed by one hand one time. Have them count as they go: ten, 20, 25. Don't forget to teach them the motion for "Give me a penny." Have them say, "One cent!" and touch two index fingers together!

Wanda Rikli—Gr. K
Southern Valley School
at Beaver City
Beaver City, NE

Counting to 100

Stamping to 100

Provide a variety of mini rubber stamps and ink pads to help youngsters make these headbands for the 100th day of school! To prepare, duplicate the 100 pattern on page 68 to make a class supply. Point out the "frames" of ten boxes on the numbers and the exclamation point. Have a child choose a stamp and stamp it one time in each box as he counts to ten. Then have him switch stamps or ink colors and fill another frame of ten. Have him continue until he's filled in all the frames and stamped 100 times. Then staple or glue the completed design to a sentence strip headband for your kindergarten counter to proudly wear!

Candee Conklin—Gr. K
School #35
Rochester, NY

Math Skills

Grouping
Counting

Group and Count

Let's see... What can your little ones count today? How about themselves? Just call out a number and instruct students to gather themselves into groups that equal it. For example, if you call out, "Five," your students must gather into groups of five. Then have the class count by fives as you point to each group. Call out a different number, and repeat the process.

Jennifer Rossano—Gr. K
The Caedmon School
New York, NY

Addition

Ice-Cube-Tray Addition

Help your kindergartners practice adding numbers with the help of some ice cube trays and colored counting chips. Provide each child in a small group with an ice cube tray and a supply of chips. Give her a problem to solve, such as 6 + 4. Show her how to put six chips in the top row of her ice cube tray and four chips in the bottom row. Then have her count all the chips to determine the answer. After students are comfortable using the chips to solve problems, write the problems on your board so that little ones can begin to see the connection between the objects and the written number sentence.

Bill Walker—Gr. K
Andrew Jackson Elementary
Jackson, TN

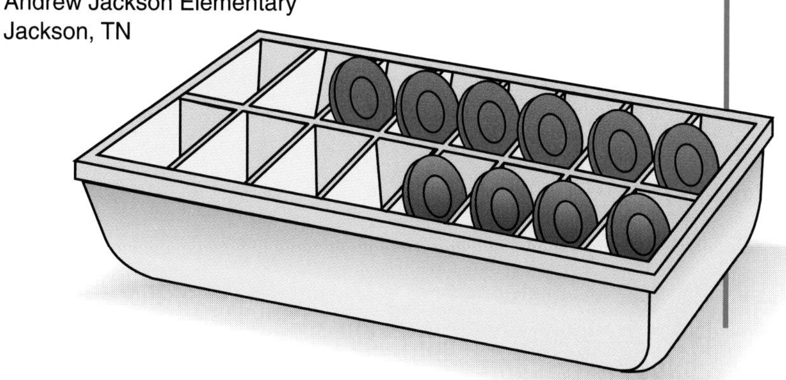

Identifying coins
Understanding coin values

Flip a Coin

Learning about Lincoln? Remind students that he appears on the penny with this fun coin-flipping activity—and toss in some learning about other coins, too! Purchase a black plastic top hat at your local party store. Put this version of Lincoln's hat upside down on a tabletop. Then gather a small group of students and give them a pile of coins. Have a child take a coin and tell you its name and/or its value. If he is correct, he may try to flip the coin off his thumb and into the hat.

Sue Lein
Wauwatosa, WI

Sorting
Tallying

Jelly Bean Tally

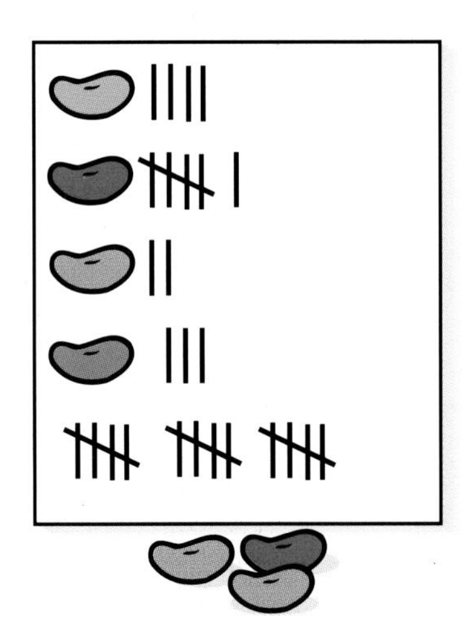

Yum! What could be tastier than using jelly beans to practice math? Give each child a clear plastic baggie of assorted jelly beans. Ask her to dump her beans out on a tabletop and then sort them by color. Give her a sheet of paper and ask her to record each color in her collection by drawing and coloring a jelly bean. Have her draw the beans in a line down the left side of her paper. Then have her make tally marks next to each color to show the corresponding number of beans. Next, have her mix up the colors and make a new set of tally marks at the bottom of her paper to represent the total number of jelly beans she has.

Cindi Zsittnik
Boonsboro, MD

Counting
Graphing

Pool to Pond

Studying pond life? Bring a pond into your classroom! Actually, bring in a small plastic or inflatable pool. Fill it with blue Easter grass; then add small plastic or vinyl pond animals. Working with a small group of students, ask each child to find a particular number of animals. When each child has counted her animals, make a graph to compare the quantities of each one. Will there be more fish or frogs in the pond today?

Gloria Thudium
Baton Rouge, LA

Recognizing coins
Understanding coin values

Ticket, Please

Want to improve youngsters' money skills? This idea is just the ticket! Make a supply of tickets—small rectangles of paper—with various coins stamped on them. As students line up to go to lunch or outdoor playtime, give each child a ticket. Ask her to identify the coin and/or give its value before she gets in line. Once students have mastered this activity, progress to more of a challenge! Using tickets stamped with nickels, dimes, or quarters (not pennies), have a student tell you the value of the coin on her ticket. Then have her tell you what other coins also equal that amount, such as two nickels equal a dime.

Jannelle Weiss—Gr. K
Carousel School
Rancho Cordova, CA

Math Skills

Nonstandard measurement

Jump!

After sharing the story *Jump, Frog, Jump!* by Robert Kalan, invite your kindergartners to see how far they can jump! Have each child stand behind a line and jump as far as he can. Record the distance by cutting a corresponding length of adding machine tape. Then have the child sit down at a table with the tape, a copy of the recording sheet on page 68, and the manipulatives listed on the reproducible: Unifix cubes, links, and some other type of counters. (Frog counters would be perfect!) Have the child lay the cubes end to end to cover the length of the tape and then count them and record the number on the recording sheet. Have him repeat the procedure with the links and the counters. Then attach the adding machine tape to the child's reproducible. Display all the strips and recording sheets from shortest to longest jump.

Jennifer Woods
Alma Primary School
Alma, AR

Matching numerals and number words
Counting

Easter Egg Math

This activity is "eggs-actly" right for helping youngsters match numerals to number words! Gather a dozen plastic Easter eggs with separating halves. Label one half of each egg with a numeral; then label the other half with the corresponding number word. Pull the halves apart; then store the eggs in a large zippered plastic bag at your math center, along with a supply of jelly beans. Have a child at this center match the numerals and number words to assemble the eggs and then place the corresponding number of jelly beans inside each one.

Shannon Smith—Gr. K
Westridge Elementary
Provo, UT

Addition

Name Number Sentences

This addition idea couldn't be easier! Simply choose a student's name and write it on your board. Together, count the vowels and record the number below the name. Then count the consonants and record that number too. Put a plus sign between the two numbers and an equal sign after. You have a number sentence that's ready for your young mathematicians to solve!

Allison
3 + 4 =

Elaine Gifford—Gr. K, Estill Elementary, Estill, SC

Name________________________________

Graph 'n' Snack

8				
7				
6				
5				
4				
3				
2				
1				

 Note to the teacher: Use with "Graph 'n' Snack" on page 56.

Name ____________________

Got It!

Roll the dice.

Count the dots.

Find a match.

Note to the teacher: Use with "Got It!" on page 61.

100 Patterns

Use with "Stamping to 100" on page 62.

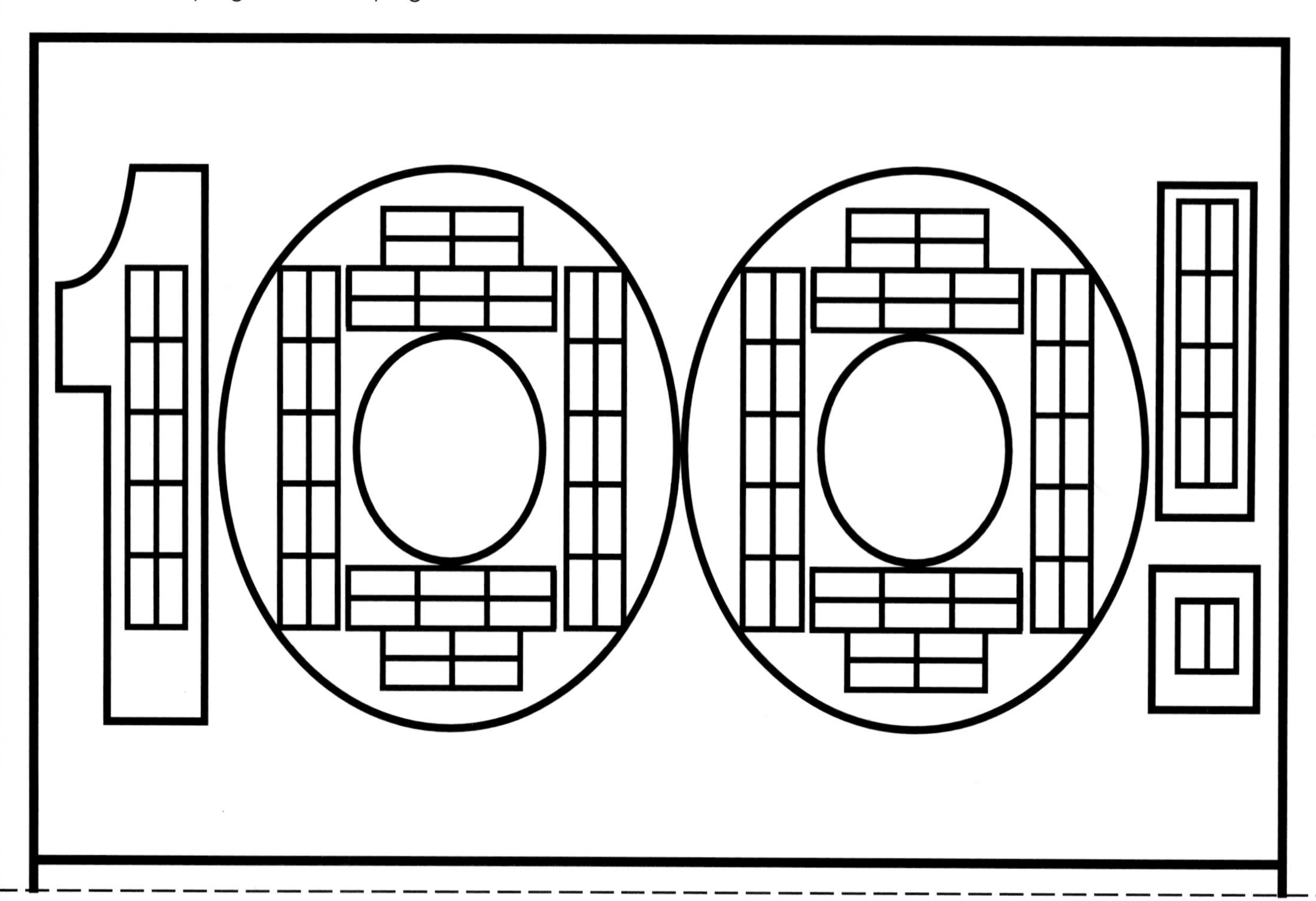

Recording Sheet

Use with "Jump!" on page 65.

Jump, ______________________, Jump!

(child's name)

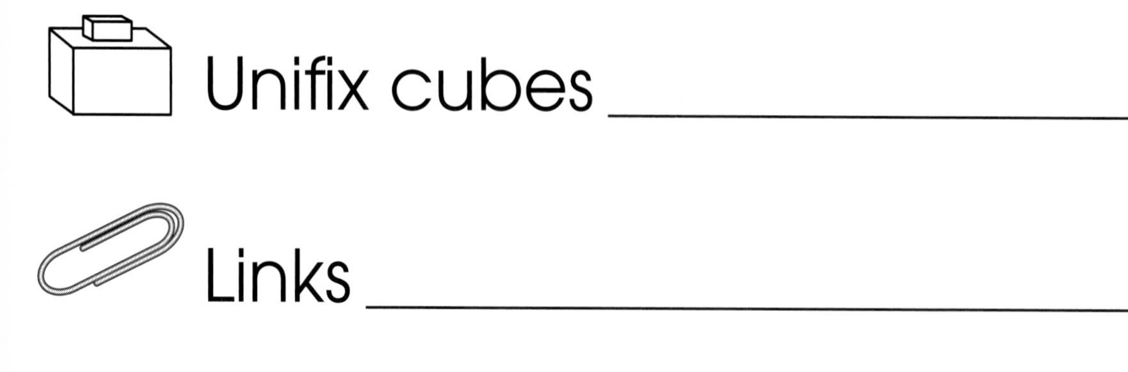

Unifix cubes ______________________

Links ______________________

Counters ______________________

Classroom Displays

Use your school's die-cutter to make this interactive bulletin board. Make a supply of colorful cutouts in a variety of shapes similar to those shown. Laminate the cutouts for durability. Attach rows of patterned cutouts to a bulletin board within students' reach. Remove a cutout from each row and attach the hook side of a Velcro dot in its place. Then put the loop side of the Velcro dot on the back of the cutout. Title the board as shown. Invite students to complete the patterns by positioning the cutouts in the correct places.

Melissa Auchenbach—Gr. K
Lower Gwynedd Elementary
Ambler, PA

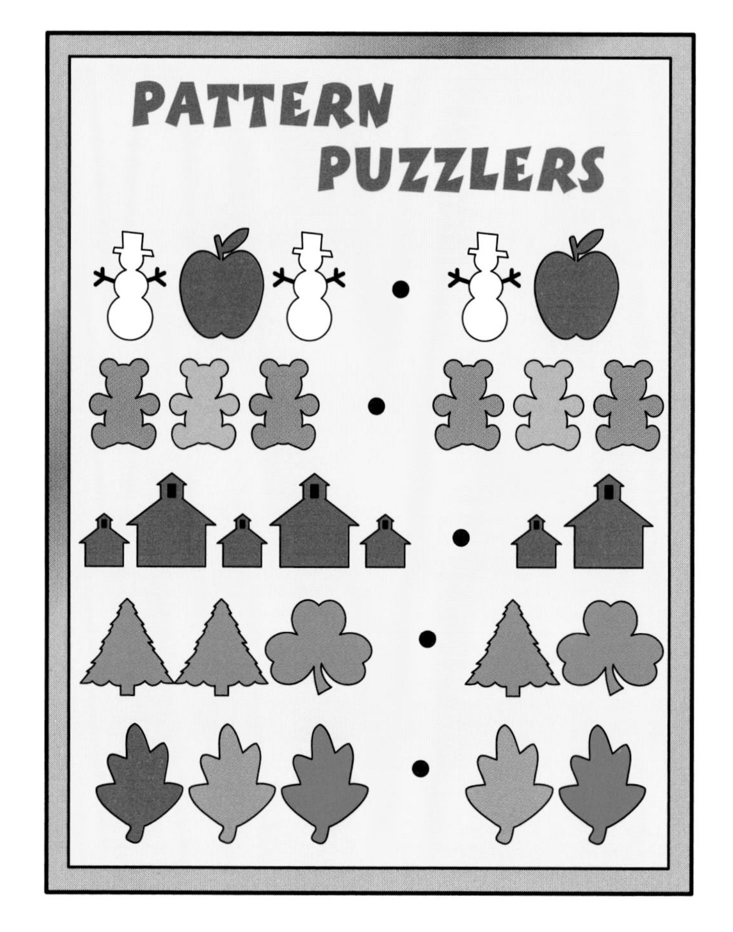

To prepare this simple seasonal display, staple two lengths of gray yarn vertically and horizontally to a bulletin board. Then, working with a long length of yarn and moving in a diamond pattern, staple the yarn to the board each time it crosses an intersecting line. Add a large spider decoration to the center of the web and the title shown. Slip good work behind the web and staple it in place.

Treena L. Ferguson—Gr. K, Edgewood Elementary, Pottstown, PA

Reinforce positive behavior with this gobblin' good display. Have each child color a small Styrofoam cup with a brown marker. Then hot-glue a large pom-pom to the cup as shown. Next, have the child cut out a construction paper beak, wattle, and eyes and then glue them to the pom-pom. Attach each turkey cup to the wall. Drop craft feathers in the cup of each student who shows good behavior. On a designated day, reward students' efforts with a treat of corn—candy corn!

adapted from an idea by Beverly Nordin—Gr. K, Sykes Elementary, Jackson, MS

All you need for this jazzy bulletin board is a class set of free Internet CDs and student photos! Cut each photo to fit the center of a CD and then glue it in place. Use a permanent marker to label each disc with the student's name. Attach the CDs to a bulletin board using double-sided tape, and add the title shown. Now that's hip!

adapted from ideas by

Lisa Cohen—Gr. K
Laurel Plains Elementary
New City, NY

Bonnie Keller—Gr. K
Moore Elementary
Clarksville, TN

Use this bulletin board idea to encourage your little ones to curl up with a good book! In advance, take a photograph of each child wrapped in a blanket, holding a teddy bear, and looking at a favorite book. Staple the photos to a bulletin board; then attach a bear and book cutout along with the title shown.

Judy Ruiz—Gr. K, Holaway Elementary, Tucson, AZ

Your students' faces will light up when they see this bright and shiny tree display! To begin, put a small amount of inexpensive hair gel and one or two drops of food coloring in a resealable plastic bag for each child. Seal the bags. Have each youngster rub his bag to mix the contents. Next, cut a large tree shape from green bulletin board paper. Then cut a two-inch circle in the tree, as shown, for each child. Tape a bag behind each hole and then tape the tree to a sunny window. What a beautiful tree!

Sheila Crawford—Five-Year-Olds
Kids Kampus
Huntington, IN

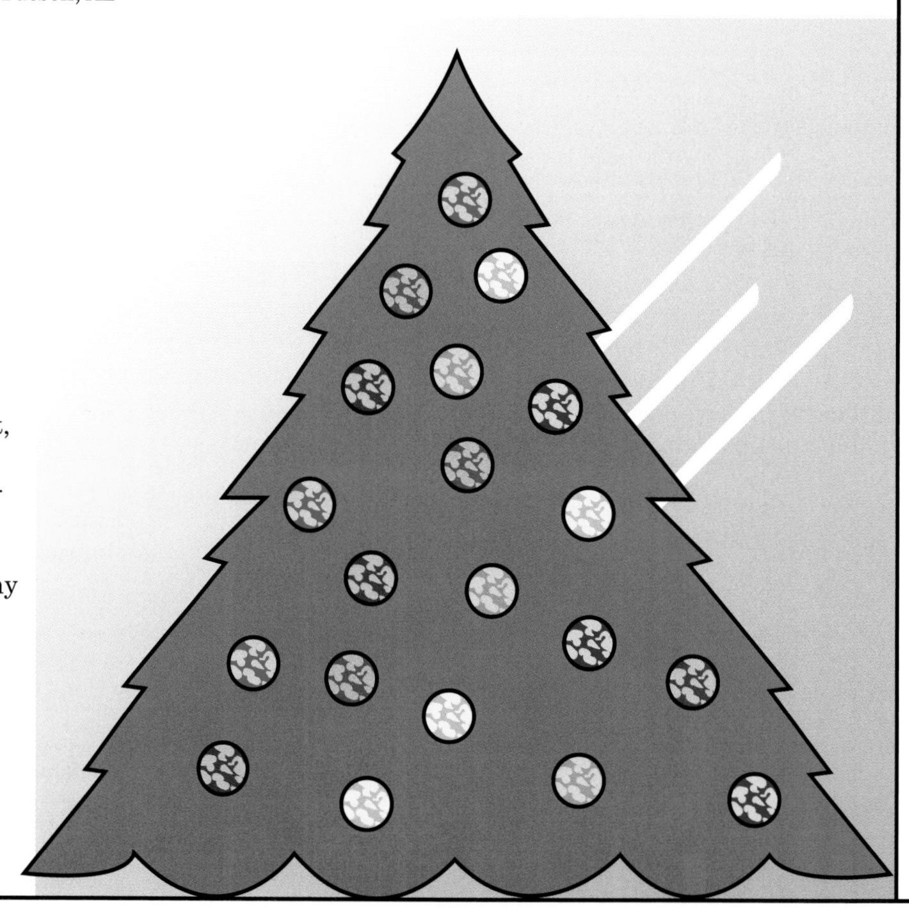

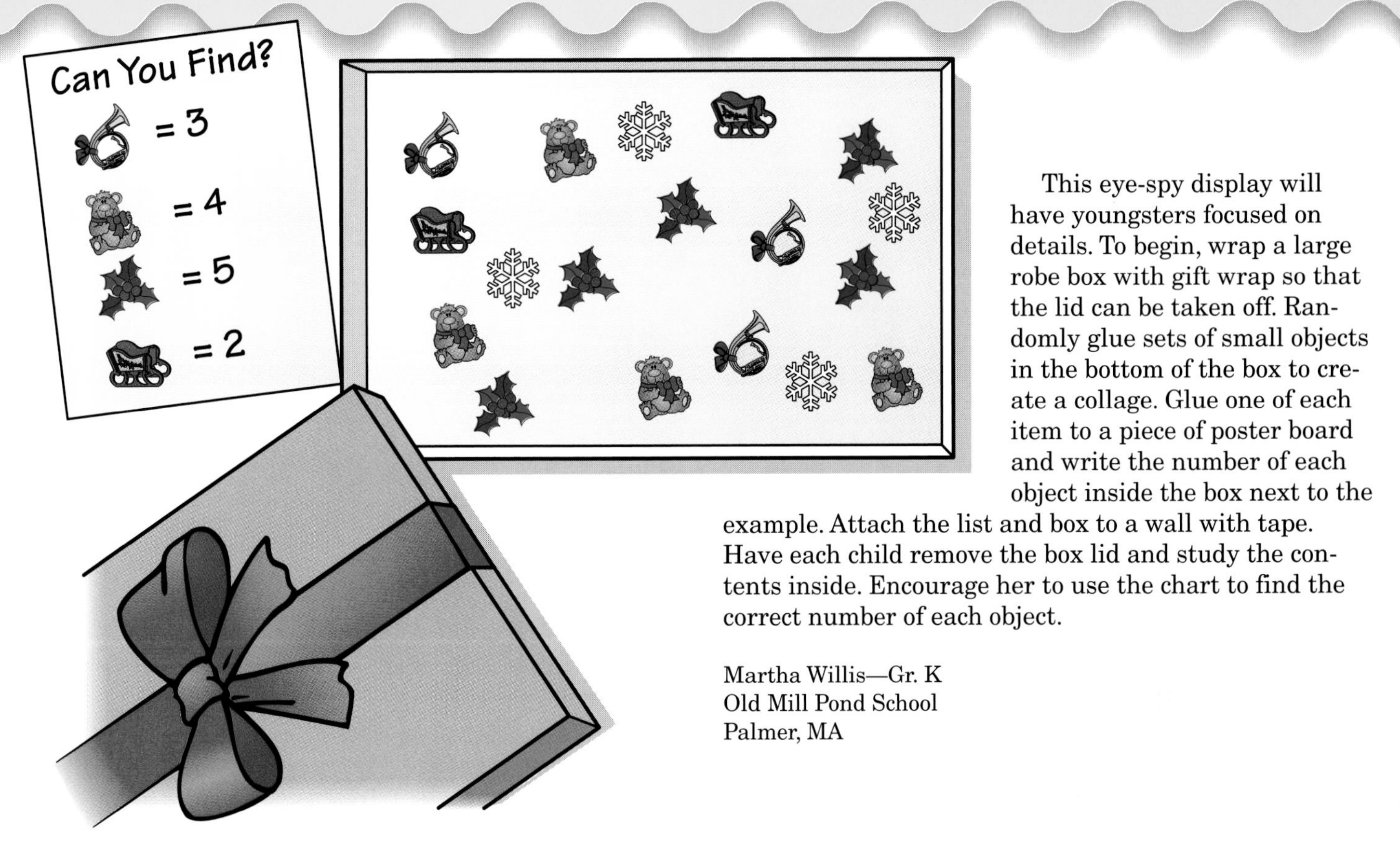

This eye-spy display will have youngsters focused on details. To begin, wrap a large robe box with gift wrap so that the lid can be taken off. Randomly glue sets of small objects in the bottom of the box to create a collage. Glue one of each item to a piece of poster board and write the number of each object inside the box next to the example. Attach the list and box to a wall with tape. Have each child remove the box lid and study the contents inside. Encourage her to use the chart to find the correct number of each object.

Martha Willis—Gr. K
Old Mill Pond School
Palmer, MA

This interactive bulletin board will have little ones matching numerals to picture sets. To prepare, glue numeral cutouts to one side of a large piece of white bulletin board paper and randomly add sticker sets to the opposite side of the paper. Then draw lines to separate each set. Laminate the paper for durability. Staple the paper to a low bulletin board or to the wall within students' reach. Tie a water-based marker to a length of yarn and then attach it to the wall near the board. Have each child count each set of stickers and use the marker to draw a line from the set to the corresponding numeral. After a youngster has matched all sets and numerals, have him use a damp paper towel to erase his lines.

Melissa Auchenbach—Gr. K, Lower Gwenydd Elementary, Ambler, PA

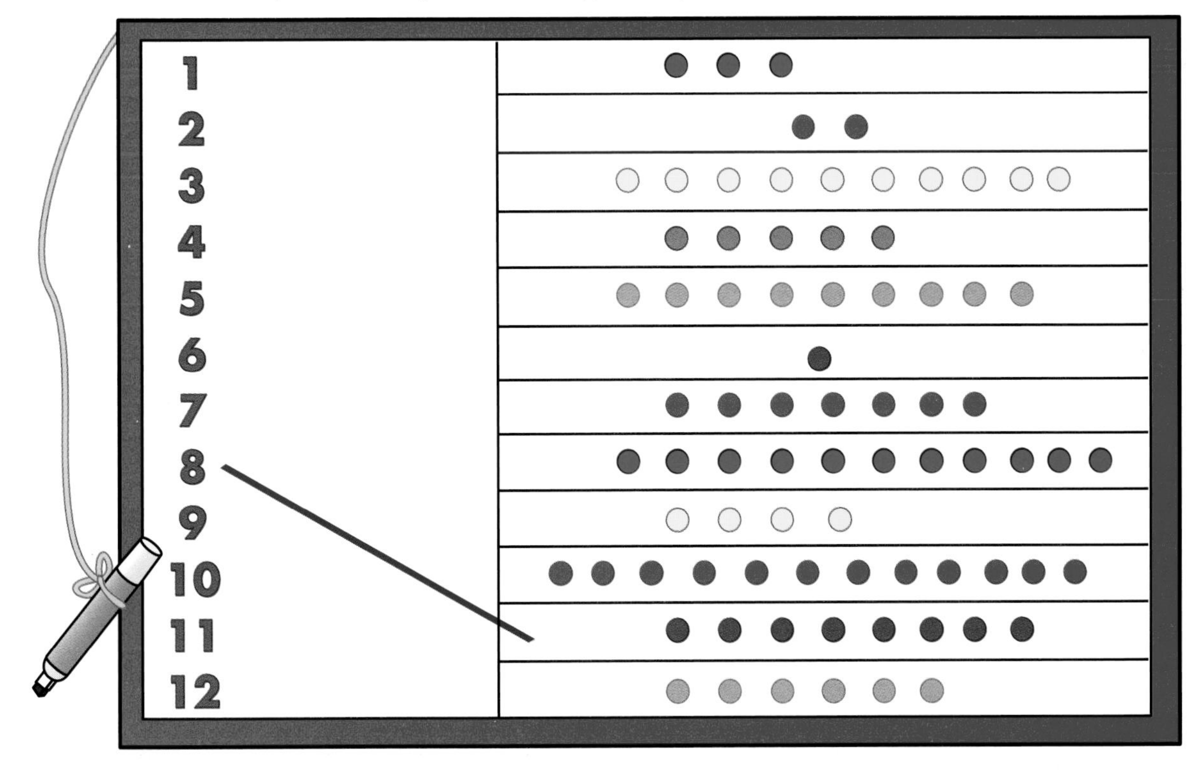

Patterns make this display extra pretty! Give each child a nine-inch square of construction paper. Have her use heart-shaped sponges and paint to create a pattern on her paper. Cut a large heart from bulletin board paper. Position the patterned squares on the heart and then glue them in place. Trim the outer edges of the heart and staple it to your wall. Finally, add a ruffled edge of crepe paper and the title shown. What a sweet heart!

Lora Lancaster Krpejs—Gr. K, Trinity Elementary School, High Point, NC

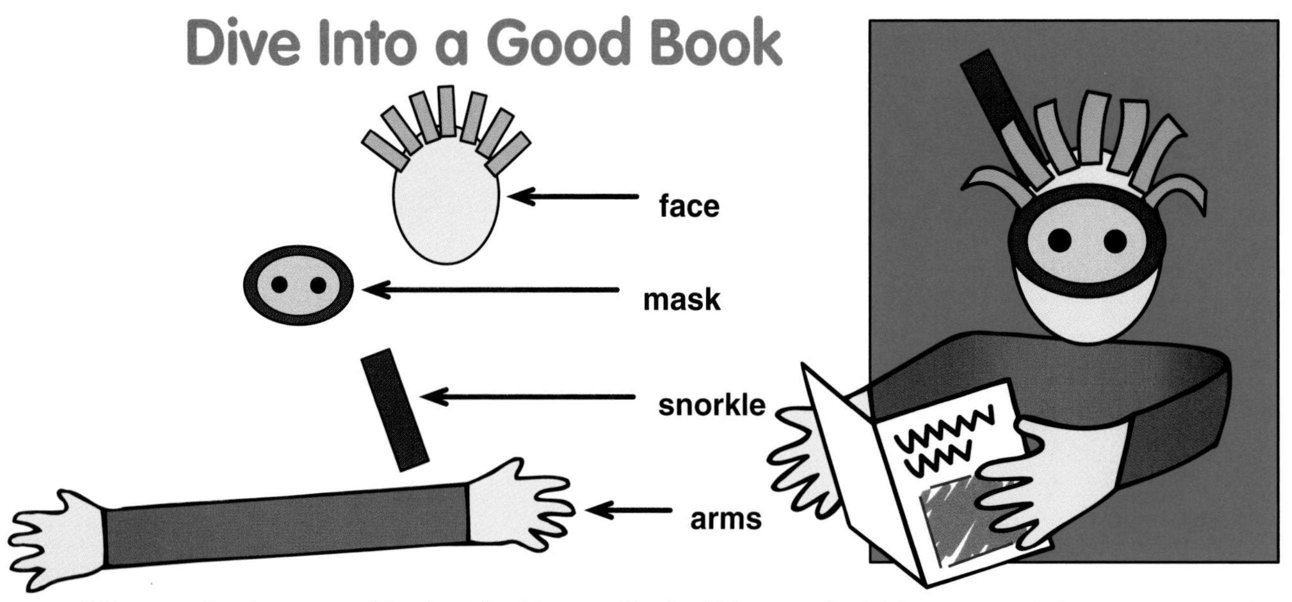

Why not dive into a good book with this cute display? Have each child cut an oval from an appropriate color of flesh-toned construction paper and then glue on strips of construction paper hair. Next, have him glue on a mask made from a small light blue construction paper oval glued to a larger black construction paper oval. Have each child cut black circle eyes and a snorkel tube. Glue the eyes to the mask and the tube behind the head. Have each youngster trace his hands and then cut out the shapes. Have him glue the shapes to a 3" x 18" strip of paper as shown. Give each child a sheet of white construction paper and have him illustrate the cover of his favorite book. Assemble the pieces as shown and attach them to a sheet of blue construction paper. Display the divers with the title shown.

Johanna Litts—Gr. K, North Central Elementary, Hermansville, MI

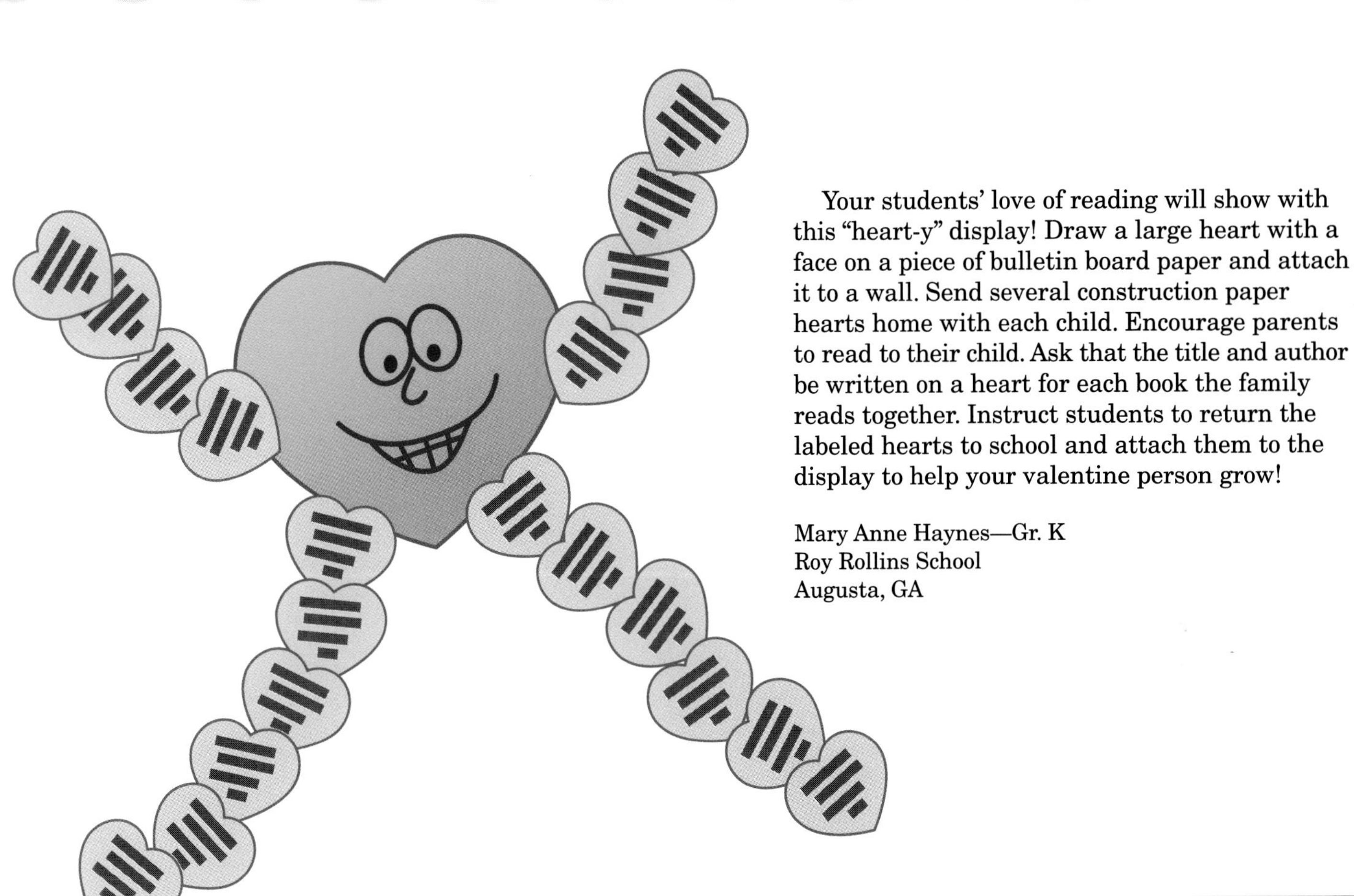

Your students' love of reading will show with this "heart-y" display! Draw a large heart with a face on a piece of bulletin board paper and attach it to a wall. Send several construction paper hearts home with each child. Encourage parents to read to their child. Ask that the title and author be written on a heart for each book the family reads together. Instruct students to return the labeled hearts to school and attach them to the display to help your valentine person grow!

Mary Anne Haynes—Gr. K
Roy Rollins School
Augusta, GA

Your youngsters will stick to the five senses with this bulletin board idea. Cover a small bulletin board with felt. Label the board as shown. Cut pictures from discarded magazines that show the senses being used or pictures in which you could use your senses. Laminate each one and then add a piece of Velcro (the hook side) to the back. Place the pictures near the bulletin board and encourage students to position them on the board next to the appropriate sense.

Melissa Auchenbach—Gr. K
Lower Gwynedd Elementary School
Ambler, PA

CLASSROOM DISPLAYS

Here's a springtime project for all the kindergartners in your school! Draw, color, and cut out a hound dog from white poster board; then cut it in half. Next, make a body section for each kindergartner. Number each body piece; then distribute them for the children to color with markers or crayons. When the remaining number of school days and the number of kindergartners correspond, put the display up in a hallway. As each day passes, have a child remove her section, moving the back end of the hound a bit closer to the front, and moving everyone closer to the end of school!

Sandy Agne—Gr. K
Tipton Elementary School
Tipton, IA

Put colorful plastic jug lids to good use this spring! For each child, glue several lids to blue background paper to make a flower shape; then glue the child's picture to the center. Use green paint to add a stem, leaves, and grass. Then have students draw and cut out insects to complete the display.

Stacy Wingen—Gr. K, Howard Elementary, Howard, SD

For a fresh follow-up to Eric Carle's *The Very Hungry Caterpillar,* mount green paper circles on a wall in the shape of a caterpillar; then add a face as shown. Give each child a sheet of copy paper with the sentence starter shown. Have her dictate an ending to the sentence and draw a picture. Mount the papers on the caterpillar background.

Pat Ostrowka—Gr. K, Pilot Elementary, Greensboro, NC

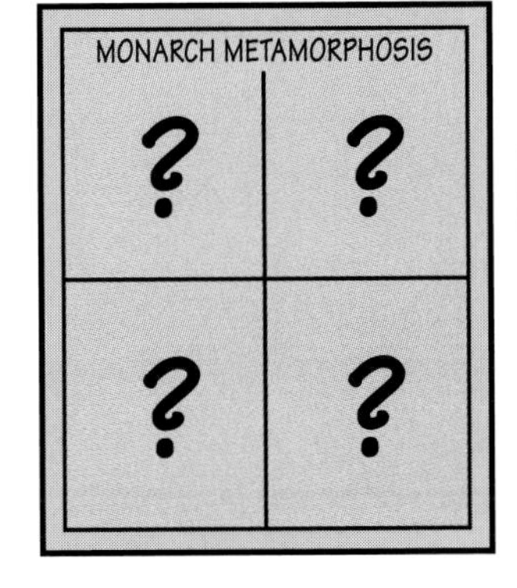

Make this mystery display to introduce the concept of *metamorphosis.* Divide a bulletin board with the title shown into four sections; then mount a question mark cutout in each space. Bring in caterpillars for students to observe; then every few days replace a question mark with one of the labeled stages of metamorphosis as directed below:

Box 1: Display a paper leaf and half of a Styrofoam egg shape.
Box 2: Display a paper leaf and half of a painted cardboard egg carton.
Box 3: Display a paper leaf and a chrysalis cut from paper.
Box 4: Have students decorate butterfly cutouts to place in the last box.

Diana Phillips—Gr. K
Washington Elementary School
Jacksonville, IL

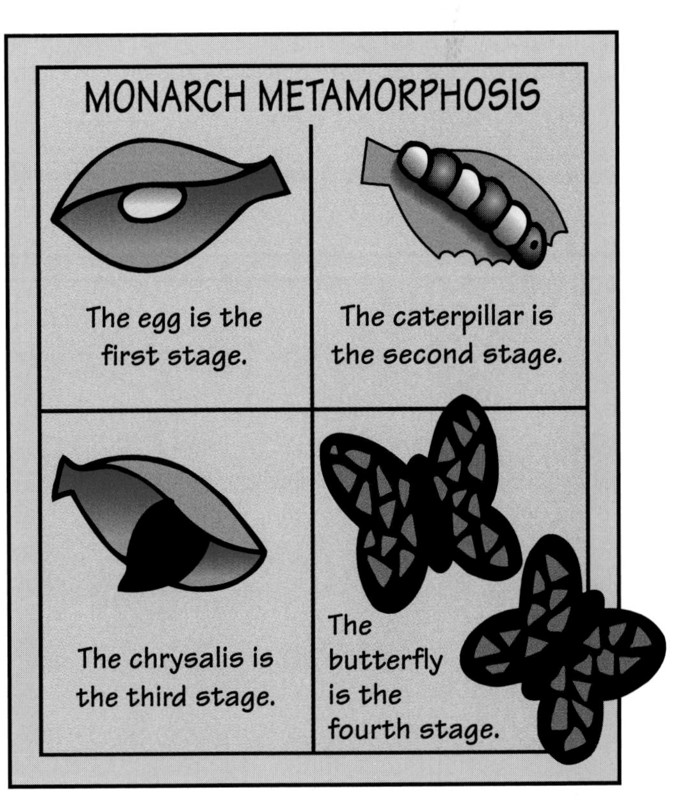

This mouthwatering display will send students on their way to summer! Have each child use craft foam shapes, confetti, sequins, or other craft materials to decorate a construction paper scoop of ice cream. Attach each scoop to a triangle of tan paper, crosshatched to resemble a cone. Display all the ice-cream creations with the title shown.

Michelle LeMaster-Johnson—Grs. K–4/K–5, Windlake Elementary, Milwaukee, WI

Make this grand ol' flag to celebrate the Fourth of July! On a large piece of white bulletin board paper, pencil in the stripes and the field of blue. Have students sponge-paint or make red paint handprints to create the red stripes. Add blue paint in the corner. When it's dry, have each child help add white sponge-painted stars. If desired, enhance some of the stars by mounting a child's photo in the center of each one.

Ellen Moser—Gr. K
South Kortright Central School
South Kortright, NY

Heather Tulak—Gr. K
Labadieville Primary School
Labadieville, LA

Getting Your Ducks in a Row

Getting Your Ducks in a Row

Management Tips for the Classroom

Action-Packed Scavenger Hunt

When your new kindergartners visit your classroom just before the start of the school year, send them on a scavenger hunt! Make a simple scavenger hunt sheet (similar to the one shown), listing places in the classroom you want students to see. Duplicate the list for each child. Make the hunt more active by posting a sign at each spot that asks youngsters to perform an action. For example, post a sign near the pencil sharpener that says "Can you sharpen your pencil?" Near the soap dispenser at the sink, post a sign that says "Can you make the soap come out?" Little ones will become familiar with their new classroom and gain a sense of accomplishment.

Lisa Wilkinson—Gr. K, Loveville School, Loveville, MD

Slipcover Storage

Looking for a convenient place for youngsters to store their supplies? How about on the backs of their chairs? Purchase some sturdy twill fabric with a colorful design; then sew a simple slipcover to place over the back of each child's chair. Sew a pocket onto each slipcover, inserting a length of elastic in the top hem. The pocket will securely hold a box of school supplies, and keep tables clear and cubbies uncluttered!

Janice Harford—Gr. K, Kelowna, British, Columbia, Canada

Plants With a Purpose

A potted ivy plant in the center of each of your group tables will add to your classroom decor, and it can serve as a teaching tool! Insert a florist's cardholder in each plant. Then display cards showing colors, numbers, letters, or sight words to name each table. Call students to group time or to line up by the table name specified on their plant. Change the table names as often as you desire to help reinforce various skills. Your little ones will enjoy caring for the plants and watching them grow. And at the end of the year, the plants make wonderful gifts for parent helpers!

Toni Osterbuhr—Gr. K
Price-Harris School, Wichita, KS

Positive Pockets

Keep your students on their best behavior by having them collect a pocketful of craft sticks! To store the craft sticks, cut the pockets from several pairs of old jeans. Hot-glue the pockets—one per child—onto a large piece of denim fabric. Tape a name card to the front of each pocket; then hang the piece of fabric on a wall within students' reach. Once a student has accumulated five sticks for good behavior, present her with a prize, such as a trip to a treasure box full of inexpensive goodies. Yippee! It's time to cash in!

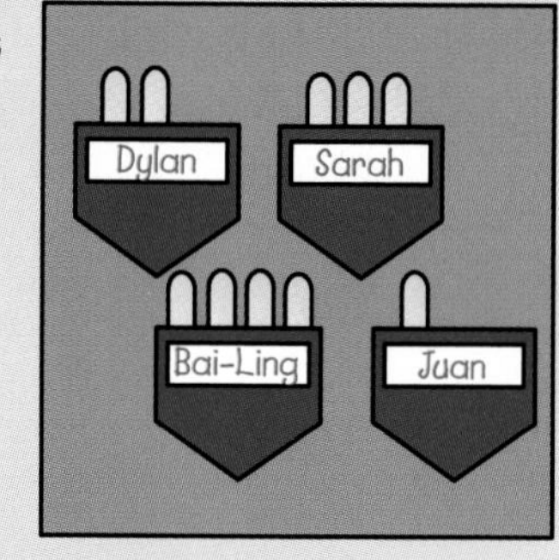

Erica Cerwin—Gr. K
Thornton Elementary, San Antonio, TX

From Home to School

Take attendance each day with this easy display! To prepare, cut out a large house and a large school building from poster board. Color the cutouts and add details as you desire. Display the cutouts on a wall or bulletin board within children's reach. Next, write each child's name on a separate strip of tagboard. Add self-adhesive Velcro to the backs of all the name strips and to the house and school shapes. Place all the name strips on the house shape. As each child arrives, ask him to move his name from the house to the school. Then as he leaves each day, have him move his name back to the house shape. Students will be learning to recognize their names, and you can see at a glance who's at school!

Johnna Lewis—Preschool/Kindergarten
St. Agnes Central School
Mingo Junction, OH

Getting Your Ducks in a Row

Management Tips for the Classroom

Save the Soap!

Are your little ones a bit overzealous with the soap from your hand-pump dispenser? Twist a thick rubber band around the neck of the pump. This will control the amount dispensed with each pump and still allow enough soap to get little hands squeaky clean!

Anne Marie Chemi—Gr. K
Culpepper, VA

Soda Cans at the Easel

Here's an inexpensive alternative to plastic paint cups for your easel. Use soda cans with wide mouths. Simply rinse out the cans and pull the pop-tops completely off. Add a bit of masking tape around each can opening to eliminate any sharp edges. Tape a piece of construction paper around the can to correspond with the paint color you'll be putting inside it. Then half-fill the cans with paint and slip in your favorite brushes!

Kathie Clark—Gr. K
Arrowhead School
Copley, OH

The Silly Box

Help your kindergartners with self-control by creating a Silly Box. Cover a cardboard box with bright bulletin board paper and place it near your classroom door. Each day when students arrive, ask them to drop their sillies in the box. If a child is acting silly at an inappropriate time, remind him to drop his sillies in the box. In fact, little ones will soon be reminding one another! Of course, you'll want to periodically invite each child to retrieve his sillies from the box for a scheduled silly time!

Lee Ann Wilson—Gr. K
Lone Star Elementary
Keller, TX

Border Storage

Binder clips will help keep your bulletin board borders in easy reach. Secure each set of borders with a medium or large binder clip. Then place some self-adhesive hooks along a wall in your classroom storage closet. Simply hang the clips on the hooks, and you can find your borders whenever you need them!

Annemarie Hodge—Gr. K
Ocee Elementary School
Alpharetta, GA

Please Return

Want to make sure parents see important papers that must be returned to school? Choose one color to be used *only* for papers that must be returned, such as field trip permission slips, emergency forms, or school surveys. Tell parents about your color-coded system, and they'll soon learn to keep an eye out for those most important papers.

Shelly Fales—Gr. K
Whittemore-Prescott Early Childhood Center
Whittemore, MI

Getting Your Ducks in a Row
Management Tips for the Classroom

Roll Card
Afraid that you might forget to grab your roll book during a fire drill or that you might be outside and not have it available? Solve the problem by keeping a class list handy at all times. Simply type the names of all your students on a mailing label and stick the label to the back of your identification badge or a laminated card you keep in your pocket all the time. You can make sure all your little ones are safe and sound—anytime, anywhere!

Christy DeLashmit—Gr. K
Brighton Elementary
Brighton, TN

Paint Dispenser
Encourage independence at center time by mounting a paint dispenser on the wall of your art area. Purchase a dispenser for liquid soap, shampoo, and lotion at your local discount store. Fill the compartments with different colors of paint and provide small margarine tubs at your art center. Show youngsters how to dispense a small amount of paint into a tub. If desired, add a chart nearby showing how to mix primary colors to make secondary colors. Now they can help themselves to paint during center time!

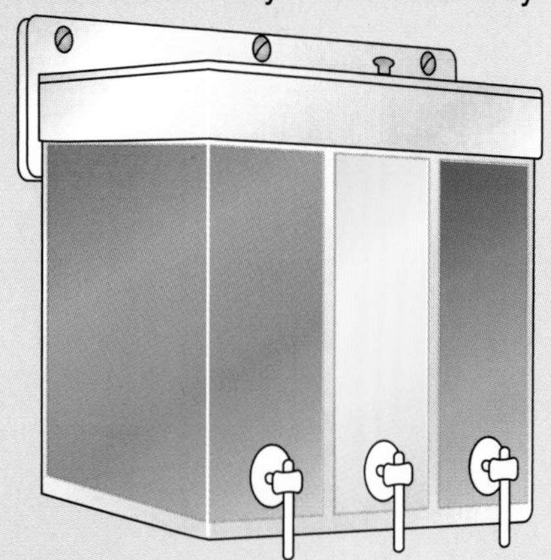

Lindsey A. Vail—Gr. K
Quincy, MA

A Sticky Note
Need to make sure Mom and Dad see a note or reminder? Type the note on your computer; then print it out on label paper. Stick the label onto a child's clothing to transform him into a walking reminder! If you're worried the child may remove the note, stick it onto his back.

Niki Frew—Gr. K
Coquihalla Elementary
Hope, British Columbia, Canada

Medicine Reminder
If you have a student who needs to take medicine at a certain time each day, try this tip! Bring in a digital alarm clock and set it to remind you when it's medicine time. When the alarm rings, send the child to the nurse to receive her dose. Then reset the clock so that it will ring the next day at the appropriate time. Keep a stack of preprinted slips near the clock and fill out one each day to assure parents the child received her medicine.

Johnna Young—Gr. K
Rocky Gap Elementary
Rocky Gap, VA

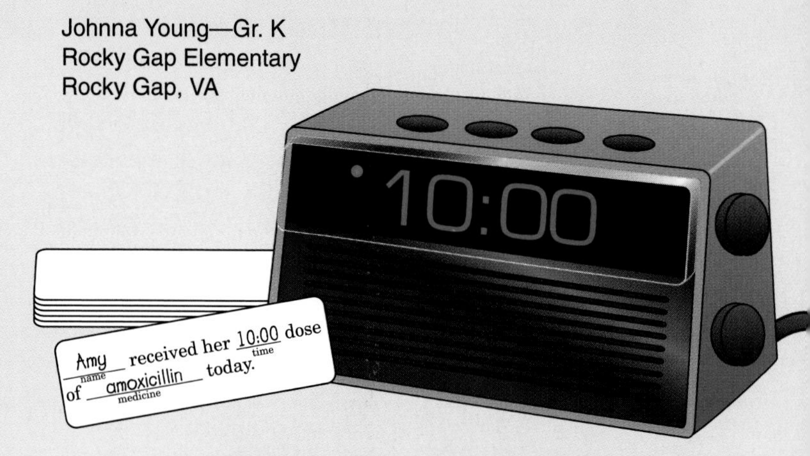

Flash Card Storage
Here's a clever way to store your supply of teacher-made flash cards—place them in a recipe file box! Use the tabbed dividers that come with many such boxes to separate the flash cards by subject or skill.

Melissa Merritt—Gr. K
East End Elementary
Humboldt, TN

Getting Your Ducks in a Row

Management Tips for the Classroom

Audiotapes at Hand

Want a handy way to store your audio cassette tapes? Try check boxes! Simply empty out the books of checks from their box. Now you have a sturdy holder for up to 12 cassette tapes in their plastic cases! Just stand the cassette boxes upright inside the check box. The titles will be easy to read, and the box won't take up much space in your listening center.

Julia F. Simmons
Aberdeen Elementary
Chesapeake, VA

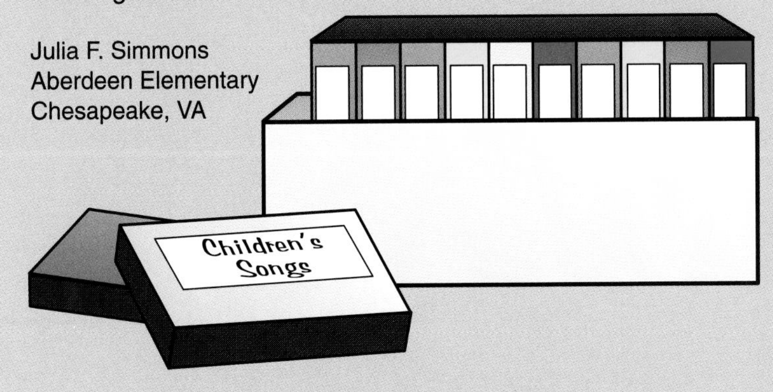

Personalized Game Pieces

Make board games more fun with these picture-perfect game pieces! Attach the loop side of a small piece of Velcro to each Candyland game piece; then make a set of small class pictures with the hook side of the Velcro on the back of each one. When a group is set to play a game, have each child attach her picture to a game piece. No more forgetting if she's red or blue in the middle of the game!

Elizabeth DeChellis—Gr. K
Victor Mravlag School No. 21
Elizabeth, NJ

Don't Pop That Bubble!

Need your students to stay quiet for a minute or two? Ask them to put bubbles in their mouths! Encourage each child to puff up his cheeks and hold on to the bubble of air by keeping his mouth closed. When it's okay to talk again, have everyone make a little popping noise!

Pam Sistrunk—Gr. K
South Leake Elementary
Walnut Grove, MS

Disposable Aprons

These paint aprons are easy—and free! To make one, cut off the bottom of a plastic grocery bag; then cut straight down the center of one wide side. Have the child slip his arms through the handles so that the still-intact side of the bag covers his front. Hold the back closed with a clothespin. When the painting's done, just toss the grocery-bag apron into a recycling bin that accepts plastic bags!

Bobbie Beasley—Gr. K Teacher's Aide
Weimer Elementary
St. Albans, WV

The Quiet Game

Try this supersimple game to keep youngsters quiet while waiting in line or when you need to speak to a colleague or parent. Choose one child who is standing or sitting quietly to stand in front of the group and be the Quiet Leader. That child then gets to choose someone else who is being quiet and well behaved, and the first Quiet Leader returns to his place. The game continues for as long as necessary, and others will marvel at your group's composure!

Shelly Kidd-Hamlett—Gr. K
Helena Elementary
Timberlake, NC

A Handy Book "Dish-play"!

Make picture books easily accessible for little hands by displaying them in a dish-drying rack! Purchase an inexpensive plastic or wire drying rack; then slide a picture book into each slot. Choosing and putting away books has never been easier!

Sherri Woodard—Gr. K
Wayne Grey Elementary
Addison, MI

Individual Writing Boards

Save paper with these convenient and clever dry-erase boards! Purchase an inexpensive sheet of 1/8-inch white tile board at your local hardware store. Request that the store cut the tile board into 9" x 12" pieces. (If the store does not cut tile board, it can be cut easily with a table saw). Have children use dry-erase markers directly on the tile board for a paper-saving portable desk! To use each piece as a clipboard, place a large binder clip at the top of the tile board as shown.

Sandra Miller—Gr. K
Mt. Calvary School
Erie, PA

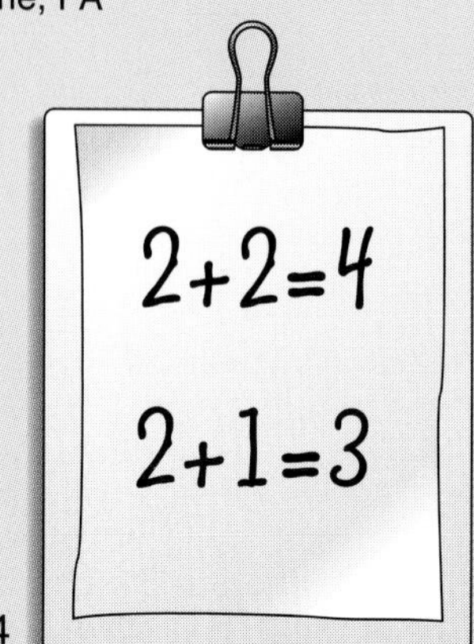

File Folder Holders

Looking for an inexpensive way to store file folders? Pop them into an empty 12 or 24-pack soda box! Simply remove the top of the box as shown; then slide file folders into the opening. If desired, cover the box with Con-Tact paper. Neat!

Shandra Hathaway—Gr. K
Haverhill Elementary
Fort Wayne, IN

Reusable Name Holders

Labeling cubbies and coat hooks is a snap with this handy timesaver! Purchase binder label holders at your local office supply store. Stick each self-adhesive plastic sleeve next to a cubby or coat hook. Write each student's name on an insert and then slip each one into a different plastic sleeve. Before school starts for a new year, program another set of inserts and place them in the sleeves. Voilà... You're ready for a new class of smiling faces!

Chris Zigment—Gr. K
Pauline Memorial Catholic School
Colorado Springs, CO

A Book Review for You!

All it takes is a click and a flash to review a year of class-made books! Lay the class-made books on a table with the titles showing. Then take a photograph of the books. Keep the picture handy as a reminder of the books completed that year and refer to it for future planning. Click! Flash! Finished!

Jennifer Barton—Gr. K
Elizabeth Green School
Glastonbury, CT

Kindergarten Café

Kindergarten Café

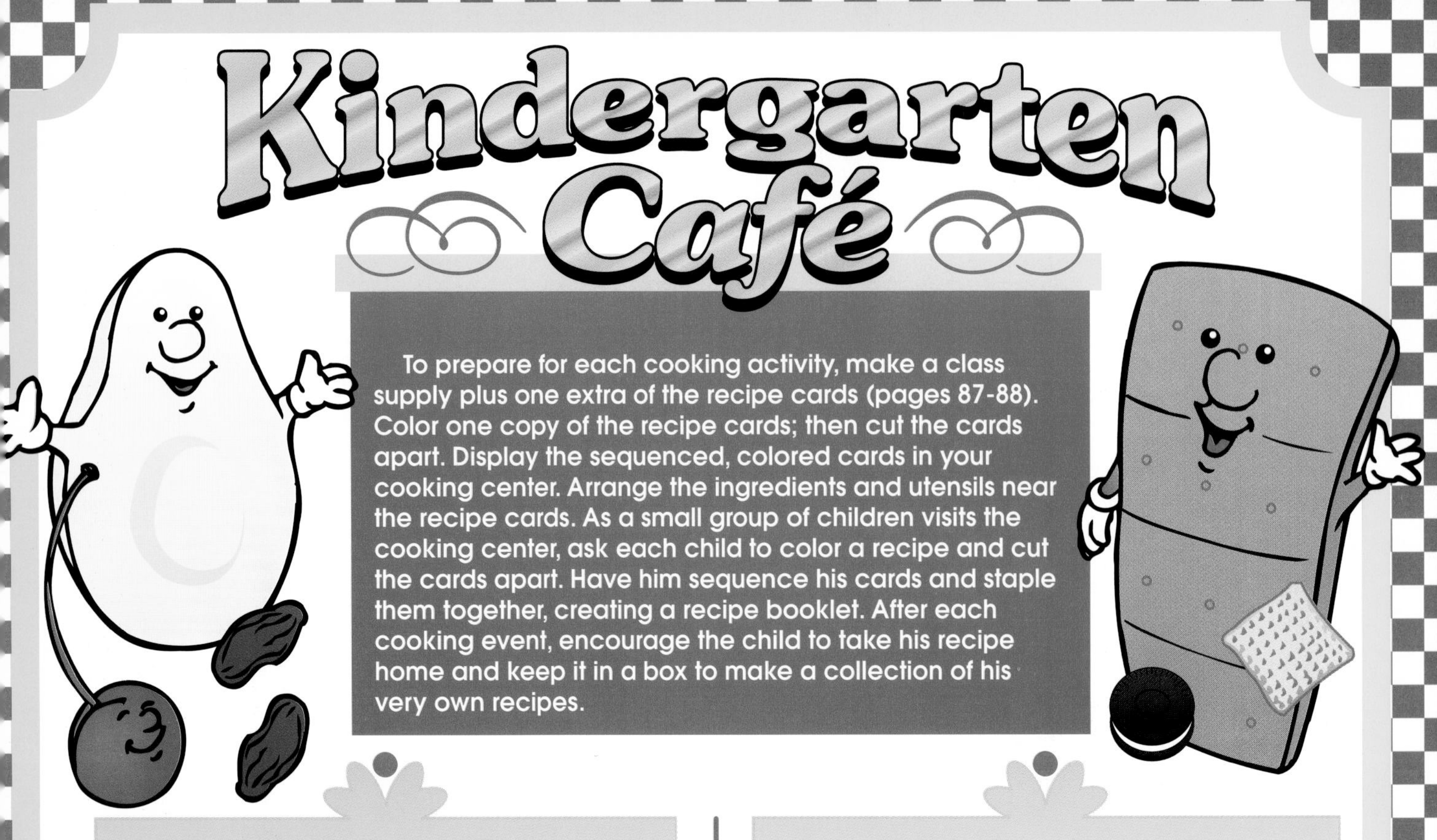

To prepare for each cooking activity, make a class supply plus one extra of the recipe cards (pages 87-88). Color one copy of the recipe cards; then cut the cards apart. Display the sequenced, colored cards in your cooking center. Arrange the ingredients and utensils near the recipe cards. As a small group of children visits the cooking center, ask each child to color a recipe and cut the cards apart. Have him sequence his cards and staple them together, creating a recipe booklet. After each cooking event, encourage the child to take his recipe home and keep it in a box to make a collection of his very own recipes.

Funny Fruit Face

Ingredients for one:
shredded cheese (hair)
canned pear half (head)
2 raisins (eyes)
maraschino cherry half (nose)

Utensils and supplies:
paper plate for each child
plastic fork for each child

Teacher preparation:
- Drain pears.
- Cut maraschino cherries in half.
- Arrange the ingredients, utensils, and supplies for easy student access.

Allison Pratt—Gr. K
Eagle Bluff Kindergarten
Onalaska, WI

School Bus Snack

Ingredients for one:
graham cracker (4 sections)
yellow-tinted vanilla frosting
4 pieces of Chex cereal
2 Mini Oreo cookies

Utensils and supplies:
paper plate for each child
plastic knife for each child

Teacher preparation:
- Tint vanilla frosting with yellow food coloring.
- Arrange the ingredients, utensils, and supplies for easy student access.

Melissa Hauck—Grs. PreK-1
Pear Tree Point School
Darien, CT

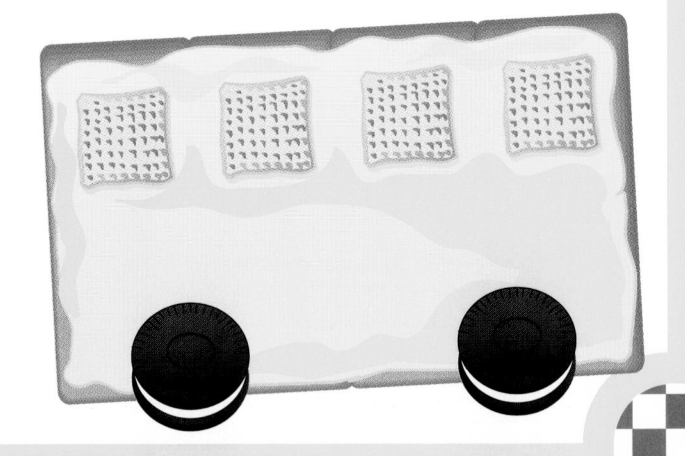

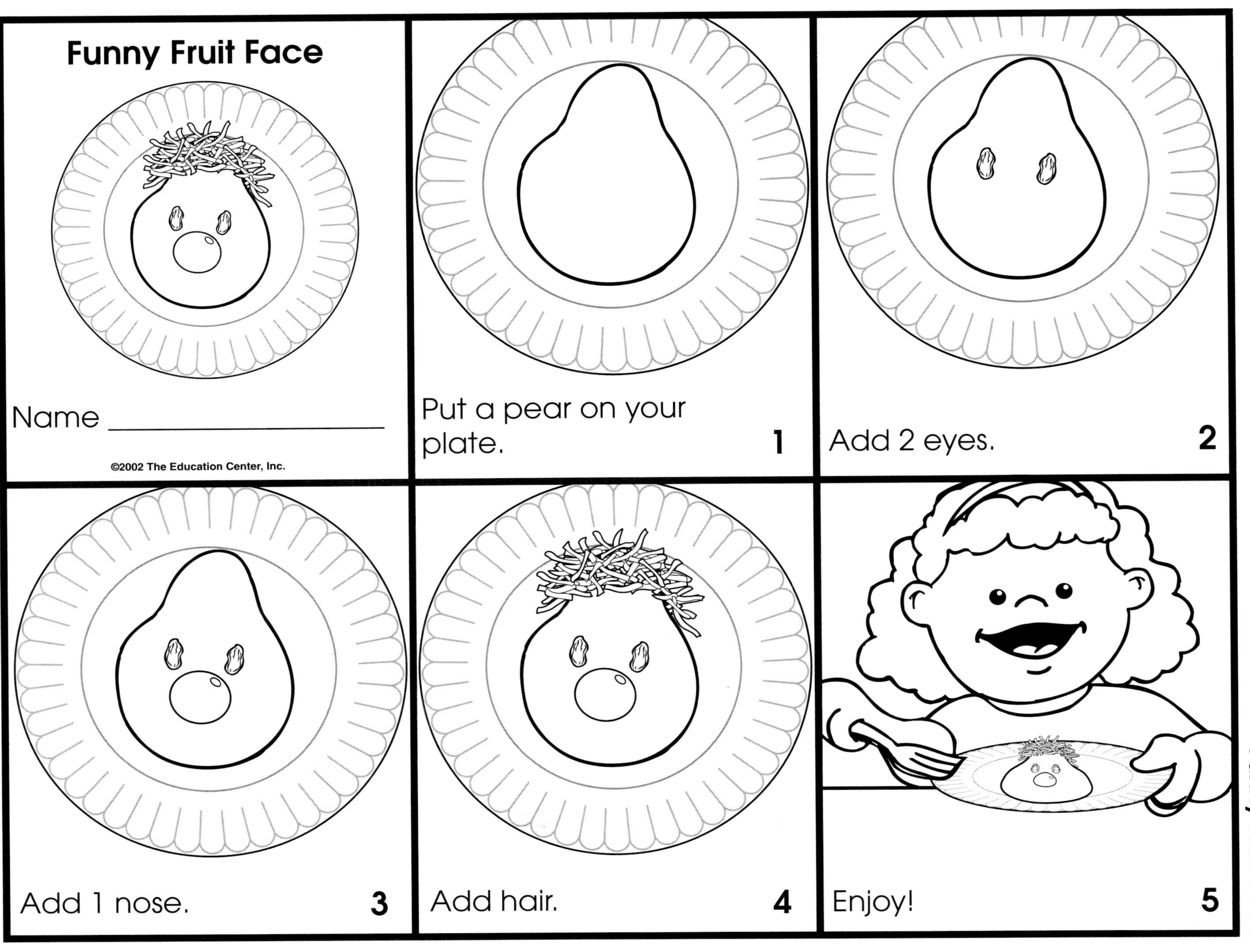
Funny Fruit Face
Name ________
©2002 The Education Center, Inc.
Put a pear on your plate.
1
Add 2 eyes.
2
Add 1 nose.
3
Add hair.
4
Enjoy!
5

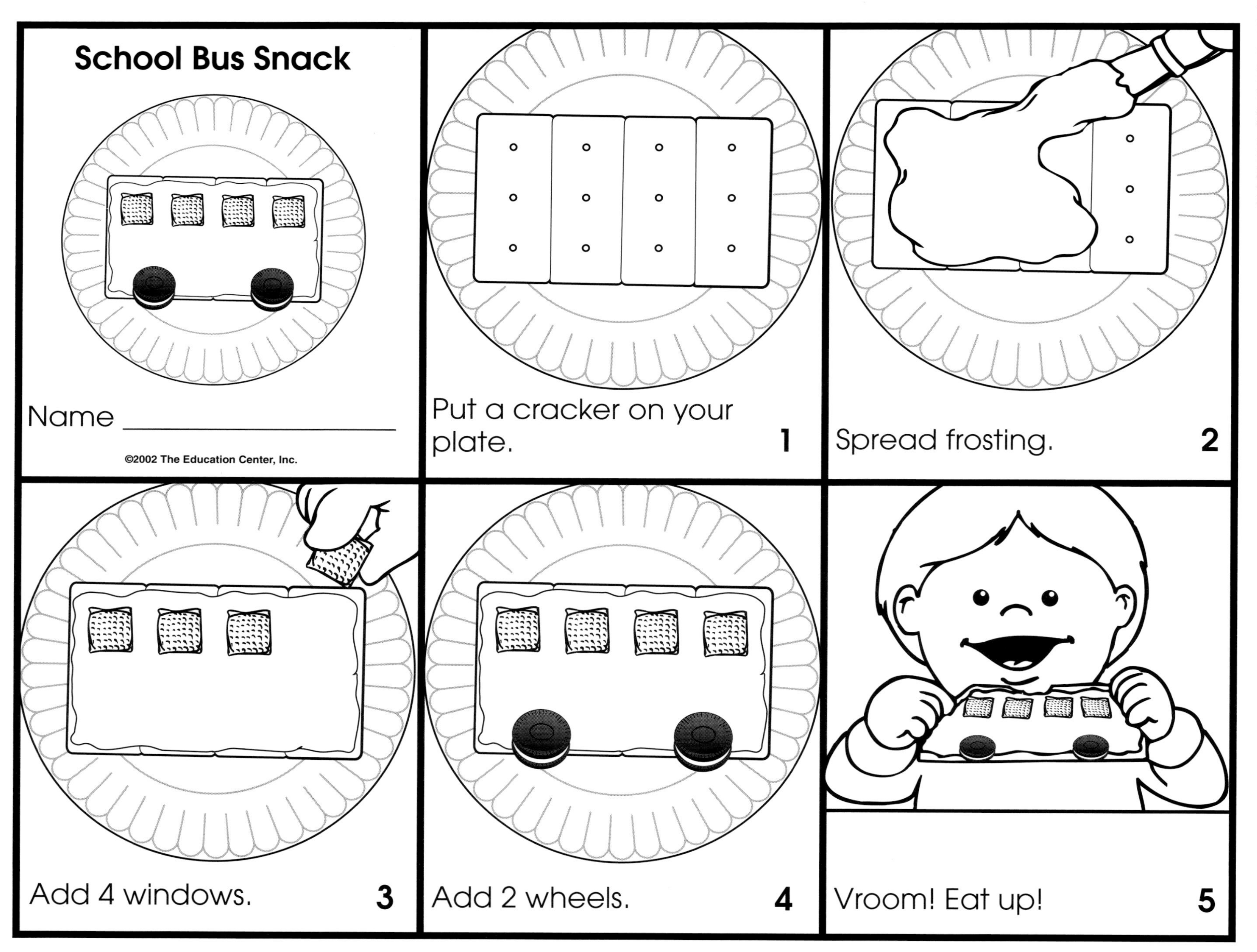
School Bus Snack
Name ________
©2002 The Education Center, Inc.
Put a cracker on your plate.
1
Spread frosting.
2
Add 4 windows.
3
Add 2 wheels.
4
Vroom! Eat up!
5

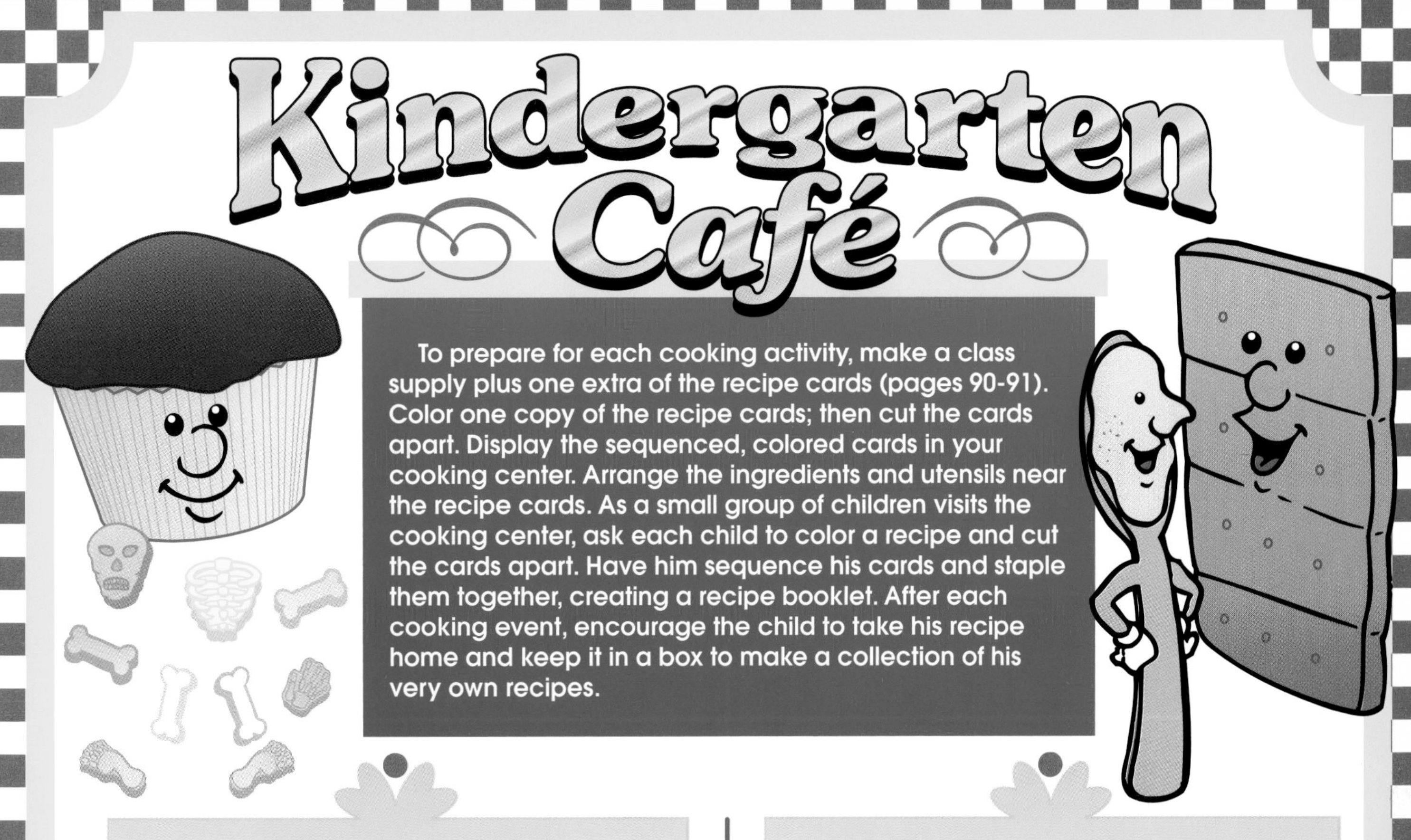

To prepare for each cooking activity, make a class supply plus one extra of the recipe cards (pages 90-91). Color one copy of the recipe cards; then cut the cards apart. Display the sequenced, colored cards in your cooking center. Arrange the ingredients and utensils near the recipe cards. As a small group of children visits the cooking center, ask each child to color a recipe and cut the cards apart. Have him sequence his cards and staple them together, creating a recipe booklet. After each cooking event, encourage the child to take his recipe home and keep it in a box to make a collection of his very own recipes.

Skeleton Snack

Ingredients for one:
cupcake
chocolate frosting
Brach's Dem Bones® candy

Utensils and supplies:
paper plate per child
plastic knife per child

Teacher preparation:
- Bake cupcakes according to package directions.
- Arrange the ingredients, utensils, and supplies for easy student access.

adapted from an idea by Sue Lewis Lein—Gr. 4K
St. Pius X Grade School
Wauwatosa, WI

Upside-Down Pumpkin Pie

Ingredients for one:
1/3 cup vanilla pudding flavored with pumpkin pie spice
1 tsp. canned pumpkin
2 tsp. graham cracker crumbs

Utensils and supplies:
clear plastic cup per child
plastic spoon per child
1/3-cup measuring cup

Teacher preparation:
- Prepare pudding according to package directions.
- Mix in one-fourth teaspoon of pumpkin pie spice per box of pudding.
- Crush graham crackers.
- Arrange the ingredients, utensils, and supplies for easy student access.

Cynthia Jamnik—Gr. K, Our Lady Queen of Peace School
Milwaukee, WI

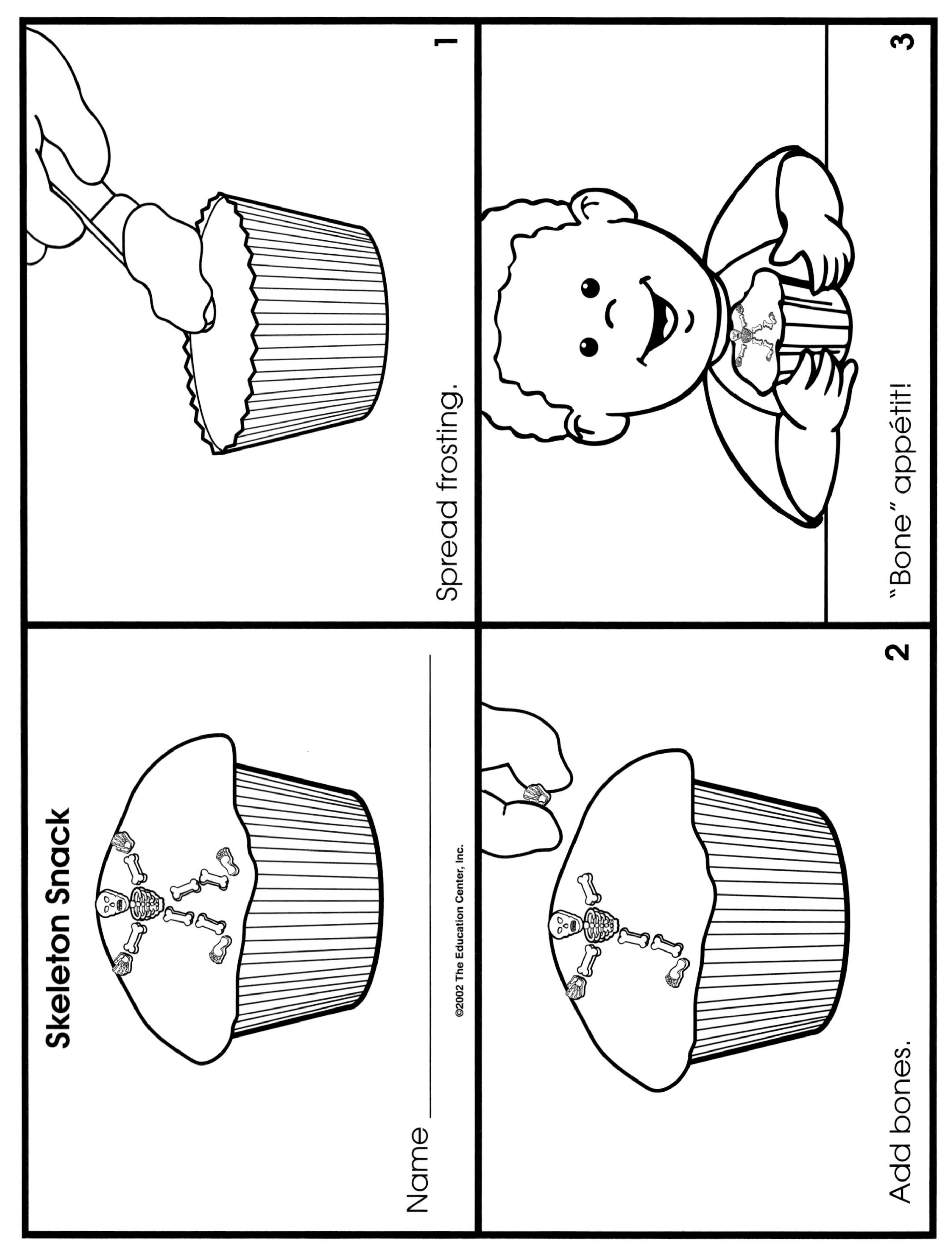
Skeleton Snack
Name
©2002 The Education Center, Inc.
1
Spread frosting.
2
Add bones.
3
"Bone" appétit!

Upside-Down Pumpkin Pie
Name ________
©2002 The Education Center, Inc.
$\frac{1}{3}$ cup
Put $\frac{1}{3}$ cup of pudding in your cup.
1
Add 1 spoonful of pumpkin. Stir.
2
Add crumbs. Dig in!
3

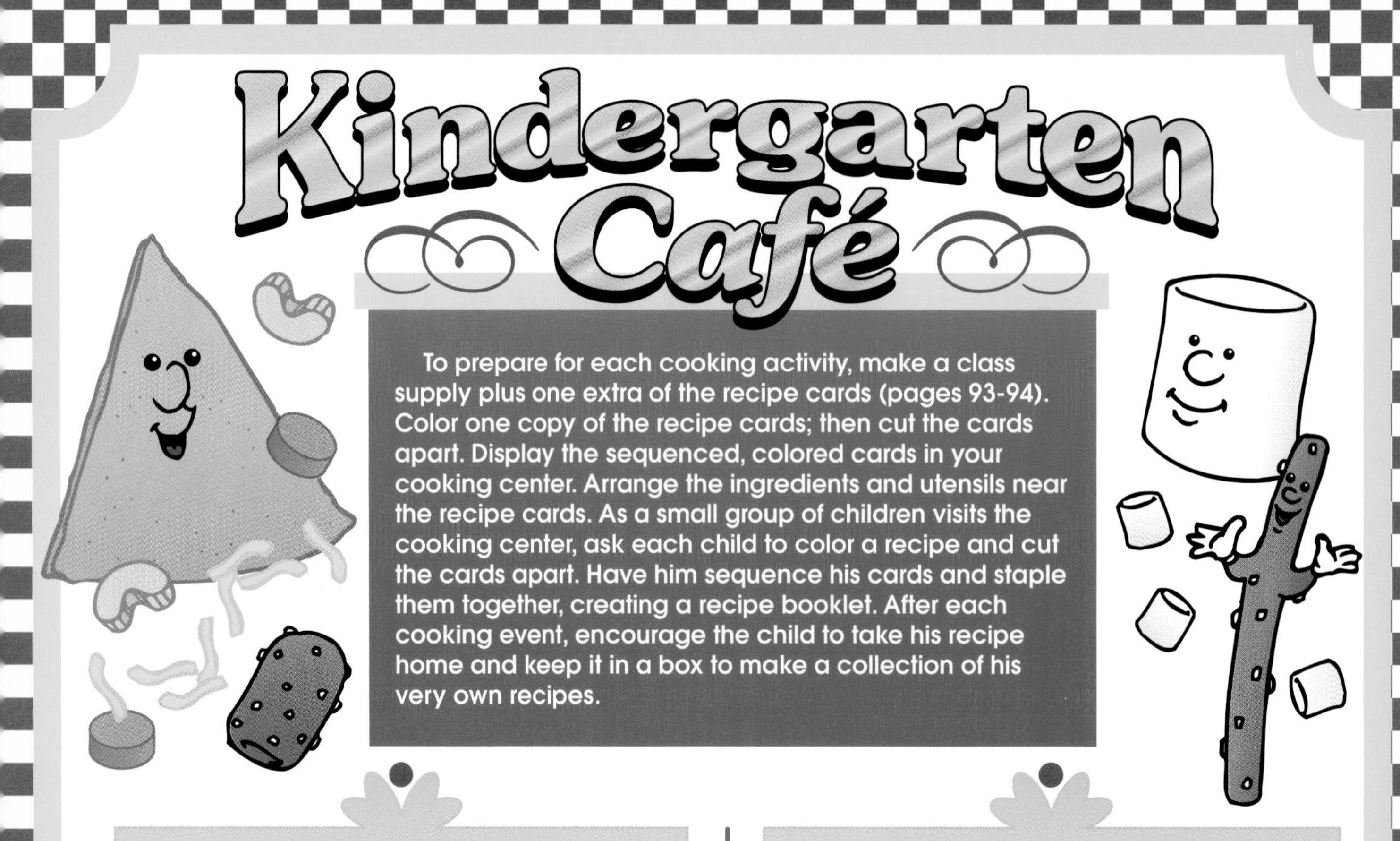

Kindergarten Café

To prepare for each cooking activity, make a class supply plus one extra of the recipe cards (pages 93-94). Color one copy of the recipe cards; then cut the cards apart. Display the sequenced, colored cards in your cooking center. Arrange the ingredients and utensils near the recipe cards. As a small group of children visits the cooking center, ask each child to color a recipe and cut the cards apart. Have him sequence his cards and staple them together, creating a recipe booklet. After each cooking event, encourage the child to take his recipe home and keep it in a box to make a collection of his very own recipes.

A Tortilla Tree

Ingredients for one:
$^1/_4$ spinach tortilla
pretzel nugget (trunk)
carrot slices (ornaments)
celery slices (ornaments)
ranch dressing (garland)
shredded cheese (tinsel)

Utensils and supplies:
paper plate for each child

Teacher preparation:
- Cut spinach tortillas into triangle-shaped quarters.
- Slice carrots and celery.
- Put ranch dressing in a squeeze bottle with a narrow opening, such as a ketchup bottle with a pointed tip.
- Arrange the ingredients, utensils, and supplies for easy student access.

Judi Lesnansky—Title I
New Hope Academy
Youngstown, OH

Sweet Snowflakes

Ingredients for one:
large marshmallow
6 pretzel sticks
6 miniature marshmallows
vanilla frosting

Utensils and supplies:
paper plate for each child
plastic knife for each child

Teacher preparation:
- Arrange the ingredients, utensils, and supplies for easy student access.

Jessica Hines—Gr. K
Clarksville Elementary
Clarksville, TX

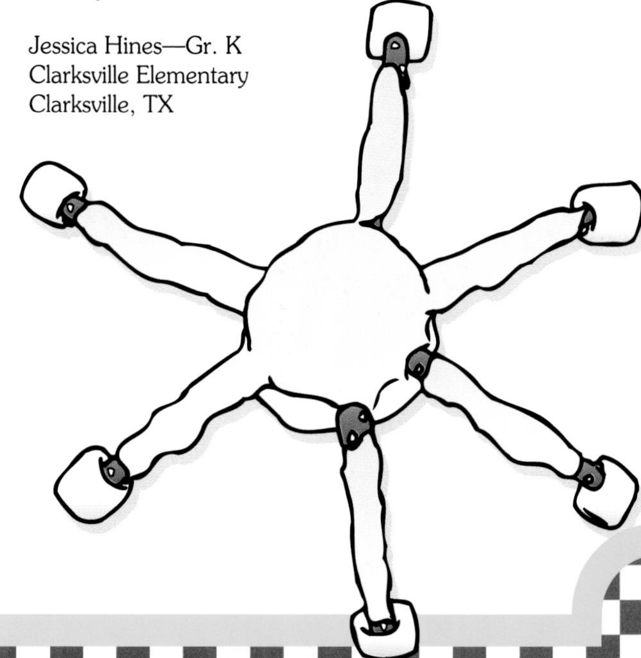

A Tortilla Tree
Name ____________
©2002 The Education Center, Inc.
Put a tree on your plate.
Add a trunk.
1
Add ornaments.
2
Add garland.
3
Add tinsel.
4
Taste your tree!
5

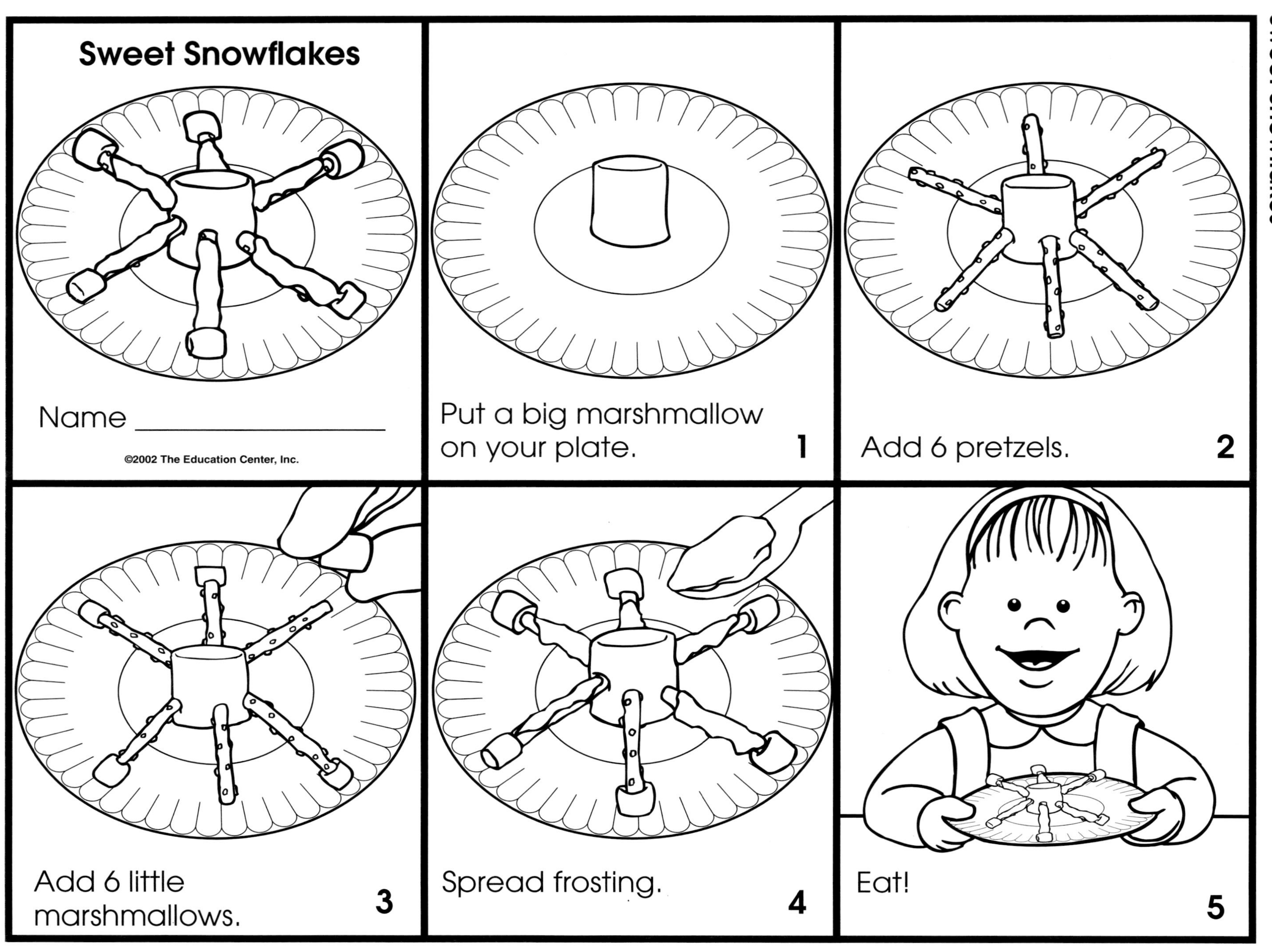
Sweet Snowflakes
Name ______
©2002 The Education Center, Inc.
Put a big marshmallow on your plate.
1
Add 6 pretzels.
2
Add 6 little marshmallows.
3
Spread frosting.
4
Eat!
5

Kindergarten Café

To prepare for each cooking activity, make a class supply plus one extra of the recipe cards (pages 96–97). Color one copy of the recipe cards; then cut the cards apart. Display the sequenced, colored cards in your cooking center. Arrange the ingredients and utensils near the recipe cards. As a small group of children visits the cooking center, ask each child to color a recipe and cut the cards apart. Have him sequence his cards and staple them together, creating a recipe booklet. After each cooking event, encourage the child to take his recipe home and keep it in a box to make a collection of his very own recipes.

Lovebug Cookie

Ingredients for one:
large sugar cookie
strawberry-flavored frosting
2 pretzel sticks (antennae)
2 conversation hearts
2" piece of red licorice lace (mouth)
2 M&M's candies (eyes)
mini chocolate chip (nose)

Utensils and supplies:
paper plate for each child
plastic knife for each child
2 doily quarters (wings)

Teacher preparation:
- Cut licorice into two-inch lengths.
- Cut white doilies into quarters.
- Arrange the ingredients, utensils, and supplies for easy student access.

Peggy Stratton
Okeechobee, FL

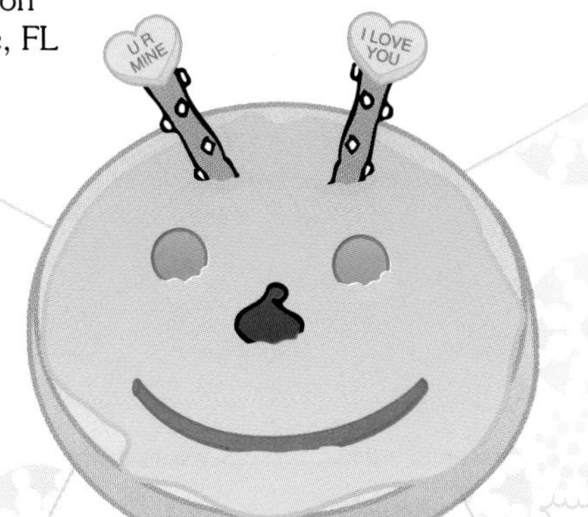

Cat in the Hat Snack

Ingredients for one:
scoop of vanilla ice cream
mini ice-cream cone wrapped with a strip of red Fruit by the Foot snack
3 M&M's candies
six 1" pieces of black or red licorice lace

Utensils and supplies:
paper plate for each child
plastic spoon for each child

Teacher preparation:
- Use an ice-cream scoop to scoop balls of ice cream onto a cookie sheet and then place the sheet in the freezer.
- Cut licorice into one-inch lengths.
- Cut red Fruit by the Foot snack into four-inch strips. Wrap one strip around each cone.
- Arrange the ingredients, utensils, and supplies for easy student access.

Terry Schreiber—Gr. K
Holy Family School
Norwood, NJ

Lovebug Cookie
U R MINE
I LOVE YOU
Name ________
©2002 The Education Center, Inc.
Put 2 wings on your plate. Add a cookie.
1
Spread frosting.
2
Add 2 antennae. Add 2 hearts with frosting.
3
Add 2 eyes. Add 1 nose.
4
Add a mouth. Buzz!
5

Cat in the Hat Snack
Name ______
©2002 The Education Center, Inc.
Put ice cream on your plate.
1
Add a hat.
2
Add 2 eyes.
Add 1 nose.
3
Add 6 whiskers.
4
Now snack on your Cat in the Hat snack!
5

Kindergarten Café

To prepare for each cooking activity, make a class supply plus one extra of the recipe cards (pages 99-100). Color one copy of the recipe cards; then cut the cards apart. Display the sequenced, colored cards in your cooking center. Arrange the ingredients and utensils near the recipe cards. As a small group of children visits the cooking center, ask each child to color a recipe and cut the cards apart. Have him sequence his cards and staple them together, creating a recipe booklet. After each cooking event, encourage the child to take his recipe home and keep it in a box to make a collection of his very own recipes.

Muddy Boots

Ingredients for one:
1/2 c. chocolate pudding (mud)
2 graham cracker sections (boot tops)
2 Vienna Fingers creme-filled sandwich cookie halves (boot bottoms)

Utensils and supplies:
disposable bowl for each child
plastic spoon for each child
1/2 c. measuring cup

Teacher preparation:
- Prepare chocolate pudding according to package directions so that each child will have one-half cup.
- Break Vienna Fingers creme-filled sandwich cookies in half.
- Arrange the ingredients, utensils, and supplies for easy student access.

Chicken Licken

Ingredients for one:
2 Ritz crackers (head, body)
2 Vienna Fingers creme-filled sandwich cookies (wings)
2 pretzel stick halves (legs)
2 M&M's brand mini baking bits (eyes)
cheese triangle (beak)

Utensils and supplies:
paper plate for each child

Teacher preparation:
- Slice cheese into small triangles.
- Arrange ingredients, utensils, and supplies for easy student access.

Muddy Boots
Name ____________
©2003 The Education Center, Inc.
$\frac{1}{2}$ cup
Put $\frac{1}{2}$ cup of mud in your bowl.
1
Add boots.
2
Dig in!
3

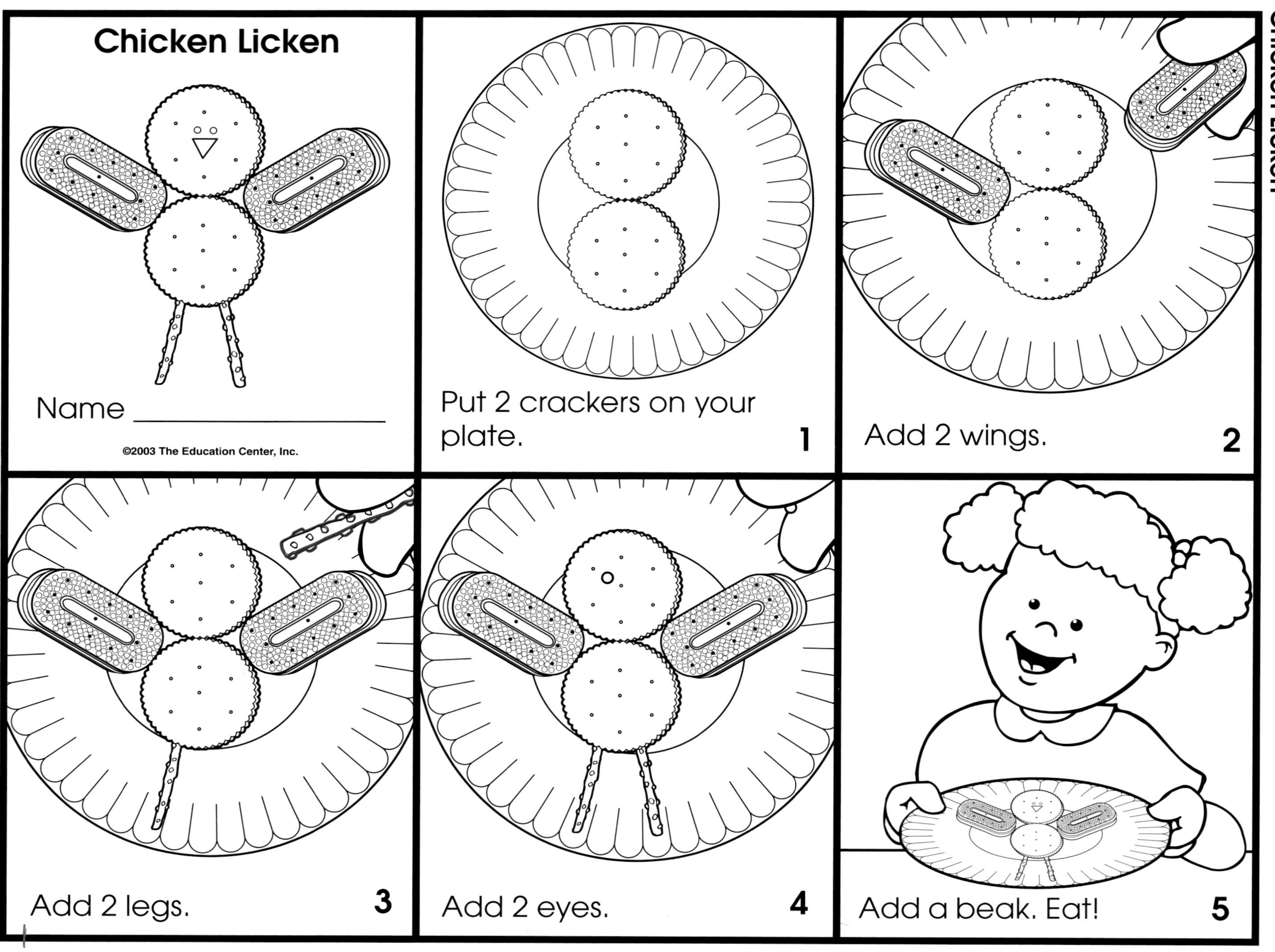
Chicken Licken
Name
©2003 The Education Center, Inc.
Put 2 crackers on your plate.
1
Add 2 wings.
2
Add 2 legs.
3
Add 2 eyes.
4
Add a beak. Eat!
5

Learning Centers

Learning Centers

Literacy Center

Straw Letters

Help youngsters practice letter formation with the help of some inexpensive drinking straws. To prepare, write large letters on separate 4" x 6" index cards. (You may wish to use letters without curved lines for this activity.) Place these in your literacy center, along with a large supply of drinking straws cut into one- to two-inch pieces. Have a child at this center glue the straw pieces over the lines to form the letters. Easy!

Millie Morris—Gr. K
Berkmar United Methodist School
Lilburn, GA

Science Center

Sorting Animals

Boost beginning classification skills with this idea! Gather a variety of small plastic or vinyl animals, including some farm animals. Make a chart with the headings "Farm Animals" and "Not Farm Animals." Place the chart and animals in your science center, along with some nonfiction books about farm animals. Have students examine the animals and sort them onto the chart, using the books for reference if needed.

Kim Lockley—Gr. K
Hawk Ridge Elementary
Charlotte, NC

Snack Center

Snack and Learn

Serve up some math and reading practice at snacktime each day! Designate a spot in your classroom as the snack station. Equip the area with a small dry-erase board and a large bowl. Each day, place all the snack in the bowl and estimate how much of the snack each youngster may have. Then write instructions on the dry-erase board. At the beginning of the year, use numerals and picture cues. Later, introduce number words, color words, sight words, and number sentences. For example, you might write "You may have three white crackers and four brown crackers." What a yummy way to incorporate math and reading skills!

Sheryl Gunning—Gr. K
Cheatham Hill Elementary
Marietta, GA

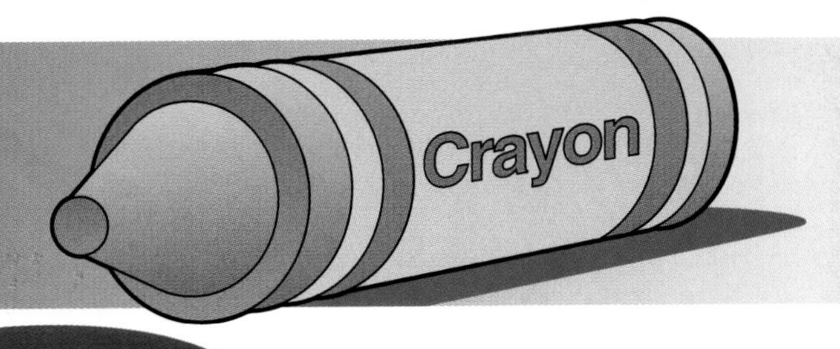

Math Center

Big, Bigger, Biggest!

Help youngsters make size and length comparisons with these easy-to-make workmats for your math center. On a large sheet of construction paper, write the words "Big," "Bigger," and "Biggest," using corresponding letter sizes as an additional clue for nonreaders. Laminate the mat for durability. Then gather or make a collection of items in three sizes—such as blocks or paper cutouts—for little ones to sort onto the mat. If desired, make the collection seasonal or thematic. Vary the activity by creating mats for small, smaller, and smallest or long, longer, and longest.

Carrie Herzog—Gr. K
Lincoln Elementary
West Allis, WI

Reading Center

Match the Fish

After sharing the book *One Fish, Two Fish, Red Fish, Blue Fish* by Dr. Seuss, create this file folder activity to extend the story and reinforce sight words. Glue four library pockets inside a file folder and one pocket to the back of the folder. Label each pocket with a type or group of fish found in the story. Then draw the corresponding fish on a plain index card. Place all the cards in the library pocket on the back of the folder; then print the title of the book on the front. To play, a child removes all the cards and sorts them into the corresponding pockets on the inside of the folder. Two fish, one fish—reading fun fish!

Karen Smith—Grs. K–1
Homeschool
Pace, FL

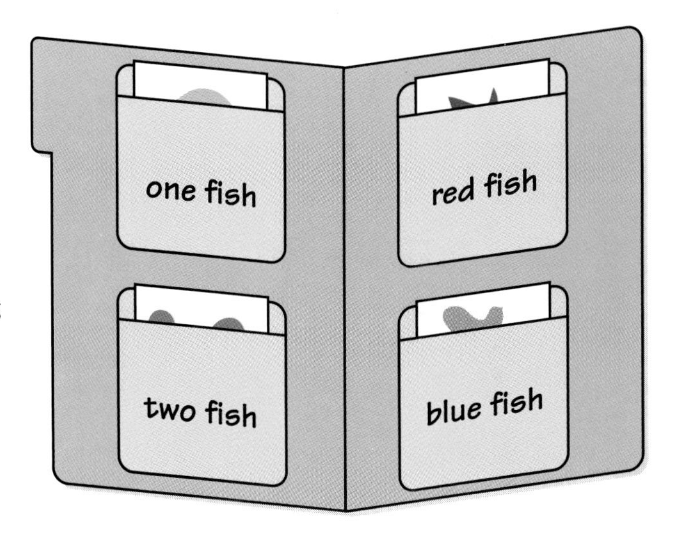

Fine-Motor Center

Just A Dot

Do your new kindergartners need some gluing practice? Try making some dazzling dots to reinforce that just a bit of glue is plenty! First, talk with students about why they only need a small dot of glue for most gluing projects. Have them chant "Not a lot, just a dot!" several times. Then bring out a supply of 1" x 6" construction paper strips. Invite each youngster to make dots of glue on a strip. If any dots turn into puddles, toss the strip and give the child a new one. Reward all those just-right dots of glue with a sprinkle of glitter. Then, when the glue dries, staple the strip around the child's wrist so he may wear it home. If desired, coordinate the paper strip and glitter to match your school colors!

Toni Osterbuhr—Gr. K
Price-Harris School
Wichita, KS

Learning Centers

Math Center

Pecan Pies

This Thanksgiving-themed center will be a hit—you can count on it! To prepare, glue five small foil tart pans to individual squares of tagboard. On each square, write a numeral from 1 to 5 (or from 6 to 10 if you choose). Place the tart-pan squares, some tan play dough, and a bowl of unshelled pecans at the center. Have a child press some play dough into the bottom of each tart pan to make a piecrust. Then have him add the number of pecans to each pie that matches the number on its card. Ahhh…perfect pies!

Jennifer Barton—Gr. K
Newington, CT

Sensory Table

Candle Makers

Here's a fun twist for your sensory exploration center! Pour a different color of wax crystals (found at your local craft store) into each of several shoeboxes. Provide plastic spoons or small shovels, funnels, a variety of cups or containers, and candlewicks. Encourage each youngster to fill a container with crystal colors of her choice to create a unique candle. Then have her push a piece of candlewick down through the center of the candle. If you'd like little ones to be able to take a candle home, give each one a baby food jar. Have her fill it with crystals and add a wick before screwing on the top of the jar. Also send home a note explaining that the candle should be burned only under adult supervision, and that the wax crystals will melt when the wick is lit.

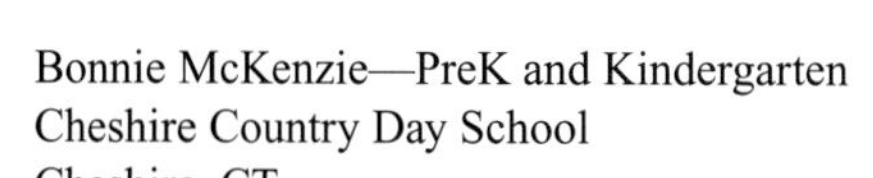

Bonnie McKenzie—PreK and Kindergarten
Cheshire Country Day School
Cheshire, CT

Dramatic-Play Area

In the Mail Room

Put sorting skills to work when you invite youngsters to play the part of mail room workers. Stock your dramatic-play area with old letters and postcards, magazines, large envelopes, mailing tubes, and boxes wrapped in brown kraft paper. Have youngsters sort the mail by type into various plastic tubs or baskets. They'll have all sorts of fun!

Karen Bryant
Rosa Taylor Elementary
Macon, GA

Literacy Center

Letter Detectives

Youngsters will be keeping one another in suspense as they practice letter formation in your literacy center! Provide a variety of materials, such as craft sticks, toothpicks, wooden cubes, pipe cleaners, and clay. Also provide a stack of large index cards, each with a different letter written on it. Have each child at the center choose a material and a letter card, without letting others at the center see his chosen letter. Have each child use his material to form the letter on his card. Then, one by one, have youngsters show their handiwork to the others. Have your little letter detectives determine which letter each child formed.

Dayle Timmons—Gr. K, Chets Creek Elementary
Jacksonville Beach, FL

Math Center

Graphing Is Great!

Provide individual graphing practice at your math center with some simple-to-make graphing cards and fun collections! Make a supply of individual graphing mats similar to the one shown; then laminate the mats for durability. Next, put together several small collections of items for little ones to graph, and place each collection in a separate container. Seasonal mini erasers in different designs, bingo chips in different colors, buttons, or birthday candles—any small items will do! Have a child at this center sort a collection on a graphing mat. Then ask questions about her completed graph such as the following: "Of which item did you have the most? The fewest? Are there more blue or red? How many more?" Your youngsters will agree—graphing is great!

Linda Havens—Gr. K, Oakwood Elementary, Kalamazoo, MI

Science Center

Magnet Investigation

Set up this testing center for some fun with magnets! To prepare, print the word *yes* on six index cards and the word *no* on six more. Collect six items that will stick to a magnet and six that will not. If desired, use seasonal items. Place the items in a basket at the center, along with a strong magnet. Next, draw pictures of the 12 items on a piece of poster board, randomly placing the items that can and cannot be picked up with a magnet.

At the center, a child chooses an item and predicts whether it will stick to the magnet. She tests her prediction; then she places either a yes card or a no card over the item's picture on the poster board to show the actual result. She continues until she has tested all 12 items.

Sandy Kennedy—Developmental Kindergarten
Cincinnati Hills Christian Academy, Cincinnati, OH

Learning Centers

Block Center

LEGO on the Wall

Help your kindergartners see buildings from a whole new perspective with this idea! To prepare, glue together several LEGO building bases onto a thin piece of plywood. Then screw or nail the edges of the plywood to the wall in your block area. Invite youngsters to build LEGO structures *out* from the wall instead of *up* from the floor!

Lindsey A. Vail—Gr. K
Highlands Elementary
Braintree, MA

Science Center

Making an Impression

Focus youngsters' attention on texture and pattern with an activity that uses a classroom favorite—play dough! To prepare, gather a variety of objects with interesting textures, shapes, or raised designs. Place the objects at your science center, along with a supply of play dough. Encourage students at this center to make a small ball of dough and then press one of the items into the ball to make an impression. Have her continue with other items.

If desired, make this a partner activity. Have one child close her eyes while her partner chooses an item and makes an impression of it in the play dough. Then have the child open her eyes and guess which item made the imprint.

Heather Miller—PreK
Creative Playschool
Auburn, IN

Math Center

Manicure Math

This addition activity will be a favorite—hands down! To prepare, trace a child's hands on a sheet of white paper. Below the hand shapes, write an addition sentence as shown, leaving blanks for the numbers. Laminate the paper and place it in your math center, along with a supply of dry-erase markers. Use a white sticky dot to mask the six-dotted side of a die. Place the special die in the math center too.

To use this center, a child rolls the die and paints nails (with a marker) on the corresponding number of fingers on the left hand. Then she rolls again and paints the indicated number of nails on the right hand. (If she rolls a blank, she counts it as a zero.) Then she fills in the corresponding numbers to complete the addition sentence. Have her wipe the paper clean and give another manicure for more math fun!

Heather Miller—PreK

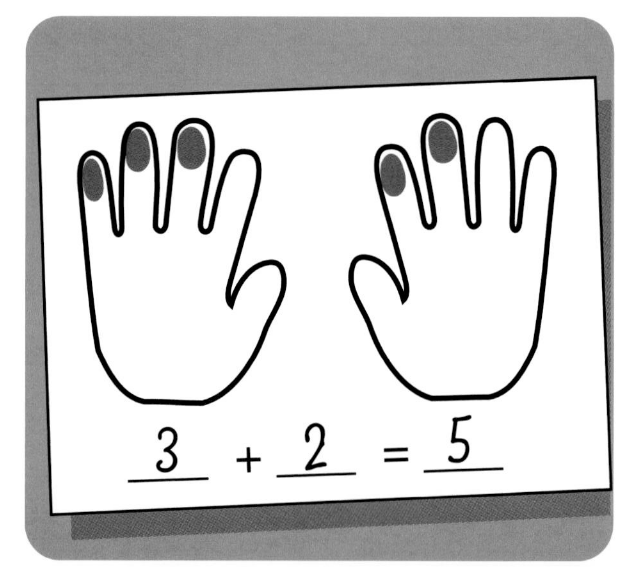

Dramatic-Play Center

Travel Agency

Send your kindergartners on a dramatic-play journey when you transform your housekeeping area into a travel agency! Check with local travel agents or on the Internet to find free travel brochures; then arrange them on shelves for "customers" to peruse. Add a child's desk and chairs, an old phone or play phone, paper, pencils, and perhaps an old computer monitor and keyboard. Make a list of hotels, airlines, rental car agencies, and cruise lines with pretend phone numbers so that "agents" can call for information and bookings. Post a world map on the wall and display travel posters (or pictures cut from travel magazines). Add yarn linking each poster with its spot on the map.

Model how to use the center; then invite youngsters to role-play agents and customers deciding on desirable destinations!

Shannon Adams—Gr. K
Waxahachie Faith Family Academy
Waxahachie, TX

Literacy Center

Gifts From *A* to *Z*

Wrap up beginning-sounds skills with a center idea that's perfect for the holiday season! To prepare, collect a set of 26 jewelry-sized gift boxes. Label each one with a letter from *A* to *Z;* then stick a miniature gift bow on top. Next, collect a set of clip-art pictures so that you have one for each letter of the alphabet.

To use this center, a child identifies the beginning sound of the item in a picture. He then places the picture inside the corresponding gift box. When all the pictures are in the boxes, it's a wrap!

Lara Bronson—Gr. K
Woodcrest Elementary
Fridley, MN

Writing Center

Cookie Sheet Sentences

Your young writers will enjoy this "attractive" way to write sentences! To prepare, drill holes in the corners of old cookie sheets; then screw the cookie sheets to the wall of your writing area. Provide a set of magnetic words for youngsters to use as they "write" sentences on the cookie sheets. This is one activity they'll be sure to stick to!

Lindsey A. Vail—Gr. K
Highlands Elementary
Braintree, MA

Learning Centers

Pretzels, Get Your Pretzels!

Here's a twist for your dramatic-play area—transform it into a pretzel shop! Provide youngsters with aprons, chef's hats, recipe cards, a cash register, order pads, pencils, some empty salt shakers, and a supply of brown rug yarn to twist into pretzel shapes! Invite your kindergartners to role-play making, selling, and buying pretzels. What yummy fun!

Judy Patterson—Preschool and Gr. K
Our Hope Lutheran School, Wayne, IN

Brush Your Molars

This small-group center activity is perfect for Dental Health Month in February! To prepare, gather a supply of small mirrors, toothbrushes, and the bottoms from plastic soda or water bottles (the ones that have indentations, not the smooth ones). Gather a group around a table and give each child a mirror. Ask her to examine her teeth, including the teeth in the back called *molars.* Talk about how these teeth help us to chew. Then put the mirrors away and give each child a toothbrush and a bottle bottom turned upside down to resemble a molar. Explain that students will practice brushing their molars by brushing these giant teeth! Spread a bit of peanut butter or ketchup onto each child's plastic tooth. Then ask her to dip her toothbrush into a container of water and brush the tooth clean. To help with the cleaning, give each child a squirt of toothpaste.

Joy Meyer—Gr. K
Fox Prairie Elementary, Stoughton, WI

Math Center

Candy Heart Patterning

Little ones will be sweet on this math activity! Place a bowl of multicolored candy conversation hearts on the table in your math center. Have each child at this center make a pattern with various colors of hearts. When the pattern's done, have extra hearts on hand and let the eating begin!

Jenny Kamerman—Gr. K
Dunnville Christian School, Dunnville, Ontario

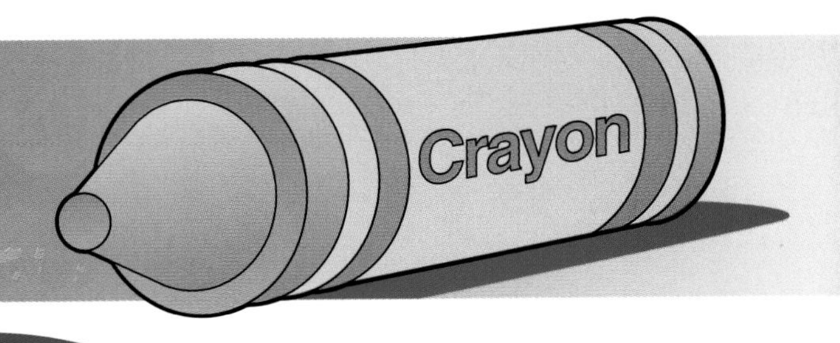

Game Center

Valentine Memory

Purchase some inexpensive valentines—or save the ones your youngsters give you each year—to create this memory game. Find duplicates among your valentines; then mount each one and its match on separate squares of red construction paper. Laminate the resulting cards for durability. Place the cards in a heart-shaped candy box at your games center. Invite youngsters to shuffle the cards and place them facedown in rows. Have each player take a turn turning over two cards, trying to find a matching pair. If the cards match, he keeps the pair. If the cards don't match, he turns them facedown again. When all the pairs have been found, the player with the most pairs wins!

Suzanne Ward—Junior and Senior Kindergarten
Seneca Unity Public School, Caledonia, Ontario

Math Center

French Fry Math

Use french fries to help your kindergartners with numeral recognition and counting? What a *hot* idea! Ask a local fast-food restaurant to donate 20 french fry bags. Label each bag with a number from 1 to 20. Then gather a supply of craft sticks to represent french fries. At this center, one child plays the part of the customer and asks for a particular number of fries. Another student plays the worker. He finds the bag with the corresponding number on it and fills it with that number of craft-stick fries. Order up!

Launa Mair, Gloria Alonso, and Mindy Rasmussen—Gr. K
W. Russel Todd School, Roosevelt, UT

Literacy Center

Beanbag Alphabet

This alphabet puzzle is as easy as ABC! To prepare, label each of 26 plain beanbags with a different capital letter. Die-cut letters from craft foam and use hot glue to attach them to the beanbags, or die-cut them from self-adhesive felt and simply stick them in place. Then make an alphabet strip, as shown, so that each beanbag has an identically sized square labeled with a lowercase letter. Have students at this center place the matching beanbag atop each square on the strip.

Elizabeth DeChellis—Gr. K
Victor Mravlag School No. 21
Elizabeth, NJ

Learning Centers

Spelling Center

Shake and Spell

Shake up spelling practice with this center idea! Cover the outside of a powdered drink canister or potato chip can with solid-colored construction paper or Con-Tact covering. Find clip art or stickers that depict simple CVC (consonant, vowel, consonant) words; then stick three or four of them on the outside of the can. Put the magnetic letters needed to spell each CVC word inside the can; then put on the lid. Have a child shake the can and spill the letters out onto a tabletop. Then have him arrange the letters to spell each word depicted on the can.

Jeanne Jackson—Gr. K
Northside Primary
Palestine, TX

Dramatic-Play Area

Pizza, Please

Invite youngsters to role-play pizza makers in your dramatic-play center with the help of a few props. Make a pizza base by gluing a tan felt crust and red felt sauce to the inside bottom of a clean pizza box. Then fill disposable bowls or small bins with toppings, such as small brown pom-poms for sausage, metal washers painted green and black for olives, red counting chips or buttons for pepperoni, and dried lima beans for mushroom pieces. Then encourage students to role-play customers, waiters, cashiers, and bakers. Let's make some pies!

Angela Van Beveren
Alvin, TX

Science Center

It's a Wash

What can we learn from laundry? A lot! To prepare for doing this laundry-drying experiment at your science center, give youngsters tagboard templates in the shapes of shirts, pants, and dresses. Have them trace the patterns onto various types of paper, such as paper towels, wrapping paper, wallpaper, or copy paper. At the center, put out a washtub (a container of water) and have little ones dip the paper clothing into it. Provide miniature clothespins and string a clothesline nearby. Have youngsters hang the wet clothes; then have them check back throughout the day to make observations and see which items dried more quickly and which dried more slowly.

Shirley Tanaka—Gr. K
Francis Scott Key Elementary
San Francisco, CA

Reading Area

Flannelboard Clouds

Is it an ice-cream cone? A sheep? A birthday cake? No—it's an easy way to help youngsters retell the story *It Looked Like Spilt Milk* by Charles G. Shaw! Purchase some interfacing at your local fabric store; then lay it over the cloud shapes in the book. Trace the shapes onto the interfacing. Cut out the cloud shapes and use them to tell the story at your flannelboard. Then leave the flannelboard and pieces available for your kindergartners to use independently.

Linda Rasmussen—Gr. K
Donner Springs School
Reno, NV

Math Center

These Are "Thumb" Bugs!

Combine art and math in this great graphing activity! Have each child glue strips of white copy paper to a sheet of light blue construction paper, as shown, to create a fence. If desired, add more background features—such as grass, a sun, or clouds—with paper scraps or markers. Next, have each child make any number of thumbprint insects on her picture. Show her how to press her thumb onto an ink pad, then onto the paper. Have her use a fine-tipped black marker to add features and transform the thumbprints into bees, butterflies, or ladybugs. Next, give her a copy of a graph on page 114. Have her count and color how many of each type of insect she included in her picture.

Lin Attaya—Gr. K
Hodge Elementary
Denton, TX

Literacy Center

Coupons *A* to *Z*

Clip those coupons from your Sunday paper to help your students with alphabetizing skills! Put a number of coupons inside a coupon caddy; then store the caddy at your literacy center, along with an alphabet strip. Invite a child at this center to order the coupons by the first letter in the product name, using the alphabet strip for help if necessary.

Denise Voight
High Point, NC

Learning Centers

On the Water

Transform your dramatic-play center into a water wonderland! Set up a small inflatable boat and then add life jackets, plastic oars, toy fishing poles, inflatable beach toys, and beach towels. Encourage youngsters to role-play boating, fishing, swimming, and other water activities. What a perfect opportunity to help your little ones learn about water safety too!

Shelly Fales—Gr. K
Whittemore-Prescott Early Childhood Center
Whittemore, MI

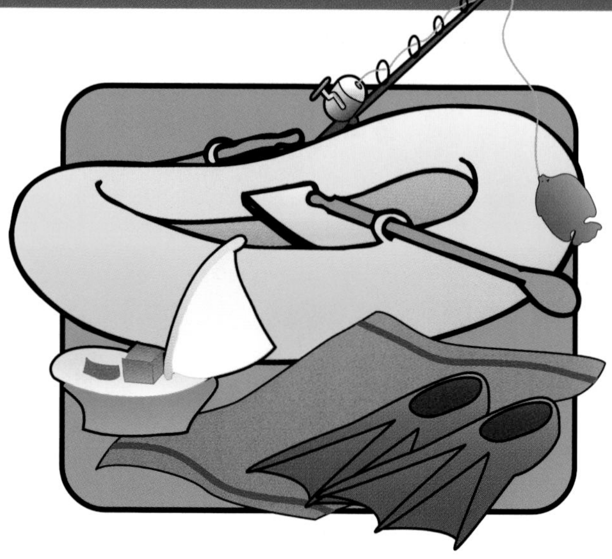

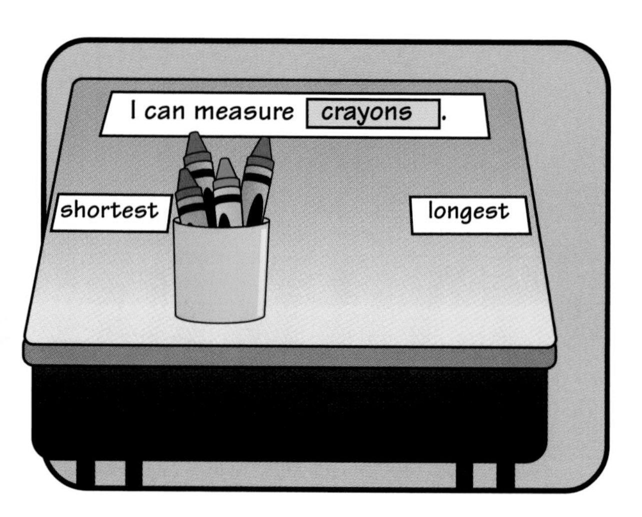

Math Center

Measurement Station

Give students ongoing practice with seriation by setting up a measurement station in your math area. Label two sides of a desk or tabletop with the words *shortest* and *longest.* Then program a sentence strip, as shown, inserting the word for whatever items you provide at the center. Place a cupful of pencils, crayons, sticks, carrots, or other items on the desk. Then ask a child to compare the items and line them up on the tabletop from shortest to longest. Keep a list of student names nearby so that each child can check off her name as she visits the station. Change the measurement item weekly to keep student interest high.

Karen Walker—Gr. K
LaCroft Elementary
Liverpool, OH

Writing Center

Picnic Grocery List

Who doesn't love going on a picnic in warm weather? Encourage young writers to prepare lists of what they'd like to take on a picnic! Stock your writing center with local grocery store flyers, pencils, and paper cut into long rectangles. Invite each child at this center to peruse the flyers, choose picnic items, and copy them down to make a list. Mmm! Let's eat!

Judi Lesnansky—Title I
New Hope Academy
Youngstown, OH

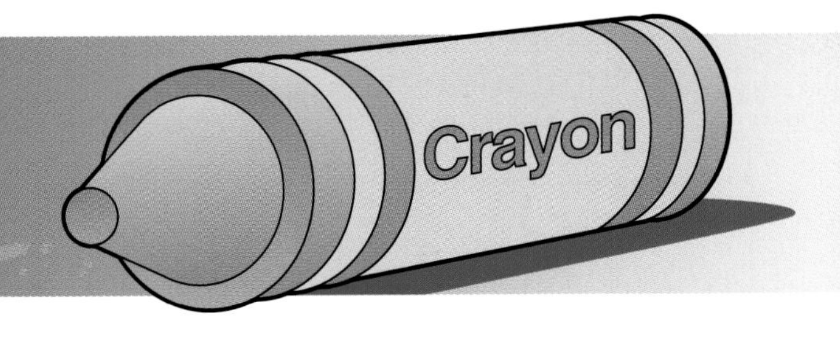

Math Center

Pasta for Practice

Give youngsters practice with estimating skills with this center idea. Provide several different types and sizes of dry pasta, as well as a few different measuring cups. Have a student estimate how many of one type of noodle will fill a particular measuring cup. Have him record his estimate on a recording sheet similar to the one shown before counting to determine the actual result. If desired, graph students' estimates and actual measurements for more math practice. Now that's using your noodle!

Karen Smith—Grs. K– 1, Pensacola, FL

Reading Center

Popcorn Words

Here's a twist on discovery bottles that will have your students popping with excitement about sight words! Fill a completely dry soda bottle about three-fourths full with popcorn kernels. Sketch a popcorn bag or a large bowl on a sheet of paper. Next, cut out several small, puffy popcorn shapes from white craft foam. Label each one with a sight word; then slip them into the bottle. Tightly secure the bottle top and give the bottle a shake! Write all the words you've hidden in the bottle on the bag or bowl. Duplicate the list; then put the copies in your reading center along with the bottle of popcorn words. Ask a child at the center to locate words and then highlight each one she finds on a copy of the list.

As a variation, write the words on simple rectangles or on other shapes and fill the bottle with sand, salt, rice, or another filler.

Jo Montgomery—PreK and Gr. K, John C. French Elementary
Cuero, TX

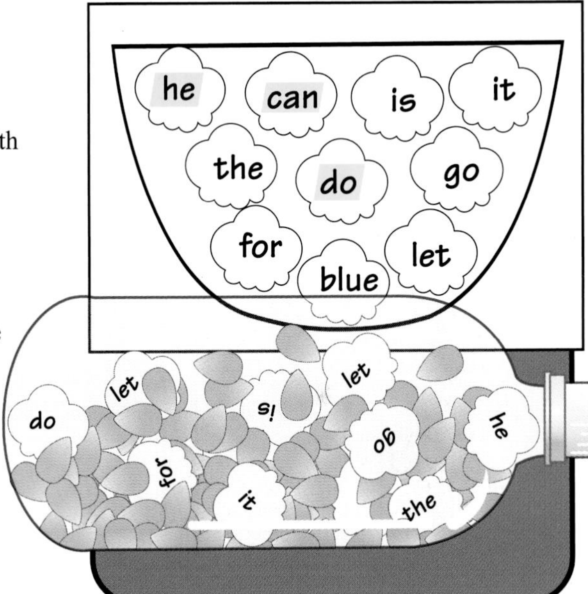

Science Center

Concept Chomper

Make reviewing science concepts fun when you toss in this center idea! To prepare, paint a small trash can to resemble a person's body. Paint or color a poster board head and attach it to the back of the trash can. This is your Super Scientist Concept Chomper! Next, label a supply of Ping-Pong balls or small foam balls with words or pictures to test a science concept. For example, label the balls with examples of living and nonliving things. Then put all the balls in a basket near the Chomper.

To use the center, a child pulls a ball from the basket, identifies the thing shown on it as living or nonliving and if correct, he tosses the ball into the Chomper. Vary the center for other concepts, such as hot and cold, types of animals, or plant-eating and meat-eating dinosaurs. Youngsters will be eager to show you the science facts they know for chances to fill the Super Scientist Chomper!

adapted from an idea by Shannon Martin—Gr. K
Provena Fortin Villa, Bourbonnais, IL

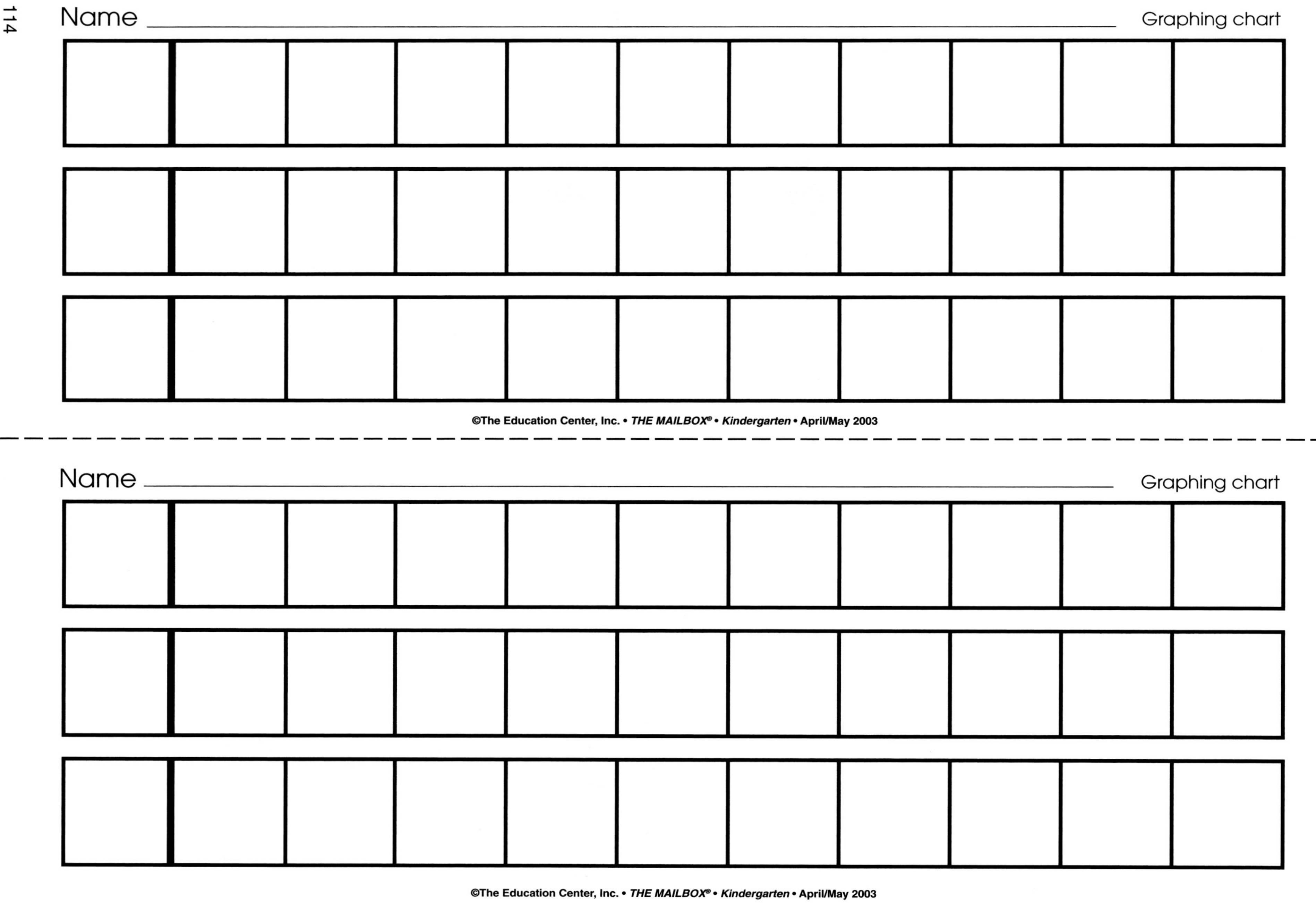

©The Education Center, Inc. • *THE MAILBOX®* • *Kindergarten* • April/May 2003

Note to the teacher: Use with "These Are 'Thumb' Bugs!" on page 111.

Lighting the Way to Literacy

Rainbow Letters

Help your new kindergartners practice writing their names with this colorful idea! Use a yellow highlighter to print a child's name on a sheet of paper. Then have the child trace the letters using three different colors of crayons. Students will get lots of practice as they write their names repeatedly, and they'll love the rainbow effect! Try printing rainbow numbers too!

Kiva English, Cato-Meridian Central School, Cato, NY

Printing Progress

Keep track of youngsters' progress in printing their names with these easy-to-make booklets. Create a master booklet with ten half sheets of paper. Each booklet page should read: "In [month], I printed my name like this." Write a different month of the school year on each page; then add a line for printing below the text. Duplicate the booklet pages for each child. Each month, have the children print their names in their booklets. After each student writes her name on the final page, invite her to review her progress. Then send the booklets home to delight and astound parents!

Jean Ricotta—Lead Teacher, Signal Hill Elementary, Dix Hills, NY

Building Letters

How do you build an *A?* With blocks, of course! Use the wooden blocks in your block area to help little ones practice letter formation. To prepare, make a building plan for each letter of the alphabet. Choose blocks to form the letter, lay them on a sheet of tagboard, and then trace around them. Laminate all the letter-building plans and put them in your block center. Invite each child to choose a letter card and lay the corresponding blocks atop the traced shapes to form the letter. Encourage little ones to come up with their own building plans by including a few blank sheets of tagboard at the center too.

Beth Edwards—Exceptional Kindergarten
Wintergreen Primary School
Greenville, NC

Lucia Kemp Henry, Fallon, NV

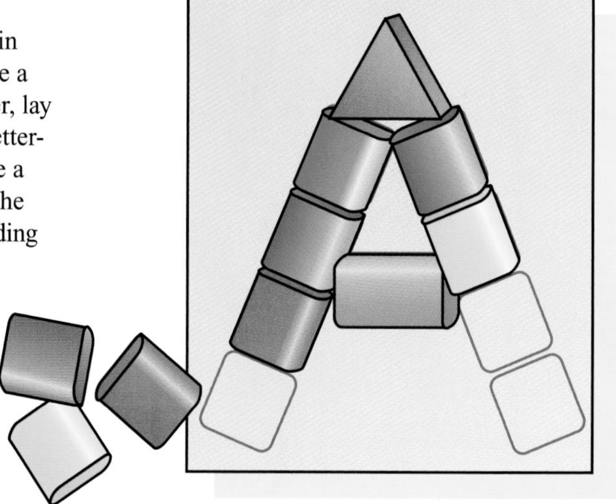

Letter of the Week Posters

Reinforce the letter you are teaching each week with this poster-perfect idea! On a sheet of chart paper, use a light color of marker to draw an item that begins with the featured letter. Have students guess what you are drawing; then have them identify the item's beginning letter. Ask youngsters to name other words that begin with the same letter; then record their responses on the chart. Display the finished poster on your classroom door so that everyone will know your letter of the week. Then, when you begin a new letter study, display the poster in your room for students to review.

Lisa Cohen—Gr. K
Laurel Plains Elementary
New City, NY

"E" Words

elephant excellent
excited egg even eye
exclusive explosive
extra eagle equals eat
expert ear eight eraser
envelope

Eye Spy

Little ones will be keeping an eye on the alphabet when they follow your clues in this fun activity! For each child, create an eye-spy stick by hot-gluing a large wiggle eye to one end of a wooden craft stick. Give each child a stick and an individual alphabet chart. Supply clues for a particular letter and ask youngsters to look for that letter. Have students use eye-spy sticks to point to the letter. Clues might be "I am the fifth letter of the alphabet. I make the /e/ sound. I begin the word *elephant*." Hey—that's the letter *E!*

Rhonda L. Chiles—Gr. K, South Park Elementary, Shawnee Mission, KS

Camouflaged Chameleon

After sharing Leo Lionni's *A Color of His Own*, give your youngsters a chance to create some camouflage of *their* very own! First, discuss the concept of camouflage and have youngsters look carefully at Lionni's illustrations. Then give each child a precut white paper chameleon and a wallpaper sample. Have the child glue the chameleon cutout onto the wallpaper. Then ask her to use crayons to make the chameleon blend in with its new background. Hmmm...where *is* that chameleon hiding?

Kathy Massengale—Gr. K
Woodward Academy
Riverdale, GA

The Story Can

Just finished reading a story? Bring out the story can! Simply cover a clean, empty can with construction paper and the decorations of your choice. On each of several wooden craft sticks, print key words—such as *characters, setting, problem, solution, beginning,* and *ending*—to help youngsters discuss stories. Put the sticks in the story can. After reading a story aloud, show youngsters the can and explain the meanings of the words on the sticks. Then model how to draw one stick and talk about the element of the story indicated. Once students understand the concept, have volunteers draw sticks and discuss the story with the group. Use as many or as few sticks as you like after each story.

Karen Saner—Gr. K, Burns Elementary, Burns, KS

Who Let the Letter Out?

Reinforce letter sounds with this fun chant modeled after the popular song "Who Let the Dogs Out." Put a supply of magnetic letters in a large coffee can. Ask a child to pull out one letter and show it to the class. Have the class respond, "Who let the [letter] out?" and follow the question with a succession of the letter's sounds. For example, if the child pulls out a *B,* the class would chant, "Who let the *B* out? /b/, /b/, /b/, /b/, /b/!"

Karen Angell—Gr. K
Mary Walter Elementary
Bealeton, VA

A Colorful Rhyme

Focus your kindergartners on color words and rhyming with this fun activity! After sharing the traditional rhyme "Miss Mary Mack" with your students, recite this version in which the color word and clothing have been changed:

Miss Mary Mack, Mack, Mack,
All dressed in *[blue, blue, blue],*
With silver buttons, buttons, buttons,
All down her *[shoe, shoe, shoe]!*

Then challenge youngsters to adapt the rhyme using other color words in the second line and appropriate rhyming words in the last line. Wow—we're rhyme writers!

Gloria Thudium—Gr. K, Ryan Elementary, Baton Rouge, LA

Licorice Letters

Want to motivate your kindergartners to learn letter formations? Bring in some yummy licorice laces! Have youngsters use licorice to form letters as instructed. Then reward their efforts by inviting them to eat the licorice letters!

Teresa Purpura—Gr. K
Jason Lee Elementary
Portland, OR

Books on a Bedsheet

Encourage little ones to share details about books they've read or listened to at home with a book-sharing sheet! Use a marker to divide a plain bedsheet into enough squares for each child to have her own square. Lay the sheet on the floor; then provide markers, yarn, fabric scraps, buttons, fabric glue, and any other appropriate craft materials. Invite each child to decorate her square on the sheet to illustrate a favorite part in her chosen book. Complete her square by adding the book's title and author, as well as the line, "This book was read by [child's name]." Display the completed sheet for everyone to see; then invite each child to tell about her square—and her book!

AnnaLisa R. Damminger
West Jersey Child Development Center
Voorhees, NJ

Backward ABCs

Help youngsters recognize letters and understand that letters make individual sounds with this activity. Each day, invite a helper to point to the letters as your class sings the familiar "Alphabet Song." Then have the child point to the letters in reverse order, and have the class sing the song *backward!* Next, have your helper point to each letter as the class makes the letter's sound. Do this in reverse alphabetical order too!

Melissa Merritt—Gr. K
East End Elementary
Humboldt, TN

Story Element Bins

Help kindergartners understand basic story elements by sorting them all out at storytime! To prepare, set up three small bins or baskets—one labeled "characters," one labeled "setting," and one labeled "events." Cut out slips of paper and list a different element from the particular story you'll be reading on each one. Then place all the slips in an envelope.

After sharing the story, have a student volunteer draw a slip of paper. Read to the class what the slip says and talk about whether it describes the story's characters, setting, or events. Have the child place the slip in the corresponding bin. Then continue by sorting the other elements into the appropriate bins.

Jennifer Hyman—Gr. K, Hayshire Elementary
York, PA

Sipping Once, Sipping Twice…

Warm up on a cold winter day with this follow-up to Maurice Sendak's *Chicken Soup With Rice.* Give each student a plain white paper circle. Ask him to imagine that the circle is a bird's-eye view of a soup bowl and have him draw his favorite soup inside the bowl. Then give him a plastic spoon to tape onto the bowl rim. Have each child dictate the type of soup in his bowl for you to write on a sentence-strip label. Display the soup bowls and labels on a large bulletin board graph with the title "Sipping Once, Sipping Twice…" What soup is the class's favorite?

Judi Lesnansky—Title I, New Hope Academy
Youngstown, OH

What's the Word?

Hop, top, pop, mop…Little ones will hear plenty of rhyming words when you play this guessing game! To prepare, cut out a number of clip-art pictures of objects whose names are easy to rhyme. Mount each picture on a construction paper square, punch holes at the top, and thread yarn through the holes to make a necklace.

To play the game, place a necklace on a student volunteer. Make sure that the picture is on her back, so it is not visible to her but can be seen by the rest of the group. Have children in the group raise their hands if they can think of words that rhyme with the picture. Have the child wearing the necklace call on students and listen to the words they tell her until she correctly guesses the object pictured on her necklace. Then begin again with a new volunteer and a new necklace!

Theresa Banaag—Gr. K, John Muir Elementary
Glendale, CA

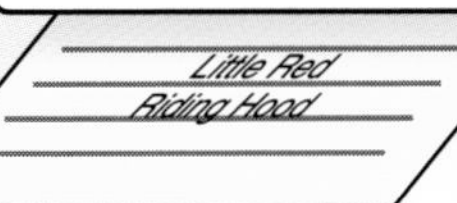

Flannelboards to Go

Here's a flannelboard idea that really delivers! Ask a local pizzeria to donate some small pizza boxes. Hot-glue a piece of flannel to the top of each box. Then stow the flannelboard pieces for a particular story inside the box, labeling the inside lid with the story's title. Students can use the small flannelboards to retell stories at center time!

Lindsey A. Vail—Gr. K
Quincy, MA

And

Youngsters will quickly learn the sight word *and* when you try this creative activity! Purchase a long length of wide pastel ribbon. Use a black permanent marker to write the word *and* on the ribbon two times, spacing the words as shown. Ask three students to stand and hold the ribbon in front of the group. Ask a child to make up a sentence about the three children, such as "John and Lin and Carly are in a row." Point to the students named and to the word *and* as the sentence is repeated by the whole group. Keep going with other students and new sentences until everyone has had a turn. For added fun, ask a fellow teacher or staff member to take a place behind the ribbon!

Judi Lesnansky—Title I, New Hope Academy
Youngstown, OH

Guess the Gift

Use the excitement of a holiday surprise to fuel little ones' writing and prediction skills! Each week during December, purchase a set of small, inexpensive gifts for everyone in your class. You might buy candy canes, seasonal erasers, mini notepads, or plastic holiday rings. Wrap the set of gifts in one box. Show youngsters the box and ask them to predict what is inside. Remind them that the box contains enough items for everyone to have one. Ask each child to draw and label his prediction on a small square of paper. Staple the finished squares atop one another on a sentence strip as shown. Then let the excitement build until Friday, when you have one child open the gift and reveal the contents. As your helper distributes the gifts, revisit the predictions. Did anyone guess correctly?

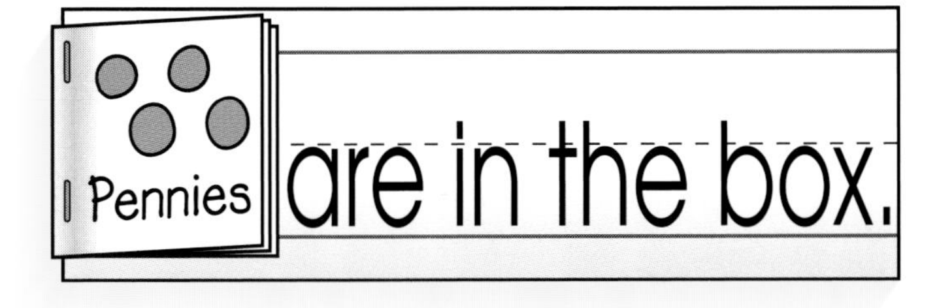

Bobbie Hallman—Gr. K, Burbank Elementary
Merced, CA

X Marks My Spot

Reinforce uppercase and lowercase letter matching with this daily routine. At each seat in your classroom, place a colorful uppercase letter sticker. Put a matching lowercase letter sticker on a small index card. Put all the cards in a box or basket and place it near your cubbies. When children arrive, have each of them draw a card from the basket and then find the seat with the matching uppercase letter. That seat becomes his seat for the day. Children can have a different seat each day, as determined by the letters they draw each morning. What a fun way to match letters and get to know friends better!

Sharon Vandike—Gr. K
Visitation Inter-Parish School
Vienna, MO

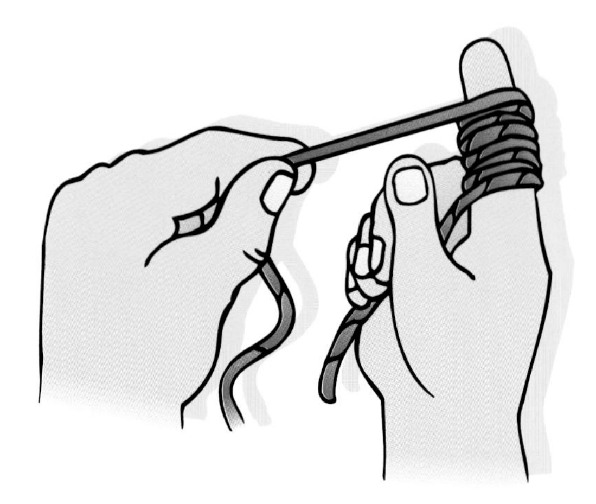

A Yard of Yarn

How fast can your kindergartners recite their ABCs? Give them some practice with this fun activity! Give each child a yard length of yarn. Demonstrate how to wind the yarn around a finger. Then have each child wind the yarn around her finger while she says the alphabet! Can youngsters get to the letter *Z* before they run out of yarn? Bet they can with a little practice!

Sadie Day—Gr. K
Carbondale Attendance Center
Carbondale, KS

A Valentine Book

Wondering what to do with all the valentines your little ones give you? Make them into a class book! Type the following sentence onto the bottom of a blank piece of copy paper: "_______ gave me a ________ valentine." Duplicate the programmed page to make a class supply. Then tape a valentine onto each page, personalizing it with a child's name and the type of valentine he gave you. Bind the pages together behind a cover and add the book to your reading center for all your little valentines to enjoy!

Jill Davis—Gr. K
Kendall-Whittier Elementary
Tulsa, OK

The "-at" Hat

Celebrating Dr. Seuss's birthday in March? Invite each of your students to make a rhyming book that resembles the famous hat of the Cat in the Hat! For each child, cut several sheets of red and white construction paper into different widths so that they stack together to form a flip book as shown. Add a long rectangle of paper to the bottom sheet to form the brim of the hat. Then print the title on the top sheet of paper. Have youngsters think of words ending in the *-at* rime to draw and write on each page. Invite each student to share his finished book with his classmates.

Jonelle Bell, Bonnie Blanck, Mary DeWitt, and Jackie Mayer—Gr. K
J. F. Dumont School
Madeira, OH

Weekly Class Books

Encourage student writing by having your kindergartners write about themselves every week! Over the course of each week, take an action shot of each of your students with a digital camera. Print out the pictures and ask each child to glue her photo to a sheet of story paper. Have her write about what she is doing in her picture. After the writing is shared with the class, compile each week's pages into a class book and keep it in your reading center. At the end of the year, invite each child to take one of these class favorites home to keep!

Lisa Libfeld—Gr. K
Jonathan Burr Elementary
Chicago, IL

A	B	C	D	E	F	G	H	I	J	K	L	M
a at ate are am	be been boy by	can cow could	do day did	eat	for	go	how	it I			like	me

N	O	P	Q	R	S	T	U	V	W	X	Y	Z
no	on out	pop		red	sit stop	to			wet			

A Shower of Words

Looking for an interesting way to create a word wall? How about using a shower curtain! Use a permanent marker to divide a solid-colored shower curtain into 26 sections (two rows of 13 boxes works well). Label each box with a different letter of the alphabet. Then write inside the box sight words and high frequency words that begin with that letter. Hang the curtain on a rod in your classroom. When you're not using it, you can just slide it aside!

Michele Galvan—Gr. K
Roosevelt Elementary
McAllen, TX

Leprechaun's Gold

Use a leprechaun's treasure to help your kindergartners be good as gold with ending sounds! To prepare, cut a supply of large yellow construction paper circles (coins). On one side of each coin, write a different ending sound you want your students to practice. On the opposite side of each coin, glue a clip art or magazine picture that has the corresponding ending sound. At your literacy center, have a child lay the coins on a tabletop, picture side up. Have him choose a coin, name the picture, and then say the ending sound. Then have him flip the coin over to check. As a variation, have students group coins with matching ending sounds.

Brenda Saunders—Gr. K
Beale Elementary
Gallipolis Ferry, WV

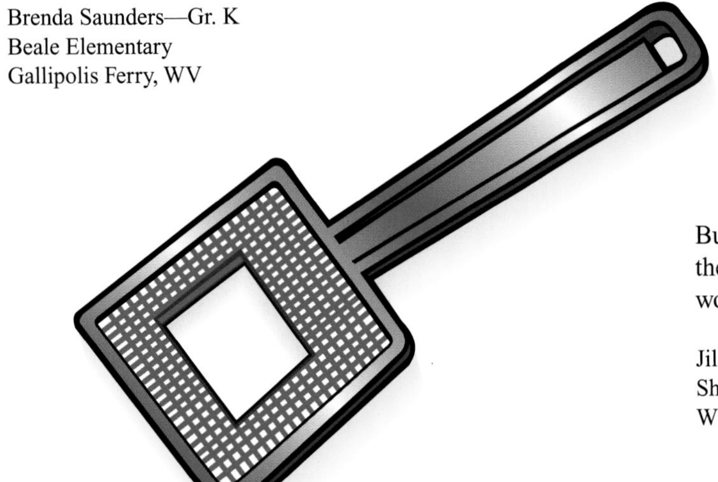

Swat That Word!

Here's a fun twist to help youngsters enjoy reading your room! Buy a new plastic flyswatter; then cut out a square in the center of the plastic. Have a child use the swatter to swat (locate) sight words, color words, or any other words of your choice!

Jill Berisford—Gr. K
Sherrard Elementary
Wheeling, WV

Very Important Big Book

This big book features some very important people—your students! After featuring each child as your student of the week, make a big book page full of information on that person. Keep adding to the book until it contains a page for each student. When it's a child's turn to be featured, send home a copy of the information request sheet on page 128. Transfer the information parents provide onto die-cuts, such as a birthday cake for the child's birthday or a house for his address. Display the die-cuts—as well as any photos or favorite items—during the week; then glue the die-cuts onto a large sheet of art paper. Add a photo you've taken of the child (since you'll want to return family photos); then laminate the page for durability. Bind the pages together with metal rings and watch as this book becomes the most popular one in your room!

Cheryl M. Howard—Gr. K
Pulaski Elementary School
Hawkinsville, GA

I Can Read!

Reinforce the reading of environmental print with a collection of "I Can Read" books! Take photographs of traffic signs, familiar restaurant signs, or familiar packaging from the grocery store. Enlarge each photo; then mount it on sturdy paper. Bind the photos together by theme and add a cover with a title such as "I Can Read Signs" or "I Can Read Foods." There's no stopping this reading success!

Bernadette Griffin
St. Michael's Country Day School
Newport, RI

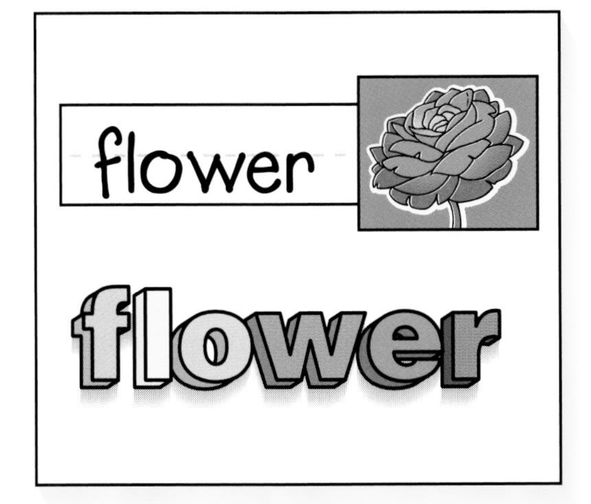

Stick to Spelling

Use a magnetboard in your literacy center to help your kindergartners stick to spelling! To prepare, cut out clip art or magazine photos of familiar items, such as a cat, a fish, a car, a flower, and a chair. Glue each picture to an individual sentence strip; then write the corresponding word on the strip. Put magnetic tape on the backs of the strips and store them in your literacy center, along with a magnetboard and a supply of magnetic letters. Invite a child to choose a strip, display it on the board, and then use the magnetic letters to spell the word by herself.

Amy Cole—Gr. K
Daphne Elementary
Daphne, AL

A Colorful Butterfly

Here's a springtime writing project that's sure to fly! To prepare, cut out a large butterfly shape from poster board or bulletin board paper. Then choose a color and ask students to brainstorm as many things as they can that are that color. Invite each child to write the name of one of the items in a space on the butterfly's wings. Then have students decorate around the spaces by gluing on crumpled tissue paper of the matching color. Use markers or decorative paper to color the butterfly's body; then add large wiggle eyes and pipe cleaner antennae to complete this colorful creation!

adapted from an idea by Phoebe Sharp—Grs. K and 1
Gillette School
Gillette, NJ

Word Family Cube

Toss some fun into learning to spell simple words when you use a word family cube! Cover a cube-shaped box with paper; then label each of the box's six sides with a different rime. Have a child toss the cube and see which word family lands on top. Have him think of a word in that family; then encourage him to spell the word by giving the letter for the initial sound and the letters of the rime. Easy!

Naomi Nussbaum—Gr. K
Barnert Temple School
Franklin Lakes, NJ

Word Detectives

Are your budding readers beginning to recognize words in print? Help them practice this new skill with some cellophane word finders. Make one by cutting a rectangle from a tagboard strip as shown; then tape a small piece of colored cellophane over the opening. During independent reading time, invite each youngster to be a word detective and find words he knows with a word finder. Keep a running list of words that each child recognizes to help you assess his reading skills.

Chris Foedisch—Gr. K
Paul Fly Elementary
Norristown, PA

Our Favorite Restaurants

Encourage young writers with a topic they're sure to eat up—talking about their favorite restaurants! Give each child a 6" x 6" square of writing paper. Have her name her favorite place to eat and write about why she likes it. Compile the pages between two construction paper covers and staple the book along the left side. Then glue the back cover to the center of a colorful paper plate. Glue the plate to a vinyl placemat, along with a napkin and a plastic fork. Then add this creative class book to your classroom library and watch the restaurant reading begin!

Shelly L. Kidd-Hamlett—Gr. K
Helena Elementary
Timberlake, NC

Summer Think Books

Encourage your kindergartners to keep their writing skills sharp over the summer with a simple gift! For each child, prepare a blank journal of about ten pages with a cover that reads "My Summer Think Book." Together, brainstorm ideas for topics students might write about during the summer, such as vacations they take, camps they attend, books they read, family members they visit, or new foods they try. Give each child a journal. Ask him to illustrate and personalize the cover. Then have each child take his journal home and write in it once a week. Motivate students by explaining that anyone who brings you a completed journal at the beginning of the next school year will receive a special reward!

Robin DiMaggio—Gr. K
Berry Hill Elementary
Syosset, NY

Words All Around

Make a set of "I Can Read" folders to help youngsters realize how many words in the environment they know. Label each folder "I can read [topic] names." Add a topic, such as the following: restaurant, store, candy bar, cereal, or toothpaste. Inside each folder, place labels, wrappers, or clippings from grocery store flyers or newspaper ads showing the names of the places or products indicated on the folder. Encourage youngsters to read the words in the folders and to refer to them for spelling help during writing time.

Vickie Crawford—Grs. K–2
Elkmont School
Elkmont, AL

Four Steps to a Story

This four-step formula makes story writing a snap! Encourage a child to write endings to the four sentence starters below to create a simple story. To make a book, instruct each child to number her pages, write each of the four sentences on a separate book page, and then add illustrations. Who's ready to sit in the author's chair?

Page 1: One day…
Page 2: And then…
Page 3: Next,…
Page 4: Finally,…

Carol Aitken
Deer Park Elementary
New Port Richey, FL

Student of the Week

Dear Family:

It's your child's turn to be featured as our Student of the Week! Please help your child fill out this information form. Return the form to school by ____________ (date), along with any pictures of your child or family you'd like to send. You may also send in some of your child's favorite items for us to display, such as a favorite T-shirt or a small toy. The photos and items will be returned to you. Thank you!

My full name is ______________________________.

My birthday is ______________________________.

My parents' names are ______________________________.

I have _________ brother(s) and _________ sister(s).

Their names are ______________________________.

I live at ______________________________.

I have a pet or pets named ______________________________.

______ I don't have any pets.

My favorite color is ______________________________.

My favorite food is ______________________________.

My favorite sport is ______________________________.

My favorite thing to do is ______________________________.

Note to the teacher: Use with "Very Important Big Book" on page 124.

Literature Units

Let's Be Friends!

Buddies, pals, amigos—whatever you call them, friends are an important part of life! Share these books about friends to help your students consider what friendship is all about.

by Ada Goren

Chester's Way

Written and Illustrated by Kevin Henkes

Chester and Wilson are like two peas in a pod. They do everything together and like all the same things. When exuberant Lilly moves to town, Chester and Wilson don't know what to think of her. But they soon find that Lilly's quirky character makes a fine addition to their friendship!

Friends usually have lots in common, just as Chester and Wilson do in this story. But sometimes friends can like different things too. Pair your kindergartners for a getting-to-know-you activity that will explore likenesses and differences. Give each child a copy of the information sheet on page 133. Have them talk to one another for a few minutes about some or all of the things on the sheet. Then instruct each child to color his sheet to show his new friend's preferences. Invite each pair to tell the group what they have discovered about one another. Which things do they have in common? On which things do they differ? After each pair has shared, remind students that good friends can be both alike *and* different!

Leon and Bob

Written and Illustrated by Simon James

Leon has just moved to town. He spends most of his time with Bob, his imaginary friend. But when a new boy moves in next door, will Leon have the courage to make a real friend?

Making a friend can be scary! When you share this story with your students, pause before Leon rings the bell at Bob's house. Ask youngsters to predict what Leon will do. Then read the rest of the story and discuss the ending. Afterward, ask youngsters to brainstorm other things Leon could do to become friends with Bob. Then give your students time to talk about their own experiences of making new friends.

Poppy and Ella: 3 Stories About 2 Friends

Written and Illustrated by Jef Kaminsky

Follow feathered friends Poppy and Ella through three short and simple stories. You'll see that even though these two bird buddies don't always see beak to beak, they support one another through thick and thin!

Your students are sure to agree that good friends help one another, just as Poppy and Ella do in all three stories. Review the problem in each of the three stories and discuss how one friend helps to solve it. Then present the situations below and ask student volunteers to tell how a good friend might react in each situation. If desired, have student pairs act out the situations for the class.

- You and your friend get ice-cream cones. Your friend's ice cream falls off the cone.
- You and your friend want to ride bikes. But your friend's bike has a flat tire, and no one can fix it right now.
- Your friend is playing at your house, and it begins to storm. Your friend is scared of the thunder.
- Your friend wanted to paint a picture at school, but never got a turn at the easel. Your friend is sad.

Jessica

Written and Illustrated by Kevin Henkes

Ruthie and Jessica, Jessica and Ruthie—they go everywhere together. The only problem is that Jessica's not real! Will Ruthie's imaginary friend get in the way of her making a real friend in kindergarten?

Ruthie meets the real Jessica on the first day of school, while waiting in line. Try this first-day-of-school idea to help your kindergartners meet some new, *real* friends of their own! Share the book a short time before you need to move to an activity outside your classroom, such as playground time or lunch. Then have students stand in a circle. Ask one child to walk around the outside of the circle while the class sings the song below. At the end of the song, have the child stop and introduce herself to the child nearest her. Have the child in the circle introduce herself; then ask the two to stand together in line. Repeat the song while another child walks around the circle to find a friend. Continue until all your kindergartners are paired up and ready to go!

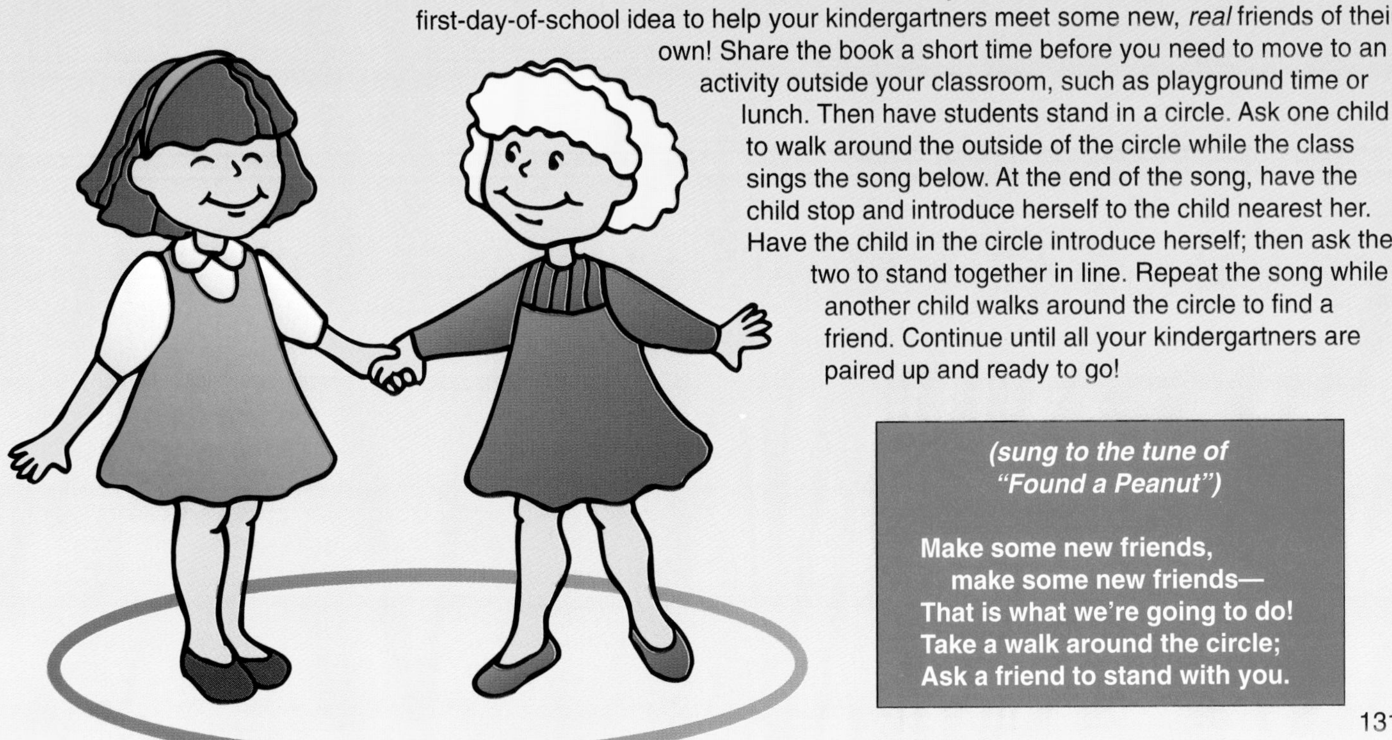

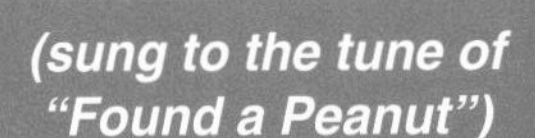

(sung to the tune of "Found a Peanut")

Make some new friends,
make some new friends—
That is what we're going to do!
Take a walk around the circle;
Ask a friend to stand with you.

Wanted: Best Friend

Written by A. M. Monson
Illustrated by Lynn Munsinger

When Cat and Mouse have a falling-out, Cat advertises for a new best friend. But he doesn't have much in common with the friendly applicants who show up at his door. With a new appreciation for his best buddy, Cat runs another ad and hopes to bring back Mouse.

Invite your students to compose their own ads for friendship! Give each child a copy of the ad on page 133. Have him dictate a few of his favorite things (such as foods, games, sports, and things to do on a rainy day). Also have him dictate his description of the type of friend he'd like. Then have him draw a self-portrait in the space provided. After sharing each child's finished ad with the group, post all the ads on a bulletin board. Add a border of newspaper strips cut from your local paper's classified advertising section and the title "Wanted: Friendly Kindergartners!"

Charlie the Caterpillar

Written by Dom DeLuise
Illustrated by Christopher Santoro

No one wants to play with Charlie the caterpillar—until he becomes a beautiful butterfly! But Charlie is wise enough to flutter past those who love him only for his looks and search for something more—a true friend.

Invite student pairs to make a cooperative craft that's sure to remind them of beautiful Charlie! Have each child use clear tape to attach a small picture of herself to one end of a bumpy pipe cleaner. Also have her tape two thin strips of paper to the back side of her photo to resemble antennae. Then explain how each child will turn this caterpillar version of herself into a stunning butterfly with the help of a friend!

Pair students; then give each child a simple butterfly shape cut from a 9" x 12" sheet of construction paper. Set out a variety of tempera paints. Have a child choose one color of paint and place a small blob on each of her butterfly's upper wings. Ask her friend to choose another color of paint and dot it on the butterfly's back wings. Have the child fold the paper; then have both children smooth their hands over the wings to spread the paint. Unfold the paper to reveal the butterfly design. Repeat the process with her partner's butterfly shape. Finally, trim each pipe cleaner "body" to the right length and use tacky glue to attach it to the center of the butterfly shape. Display these partner projects with the title "Good Friends Help You Spread Your Wings!"

Advertisement
Use with *Wanted: Best Friend* on page 132.

Friends Wanted

My name is ________________________________.

I like ________________________________,

________________________, and

________________________.

I want a friend who ____________

________________________.

All for One and One for All—Family

Extended family, nuclear family, big family, small—books about families offer good reading for us all!

by Suzanne Moore

Julius, the Baby of the World

Written and Illustrated by Kevin Henkes

Lilly is convinced that her new baby brother, Julius, is disgusting and that he should just go away. But she has a change of heart when she hears her cousin say some not-so-nice things about Julius!

Help reinforce positive feelings toward siblings with this engaging activity. After reading the story, discuss with students Lilly's feelings both before and after Cousin Garland's comments. Encourage youngsters to think of positive ways Lilly could spend time with Julius. Then wrap a stuffed mouse toy in a baby blanket and invite each child to hold Baby Julius and pretend to be Lilly. Have the child act out a positive thing she could do with Julius. Before you know it you'll see lots of brotherly and sisterly love in your classroom!

Octopus Hug

Written by Laurence Pringle
Illustrated by Kate Salley Palmer

Exactly what is an octopus hug? Becky and Jesse find out from their energetic dad when their mom goes out for the evening.

This lively book celebrates the fun and imaginative play that a father and his children can have together. After sharing the story, invite each youngster to share the experiences he's had with his dad (or another male caregiver) when his mom's been gone for a while. Then have small groups of students engage in some not-so-rough horseplay of their own. Provide each group with stuffed animals and encourage them to invent their own octopus-type hugs. To conclude this energetic activity, invite the entire class to join in a big group hug!

The Seven Silly Eaters

Written by Mary Ann Hoberman
Illustrated by Marla Frazee

Mr. and Mrs. Peters love their children. But as their family grows, so do their problems! You see, each of the Peters children is an extremely picky eater—until one day when they solve their eating problems themselves.

Nearly every child has been a silly eater at one point or another—even youngsters in your class! In advance, program a class supply of nine-inch paper plates as shown. After sharing the story with students, discuss their silly eating habits. Then have each child complete a silly eater's place setting. Provide each youngster with a programmed plate, a 12" x 18" sheet of construction paper (placemat), a plastic fork and spoon, a napkin, scissors, and glue. Have each youngster look through discarded magazines for pictures of foods he liked to eat as a young child. Then instruct him to cut out the pictures and glue them to his plate. Next, have him glue his plate, fork, spoon, and napkin to his placemat. Have him dictate to you the ending of the sentence programmed on the plate. Display the finished projects on a bulletin board titled "Silly Eaters in [your name]'s Class."

Kool-Aid Dough

Ingredients:

- $2\frac{1}{2}$–3 c. flour
- $\frac{1}{2}$ c. salt
- package unsweetened Kool-Aid
- 1 tbsp. alum
- 2 c. boiling water
- 3 tbsp. corn oil
- 1 c. additional flour

Preparation:

Mix the first six ingredients to make a dough. After the dough cools, knead it—adding small amounts of the additional flour if necessary—until it reaches the desired consistency. Store the dough in an airtight container.

Mmm, Cookies!

Written by Robert Munsch
Illustrated by Michael Martchenko

Are those real cookies or ones made out of play clay? Find out what happens to Christopher, who serves Mom and Dad some not-quite-real cookies.

Get your little ones set for some squishing and squashing as they make their own cookies—well, pretend cookies—with this center idea. Make several different batches of scented play dough using the recipe above. Place the dough, old cookie cutters, rolling pins, plastic knives, plastic forks, and old garlic presses at a center. Invite each child to visit the center and make a play dough cookie. Have her place her cookie on a small paper plate labeled with her name. Allow the cookies to dry for several days. After the cookies have completely dried, hot-glue a heavy-duty magnet to the back of each one. Have each child place her cookie in a snack bag and then staple a copy of the cookie poem from page 158 to the bag. Then send the cookies home. Parents will be delighted with this treat—a visual treat, that is!

Me and My Family Tree

Written by Joan Sweeney
Illustrated by Annette Cable

Join a young girl as she explores how her brother, parents, grandparents, and other assorted relatives end up on her family tree.

Everyone has a family tree, and this book will inspire your young genealogists to create family trees of their very own! In advance, make a class set of the apple patterns and poem on page 138. To make a tree, paint a child's forearm with brown paint and then help her press her arm onto a 12" x 18" sheet of light blue construction paper to make a trunk. Then paint her hand with green paint. Have her make several handprints at the top of the trunk to represent the leaves and branches, repainting her hand as needed. Instruct each child to color and cut out the poem on her copy of page 138 and then glue it to the bottom of her family tree. After the trees have dried, send them home with students along with their apple patterns. Encourage each family to help its child complete the family tree by labeling the apples and then gluing them onto the tree. Have students return the trees to school on a designated day. Invite each youngster to share her family tree with the class. What a nice orchard of family trees!

A Quiet Night In

Written and Illustrated by Jill Murphy

It's Mr. Large's birthday! Who will stay up to eat the delicious birthday dinner? And just who will go to bed early?

A birthday can be celebrated in many ways—with a party, a special dinner, or a quiet night in! To begin, have students discuss how their families celebrate birthdays. There's no doubt that gifts will be mentioned. After discussing birthday traditions, give your youngsters some fine-motor practice by setting up a gift-wrapping center. Place a supply of boxes in various sizes at a center, along with sheets of comics from the newspaper (or birthday-themed wrapping paper), bows, scissors, and tape. Invite each youngster to choose a box and wrap it using the supplies at the center. After all of the boxes have been wrapped, have students unwrap them and start all over again!

Come Out and Play, Little Mouse

Written by Robert Kraus
Illustrated by Jose Aruego and Ariane Dewey

Little Mouse accepts Cat's treacherous invitation to come play. Who will rescue him? The results are surprising!

Big Brother Mouse certainly took care of his little brother in this tale! Have students say thanks to those who care for them with this project. In advance, make a class set of the thank-you cards on page 158. After sharing the story, discuss how Big Brother Mouse cared for Little Mouse. Have students think about a way that a family member showed she cared. Then give each youngster a thank-you card and have him cut it out. Help each child fold his card and use an ink pad to make a thumbprint in the *o* position of the word *you*. Instruct him to use a fine-tip pen to draw eyes, ears, and a tail on the print to transform it into a mouse. Have him color the rest of the card. Help him write the name of the recipient on the cover and a thank-you sentence on the inside of the card. Encourage each youngster to take his thank-you card home and deliver it to his special family member.

The Relatives Came

Written by Cynthia Rylant
Illustrated by Stephen Gammell

Here they come—the relatives from Virginia! When this extended family gets together, there's bound to be lots of hugging, laughing, and eating going on until it's time to head home!

Your youngsters will be eager to make these personalized booklets after hearing Cynthia Rylant's happy story. To prepare, make a class set of the booklet patterns on page 139 and cut a 6" x 20" strip of white bulletin board paper for each child. Accordion-fold each strip to make four equal sections. Have youngsters think of a time when relatives came to visit. Instruct each child to draw a picture of his relatives on the sections of his strip, using the back of each section if necessary. Help each child label the pictures on his strip. Have him color and cut out his car patterns. Help him tape the front and back patterns of his car to the ends of his strip as shown. Invite each child to share his book with the class and tell about a time when his relatives came to visit.

Apple Patterns and Poem

Use with *Me and My Family Tree* on page 136.

My Family Tree

I made a tree that's special. It's special just for me.
It's full of hugs and care and love. It's my family tree!

Use with *The Relatives Came* on page 137.

Deck the shelves with this collection of holiday books because 'tis the season for great stories!

by Jana Sanderson, Rainbow School, Stockton, CA

Color recognition
Reading

Sammy Spider's First Hanukkah

Written by Sylvia A. Rouss
Illustrated by Katherine Janus Kahn

Sammy Spider is fascinated by the traditions of Hanukkah. He lowers himself down a silken thread to take a closer look at the candles on the menorah and the colorful dreidels spinning below him. This darling holiday story is sure to warm hearts—and for Sammy, his feet!

blue
red
yellow
green
purple
orange
rose
brown

After a reading of the book, use this fun spin-off activity to have students' heads whirling with colors. In advance, gather a supply of cake pans, one for each group of four children. Photocopy page 143 to make a class set. Cut out a white paper circle to fit in the bottom of each pan. Use a marker to divide each circle into eight wedges. Then color each wedge using the colors from the story. Provide each group with a cake pan, a dreidel, and a set of crayons matching the colors from the story. Give each child a copy of page 143.

Have each student in the group, in turn, spin the dreidel in the bottom of the pan. When it stops spinning, have him identify the color the dreidel landed on and then color the section of his paper labeled with the corresponding color word. Play continues until each child has completed his paper. What colorful dreidels!

Fine motor
Writing

I wish for a vacation for my mom.

Toot & Puddle

I'll Be Home for Christmas

Written and illustrated by Holly Hobbie

A lucky nut and a sleigh ride from an unexpected holiday stranger lead to the reunion of two friends on Christmas Eve. This is a delightfully charming story about friendship and sharing a magical holiday together!

Have you been wishing for a unique writing activity? You're in luck! To prepare, cut two walnut shapes from brown paper grocery bags for each child. Then, as you share this story, have each youngster think of a wish. After you've finished reading, help each child record her wish on a slip of paper. Give each youngster two walnut shapes. Have her crinkle, fold, and crease the shapes. Then staple each child's nut halves together, leaving an opening at the top. Have each child stuff her nut with newspaper and then place her wish inside. Staple each opening closed. Encourage each child to take her nut home and open it with her family to reveal her wish. Happy wishes to you!

Following directions
Craft

The Christmas Cobwebs

Written by Odds Bodkin
Illustrated by Terry Widener

An immigrant family cherishes a box of Christmas ornaments brought from their homeland, but misfortune causes them to part with the ornaments. Thanks to some busy spiders, the family's Christmas tree is beautiful once again and their new house feels like home.

Capture the spirit of Christmas with these cobweb ornaments. To prepare, use a permanent marker to draw an ornament outline on a piece of waxed paper for each child. Cut white yarn into one-yard lengths to make a class set. Thin glue by mixing two parts glue with one part water. Provide each child with a programmed piece of waxed paper, a length of yarn, and access to the thinned glue. Instruct him to dip his yarn in the glue mixture and then squeeze off the excess. Have him lay the yarn along the ornament outlines on his paper. Then instruct him to zigzag and swirl the remaining length of yarn across the outline. Allow the yarn to dry completely. Peel each cobweb ornament from its paper. Surprise your students one morning by hanging the ornaments on a tree for all to see!

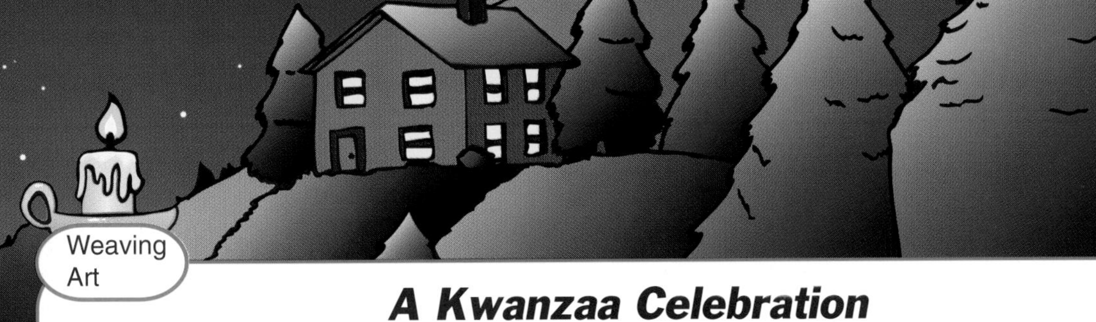

Weaving
Art

A Kwanzaa Celebration

Written by Nancy Williams
Illustrated by Robert Sabuda

Through symbols, traditions, and the vivid brush strokes of the images, an African American holiday is celebrated with pop-up pages.

Extend the idea of this pop-up book by having youngsters combine two traditions of Kwanzaa into a 3-D design. To prepare an *mkeka,* or placemat, for each child, cut slits $1\frac{1}{2}$ inches apart on the fold of a 12" x 18" sheet of black construction paper as shown. Then cut a large supply of $1\frac{1}{2}$" x 12" strips of red and green construction paper. Have each child weave strips through the slits of her black paper. Have her add a dab of glue to each end of each strip to secure it to the black paper.

To prepare a kinara for each child, cut out a candleholder from a folded 6" x 15" piece of brown construction paper as shown. Unfold each holder. Then cut red, green, and black construction paper into 1" x 6" strips so that each child will have three red strips, three green strips, and one black strip. Have each student cut one end of each strip into a point and then add gold glitter glue to the point to represent a flame. Instruct her to glue her candles to the holder as shown. Then staple the mkeka and the kinara together to create a freestanding project. Happy Kwanzaa!

Numeral recognition
Counting

Gingerbread Baby

Written and illustrated by Jan Brett

In classic Jan Brett style, a gingerbread baby jumps from the oven and leads a comical chase throughout the countryside. The beautifully detailed illustrations introduce a new twist to this popular fairy tale.

No one will be running away from this fun math activity once they smell the spices of the gingerbread! In advance, fold two corners of a napkin and secure them with tape to create a house shape, as shown, for each child. Program 20 index cards each with a different numeral from 1 to 20. Then draw a gingerbread man or place a gingerbread man sticker on two blank cards. Put the number cards and gingerbread man cards in a paper bag and shake the bag to mix the cards. Provide a small group with a supply of cereal pieces, gingerbread men cookies, and napkin houses.

In turn, have each child draw a card from the bag. If a numeral card is drawn, instruct the child to read the numeral, place the appropriate number of cereal pieces on his house, and then return the card to the bag so play can continue. If a gingerbread man card is drawn, have the student add a gingerbread man to his house, return the card to the bag, and then take another turn. Each youngster is a winner when his house is covered with cereal and gingerbread men. It's time to snack!

Counting
Numeral recognition
Telling time to the hour

P. Bear's New Year's Party: A Counting Book

Written and illustrated by Paul Owen Lewis

What's black, white, and read all over? It's this unique counting book. Black-and-white illustrations with simple text allow young children to count P. Bear's best-dressed friends as they arrive around the clock in preparation for his New Year's party!

This activity leads to round-the-clock fun! Program a supply of index cards with black sticky dots to represent the numbers one through 12. Make a large clockface on bulletin board paper and draw the minute hand pointing to 12. Then cut out a shorter hour hand from tagboard and attach it to the center of the clock with a brass fastener. In turn, invite each child to choose a card from the stack. Have her count the dots on her card and then move the hour hand on the clock to the corresponding number. Then instruct her to form a sentence similar to those in the book, such as "At 7:00, seven deer ate dinner in the forest." Record each child's sentence on a sheet of paper and then have her illustrate the page. Stack the pages in chronological order and bind the pages between construction paper covers. Finally, title the book "Ticktock Counting Round the Clock."

Name ________________________________ Reading color words

A Colorful Dreidel

blue

red

yellow

green

purple

orange

rose

brown

Note to the teacher: Use with *Sammy Spider's First Hanukkah* on page 140.

Use this selection of books to introduce your students to some of the many feelings they can experience on any day!

by Rhonda L. Chiles, South Park Elementary, Shawnee Mission, KS

Identifying feelings

TODAY I FEEL SILLY & OTHER MOODS THAT MAKE MY DAY

Written by Jamie Lee Curtis
Illustrated by Laura Cornell

Follow along as a little girl delightfully describes the emotions she feels as she experiences each day. Kindergartners will love the simple rhyming verse and charming illustrations of this book.

After reading the story, have each youngster make a feelings character. To prepare, photocopy page 147 to make a class set. Prompt students to discuss a variety of feelings. Have each child use facial expressions to illustrate each feeling. Then give each child a copy of page 147 and have him color and cut out the character pattern and feelings wheel. Help each child cut out the facial area of his character. Attach the feelings wheel to the back of the character, as shown, using a brass fastener. Then reread the book. Have students turn their wheels to show each feeling that is mentioned in the story. Pair students and instruct each child to turn his wheel and describe a time when he felt the feeling shown on the character's face. I felt happy the day I lost my tooth!

Count to ten
Walk away
Talk things out
Exercise
Take a deep breath

FRANKLIN'S BAD DAY

Written by Paulette Bourgeois
Illustrated by Brenda Clark

Franklin is having a bad day because his good friend moved away. Mad and sad, he talks to his father and, together, they find a way to make Franklin feel better.

Your little ones will get a kick out of pretending to be Franklin with this pantomime activity. After listening to the story, encourage youngsters to scrunch up their faces and act out parts of Franklin's bad day. Then lead students to discuss things they can do when they want to change the way they are feeling—for example, count to ten, walk away from the situation, talk things out, squish clay, take a deep breath, or exercise. Write students' responses on a turtle-shaped chart. Post the chart in your classroom to remind students that, just as Franklin discovers, there are things we can do to help turn a bad day into a glad day!

FEELINGS

Completing a craft
Writing color words

Go Away, Big Green Monster!

Written and illustrated by Ed Emberley

Through descriptive text and bright colors, Big Green Monster grows on each page of this die-cut book. Then, in the second half of the story, readers watch as he slowly disappears—no more monster!

After reading the story, lead students to discuss things that scare them. Then have the group substitute each youngster's response in the following sentence: "Go away, [storms]!"

Next, make these colorful monster posters. Give each child a copy of page 148, a 12" x 18" sheet of black construction paper, a 9" x 12" sheet of construction paper in any color (for the face), and several smaller pieces of construction paper in a variety of colors. Instruct him to glue his copy of page 148 to his large sheet of construction paper as shown. Instruct him to use scissors to round the corners of his 9" x 12" sheet of construction paper to make a head shape. Then guide each child to cut out the appropriate number of facial features for his monster. Have him glue the features to his head shape to create a monster face. Next, instruct him to observe the colors used to make his monster's face and then complete his reproducible by writing the appropriate color word on each line. Go away, Monster, and don't come back!

The Happy Hedgehog Band

Written by Martin Waddell
Illustrated by Jill Barton

Harry and the other hedgehogs love to bang on their drums. The other forest animals want to join in, but can't find any drums. Together the animals come up with a plan so that all the animals can play along with the hedgehog band.

Sing this little ditty with your youngsters to illustrate how music can make them happy! As students sing, encourage them to add more sounds to the music by tapping a pencil, clapping to the beat, or snapping their fingers. Then have youngsters stand up and dance. You'll see lots of smiles as your happy kindergarten band sings, claps, and dances around the room!

(sung to the tune of "Kiss Him Goodbye")

Tum-tum-te-tum,
Diddle-diddle-dum,
Ratta-tat-tat,
And BOOM!

Guess How Much I Love You

Written by Sam McBratney
Illustrated by Anita Jeram

Little Nutbrown Hare loves his father very, very much. As he describes his love in this enchanting tale, Little Nutbrown Hare discovers that he is loved even more.

After sharing the story, have students think of someone they love very much. Then instruct each child to stretch out his arms and say, "I love you this much!" Have students continue to profess their love using other movements from the book, such as "I love you as high as I can reach," "I love you all the way up to my toes" (students lie down on the floor with their feet in the air, then stretch toward their toes), and "I love you as high as I can hop." Then photocopy page 149 to make a class set. Give each child a copy and have him draw a self-portrait on the first toe print, a heart on the second toe print, and a picture of someone he loves on the third toe print. Then help each child complete the sentence on the footprint. Post the papers on a bulletin board titled "[Your name]'s class is so loving!"

Following directions
Making a snack

Mrs. Rose's Garden

Written and illustrated by Elaine Greenstein

Mrs. Rose never wins a blue ribbon at the county fair until one year she uses a special fertilizer mix. Her vegetables become enormous, big enough to win all blue ribbons. Now winning doesn't seem quite so fun. Then she has an idea to help her friends receive ribbons at the fair. Mrs. Rose wins a special ribbon for having the biggest heart!

Mrs. Rose has a big heart. Helping her friends makes her feel good. Lead a class discussion about caring for others and about how good helping someone can make us feel. Encourage youngsters to share how they have helped others. Then make a heart garden in honor of Mrs. Rose. Provide each child with a graham cracker (the ground), a plastic knife, access to chocolate frosting (special fertilizer mix), and several candy hearts. Have her spread her cracker with frosting and then place (plant) her hearts on it to complete the garden. Mrs. Rose would be so proud!

Feelings Wheel and Character Pattern

Use with *Today I Feel Silly & Other Moods That Make My Day* on page 144.

Go Away, Big Monster

With two ______________ eyes,

A long ______________ nose,

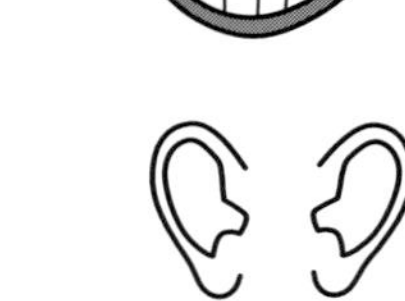

A big ______________ mouth,

With sharp ______________ teeth,

Two little ______________ ears,

Scraggly ______________ hair,

And a big ______________ face.

And Don't Come Back!

Note to the teacher: Use with *Go Away, Big Green Monster!* on page 145.

Name ____________________ *Guess How Much I Love You*

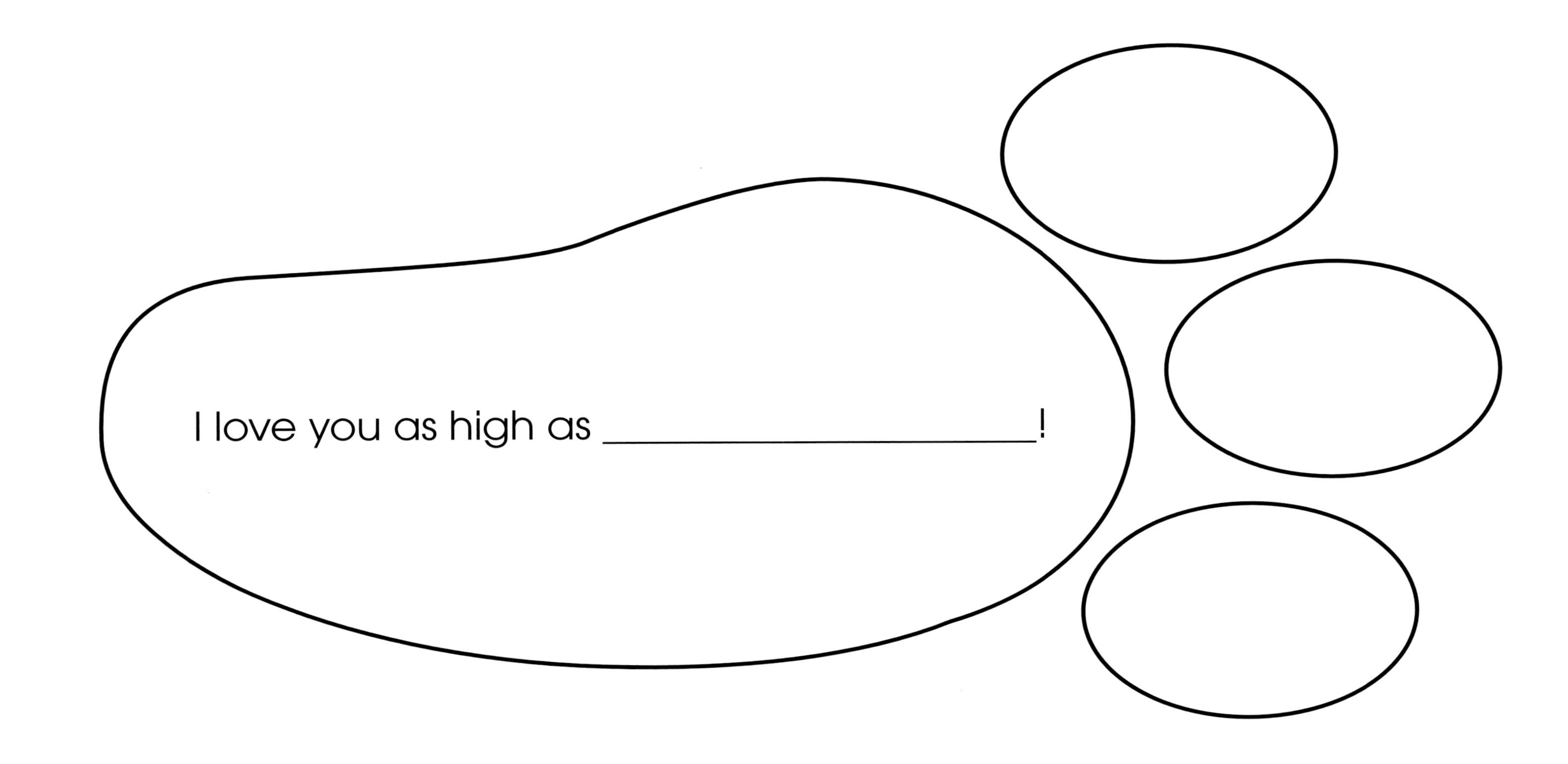

Note to the teacher: Use with *Guess How Much I Love You* on page 146.

Very Imaginative Literature

Share this collection of books with your youngsters to entertain them and inspire them to use their creative imaginations!

by Lucia Kemp Henry, Fallon, NV

Drawing
Writing

Chimps Don't Wear Glasses

Written by Laura Numeroff
Illustrated by Joe Mathieu

Can horses hang glide? Do pandas pole vault? This silly story's illustrations suppose that animals can do the things that people do! The busy critters in this tale will inspire your youngsters to conjure all kinds of impossible animal antics.

Introduce the book by showing students the cover and reading the title. Explain that even though chimps don't wear glasses, it's fun to imagine that they do! As you share the story, invite youngsters to study the illustrations to find each animal and every outrageous activity pictured. When you've finished the story, prompt each child to share the name of her favorite animal from the story and what that animal does. Ask the child to think of another unbelievable human activity the animal might imitate. Then reread the final page of the book as inspiration for an art project. To spark each child's imagination, say, "If you dreamed a scene for the book, what animal would you see? What would it do?" Give each child a sheet of paper and invite her to draw a picture to illustrate what she's imagined. Then have her write a sentence to describe her illustration. Later, bind the pages to make a class book and title it "Imagine What Animals Might Do!"

Sarah can catch the moon by grabbing a big balloon and going up.

Writing
Drawing

I'll Catch the Moon

Written and photo-illustrated by Nina Crews

Sometimes the big, bright moon looks so close it seems that it's within arm's reach. When a young girl sees the moon through her window, she wants to reach up and grab it. How can she catch the moon? With her imagination, of course!

As you share this story, have youngsters think about what is real on each page and what is imaginary. To prepare, program a sheet of paper with the story starter shown; then make a copy for each child. After reading, ask students to recall the character's imaginary uses of real objects to help her reach the moon. Prompt each child to imagine a way to catch the moon. Give each child a programmed copy and have her use paint and a round sponge to make a print on her paper to represent the moon. After the paint has dried, have her draw a picture to show her imaginative idea for reaching the moon. Then instruct her to use the story starter on the page to write a sentence about her picture. Invite each child to share her illustration and sentence with the class. Bind the completed pages between black construction paper covers decorated with foil star stickers. Use a white crayon to title the book "How to Catch the Moon." To the moon!

Problem solving

Harold and the Purple Crayon

Written and illustrated by Crockett Johnson

Harold uses a vivid purple crayon to draw things that lead him on an imaginary adventure. Some things he draws cause problems. To help solve the problems he's drawn, Harold uses his creativity and his amazing crayon in very inventive ways.

After reading the story, prompt students to discuss some of Harold's problems and how he solves them. Then extend the story by inviting each child to imagine his own purple crayon adventure! Give each child construction paper copies of pages 153 and 154. Instruct him to cut out the booklet pages and then stack them in order. Help each child staple his pages together. Have each child use a purple crayon to draw a picture that solves the problem on each page. Next, have him draw a purple crayon on the cover and write his name on the line. Invite each child to share his book with the class. Wow, what an adventure!

Role-playing

Pretend You're a Cat

Written by Jean Marzollo
Illustrated by Jerry Pinkney

How many times have you watched your youngsters pretend to be farmyard friends, pets, or animals in the zoo? This book is filled with imaginative children who reinforce the fact that pretending provides oodles of learning opportunities.

One of the most imaginative things a child can do is pretend to be an animal. As you share each page of the story, pause to allow youngsters to perform the suggested animal actions. After reading, prompt students to recall the names of the animals in the book. Record each animal name on a 3" x 5" index card, display the word cards in a pocket chart, and read each one aloud. Then place the cards in a container to use in a singing game. Have students form a circle. Invite a volunteer to draw a card from the container. Help the child read the word; then prompt her to pretend to be the animal while the rest of the class sings the song below, inserting the correct animal name in the blanks. Continue the activity until every child has had a turn. Meow!

(sung to the tune of "London Bridge")

Can you move just like a [cat],
Like a [cat], like a [cat]?
Can you move just like a [cat]?
Please, please show us!

Can you sound just like a [cat],
Like a [cat], like a [cat]?
Can you sound just like a [cat]?
Please, please show us!

Exploring alike and different
Making a craft
Writing

The Big Box

Written by Virginia Grant Clammer
Photo-illustrated by Dorothy Handelman

Two youngsters use imagination and craft materials to turn an ordinary box into something special. The best thing about the box is that it can be anything imaginable!

This book offers an opportunity to explore how objects can be alike and different. After reading, review the pictures of the box as a car and as a jet. Have students tell you how the two things are alike. Then ask youngsters to share how they are different. Extend the comparison to include the train. Next, ask students how the box could be changed to look like other things, such as a boat or a house. Then invite each child to design his own box creation. Stock a center with shoeboxes, glue, scissors, construction paper, and lots of collage materials. Have each child visit the center and use the art materials to transform a box into a car, a jet, a train, or anything else he can imagine. Later, have each child write a sentence describing his creation. Arrange the projects on a table to create an impressive display of imagination.

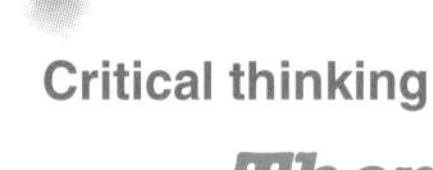

Critical thinking

There's a Nightmare in My Closet

Written and illustrated by Mercer Mayer

An imaginary monster isn't so scary when a little boy uses creative thinking to tame the nightmare critter in his closet!

Help students make the most of the story by asking questions as you read. Choose from the questions below or make up your own. After reading the story, give each child a piece of paper. Have her use crayons to draw a picture of a nightmare. Instruct her to fold a 12" x 18" sheet of construction paper in half; then help her glue her picture inside as shown. Have her glue a yellow construction paper circle to the front cover to represent a doorknob. Help her write her nightmare-taming idea on the cover. Use a stapler to attach the picture portion of each child's door to a bulletin board backed with black paper. Title the board "Taming Nightmares!" What a great way to open the doors to your youngsters' imaginations!

How do you know the boy is afraid of the nightmare?
Is the nightmare real?
What would you do to tame your own nightmare?
What would your nightmare look like after you tamed it?

Use with *Harold and the Purple Crayon* on page 151.

My Purple Crayon Adventure

by ____________________

If I saw a dragon, I would draw…

1

If I fell in the ocean, I would draw…

2

Booklet Pages

Use with *Harold and the Purple Crayon* on page 151.

Good Ol' Summertime Reading

Finally, it's summertime, and long warm days are made even better with plenty of sizzling summer books! So grab this collection of literature; then sit back, relax, and have fun reading!

by Suzanne Moore, Irving, TX

Arthur's Family Vacation

Written and illustrated by Marc Brown

When Arthur and his family go to the beach, rain interferes with their fun—or does it?

When the weather turns bad, Arthur still manages to have loads of fun. After sharing this story with students, have youngsters help you list the activities Arthur's family participates in while on vacation. Write student responses on a sheet of chart paper. Discuss each activity and have students decide on their favorite activities. Then cut the chart into strips, with one activity on each strip. Post each strip in a different location in your classroom. Review each activity and then invite each child to stand near the strip listing his favorite activity. Count the number of students in each group and then have the groups line up to make a human graph that represents the results. Finally, discuss the graph with students to determine the most popular activity.

A trip to Gatorville

Grandma Summer

Written and illustrated by Harley Jessup

Ben and Grandma head off to the family's old beach house. Ben soon finds that the house and the nearby beach are filled with history and treasures.

Hidden treasures await students when you hide ocean-swept items in your sand table. In advance, collect smooth stones, plastic teacups, shells, a large green marble to represent the Japanese glass float, and plastic seaweed and driftwood (both available from your local craft store). Hide the small items in dampened sand; then cover the sand with the driftwood and seaweed. After sharing the story, give each youngster a sheet of paper and a pencil. Then invite small groups of students to discover what's been washed ashore in your classroom's sand table. Have students document their finds by drawing pictures and writing about each one. They'll enjoy the thrill of discovery just as Ben does! After youngsters have found all the hidden treasures, encourage them to rebury the items for another small group to discover.

Pigs Ahoy!

Written and illustrated by David McPhail

What happens when a pack of piggies vacations on a cruise? Bedlam and a whole lot of fun!

The pigs in this delightful story seem to have a fabulous time no matter what problems they cause! After you share this story, ask students, "What trouble could the pigs get into at the man's house?" After a discussion of the kinds of situations the pigs could get into, have each child use a pink ink pad to make seven thumbprints on a sheet of paper. Then instruct him to use a pencil or marker to add ears, eyes, noses, and tails to the prints to transform them into pigs. Next, have him illustrate a pig-produced catastrophe around his piggy prints. Instruct him to write about his picture beneath the illustration. Then invite him to share his completed picture with the class. Bind the pages to make a book titled "Piggy Problems." Now that's a perfectly porky page-turner!

Around the Pond: Who's Been Here?

Written and illustrated by Lindsay Barrett George

With gloriously detailed paintings, the pleasure of a guessing game and a nature walk are combined in this simple story about two children's search for blueberries near the pond.

Looking at clues and guessing who left them will spark plenty of student curiosity as you share this book with your young nature lovers. Continue the guessing game in your classroom by inviting students to create this interactive bulletin board. In advance, cover your bulletin board with green paper. Mount a free-form pond shape in the center and label it "Around the Pond: Who Is Here?" Then have each student draw a picture of a pond animal (including animals not mentioned in the book) on a 9" x 12" sheet of paper. Next, discuss the guessing-game format of the book with students. Help each child write a clue for his animal picture on a second sheet of paper. (The clues can be as simple as "I look like a bandit. I live near the pond. Who am I?") Staple each clue sheet atop the matching animal picture. Then mount the completed projects on your bulletin board within students' reach. Encourage students to read the clues and then guess the hidden animals before lifting the clues to reveal the underlying animal drawing. Mystery solved!

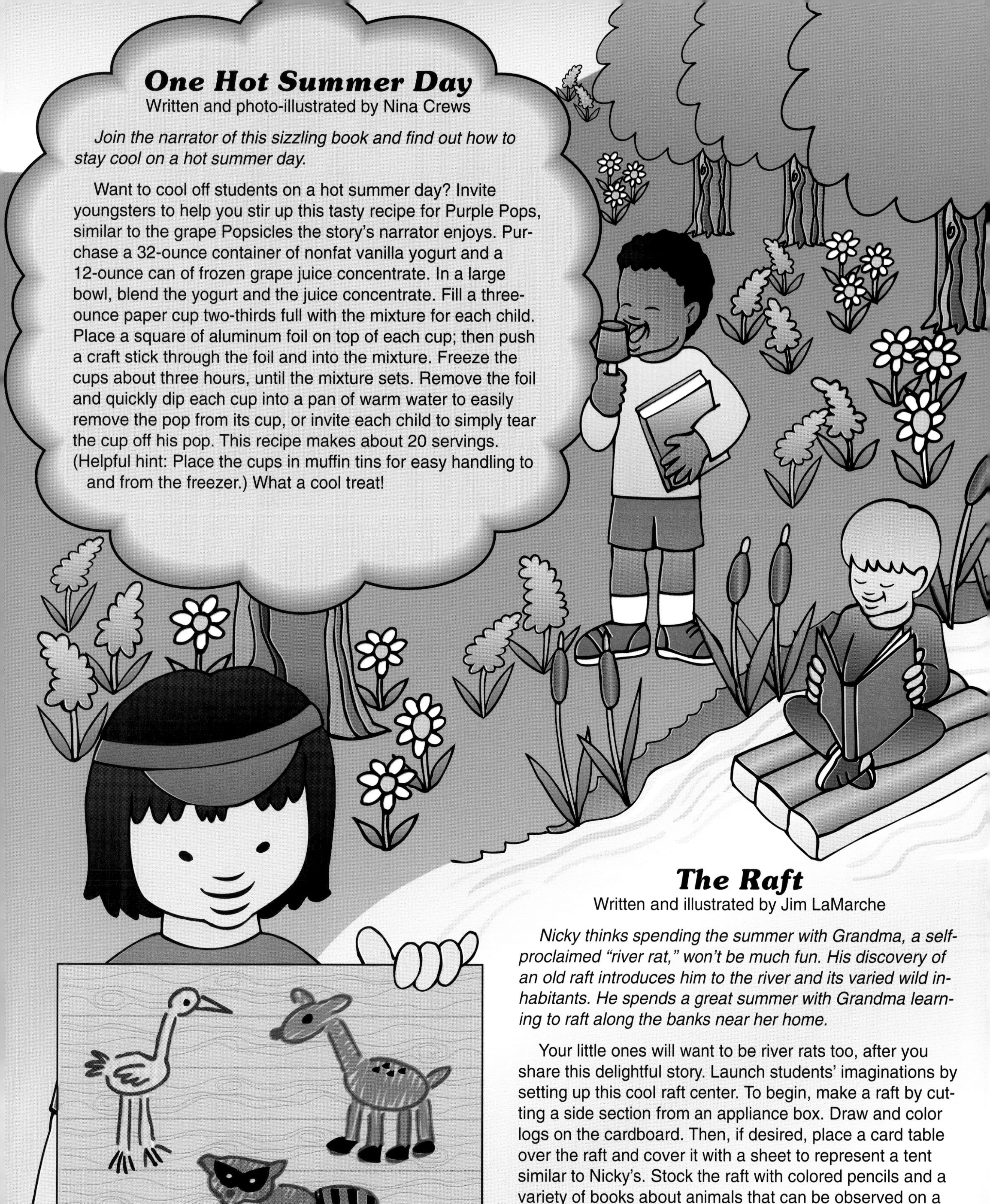

One Hot Summer Day

Written and photo-illustrated by Nina Crews

Join the narrator of this sizzling book and find out how to stay cool on a hot summer day.

Want to cool off students on a hot summer day? Invite youngsters to help you stir up this tasty recipe for Purple Pops, similar to the grape Popsicles the story's narrator enjoys. Purchase a 32-ounce container of nonfat vanilla yogurt and a 12-ounce can of frozen grape juice concentrate. In a large bowl, blend the yogurt and the juice concentrate. Fill a three-ounce paper cup two-thirds full with the mixture for each child. Place a square of aluminum foil on top of each cup; then push a craft stick through the foil and into the mixture. Freeze the cups about three hours, until the mixture sets. Remove the foil and quickly dip each cup into a pan of warm water to easily remove the pop from its cup, or invite each child to simply tear the cup off his pop. This recipe makes about 20 servings. (Helpful hint: Place the cups in muffin tins for easy handling to and from the freezer.) What a cool treat!

The Raft

Written and illustrated by Jim LaMarche

Nicky thinks spending the summer with Grandma, a self-proclaimed "river rat," won't be much fun. His discovery of an old raft introduces him to the river and its varied wild inhabitants. He spends a great summer with Grandma learning to raft along the banks near her home.

Your little ones will want to be river rats too, after you share this delightful story. Launch students' imaginations by setting up this cool raft center. To begin, make a raft by cutting a side section from an appliance box. Draw and color logs on the cardboard. Then, if desired, place a card table over the raft and cover it with a sheet to represent a tent similar to Nicky's. Stock the raft with colored pencils and a variety of books about animals that can be observed on a river. Then invite small groups of students to take pretend trips down the river. Encourage youngsters to peruse the books and then draw pictures on the raft of the animals they've seen on their float trip. Way to go, little river rats!

Cookie Poem

Use with *Mmm, Cookies!* on page 135.

Thank-You Card

Use with *Come Out and Play, Little Mouse* on page 137.

Our Readers Write

Our Readers Write

Handprint Puzzle

Here's a first-day-of-school project that parents will treasure! Visit your local craft store to purchase a class supply of blank jigsaw puzzles. Or simply use 5" x 7" pieces of poster board. Paint a child's hand with tempera paint; then have him press a handprint onto the blank puzzle or poster board. Use a permanent marker to write the child's name near the print, or have him write it himself. Allow the paint to dry. If you're using poster board, puzzle-cut the finished project. Put each child's pieces in a separate zippered plastic bag; then staple the provided poem to the bag. What a great kindergarten keepsake!

Angie Bonthuis—Gr. K
Gilbert Elementary, Gilbert, IA

First-Day Fun

There's nothing like a little science to keep your mind off first-day jitters! To prepare, fill two containers with water. Tint one with blue food coloring and the other with yellow. Make enough tinted ice cubes so that each child will have one of each color. Give each youngster two ice cubes sealed in a zippered plastic bag. Ask her to melt the ice as quickly as possible; then watch the creative solutions in action! Have her observe her bag periodically. Hey, blue ice and yellow ice make green water!

adapted from an idea by Jeanette Pauls—Gr. K
Calistoga Elementary
Calistoga, CA

"Safe-Tees"

Near the beginning of the school year, have each child bring in a plain white T-shirt. Enlist the help of some parents to help tie-dye the T-shirts using your school colors. Then have youngsters wear the shirts when your class goes on a field trip. Your students will be recognizable as part of your group, but the shirts won't give away any information about their names or school to strangers.

Jean Ricotta—Lead Teacher
Signal Hill Elementary
Dix Hills, NY

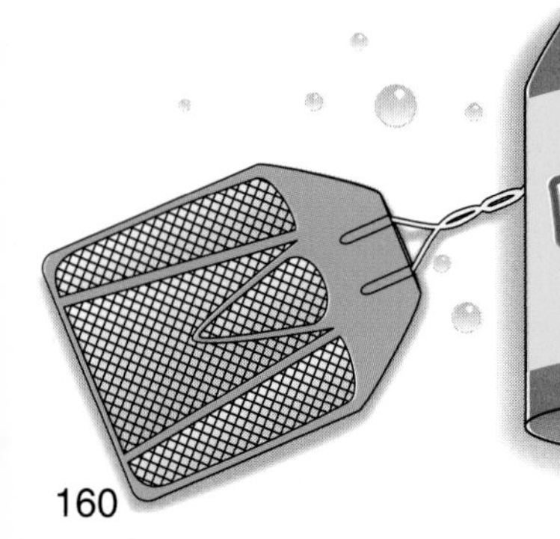

Fabulous Flyswatters

Next time your group heads outdoors for some bubble fun, take along a few new flyswatters! Dip them into shallow pans of bubble solution; then wave them through the air. You'll get a bounty of bubbles!

Leanne Gibbons—Gr. K
Sacred Heart School
Quincy, MA

Functional Foam

Want long-lasting calendar shapes, nametags, or desktags? Cut the shapes from craft foam! Your school's die-cutting machine will make the job easy, and using foam instead of construction paper cuts down on laminating!

Vivian Langston—Gr. K
Seffner, FL

Have a Seat on That...Placemat?

Yes! Durable vinyl placemats in fun shapes will help little ones keep their seats during circle time. Purchase a class supply of placemats in cute shapes, such as bears and fish. Place one on the carpet where you'd like each child to sit. Then invite youngsters to find a seat. Neat!

Cathie Rubley Hart—Gr. K
Westwood Hills Elementary
Waynesboro, VA

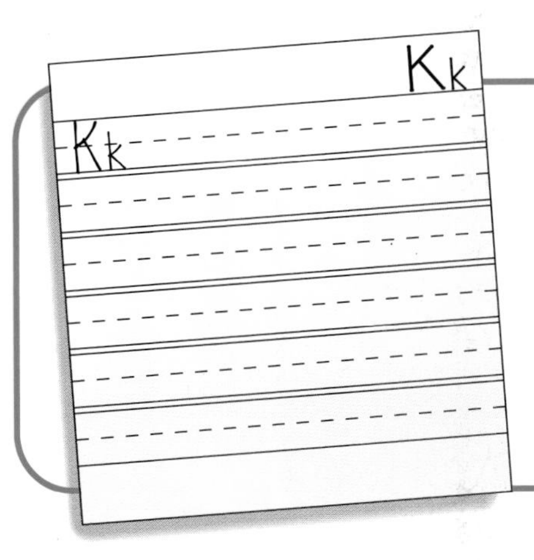

A Little Help for Lefties

Ever notice that the example on most handwriting practice sheets is on the left side? This makes it tough for left-handed students to follow the model, since their hands may cover the example. Write the model letter or word on the upper right corner of the sheet for your lefties. *Much* better!

Barbara Peek—Volunteer
Andalusia, AL

Coloring Tables

Keep young siblings busy during your open house or parent conferences by setting up one or two coloring tables. Simply cover a table with inexpensive paper and set out a basket of crayons. They'll stay busy, and you can display the family art later for everyone to enjoy!

Anne Rideout—Gr. K
Sandy Elementary
Sandy, UT

Fresh Play Dough

Tired of dried-out play dough? Ask parents to make fresh play dough each month! At a parent visitation night near the start of the year, put out a sign-up sheet for any parents who are interested in making play dough for your class. Each month, send home a play dough recipe to one or two families that have signed up, and ask them to send in the play dough within a week. You might ask for specific colors or let the parents surprise you! When the new play dough arrives, divide the old dough and send it home with students. You'll get lots of fresh play dough, and parents will get a fun recipe they can use again at home!

Barbara Cohen—Gr. K
Horace Mann Elementary, Cherry Hill, NJ

No-Cook Dough

Ingredients:
4 cups flour
1 cup salt
1 ¾ cups warm water tinted with food coloring

Preparation:
Combine the flour and salt in a bowl; then add the warm water. Knead the dough for ten minutes. Keep the dough refrigerated in an airtight container.

Columbus Day Craft

Can you make a ship from a square of paper and a craft stick? Sure! Try this easy craft to take note of Columbus Day. Show your youngsters a five-inch square of white paper with two lines drawn as shown. Cut along the two lines. Position the middle section of the paper atop a piece of blue construction paper to form the body of the ship. Then position the two triangles to make the sails. Add a craft stick mast in the center. After your demonstration, give youngsters their own supplies and have them create their own ships. Invite them to use crayons to add details to their pictures.

Cheryl Chase—Gr. K, Calvary Christian School, Derry, NH

Shower Curtain Rings to the Rescue!

If you use metal key rings to bind student books or keep sets of word cards together, you know they can get expensive. So buy shower curtain rings instead! Slim metal shower curtain rings work perfectly for book binding, charts, or word cards, and they're much less expensive than key rings.

Rita Lail—Gr. K, Sherrills Ford Elementary, Sherrills Ford, NC

Halloween Houses

Keep an eye out for stores displaying cardboard houses near Halloween. Ask if they have duplicate displays or if you can have the display when the selling season is over. Then use the house in your classroom as a fun seasonal center or an interesting reading nook.

Susan Svoboda—Gr. K, Heideman Elementary, Tustin, CA
Linda Ploch—Gr. K, Lutheran Church of the Cross Day School, St. Petersburg, FL

Teacher-Made Stencils

If your budget is tight, make your own durable stencils from reproducibles and transparencies. Simply photocopy a desired pattern onto transparency plastic. Then use a craft knife to cut out the pattern. Easy!

Pat Hardin—Gr. K, First United Methodist School, Kissimmee, FL

Color-Mixing Movement

Here's a fun and active way to teach youngsters about secondary colors! Cut a class supply of cellophane strips in the three primary colors. Give each child a strip; then invite youngsters to move freely to music. Stop the music and ask each child to find a partner with a cellophane strip in a different color. Ask each pair to tell you what color it makes together. Have the pair overlap the cellophane strips to see the color mixing up close. Then restart the music and repeat the activity with students finding different partners each time.

Karen Gelormino, Wildwood School, Aspen, CO

Scissor Starter

When you need to cut out the center of a sheet of paper, use a hole puncher to make a starter hole. Then stick the point of your scissors into the tiny hole to get the cutting started. Easy—and safer than poking your scissor blade into the paper!

Amy Hancock—Gr. K, Citizens Christian Academy, Douglas, GA

Information Motivation

Motivate your kindergartners to learn their addresses and phone numbers with a personal touch from you! First, write each child a note and place it in an envelope addressed to her. Display all the envelopes on a bulletin board with a replica of a U.S. mail collection box. When a child learns her address, have her put your letter in the mailbox replica. Then drop her letter in the real mail that afternoon. As each youngster learns her phone number, give her a call at home. Students are sure to spread the excitement when they tell of receiving their letters and calls from you!

Betsy Thompson—Gr. K, River Oaks Baptist School, Houston, TX

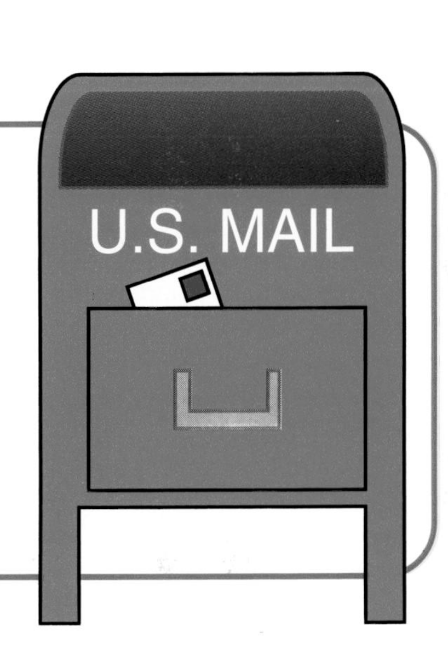

Kindergarten Date Night

Plan a special night for kindergartners and their parents—no siblings allowed. (Ask the PTA to supply baby-sitting services for parents who can't find sitters.) Have each family bring a blanket or quilt and join you for some time together to do fingerplays, sing songs, and enjoy a couple of read-aloud favorites. Then serve refreshments and invite children and parents to mingle for a while. Be prepared: Kindergarten families will probably want to repeat this fun evening again in the spring!

Peggy Campbell Rush—Gr. K, Union Township School, Hampton, NJ

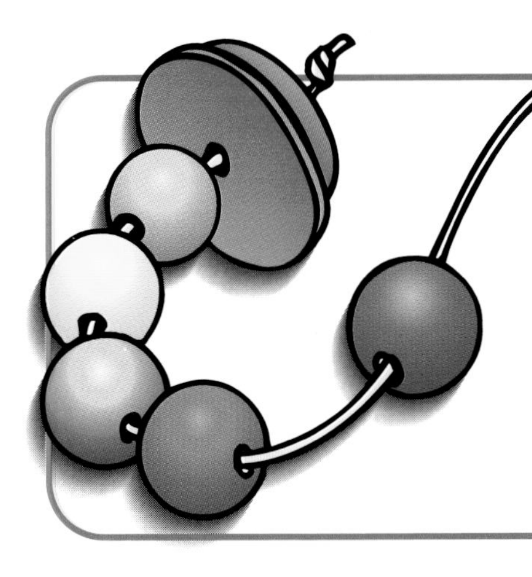

Stringing Solution

To ensure that beads won't slip off the end of a string, especially after careful patterning by a conscientious kindergartner, put a milk jug lid at the end of the string. Just poke a hole in the center of a pop-off milk jug lid or other drink lid. Slip the lid onto the string first; then tie a knot below the lid to hold it in place. When a child adds beads to the string, you can rest assured you won't have bouncing beads or the need to tie bigger and bigger knots!

Gwen Souter—Gr. K, Roscoe Wilson Elementary, Lubbock, TX

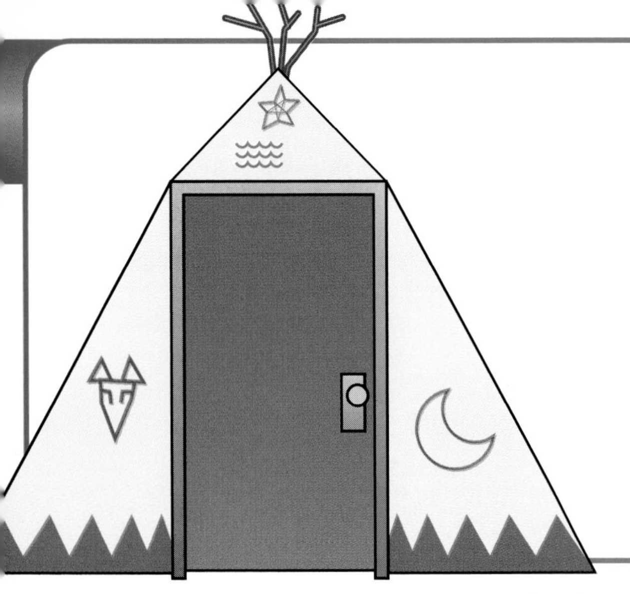

Tepee Entryway

If your kindergartners are learning about the Native Americans of the Plains, help them create this entrance to your classroom that resembles a tepee! Cut three pieces of thin muslin, two shaped liked triangles (for either side of the door) and one triangle-shaped piece to go over the door. Ask each child to choose a Native American name and picture symbol to paint onto one of the muslin pieces. When the paint is dry, use heavy tape to attach the pieces around your door. Add a final touch by taping three or four thin sticks at the tepee's top.

adapted from an idea by Renea Dickson—Gr. K, Winder, GA

Don't Toss the Tissue Box!

Cold and flu season is starting, and your little ones are bound to go through a truckload of tissues. Don't throw the empty tissue boxes away. Save them for Valentine's Day! Empty tissue boxes will make fine holders for valentines; students can simply drop their cards in the openings. If the boxes have pretty designs, just add student names. Otherwise, cover the boxes in white paper and invite youngsters to decorate them.

Angela Nolan—Gr. K, St. Mary's School, New Albany, IN

Wagons Ho!

Transform a rectangular classroom table into a covered wagon to make an imaginative play area! Set the table upside down on the floor. Use heavy-duty tape to attach large pieces of cardboard (as shown), bending the cardboard into a rounded shape as you go. Help little ones paint the cardboard to resemble the top of a covered wagon. Then attach four giant cardboard circles to the sides and paint them to look like wagon wheels. Ready? Go west, young kindergartners!

Trish Draper—Gr. K, Millarville Community School
Millarville, Alberta, Canada

Are You Game?

Hold a Board Game Week and invite your kindergartners to play simple board games during center time! Ask parents to let you borrow age-appropriate games for two, three, or four players. Have them label the games and pieces with their children's names before sending them in. During center time, divide your class into a number of groups to equal the number of available games. Your youngsters will have fun and get valuable practice with following directions, counting, and cooperative play. So let the games begin!

Marge Hardy—Gr. K, St. Wendelin School, Butler, PA

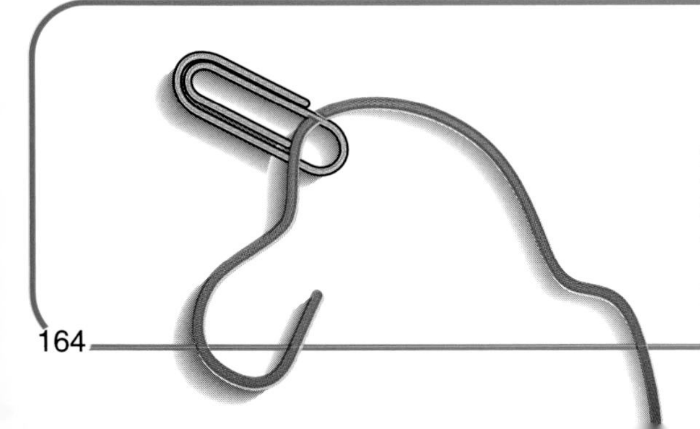

Easy Lacing

Tired of taping the ends of yarn for lacing or dipping them into glue to harden overnight? Try this tip! Slip one end of a yarn length into a small paper clip. The paper clip "needle" will make lacing a "hole" lot easier!

Melissa Wehner—Gr. K, Ritenour Early Childhood Center, St. Louis, MO

Holiday Senses

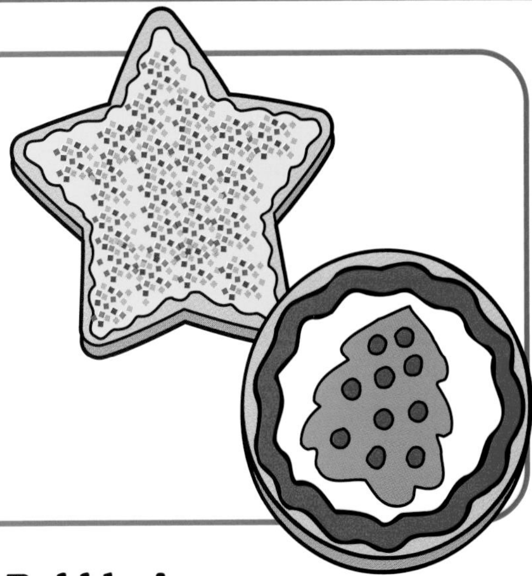

Use the three-week stretch between Thanksgiving and Christmas to teach your students about the five senses. Begin by asking youngsters to list things they see, hear, smell, touch, and taste at holiday time. Then plan activities that highlight the senses and tie into the holiday, such as:

- a Bell Show-and-Tell where every child brings in a different bell to ring
- baking and eating Christmas cookies
- graphing everyone's favorite color of gumdrop
- popping popcorn and stringing it for a Christmas tree

What a simply "sense-ational" way to get ready for the holidays!

Lynn Dobbs—Gr. K, Jasper Elementary, Jasper, TN

Brrr...Bubbles!

Is it rain? Is it snow? No—it's bubbles! Create some whimsical weather with an indoor bubble storm! Equip each child with a small individual bottle of bubbles, sold at your local craft store in the wedding section. Invite little ones to put on their mittens and hats before blowing up a batch of "snow bubbles" inside the classroom. Cool!

Elizabeth Robinson—Gr. K
Hidden Valley Elementary
Houston, TX

Year Parade

Help kindergartners learn the names and order of the months of the year with a Year Parade! Send home a note assigning each child a month of the year and requesting that parents help their children create a costume that reflects that month. For example, a child dressing to represent April might wear pastel clothing with rain boots and carry an umbrella. Practice lining up in the order of the months, with some students carrying signs labeled with the months' names. Invite parents to view the parade on the big day as your students proudly march as the months!

Sandie Ayers—Gr. K
Chesterbrook Academy
Sterling, VA

Whisper, Whisper...Shout!

Here's a fun way to reinforce months of the year and days of the week. Each day at calendar time, have your class whisper the days of the week in order. But when you reach the current day, have them shout it out! Do the same when reciting the months of the year, shouting out only the current month. Kindergartners love having permission to shout indoors, and the repetition of this activity will reinforce these important calendar concepts.

Wendy Rivilis—K4 and K5, ABC Kids Care, Inc., Grafton, WI

A Present and a Poem

Here's an inexpensive but meaningful gift you can give to your kindergartners! Purchase a class supply of shiny, reflective, spherical Christmas ornaments. To each one, attach a copy of the poem shown, along with your name and the school year. Pass out the gifts and read the poem together. Little ones will be so excited to look into their ornaments and see the special person you've written about!

Jill Nelson—Gr. K, Parkland School
Greece, NY

Placemat Project

Teach your students the joy of giving by having them make placemats for a local hospital or nursing home! To prepare, contact local hospitals or nursing homes to ask whether they'd like the placemats and to determine the size of their food trays. Cut paper to an appropriate size; then decide how you'll decorate the mats. You might use sponge-painting, potato prints, or simple crayon drawings. These merry mats are sure to bring smiles to lots of faces!

Cindy Barber, St. Cecilia's School, Thiensville, WI

From Lids to Literature

Transform box lids into book covers in a snap! Scout holiday sales for gift boxes with decorative lids, especially boxes with larger interesting art, such as a train or a Christmas tree. Then cut out the flat top of a box, laminate it, and use it as a cover for a class book!

Jackie Wright—Preschool and K
Summerhill Children's House
Enid, OK

Light the Tree

This center-time activity will add a bit of holiday cheer while improving youngsters' fine-motor skills. Draw a simple outline of a Christmas tree on a sheet of green construction paper. Cut the paper to fit over the screen of a Lite-Brite toy. Invite youngsters to decorate the tree with the colorful Lite-Brite pegs. Then hold a ceremony to light the tree by plugging in the Lite-Brite. What fun!

Marilyn Lockwood—Gr. K, Walker Elementary, Florissant, MO

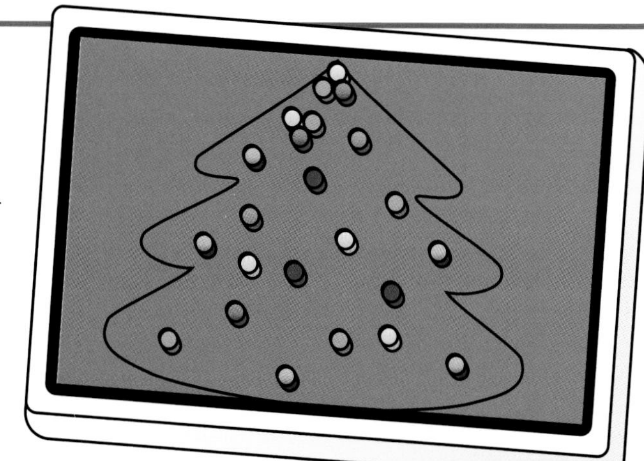

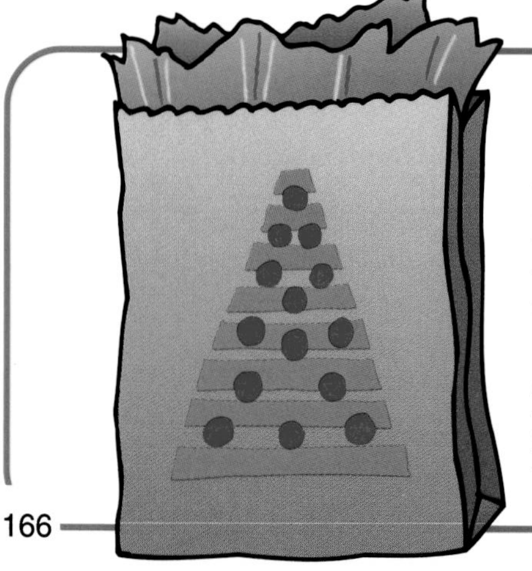

"Tree-rific" Gift Bag

Make these easy gift bags to hold holiday gifts for Mom and Dad or classroom helpers. To make one, use red and green tempera paint and a paper lunch bag. On one side of the bag, paint graduated green lines to resemble an evergreen tree as shown. Then use the red paint to add red dots for ornaments. Allow the paint to dry, and this project is all wrapped up!

Sandra O'Connell—Gr. K
M. M. Pierce School
Remington, VA

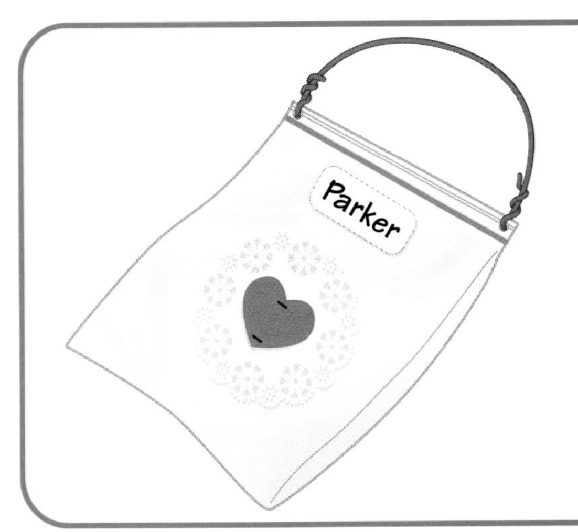

Valentine Bags in a Zip!

If you find that paper bags aren't so perfect for holding valentines, try this idea instead! Decorate a gallon-size zippered plastic bag for each child's valentine goodies. Simply staple a pretty paper doily and a red heart shape to the side of each bag. Then add a large label and print the child's name on it. If desired, add a handle by punching two opposing holes *above* the zipper. Thread a red or pink pipe cleaner through the two holes and twist the ends to hold them in place.

Alayna DiSanto—Gr. K
Lyons, NY

Deck the Halls With Hearts

Decorate for Valentine's Day with these pretty mobiles! Have each child trace and cut out four paper hearts in four sizes (6, 5, 4, and 3 inches), using seasonal colors of construction paper. Punch a hole at the top and the bottom of each heart. Have the child lay the four hearts on a tabletop with the largest heart at the top and the smallest heart at the bottom. Instruct her to thread a three-foot length of curling ribbon through all the hearts, leaving extra ribbon at the top to create a loop for hanging and extra at the bottom to be curled. Then have her use a glue stick to secure the ribbon to the hearts. When the glue is dry, hang up the hearts!

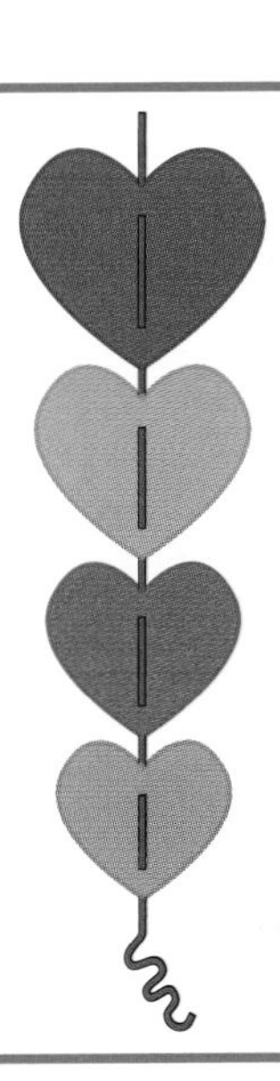

Carol Grant Barrett—Gr. K
John Adam School
Delson, Quebec, Canada

Circle-Time Shimmy

Is your group-time circle sometimes a bit too small for everyone to fit? Tell students to make room for everyone with this musical reminder! Demonstrate how to "shimmy" by scooting your bottom backward when you are seated on the floor. Then, when your circle is too small, begin singing part of that old favorite "Shimmy, Shimmy Cocoa-Pop" and have seated children shimmy backward until the circle enlarges and there's room for all! Shimmy, shimmy cocoa-pop. Shimmy, shimmy pow!

Cindy Marshaus—Gr. K, St. Gregory the Great School, S. Euclid, OH

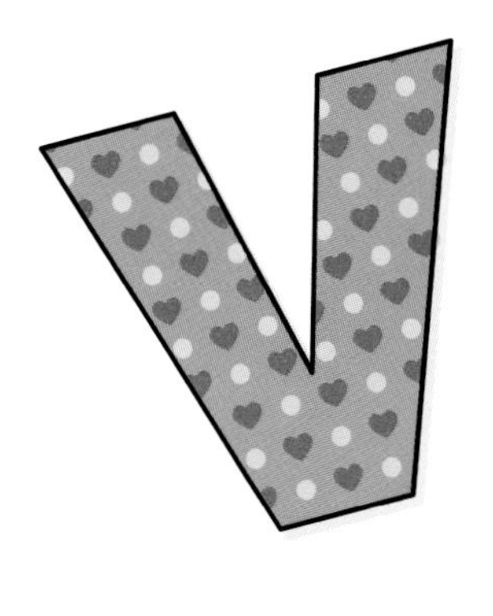

Wrapping-Paper Letters

Jazz up your bulletin boards with some inexpensive lettering! Visit your local discount store and purchase flat wrapping paper with a design that fits the current season or a favorite theme. Laminate the sheets; then die-cut letters—and borders, too!—from the laminated paper.

Trisha Collis—Gr. K
Tuscarora Elementary
Martinsburg, WV

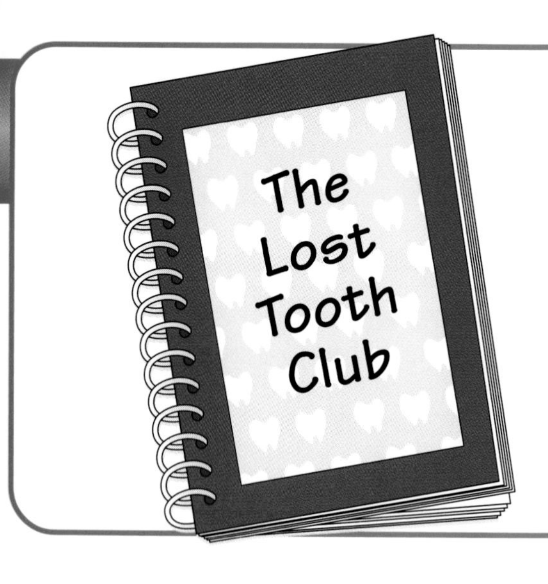

Class Book Covers

Cute covers for your class books are easy to find—just make a trip to your local craft store and check out the myriad of scrapbooking paper! You're sure to find paper to match almost any season or theme. Just mount a sheet of the decorative paper to a larger piece of construction paper; then laminate the cover for durability. Check out the scrapbooking aisle for interesting die-cuts, too. You can use these as tracers or collage materials for projects!

Gayle Begley—Gr. K
West Oaks Private School
Houston, TX

Duplicated Doilies

Stretch your art supplies dollar with this handy tip! Lay a sheet of dark paper behind a doily; then make photocopies of the doily—as many as you need for any project! If necessary, outline the edges of the photocopies with a dark marker to make cutting easier for your kindergartners. And, if you need a different size, simply reduce or enlarge the doily using the photocopier!

Kathy Blumberg—Gr. K, St. Kevin School, E. Alton, IL

Desktags That Stay—or Go!

If you're tired of scraping tape or self-adhesive desktags from your classroom tables, try Velcro instead! Stick the hook side of a length of self-adhesive Velcro fastening tape on the table at each child's seat. Then attach the loop side to the back of each child's laminated nametag. Press the two together and—voila!—a desktag that stays in place but is easy to move, too!

Tammy Vincent—Gr. K
Northern Valley Schools
Almena, KS

Pencils That Stay Put

Cut down on lost pencils with this sticky solution! Attach the hook side of a two-inch length of Velcro fastening tape at each child's workspace. Then attach the loop side of the tape to her pencil. Now that pencil will stay put when it's not in use!

Camille Smith—Grs. K–2 Special Education, Wetmore Elementary, San Antonio, TX

It's the Original!

How many times have you accidentally passed out your original from a stack of copies? To prevent this mistake, use a yellow highlighter to mark a large *X* in the center of your original. The copier won't pick up the *X*, but your eyes will when it comes time to pass out papers!

Rhianna Jenkerson—Gr. K
Desloge Accelerated Elementary
Desloge, MO

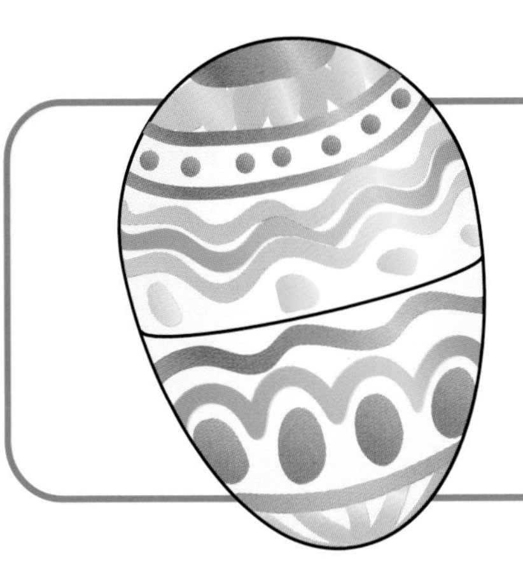

Everlasting Easter Eggs

Want to help youngsters decorate Easter eggs without the worries of boiling or breaking the eggs? Purchase white plastic eggs at your local craft or discount store; then have children use colorful fine-tip permanent markers to decorate them. These pretty eggs will last for years!

Sue Lewis Lein, St. Pius X Grade School, Wauwatosa, WI

Bunny Booklet

Your youngsters will be celebrating the season with these adorable accordion-folded booklets! To make one, cut six egg shapes from white tagboard; then use clear tape to attach them in one long strip. Have each child accordion-fold the strip, glue on two long ears, and then decorate the cover to resemble a bunny face complete with a pom-pom nose. Help her add her name and "Bunnies" to the cover. Have her unfold the booklet and program the pages as shown. Instruct her to make yellow paint fingerprints, as shown, on each page and then use a fine-tip marker to transform each one into a bunny. On the last page, simply add ears to each bunny and glue on a white dot made with a hole puncher for each tail. Finally, glue a cotton ball to the back of the booklet for a cute bunny tail!

Lucia Kemp Henry
Fallon, NV

Big-Book Storage

Here's an inexpensive way to store those cute but cumbersome big books! Purchase one or more plastic hampers at a local discount store. You can find them in an array of colors and big books fit perfectly inside!

Donna Luther, L. F. Smith Elementary, South Houston, TX

Connect Your Cubes

Save time with this simple tip! Store your connecting counting cubes in sticks of five or ten. It will be quick and easy to distribute a number of cubes to each student when you don't have to count each cube individually.

Jill Berisford—Gr. K, Sherrard Elementary, Wheeling, WV

Tins of Treats

These miniature Easter baskets will have your little ones hopping for joy! Ask parents to collect the tins from General Foods International Coffees (or similar tea tins). To make each basket, cut a strip of brown tagboard and tape the ends of it inside a tin to create a handle. Cover the outside of the tin with wood-grain or basket weave design Con-Tact paper. Then fill the tin with Easter grass and small candies. It'll hold just the right amount of Easter goodies for a kindergartner's tummy!

Lois Gordon—Gr. K, Hillandale Elementary, E. Flat Rock, NC

Classy Cups

Looking for easy, inexpensive storage for children's supplies? Ask a local restaurant to provide a class supply of plastic drink cups with lids! Put a child's crayons and glue stick inside a cup; then put the lid on. Slip a pencil through the straw hole and everything's neatly stored and ready to use!

Staci K. Royer—Gr. K, North Harlem Elementary, Harlem, GA

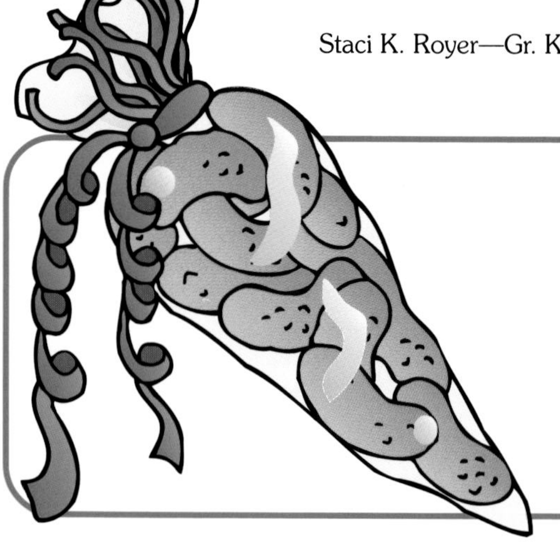

Carrots to Crunch

These springtime treats aren't filled with sweets, but *crunchy* goodies instead! To make one, fill a clear, plastic cake-decorating bag with crunchy cheese snacks, such as Chee-tos. Tie the bag closed with green curling ribbon. If desired, glue on wiggle eyes, a pom-pom nose, and some green Easter grass hair to give the carrot some character!

Robbin Kemp—Gr. K, Happy World, East Windsor, NJ

Secret Show-and-Tell

What's the secret to a successful show-and-tell? Improved listening, speaking, and thinking skills, of course! To conduct a "secret" show-and-tell, invite each child to bring in an item to share, but to keep it hidden. Then he must give three clues to help his classmates guess what he's brought without giving it away. If someone guesses correctly, that child receives a designated treat, such as a sticker or small candy. But if the child stumps the class, he may have his choice of treats.

Betty Schwartz—Gr. K, Wallace Elementary School, Hoboken, NJ

Bookmarks-s-s-s

These textured bookmarks are sure to delight your kindergartners! For each child, draw a simple snake shape on a half sheet of white paper. Have the child color the snake as she wishes. Then have her add dots of white school glue all over the snake. Allow the glue to dry; then have her cut out the snake. Invite the child to rub her fingers over the snake and feel the texture. Then have her slither her snake right between the pages of a favorite book to keep her place.

Betsy Young—Gr. K, Newman Elementary, Salt Lake City, UT

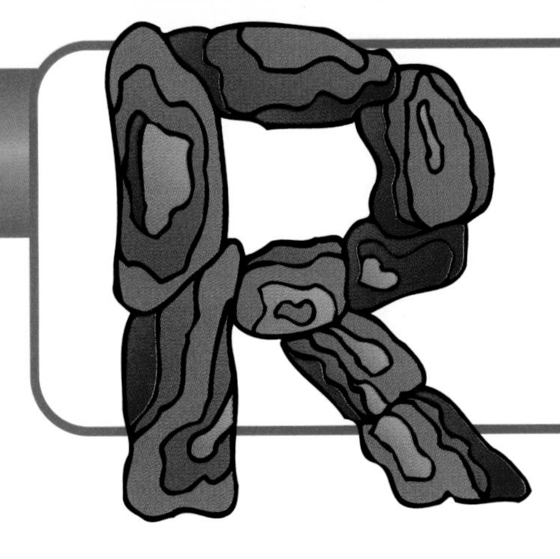

Pine Bark Letters

Give an Earth Day bulletin board a natural look with pine bark letters! Simply cut letters for your board's title from tagboard; then use hot glue to attach pieces of pine bark (purchased at your local garden center) to each letter. Hey...this wood looks good!

Angela M. Robertson, Ellisville Elementary Lower, Ellisville, MS

Tempera Glue

This paint-and-glue mixture can't be beat 'cause it stays so neat! Fill a half-full bottle of white school glue with liquid tempera paint; shake to combine. Then simply squeeze the mixture onto paper to make a painting with color *and* texture!

Judy W. Hodges—Gr. K, Rockfish Elementary School, Hope Mills, NC

Feeding Butterflies

If you're planning on hatching butterflies in your classroom this spring, try this tip. Ask a local florist to donate a few of the plastic vials used to keep single flowers fresh. When it's nearly time for the butterflies to emerge, fill each vial with water and add a fresh flower. Stick the vials into a margarine tub full of clay; then set the tub inside the butterfly box. The butterflies will have fresh flowers that will last for several days.

Shirley Schnettler—Gr. K, Ridgecrest Elementary, Largo, FL

Fun Bunnies

Ask families to collect the plastic lids from Nesquik chocolate milk bottles. Use these in the spring as game pieces for bingo or lotto. Also put some in your art center for youngsters to press into play dough or clay. The raised bunny design on the lids will make a great impression!

Annette Silvers—Special Education, Benedictine College, Atchison, KS

Mom's My Cup of Tea

Hold a Mother's Day Tea to honor the special moms of your kindergartners! Encourage youngsters to dress up for the occasion and teach them ahead of time how to serve the tea and baked goods. Then put together a PowerPoint presentation to really wow the moms! Have each child bring in a photo of him and his mom; then have him write a completion to the sentence "Mom, you are my cup of tea because…" Scan in the photos and use the children's responses as part of the presentation. Moms are sure to remember this special occasion!

Mary Jo Finnerty—Gr. K, St. Mary Magdalen School, Altamonte Springs, FL

Top Ten

Ask your current kindergartners to help you make a video entitled "The Top Ten Best Things About Kindergarten" to help you prepare next year's students! Have students decide on and rank the ten favorite things they've learned or done in kindergarten. Make a small poster for each number from 1 to 10. Videotape a child holding up the number 10 poster; then videotape 20 to 30 seconds of footage showing your class's choice for their number 10 activity. Continue counting down until you've included all ten things, which might include playground time, special classes, or centers. Show the video during a Sneak Peek or Meet-Your-Teacher Day in the fall.

Jeanne Pinkman—Gr. K, Cathedral of the Risen Christ School, Lincoln, NE

An Organizer for Dad

Here's a card for Father's Day that doubles as a handy organizer for car trips! To begin, copy the poem shown at left for each child. Allow the child to sign and illustrate the poem. Then glue each poem to the front of a two-pocket folder. Inside, attach labels for maps and phone numbers, glue on a snack-size zippered plastic bag labeled "change for tolls," and include an envelope labeled "receipts." Also add some half sheets of paper labeled "Directions to _______." Dad's sure to think of his little one every time he takes a trip!

Tina Bellotti—Gr. K, G. A. Jackson Elementary, Jericho, NY

The Be Quiet Bee

Call on some cute and cuddly critters to help groups of youngsters remember to keep quiet while you are assessing individual students. A stuffed bee, known as the Be Quiet Bee, can land on a quiet table, but it might flit away if the noise level gets too high! You might also try a Whisper Whale, a Bashful Bear, or a Gentle Giraffe. You'll be surprised how hard youngsters work to keep these quiet pals around!

Michele Galvan—Gr. K, Roosevelt Elementary, McAllen, TX

A Positive Pizza

Encourage positive behavior with some mouthwatering motivation! On a wall or bulletin board, display an untopped pizza: Simply cut a crust and sauce from bulletin board paper. Prepare a number of different topping cutouts and store them in a plastic bag near the pizza. When you see a child exhibiting positive behavior, add a topping to the pizza. When all the toppings are in place, reward the whole class with a pizza party! If desired, code the toppings for various behaviors you wish to encourage.

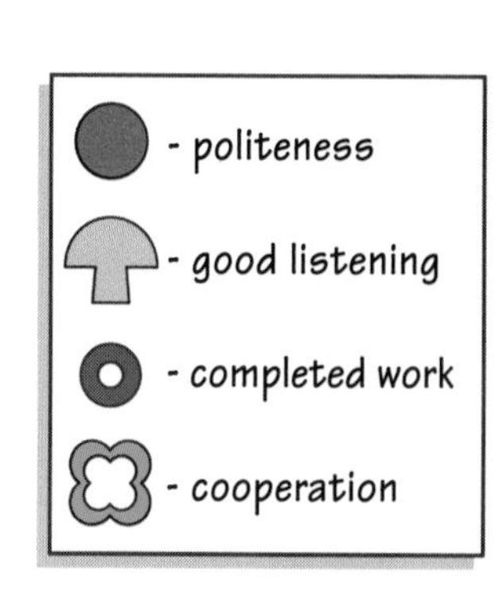

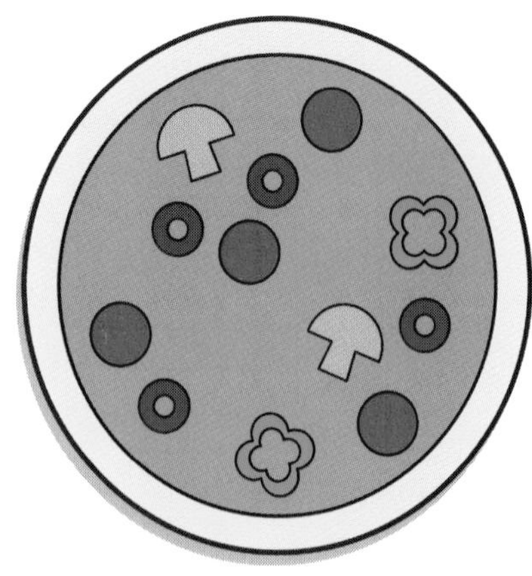

 Lynn C. Mode—Gr. K, Matthews, NC

Letters to Little Ones

Try these fun ideas for responding to students who write to you during the summer. Write back on a postcard decorated with cute stickers. Or write your response on a blank jigsaw puzzle (available at craft stores). Take the puzzle apart and mail it to the child to reassemble. Or write a letter on the back of a paint-with-water page from a paint book. Include a couple of cotton swabs in the envelope, and the student will have fun painting on your note!

Dear Lizzy,
Thanks for your letter!
I went to the beach too.
It was fun! I have lots of shells.
Love,
Mrs. S.

Chava Shapiro, Monsey, NY

Cookie Cutter Collection

Here's a useful gift for a student teacher, a parent volunteer, or a special coworker! Purchase a variety of cookie cutters to reflect the major holidays and seasons, such as an apple, a pumpkin, a turkey, a star, a heart, a shamrock, a bunny, or a flower. Before presenting the gift, tie the cutters together with pretty ribbon. The cookie cutters can be used for baking, tracing, painting, making play dough creations, and a host of other activities!

Sue Lewis Lein—Four-Year-Old Kindergarten, St. Pius X Grade School, Wauwatosa, WI

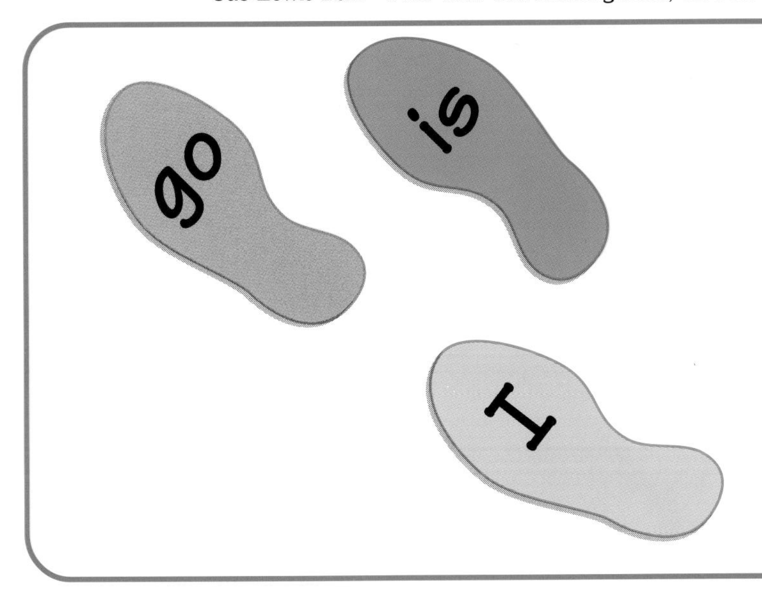

Word Walk

Students can step right up and practice sight words with this easy idea! Make a number of foot cutouts; then label each one with a sight word. Use clear Con-Tact covering to attach the feet to your classroom floor so that the footprints make a path leading to the door. Each day as students line up, have them step on each word and say it aloud. Occasionally change the order of the words on your Word Walk and add new words as students learn them.

Donna Hafner—Gr. K
Maryvale Primary School
Cheektowaga, NY

A Paperweight and a Poem

For Father's Day, have each child paint a small rock (provided by you or found on a nature walk). Have each child wrap up her decorative rock and bring it home along with a signed copy of the poem shown. (Change the word *Dad* if the gift will be presented to another significant adult.)

Joan Wittman—Gr. K
Sheldon Elementary
Varysburg, NY

Dear Dad,

This is for you; I made it myself.
You can keep it on a shelf
Or in your bedroom or with your treasure.
I hope that it will give you pleasure.

It can decorate your workspace
And keep your papers neat.
You can show it off to
All the friends you meet!

And every time you look at it,
I hope that you will know
That I'm so glad you're my dad,
And that I love you so!

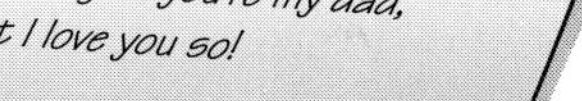

Daddy's Night at School

Sail into summer with a special night for daddies to visit your classroom! Give the evening a sailing theme with boat-shaped invitations and a challenging boat-making activity. Set out a supply of craft materials, such as construction paper, foil, play dough, craft sticks, pipe cleaners, and craft foam. Then have each child-and-father team build a boat together. Have them test their creations in a kiddie pool partially filled with water! After the launching of the crafty ships, serve refreshments and allow time for dads and kids to socialize.

Trish Draper—Grs. K–1, Millarville School, Millarville, Alberta, Canada

Nifty Negatives

Photos taken in the classroom are always fun, but what do you do with the negatives? Try this tip! Slide a strip of negatives into a filmstrip projector; then project the image of a photo onto a screen or blank wall. Youngsters will be fascinated! If desired, lay out the photos from the roll and have students match the photo to the negative you're projecting.

Wanda Spinner—Gr. K, Vanceboro Farm Life Elementary, Vanceboro, NC

Recycled Crayons

If you have lots of stubby crayons at this time of year, why not recycle them? Have students help with soaking the crayons in warm water and then peeling off any paper. Direct them to put each color separately into a tin can that's been bent to create a pouring spout. (Or make new shades by combining colors.) Then have students watch from a safe distance as you place the cans into a pan or electric skillet full of boiling water. Once the crayons have melted, pour the hot liquid into plastic candy molds and allow the wax to reharden. Ta-da! New crayons in cool shapes!

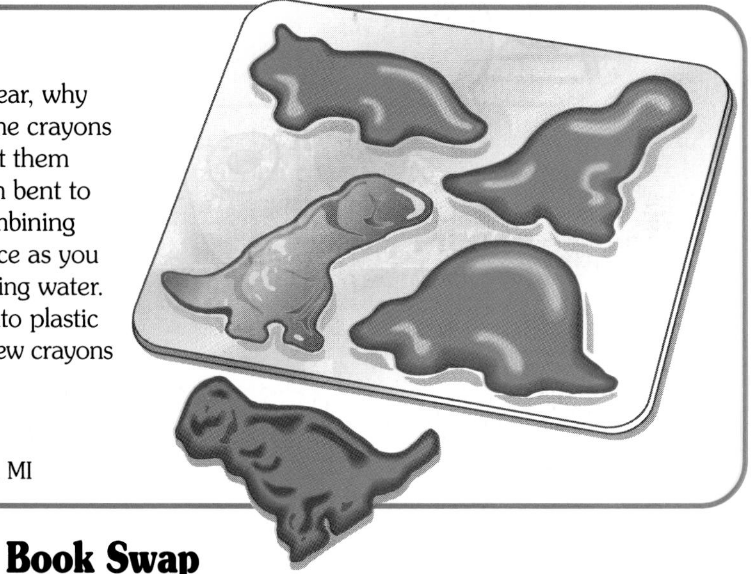

Shelly Fales—Gr. K
Whittemore-Prescott Early Childhood Center, Whittemore, MI

Book Swap

Encourage summer reading by holding a kindergarten book swap! Have each child bring in three "gently used" books to donate to the swap. (Be sure to bring in a few books in case someone forgets his donation.) Lay out all the donated books; then allow each child to pick out three new-to-him books to take home for summer reading!

Erica Cerwin—Gr. K, Thornton Elementary, San Antonio, TX

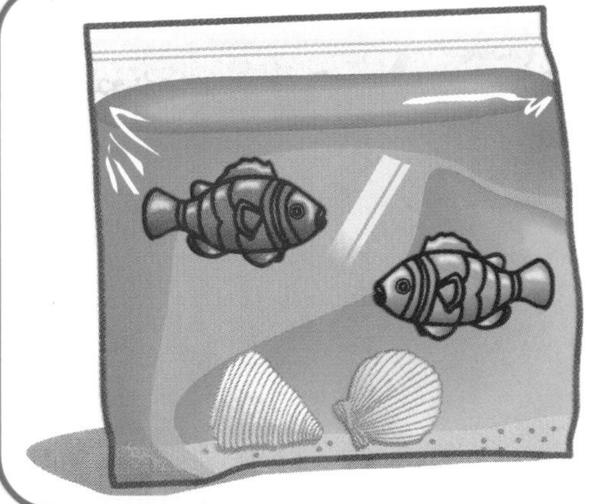

Hold the Ocean in Your Hand!

Studying the ocean? Then this project is perfect! Pour about a half inch of sand into the bottom of a plastic bag; then add a few shells. Next, mix up four batches of Knox clear gelatin according to the package instructions, using water as your liquid. (Do not use sweetened blue gelatin.) Add a few drops of blue food coloring. Gently pour the blue-tinted gelatin over the sand and shells. Slip a few plastic fish or other sea creatures into the gelatin; then put the container in the refrigerator. Once the gelatin is firm, remove the miniature ocean scene from the refrigerator, hold it in your hand, and look right through the "water"!

Sandie Ayers—Gr. K, Chesterbrook Academy, Sterling, VA

Rhythm & Rhyme Time

"Name-O"

Help students recognize and spell their names and those of their classmates with this adaptation of a traditional tune. To prepare, write each letter of a child's name on a separate card. Have students stand in front of the group holding the cards to spell the child's name. Sing the song, chanting the spelling of the child's name in the third line. Sing about one child's name each day until every child has had a turn to hear her name-o!

(sung to the tune of "Bingo")

There is a friend who's in our class,
And [Jill] is her name-o!
Chant: [J-I-L-L], [J-I-L-L], [J-I-L-L],
And [Jill] is her name-o!

Dawn Hitt—Gr. K
Burnet Elementary
Burnet, TX

Alphabet March

Step to it and teach your youngsters an alphabet song they can sing while marching around your room!

(sung to the tune of "The Ants Go Marching")

A, B, C, D, E, F, and G.
H, I!
J, K!
L, M, N, O, P, Q, and R.
S, T!
U, V!
W, X, and Y and Z—
Now I've sung my ABCs.
And I've marched around the room,
round the room,
Round the room, round the room.
Boom, boom, boom...

Christy Brammer—Gr. K
South Point Elementary
South Point, OH

It's Time for Show and Share

Get little ones prepared to listen by singing this song before sharing time. Each time the song is sung, substitute a different child's name in the last line.

(sung to the tune of "The Farmer in the Dell")

It's time for show and share!
It's time for show and share!
Sit right down and lend an ear.
It's time for show and share!

It's time for show and share!
It's time for show and share!
Sit right down and lend an ear.
It's [child's name]'s turn to share.

Toni Osterbuhr—Gr. K
Price School
Wichita, KS

Rhythm & Rhyme Time

Hey! Hey! It's Cleanup Time Today!

Just like the seven dwarfs, your little munchkins will be eager to get busy cleaning the classroom when they sing this song a few times through.

(sung to the tune of "Heigh-Ho")

Hey, Hey! Hey, Hey!
Put everything away,
In the right place where it should stay.
Hey, Hey! Hey, Hey! Hey! Hey! Hey! Hey!

Goldy Hirsch—Special Education K–2
Beacon School
Brooklyn, NY

Pick a Pumpkin

It's pumpkin-pickin' time! Get your youngsters in the mood by singing this little ditty!

(sung to the tune of "London Bridge")

Pick a pumpkin from the vine,
Pumpkin round, pumpkin fine.
Pick a pumpkin from the vine.
Let's pick pumpkins!

Pick a pumpkin from the vine.
You pick yours; I'll pick mine.
Pick a pumpkin from the vine.
Let's pick pumpkins!

Betty Silkunas—Gr. K
Lower Gwynedd Elementary
Ambler, PA

The Pizza Song

This catchy song will have your kindergartners' mouths watering for a favorite food. After singing the song once, substitute the word *cheese* in the first line with any topping your students suggest. After teaching youngsters this song, invite each child to make a mini pizza all her own by having her top a slice of Italian bread with pizza sauce and a sprinkle of cheese. Yum!

(sung to the tune of "Bingo")

There is a treat I love to eat with lots and lots of [che-ese]—
P-I-Z-Z-A,
P-I-Z-Z-A,
P-I-Z-Z-A,
And pizza is its name—yay!

Judy Patterson—PreK and K
Our Hope Lutheran School
Huntertown, IN

Rhythm & Rhyme Time

A Penguin's Wish

This tune will help your little ones remember that penguins can't fly. Teach them the accompanying motions and have a waddling good time!

(sung to the tune of "I'm a Little Teapot")

I'm a little penguin, black and white.	*Point to yourself.*
I'm good at swimming, but not at flight.	*Make swimming motions; then shake head to say no.*
When I'm in the ocean, I dive for fish.	*Make diving motion with one hand.*
Swimming's fun, but flying's my wish!	*Hook thumbs and wiggle fingers like wings.*

Jean Zeller—Grs. K–4, WCSS St. William Campus, Waukesha, WI

Calendar Song

Help youngsters understand the concepts of *yesterday, today,* and *tomorrow* by singing this song each day during your calendar time. Use a pointer to point to each day as you sing. Substitute the appropriate days of the week in each line and any appropriate information in the last line. You might mention a child's upcoming birthday, a special event at school, or a reminder that something is due.

(sung to the tune of "Mary Had a Little Lamb")

Yesterday was [Tuesday],
[Tuesday], [Tuesday].
Yesterday was [Tuesday].
Today is [Wednesday].

Tomorrow will be [Thursday],
[Thursday], [Thursday].
Tomorrow will be
[Thursday],
And [we will go to art].

Sherry Galloway—Gr. K
WaKeeney Grade School
WaKeeney, KS

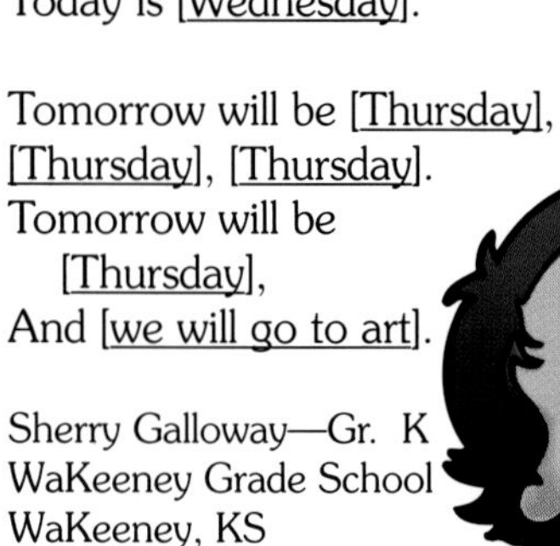

The Rudolph Prance

Welcome Santa's season with some singing and dancing—or, actually, prancing! Give each child a red sticky dot to wear on her nose as she imitates Rudolph in this song.

(sung to the tune of "The Hokey-Pokey")

You put your [hooves] in; you put your [hooves] out.
You put your [hooves] in and you shake 'em all around!
You do the Rudolph Prance and you shake it all around—
That's what the reindeer do...wooooo!

Repeat the verse, substituting antlers, red nose, *and* white tail *for the underlined word.*

Florence Paola—PreK and Kindergarten Special Needs
Jane Ryan Elementary
Trumbull, CT

Groundhog Day

Spring could be just around the corner, or your youngsters could be in store for six more weeks of winter. Either way, this little groundhog poem is appropriate! Have your little ones recite the poem below and pretend to duck in and out of a hole like a real groundhog!

Will it be winter six more weeks?
February 2nd, Groundhog peeks.
If he sees his shadow,
What will Groundhog say?
"Oh! Springtime's another six weeks away,
Yes, springtime's another six weeks away!"

Will it be winter six more weeks?
February 2nd, Groundhog peeks.
If he sees no shadow,
What will Groundhog say?
"Oh! Spring's coming early; let's go out and play!
Yes, spring's coming early; let's go out and play!"

Suzanne Moore
Irving, TX

Sit-Down Snap

Use this chant and a steady string of finger snaps to encourage your students to take a seat for circle time. Repeat the chant until all children are seated. Snap, snap, snap!

1, 2, 3, 4—push in your chairs; then sit on the floor.
Make it quiet, make it snappy,
And you will make your teacher happy!

Sherri Martin—Gr. 4K
Southland Academy
Montezuma, GA

Raw Dough!

Your play dough center will not be the same after your youngsters learn this catchy song!

(sung to the tune of "Rawhide")

Keep rollin', rollin', rollin',
Keep that clay a-rollin',
A squishin' and squashin'—raw dough!
I'm gonna cut some great shapes; you'll see elephants and apes,
Nothing compares to play dough!
So–o!

Roll it up! Roll it out!
Squish it up! Mash it out!
Now that's the song of our play dough!

Denise Erwin and Debbie Walker—Gr. K
Old Fort Elementary
Old Fort, NC

Rhythm & Rhyme Time

We Love America!

Prepare your youngsters for the Pledge of Allegiance with this wonderfully simple patriotic song!

(sung to the tune of "Skip to My Lou")

We love America; yes we do!
To our country we'll be true!
Freedom is for me and you!
Hip, hip, hooray for the red,
white, and blue!

Kellee Shuttleworth—Gr. K
Norwood Elementary School
Stonewood, WV

Alphabet Experts

Looking for a way to celebrate learning the alphabet? Invite your little ones to give themselves a pat on the back as they sing this catchy letter song.

(sung to the tune of "I've Been Working on the Railroad")

We've been working on our letters,
Learning the ABCs.
We've been working on our letters.
Just listen to us, please.

When you put letters together,
A word is what you'll get!
We will be terrific readers.
We know the alphabet!

Cindy Bowen—Grs. K–5
The Shepherd's Fold School
Hanover, PA

First Grade, Here We Come!

Help students look forward to first grade with this kindergarten review! Begin by asking children to discuss what they have learned in kindergarten; then record their ideas on a sheet of chart paper. Finally, display the chart and recite the poem below to celebrate a wonderful year of learning!

Look out first grade, here we come.
Kindergarten is all done!
We add, subtract, and read all the time.
Five cents is a nickel and ten is a dime.
We know many shapes and can tell time,
Plus opposites and words that rhyme.
Kindergarten is all done.
Look out first grade,
here we come!

Susan McGhie—Gr. K
St. Ann School
West Palm Beach, FL

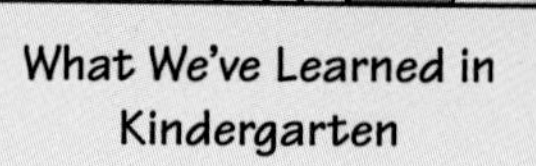

Simple Science for Kindergartners

Back to the Basics

Use these ideas to build your youngsters' knowledge of the basic needs of all living things.

by Suzanne Moore

Basic Needs: Food and Water

Help your youngsters understand the importance of food and water for survival with this little ditty. After a discussion of living and nonliving things, point out that all living things, including people, need some of the same things. Explain that two very important basic needs are food and water. Then teach youngsters the song below to reinforce this concept.

(sung to the tune of "The Bear Went Over the Mountain")

Living things need food and water,
Living things need food and water,
Living things need food and water
To keep them well and strong.

To keep them well and strong,
To keep them well and strong,
Living things need food and water
To keep them well and strong!

DID YOU KNOW?
A person drinks about 16,000 gallons of water in his lifetime!

Basic Need: Shelter

Use this demonstration to show how important shelter is for people. To prepare, locate an empty glass aquarium and put it aside.

Set up a family of plastic people and furniture on a table. Talk about some of the elements that a shelter might protect them from, such as wind and rain. Use a watering can to sprinkle "rain" over the family and then use a fan turned on high to create enough "wind" to blow them across the table. Discuss with students the effects of the rain and wind. Next, dry the people and furniture, and reset the scene. Place the aquarium over the family and repeat the demonstration. Discuss the differences the shelter makes for the family and their space.

My Basic Needs

Now that your little ones are familiar with life's basic needs, have each child make a personalized booklet. In advance, make a class set of page 183. Instruct each youngster to cut the booklet pages apart. Help him sequence his pages and then staple them where indicated. Have him write his name on the cover and then glue his picture in the space provided. Then guide him to illustrate each remaining page. Invite students to share their completed booklets.

glue
photo
here

_______________________'s

Basic Needs

I need food. 1

I need water. 2

I need shelter. 3

Spotlight on Light

Brighten your science curriculum with these glimmering ideas about light. Your young scientists will be all aglow!

by Suzanne Moore

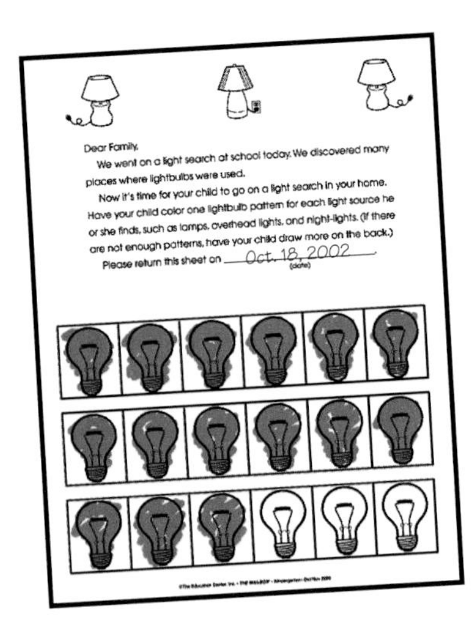

Dear Family,

We went on a light search at school today. We discovered many places where lightbulbs were used.

Now it's time for your child to go on a light search in your home. Have your child color one lightbulb pattern for each light source he or she finds, such as lamps, overhead lights, and night-lights. (If there are not enough patterns, have your child draw more on the back.)

Please return this sheet on Oct. 18, 2002 (date)

Light Search

Ignite students' curiosity about light by asking them to think about what gives us light in the classroom and what gives us light outside. Have students count the lights and windows in your classroom. Then talk about the difference between natural and artificial light. Next, take your youngsters on a walk through and around your school. Help students locate and identify the different types of light sources they see. After returning to the classroom, explain that light can come from sources such as the sun, fire, and electric or battery power. Photocopy page 185 to make a class set. Have each child take a copy home and do his own light-source search. Instruct him to color one lightbulb for each light source he finds in his home. Have students return the completed papers to school and discuss the results.

Lights Out!

Give students an opportunity to learn more about light with this bright activity. In advance, cover a table with a dark-colored blanket. Under the table, place a flashlight and a basket of materials, such as pieces of clear plastic wrap, poster board, waxed paper, tissue paper, fabric, cardboard, paper towels, aluminum foil, and cellophane. Explain to students that light can pass through some materials, but not through others. Demonstrate this fact by placing the flashlight against several different materials to see whether light will pass through them. Then invite pairs of students to sit under the table and test all of the materials to see which ones allow light to pass through them and which ones do not.

Timely Shadows

This individual experiment has youngsters measuring how the sun moves across the sky. To begin, have each child label an eight-ounce Styrofoam cup with her name. Take students outside along with their cups and several permanent markers. Instruct each child to place her cup upside down on the grass in a sunny spot. Then push a bamboo skewer through the bottom of each cup and into the ground. Have each student locate the skewer's shadow on the bottom of her cup and then trace over it with a marker. Continue to mark the shadow's movement at hourly intervals. Youngsters will be surprised to learn that the light from the sun has moved in the sky, creating new shadows on their cups.

Dear Family,

We went on a light search at school today. We discovered many places where lightbulbs were used.

Now it's time for your child to go on a light search in your home. Have your child color one lightbulb pattern for each light source he or she finds, such as lamps, overhead lights, and night-lights. (If there are not enough patterns, have your child draw more on the back.)

Please return this sheet on ______________________________.
(date)

Note to the teacher: Use with "Light Search" on page 184.

Warming Up, Cooling Down

Warm up science skills with these cool activities about temperature.

by Suzanne Moore, Irving, TX

What's Hot? What's Not?

Play this guessing game with your young scientists to get them thinking about what's hot…and what's not!

I'm thinking of something hot.
It's liquid.
Marshmallows melt in it.
What is it? *(cocoa)*

I'm thinking of something cold.
It can be different flavors.
You can eat it in a cup, a cone, or on a stick.
What is it? *(ice cream)*

Invite students to brainstorm two lists—things that are hot (such as a hot bath, fire, and the sun) and things that are cold (such as an ice cube, salad, and snow). Explain that *hot, cold,* and *warm* are words used to describe temperature.

DID YOU KNOW?

It is believed to be about 27 million degrees Fahrenheit at the center of the sun!

What's the Temperature?

This simple activity will give students practice reading thermometers, recording temperatures, and learning new vocabulary. Provide each small group with a shatterproof thermometer and a cup half-filled with room temperature water. Give each child in the group a red crayon, a pencil, and a copy of the recording sheet on page 187. In turn, invite each student to dip one finger in the water and describe how it feels. After each child has had a turn, explain that temperature is measured in degrees using a thermometer. Encourage each student to examine the thermometer; then demonstrate how to read the temperature. Place the thermometer in the water and wait a few minutes. Remove the thermometer and then help the group read the temperature. Have each student record the temperature on the "No Ice" section of his recording sheet by coloring the thermometer appropriately and writing the temperature in the blank. Place an ice cube or two in the cup and wait a few minutes. Repeat the activity and have each child record the new temperature on the "Ice" section of his paper. Way to read temperatures!

Temperature Influences

This graphing idea will have students thinking about how temperature influences their clothing choices. In advance, prepare a rebus graph featuring the following articles of clothing: pants, shirts or blouses, shorts, dresses or skirts, sandals, sweaters, shoes, coats or jackets. Discuss the clothing possibilities on the graph. Have each child think about what she wore to school. Then have her write her name on three sticky notes. Invite her to place the sticky notes in the appropriate rows on the graph. After each youngster has placed her notes, discuss the graph. What clothing was worn most? The least? Then have students describe the temperature outside. Lead students to conclude that weather influences the clothing people wear.

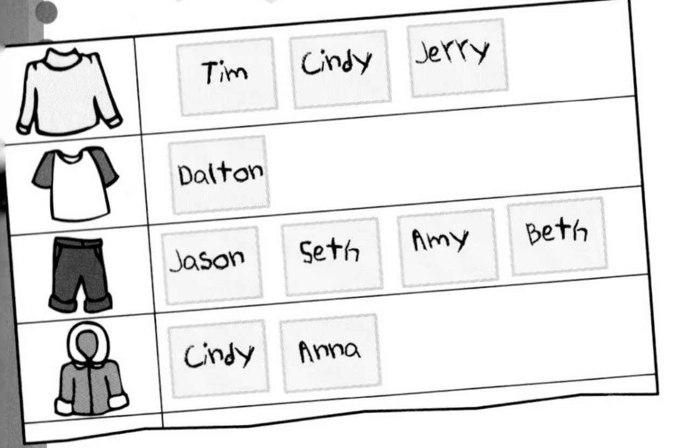

Name ________________________ Recording sheet

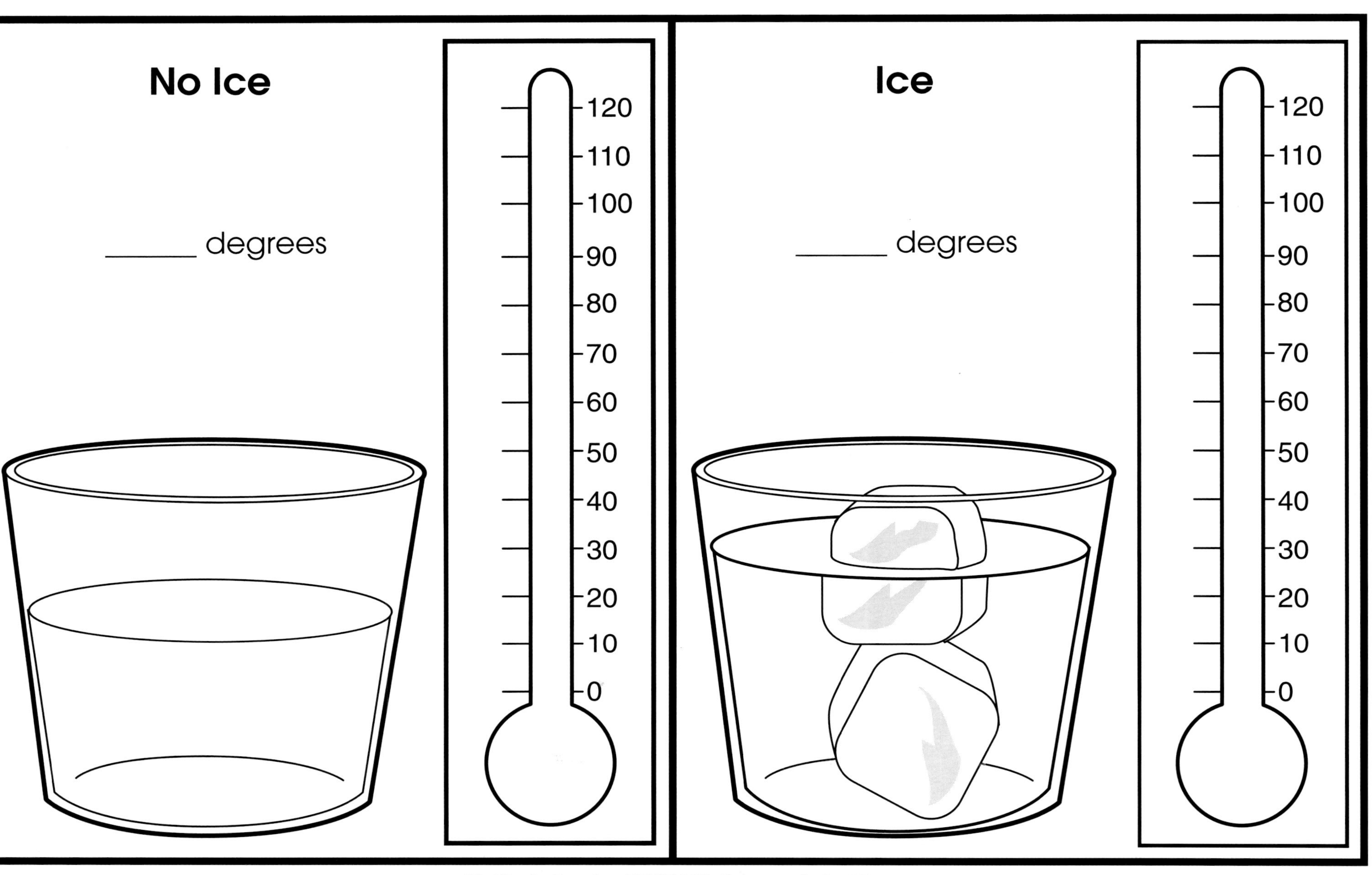

Note to the teacher: Use with "What's the Temperature?" on page 186.

Froggy Facts

Youngsters will be "hoppy" to learn these fascinating frog facts!

by Suzanne Moore, Irving, TX

Tadpole to Frog

Help your students learn about the life cycle of the frog with this cute sequencing booklet. In advance, make a class set of page 189 and gather a supply of small white sticky dots. Then have each child follow the directions to complete each page.

Directions:

Page 1: Place a sticky-dot frog egg in the water; then draw a dot in the center of it. Color the picture.

Page 2: Complete the tadpole by drawing its tail. Color the picture.

Page 3: Draw four legs on the froglet. Color the picture.

Page 4: Add sticky-dot eyes to the frog. Color the picture.

Help each child stack his pages and then staple them together. Encourage him to take his booklet home and share it with his family.

Leapin' Frogs

Frogs are known for their great leaping ability, but did you know that frogs can jump more than ten feet? Give your little tadpoles a sense of just how far a frog can jump by measuring and marking a ten-foot space in your classroom. Invite youngsters to try some frog-style jumping to see how many hops it takes for them to jump ten feet. They'll soon be amazed at just how far a frog can leap!

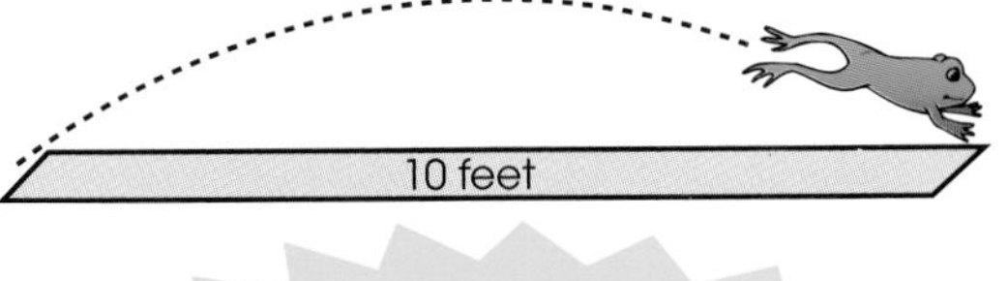

DID YOU KNOW?
When a young frog leaves the water, it's about the size of a child's thumbnail!

Froggy Started Out

Now that your students are more familiar with the life cycle of the frog, reinforce the concept with some flannelboard pieces and a song. Prepare each of the pictures on page 13 by following the directions above. Attach a piece of the hook side of Velcro to the back of each card. Then sing this little ditty with students, placing each card on the flannelboard in turn. Later, place the cards and flannelboard in your science center. Uh-huh, oh yeah, uh-huh!

(sung to the tune of "A Frog Went A-courtin'")

Froggy started out as a tiny egg. Uh-huh.
Froggy started out as a tiny egg. Uh-huh.
He started out as a tiny egg—
No hands or feet or even a leg.
Uh-huh, oh yeah, uh-huh.

Tadpole hatched from the tiny egg. Uh-huh.
Tadpole hatched from the tiny egg. Uh-huh.
Tadpole hatched, but he wasn't a whale.
He breathed with his gills and swam with his tail.
Uh-huh, oh yeah, uh-huh.

Tadpole's body grew four little legs. Uh-huh.
Tadpole's body grew four little legs. Uh-huh.
He had four legs and his little tail too;
He swam around the pond as tadpoles do.
Uh-huh, oh yeah, uh-huh.

Then one fine morning he left the pond. Uh-huh.
Then one fine morning he left the pond. Uh-huh.
He had no tail, but his little lungs grew.
He hopped on the land as froggies do.
Uh-huh, oh yeah, uh-huh.

Read aloud *Frogs* by Gail Gibbons.

A frog egg is so tiny. 1
A tadpole swims around. 2
A froglet has grown four legs. 3
A frog hops on the ground. 4
©The Education Center, Inc. • *THE MAILBOX®* • *Kindergarten* • April/May 2003

Magnet Magic

When your curious little ones experiment with these magnet ideas, they'll find science full of magical fun! In advance, make a class set of the booklet on page 191. Then guide students through the activities below to complete their booklets.

by Suzanne Moore, Irving, TX

Magnet Hunt

Want to spark instant science interest? Look no further than your collection of magnets. Give each child in a small group a small magnet and a copy of page 191. Have her cut out the pages along the dotted lines and then stack them in order. Add a 3" x $7\frac{1}{2}$" construction paper cover to each child's booklet and then staple each one along the left side. Have each youngster write "Magnets by" and then her name on the cover. Instruct her to draw her magnet on page 1 of her booklet. Then invite her to search for three items that are attracted to it and three items that are not attracted to it. Have her draw the items in the appropriate boxes. (Warn students not to test magnets on computer screens and discs, audiocassette tapes, and video tapes.) Later, gather students together to share their findings. Explain to students that magnets attract things that contain iron, steel, nickel, and certain other materials.

DID YOU KNOW?

All magnets have two poles. So, if a magnet is broken in two pieces, each piece has a north magnetic pole and a south magnetic pole.

Attraction Action

Rev up observation, counting, and communication skills with this attractive activity. Give children access to a variety of magnets and a supply of paper clips and invite small groups of students to discover which magnet will pick up the most paper clips. Have each child record her findings on page 2 of her booklet and then draw and label the magnet that picked up the most clips. After all students have visited this center, invite youngsters to talk about their observations and share their findings. Lead children to conclude that the stronger the magnet, the more paper clips it can lift.

The Great Grab

How far away can a paper clip be from the magnet and still be grabbed? Have students find out using page 3 of their booklets. Provide a large horseshoe magnet, a large disc magnet, a large bar magnet, and a small paper clip. To demonstrate this activity, place one of the magnets at the goal post. Put the paper clip on the line furthest from the goal. Does it jump to the magnet? Continue moving the paper clip closer on each successive lien. Encourage each child to test the magnets separately and discover which one grabs the paper clip from the greatest distance. Each student will record her results on booklet page 3 by drawing the strongest magnet on the left side and the paper clip on the appropriate line. This is an activity that your little learners will want to visit again and again!

Read aloud *Magnets* (Everyday Science) by Peter Riley.

These things stick to a magnet.

These things do not stick to a magnet.

Draw your magnet here.

1

How many paper clips did the magnet pick up?

Draw your magnet here.

2

Draw the paper clip.

Draw your magnet here.

3

Shake, Rattle, and Roll!

Explore the science of sound with rhythm instruments.
Sounds fun, doesn't it?

by Suzanne Moore, Irving, TX

What Do You Do?

Get your youngsters in tune with the science of sound by pulling out your rhythm instruments—both commercial and homemade. Invite each child to select the instrument of his choice. Allow time for students to explore their instruments. Encourage your little ones to play along as they sing the first three lines of the song below. When the fourth line is sung, name a rhythm instrument, such as triangle, rhythm sticks, cymbals, etc. After the last line is sung, invite students with that instrument to play. After each verse, discuss how that particular instrument's sound was made. Explain that it takes some kind of force (tapping, shaking, etc.) to make sound. Every sound—no matter how it is made—is produced by movements or vibrations.

(sung to the tune of "Ten Little Indians")

What do you do to make a sound?
Shake your instrument, roll it 'round?
What do you do to make a sound?
Play your [name of instrument] now!

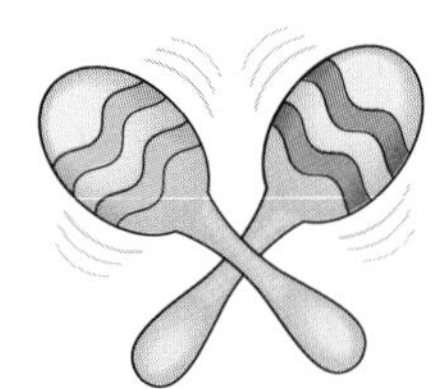

Groovy Guitars

Produce a classroom of grins galore by inviting each child to make a groovy guitar! Each child will need a clean half-gallon milk or juice carton, two unsharpened pencils, a thick rubber band, and a thin rubber band. To create a guitar, each student stretches the rubber bands around his milk carton, from top to bottom. Then have him slide the pencils under the rubber bands at each end of the carton. Invite youngsters to serenade you with their new instruments! As they pluck the "strings" of their guitars, point out how the strings differ in pitch (the high or low sound made by the vibration). Lead students to conclude that thicker rubber bands vibrate slowly, producing a lower pitch, and thinner ones vibrate quickly, producing a higher pitch.

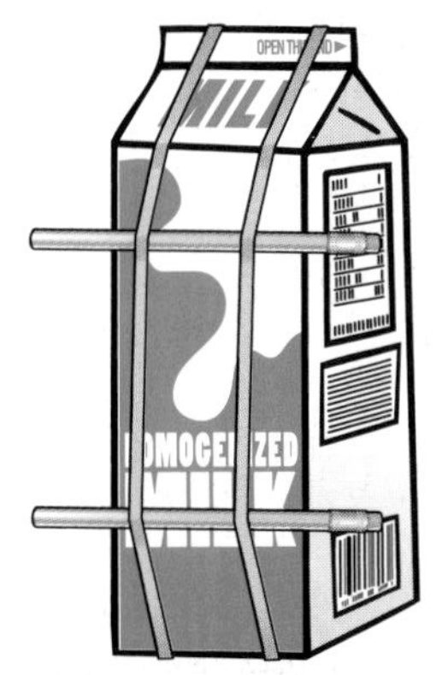

DID YOU KNOW?
Sounds travel faster through solids and liquids than through air.

Good Vibrations

How long do the vibrations last after striking a triangle or ringing a bell? How can they be stopped? Ring a handbell (or strike a triangle) and invite youngsters to softly count with you until the bell's sound can no longer be heard. Then ask youngsters to brainstorm how the bell's vibration can be stopped. After discussing student ideas, stock a center with an assortment of instruments, especially triangles, small drums, tone bars, and xylophones. Encourage students to explore each instrument to discover whether its sound lingers and, if so, how to stop it. Then explain that sound vibrations can be left free to vibrate or can be held and stopped.

Read aloud *The Science of Noise* (Science World), written by Lynne Wright.

Thematic Units and Special Features

A Warm Jungle Welcome

It's a jungle out there! Help ease beginning-of-school jitters with this welcoming unit full of creative ideas to acclimate your students to their new classroom and school.

by Angela Van Beveren

It's a Jungle in Here!

Create a jungle atmosphere in your classroom with these simple decorating ideas. First, spiral-cut large pieces of green bulletin board paper and hang them from the ceiling to resemble vines. Then make one or more palm trees for your reading area. For each tree, gather an umbrella, a large plastic pot, plaster of paris, a six-foot length of PVC pipe that is two inches in diameter, green bulletin board paper, and brown bulletin board paper. To make a tree, mix plaster of paris according to package directions and then pour it into the pot so that the pot is nearly full. After the plaster has set for a few minutes, insert the pipe in the center of the pot; then allow the plaster to completely harden. Next, wrap the pipe with brown paper and tape the paper in place to resemble the tree's trunk. Then open an umbrella and place the handle inside the pipe. Cut green paper leaves and tape them to the top of the umbrella. Your reading center has never looked so inviting!

School Safari

This indoor safari will introduce your kindergartners to their new surroundings and to the school staff with an added element of fun! In advance, leave a small stuffed jungle animal or picture card in the places you plan to visit with students. Explain to youngsters that they will be going on a safari through the school in hopes of seeing jungle animals along the way. Then don your safari hat, grab your instant camera, and guide youngsters through the school. Introduce students to the people and places that will be significant to them and have them look for "rare" jungle animals. At each stop on the safari, take a photo of the exotic animal along with the special person or place. After you return to the classroom, place the photos in an album and invite youngsters to revisit their safari tour.

Swinging Through the Day

The school day can seem long to little learners, but with this clever timeline, your youngsters will know exactly what's in store for them! Place a long strip of paper across the top of your chalkboard. Along the strip attach picture clues for each activity of the day, such as a circle for circle time, a lunchbox for lunch, a computer for computer class, and a soccer ball for P.E. Tape a length of green yarn to each picture clue as shown. Make a tan construction paper copy of one of the monkey patterns on page 198. Cut out the pattern and attach it to the beginning of the strip. As youngsters complete each part of the day, move the monkey to the next picture. Each day, change picture clues for activities that change from day to day and move the monkey back to the beginning of the strip. Your students will look forward to seeing what is next in their day!

Noble Nametags

Your little kings and queens of the jungle will be easy to spot with nametags that have royal appeal! To prepare, make a copy of the nametag on page 198 for each child. Also cut a 3" x 18" strip of construction paper for each child. On the first day of school, have each youngster color a nametag; then write his name on it. Instruct each student to glue his nametag to the center of a strip as shown. Staple each strip around the child's head so it fits like a crown. How regal!

Welcome to the Jungle

This catchy song will help your new arrivals get to know one another! Have youngsters hold hands and walk in a circle while singing the song. As the two names are sung in Line 2, have the youngsters meet in the middle of the circle and shake hands. Repeat the song until each child has been featured.

(sung to the tune of "The More We Get Together")

Welcome to the jungle, the jungle, the jungle.
Welcome to the jungle, [Miranda] and [Mike].
The animals play here, and we'll have a great day here!
So welcome to the jungle! We're glad you are here!

No Monkey Business

This attendance system will have your students practicing responsibility while reducing the amount of monkeying around during early morning exercises. To prepare, glue a class set of library pockets to a sheet of poster board. Label each pocket with a different child's name. Then make a class set of construction paper monkeys from the patterns on page 198. Laminate and cut out the monkeys. Post the pocket chart and monkeys within students' reach. Instruct each youngster to place a monkey in her pocket each morning. At a glance, you'll know who is present!

Jungle Jingle

Sing this song through a few times, and you'll learn lots about your students' favorites! Have little ones sit in a circle. Give one child a small stuffed jungle animal. Have students sing the song and pass the animal from one to another. When the song ends, have the child holding the animal answer the question from the song. Vary the question in the song by replacing the underlined word in the last line.

(sung to the tune of "Jingle Bells")

Jungle kids, jungle kids in [your name]'s class,
Let's have fun and ask someone,
"What's your favorite [snack]?"

Monkey See, Monkey Do

This whole-group game will allow your youngsters to show off their silliness and get them moving! Have the class stand in a circle. Designate one child to be the lead monkey and to stand in the center of the circle. Instruct the rest of the group to chant, "Monkey see, monkey do. Show us, [Emma], what you can do!" Have the featured child perform an action and instruct the rest of the class to repeat it. Then have the monkey in the middle choose someone to take her place and continue the game.

Pam Crane

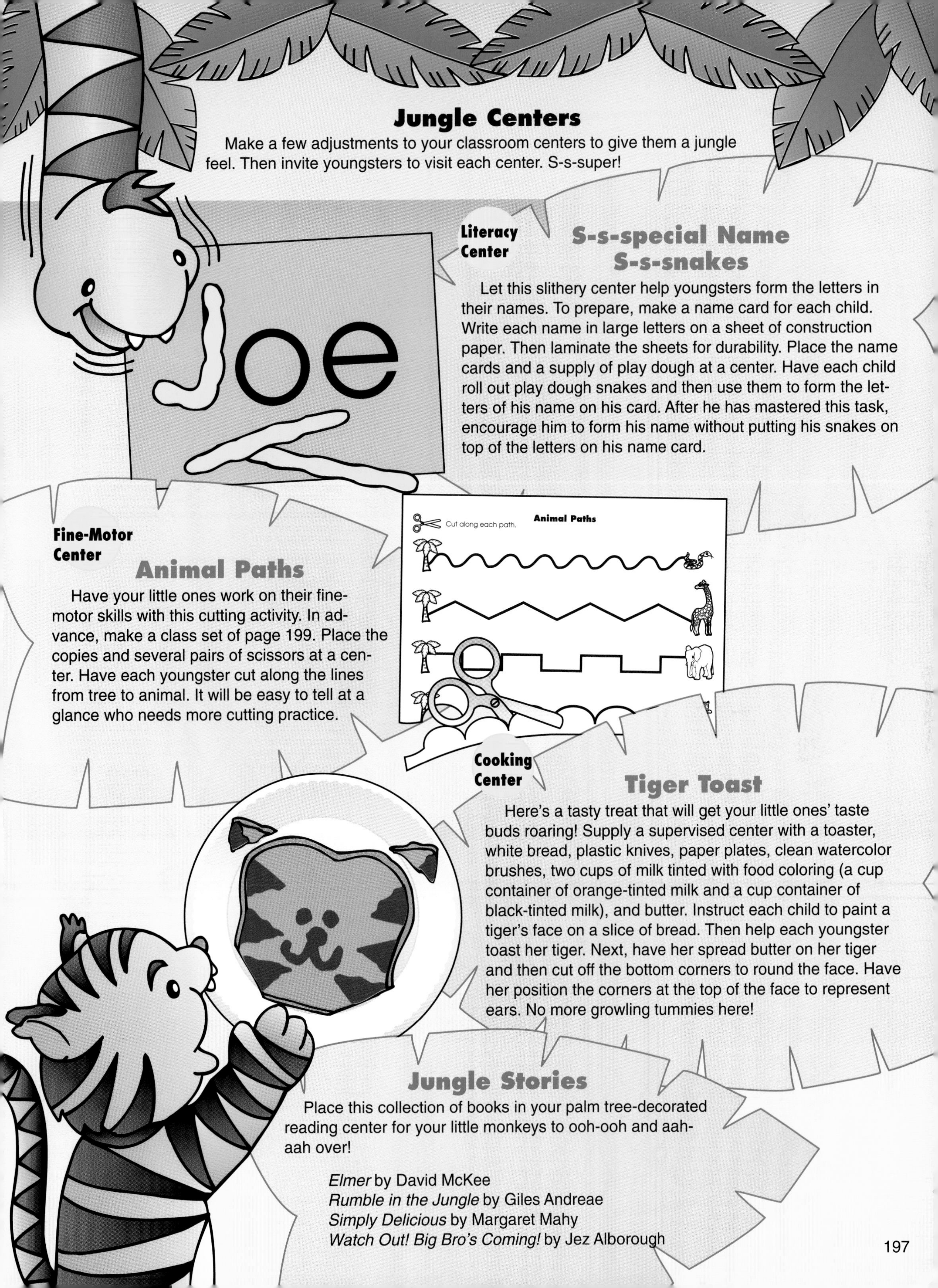

Jungle Centers

Make a few adjustments to your classroom centers to give them a jungle feel. Then invite youngsters to visit each center. S-s-super!

Literacy Center

S-s-special Name S-s-snakes

Let this slithery center help youngsters form the letters in their names. To prepare, make a name card for each child. Write each name in large letters on a sheet of construction paper. Then laminate the sheets for durability. Place the name cards and a supply of play dough at a center. Have each child roll out play dough snakes and then use them to form the letters of his name on his card. After he has mastered this task, encourage him to form his name without putting his snakes on top of the letters on his name card.

Fine-Motor Center

Animal Paths

Have your little ones work on their fine-motor skills with this cutting activity. In advance, make a class set of page 199. Place the copies and several pairs of scissors at a center. Have each youngster cut along the lines from tree to animal. It will be easy to tell at a glance who needs more cutting practice.

Cooking Center

Tiger Toast

Here's a tasty treat that will get your little ones' taste buds roaring! Supply a supervised center with a toaster, white bread, plastic knives, paper plates, clean watercolor brushes, two cups of milk tinted with food coloring (a cup container of orange-tinted milk and a cup container of black-tinted milk), and butter. Instruct each child to paint a tiger's face on a slice of bread. Then help each youngster toast her tiger. Next, have her spread butter on her tiger and then cut off the bottom corners to round the face. Have her position the corners at the top of the face to represent ears. No more growling tummies here!

Jungle Stories

Place this collection of books in your palm tree-decorated reading center for your little monkeys to ooh-ooh and aah-aah over!

Elmer by David McKee
Rumble in the Jungle by Giles Andreae
Simply Delicious by Margaret Mahy
Watch Out! Big Bro's Coming! by Jez Alborough

Nametag Pattern

Use with "Noble Nametags" on page 195.

Monkey Patterns

Use with "Swinging Through the Day" on page 195 and "No Monkey Business" on page 196.

Animal Paths

Cut along each path.

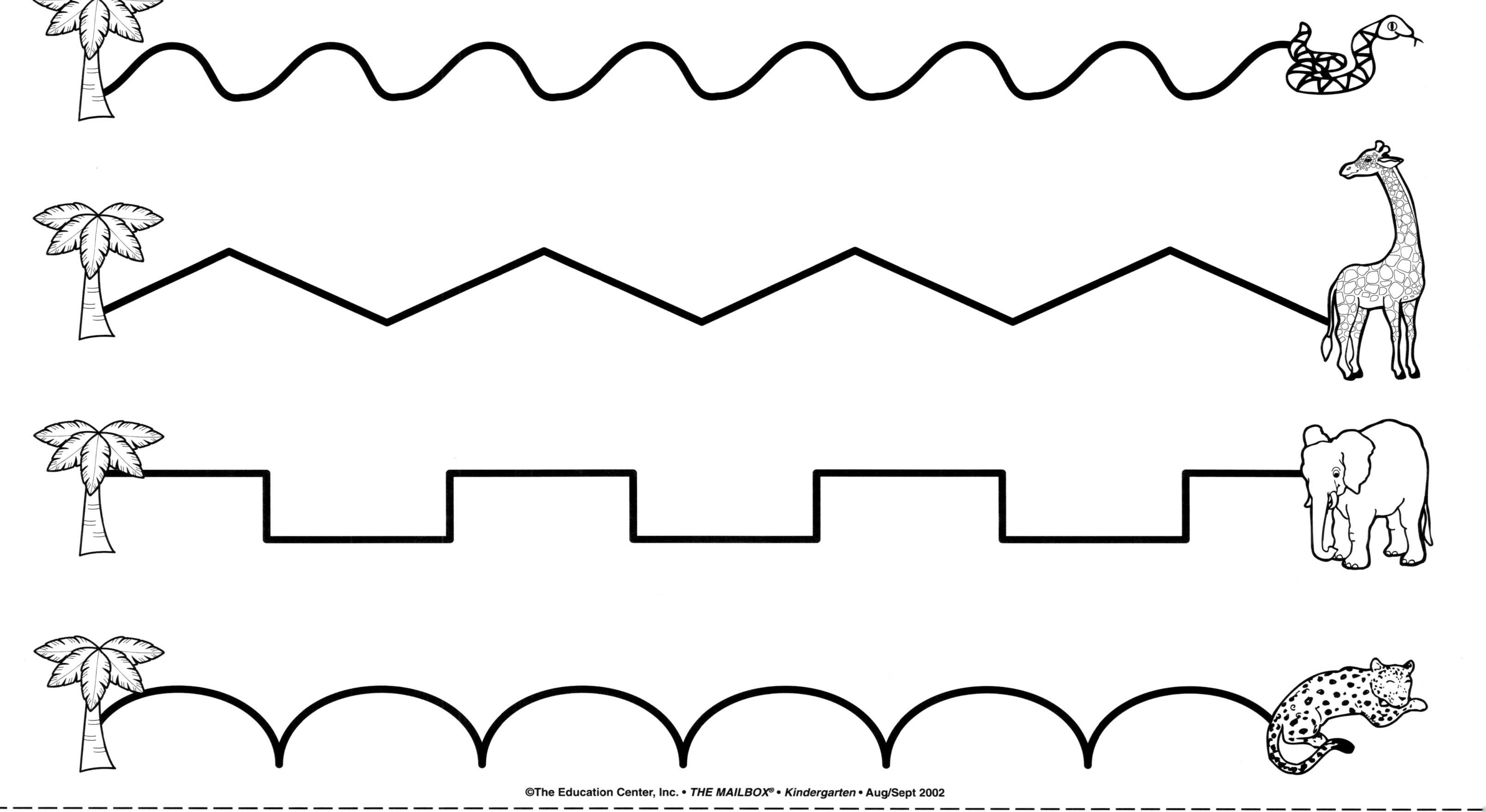

Note to the teacher: Use with "Animal Paths" on page 197.

Sounds at School

As kindergartners eagerly enter classrooms this fall, activities about your school environment offer perfect learning opportunties. Welcome your newcomers with this sampling of school-based ideas to help build essential phonological and phonemic awareness skills.

by Rhonda L. Chiles

Ms. Kirkland

Initial sounds
Rhyming

Classroom I Spy

Put a twist on the traditional game of I Spy by playing this rhyming version. Model how to play several times by substituting each object's initial sound and a rhyming word in the clues to the right. Encourage youngsters to use nonsense rhyming words when real ones aren't available. I spy…

Separating syllables

Staff Syllabication

Get ready to clap and count with this lively activity! Review the titles of school personnel with students. Then have youngsters clap the syllables of each word as you repeat it slowly. Instruct students to count the number of claps for each word. Explain that each clap is counting a syllable in the word and that all the syllables put together make up the word. After getting the hang of it, invite each youngster to call out a word for the group to clap. *"Prin-ci-pal* has three syllables!"

Phoneme identification

Listen Up!

Grab your Unifix cubes for this activity. Give each youngster a handful of cubes; then have students help you brainstorm a list of words that describe some of the things they do at school, such as read, write, cut, paste, play, and eat. Explain to students that you are going to slowly say one of the words from the list and they are to place one cube on the table for each sound they hear in the word. After one cube has been placed for each sound, have students link the cubes together. Next, instruct students to touch each cube as they repeat the word. Continue the activity using other words. One, two, three phonemes!

Blending letter sounds and word segments
Onsets and rimes

Picture Hunt

Your little ones will get into a hunt for pictures that has them blending sounds. To prepare, photocopy page 203 so that each child will have one picture mat. Laminate the mats and then cut them apart. Give each youngster a mat and eight tokens (counters, cereal pieces, or miniature marshmallows). Instruct each child to listen to your clues and then cover the appropriate picture with a token. For example, you might say, "It begins with [/b/] and ends with [/ook/]. Put it together and we say *book*." After youngsters have completed the activity as a large group, place the mats and a supply of tokens at a center. Encourage students to repeat the activity on their own during center time.

/k/,/u/,/t/

Comparing sounds

Backpack Sound Match

I have a match! You'll hear this phrase quite often as you play this game with students. In advance, gather several items found in the classroom, such as glue, a marker, a pencil, a toy, tape, and scissors; then place them in a backpack. Have students cut out two to three pictures from discarded magazines and advertisement circulars. To play, remove one item from the backpack and say its name. Have each youngster look at her pictures and decide whether any of them begin with the same sound. If so, invite her to share them with the group. Have her say the name of each picture, emphasizing the beginning sound of the word. Book—balloon. It's a match!

’s class

Phoneme identification

I Hear /l/ in Bell!

Listening skills improve as little ones decide whether they can hear certain sounds in words. Photocopy page 203 twice. Cut the pictures apart and give one to each child. Have each student hold up her picture if the letter sound you say can be heard in her picture word. For example, “Is there a /p/ in your picture’s name?” Quiz students with two to three phonemes for each picture. At a glance, you’ll be able to tell who is hearing phonemes in words. There’s a /k/ in clock!

Counting syllables

The Name Game

Syllables are counted and grouping takes place when students participate in this activity. Review with students how to clap the syllables in a word. Then have each child clap the number of syllables in his name. After each child has determined his number of syllables, have students group themselves with others who share the same number. Then count the total for each group and graph the results. That’s a lot of syllables!

Generating a rhyme

Rhyme Time

Youngsters will want to read this rhyming class book over and over again. Place a class set of items found around your classroom in a backpack. (Make sure each item rhymes with another word.) Provide each child with a sheet of paper and crayons. Invite each youngster to remove an item from the backpack. Then have her think of a word that rhymes with her item and dictate a sentence to you using the two words. Next, write the sentence along the bottom of her paper and instruct her to illustrate the page. Bind the completed pages and title the book “Rhyme Time at [your school’s name].”

Picture Mats

Use with "Picture Hunt" on page 201 and "I Hear /l/ in Bell!" on page 202.

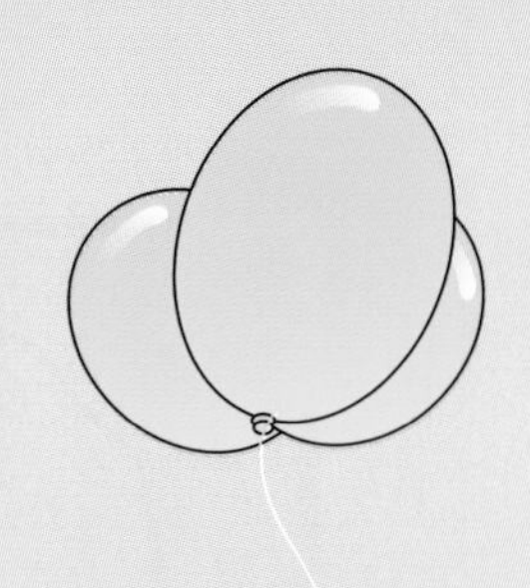

PRESENTING: The Patterns Fun Fair

The main attraction for this collection of ideas is the patterning practice your youngsters will gain while having a whole lot of fun! Come one and all to the patterns fun fair!

by Jana Sanderson

At the Gate

Get your tickets right here! Begin this unit by having students complete this patterning activity. To prepare, cut out rectangular tickets from construction paper in a variety of colors. Place the tickets in a basket. To play, have each of two students pretend to pay for a ticket and then draw one from the basket, making sure that two different colors were drawn. Instruct the youngsters to stand in front of the group and show their tickets to the class. Talk about the pattern that could be made using the two colors. Then, in turn, invite a student to choose an appropriate color of ticket to continue the pattern. For more practice, have students return the tickets to the basket and then repeat the activity to make a different pattern.

Ferris Wheel Fun

Your students will be lining up to take a turn at this Ferris wheel center, which has them making beautiful patterns. In advance, use Tinkertoy pieces to construct a Ferris wheel as shown. Glue the spokes at the center of the wheel in place with rubber cement. (You will be able to take the toys apart if this type of glue is used.) Gather a supply of colorful wooden beads that have holes large enough to fit onto the spokes. Place the Ferris wheel, beads, and eight round Tinkertoy pieces at a center. Invite students to make patterns with the beads on each spoke of the Ferris wheel. After each pattern is complete, instruct the child to add a round piece to the end of the spoke to keep the beads from sliding off. Wow! What a beautifully patterned Ferris wheel!

The Dime Toss

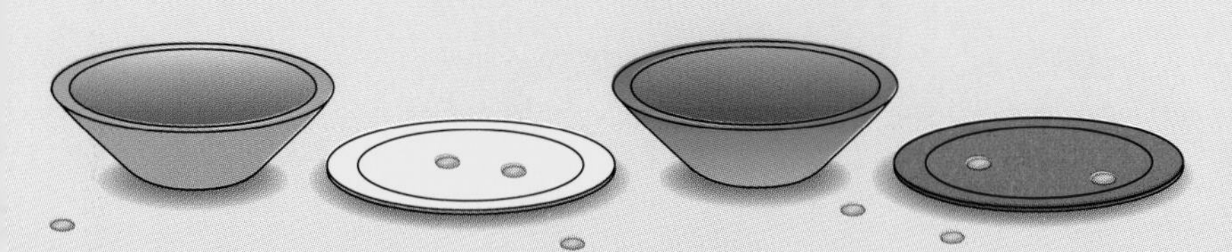

Your little ones will be eager to step right up and play this patterning game. To prepare, gather a supply of heavy plastic mugs, bowls, and plates. Have a small group of students use the dishes to create a pattern on a carpeted floor near a wall. After the pattern is complete, have students stand back and pitch dimes into the dishes. With this carnival game, everyone is a winner!

Clowning Around With Patterns

Clowning around is definitely allowed while completing this patterning activity! In advance, make a class set of the clown pattern on page 206. Then enlarge the pattern by 40 percent and copy it onto 11" x 17" paper. Color and laminate the clown, and then tape it onto a table. At the same table, place the copies, a large supply of colorful sticky dots, and a large supply of one-inch pom-poms in the same colors as your dots. Have each child visit the center and use the pom-poms to create a pattern down the front of the large clown's clothing. Have him continue the pattern by placing pom-poms between the clown's hands, as if the clown were juggling. After the child has completed the patterns, have him re-create them using sticky dots on his own clown copy. Then encourage him to color the rest of his paper. Display the papers on a bulletin board titled "Clowning Around With Patterns!"

Carousel Ride

The carousel's up and down movements are a great way to turn children on to patterns in motion. To prepare for this activity, make a tagboard copy of the horse and topper patterns on page 207 for each child. Give each youngster a copy and have her color and cut out the patterns. Staple each child's carousel topper onto a straw and then hole-punch her horse where indicated. Help her slip her straw through the holes in her horse. Next, have each student slide her horse up and down its pole as she sings the song below. Saddle up!

(sung to the tune of "The Wheels on the Bus")

The horse I ride goes up and down,
Up and down, up and down.
The horse I ride goes up and down,
On the carousel.

Clown Pattern

Use with "Clowning Around With Patterns" on page 205.

Horse and Topper Patterns

Use with "Carousel Ride" on page 205.

Go Kindergartners!

Celebrate the traditional fall sport of football while reinforcing your youngsters' awareness of long- and short-vowel sounds and rhyming skills! Use this collection of activities to kick off your unit of football fun. Touchdown!

by Rhonda L. Chiles

Vowel Chant

Football fans love to cheer and so will your little ones! Introduce your students to long-vowel sounds and rhyming words by having them repeat this chant. After completing the chant, invite students to brainstorm another list of rhyming words and then have them recite their new chant. Give me a vowel!

Give me an *A*—hey!
Give me an *E*—whee!
Give me an *I*—hi!
Give me an *O*—whoa!
Give me a *U*—ooh!

A, E, I, O, U,
I have said the vowels for you!

Perfect Pennants

Help students develop an ear for long-vowel sounds with this simple activity. To prepare, cut a triangle-shaped pennant from construction paper for each child. Label each one with a vowel; then laminate them for durability. Tape each pennant to a craft stick. Give each youngster a pennant and have him listen as you say a word that includes a long-vowel sound. Instruct him to wave his pennant and repeat the sound if he can hear his vowel sound in the word.

On a different day, introduce short-vowel sounds and repeat the activity. When your youngsters have mastered both short- and long-vowel sounds, challenge them by changing the activity to include words with short-vowel sounds and words with long-vowel sounds. Instead of having students repeat the vowel sound they hear, instruct them to say the letter name and whether it is a short or long sound. "I hear long *E*!"

Hooray for Rhymes

Bring out the pom-poms and get ready for youngsters to cheer for rhyming words! Provide each child with a pom-pom or length of crepe paper streamer. Explain to students that you will say a pair of words, and if the words rhyme, they are to stand up and cheer. If the words do not rhyme, instruct students to stay seated.

The Football Poem

Your youngsters are going to love this poem. Copy the poem onto chart paper, writing your school's mascot in the blank in line 4. After students recite the poem, invite them to circle and identify the vowels in each underlined word.

I'm going to the football <u>game</u>.
I'm going there today.
I'm going to the football game
To <u>watch</u> the <u>[your school's mascot]</u> <u>play</u>.

To the field come the <u>fans.</u>
To the field comes the <u>band</u>.
To the field come the <u>coaches</u>
Of the best <u>team</u> in the <u>land</u>.

"Let's <u>play</u>!" yell the fans.
"Let's play!" <u>yells</u> the band.
"Let's play!" yell the coaches
Of the <u>best</u> team in the land.

"Touchdown!" cheer the <u>fans</u>.
"Touchdown!" cheers the <u>band.</u>
"Touchdown!" cheer the <u>coaches</u>
Of the best team in the <u>land</u>!

Let's Cheer

This matching activity combines matching vowel sounds and rhyming words. In advance, make ten copies of the cheerleader and pom-pom patterns on page 211. Make one copy of the picture cards on page 211. Color the patterns and picture cards, if desired. Label each cheerleader's jersey with a different long- or short-vowel letter. Glue a picture card to each pom-pom. Laminate the patterns and then cut them out.

To play, have a child match each rhyming pair of pom-poms. Then have her match each pair of pom-poms to the corresponding cheerleader. Go team!

Football Pass

A soft football is all you need for this quick rhyming activity. Have youngsters stand in a circle. Gently toss the football to a student while saying a word. The child then tosses the ball back to you and says a rhyming word. Vary the activity by saying a vowel and having the child say a word that includes the vowel. Nice catch!

Short a.

Cat.

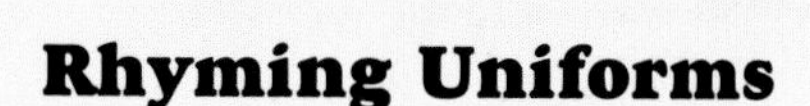

Rhyming Uniforms

This activity has youngsters getting ready for the big game—a rhyming game. Make two copies of page 212. Color the helmets and jerseys as desired. Laminate the pages and then cut out the helmets. Shuffle the cards and place them facedown between two players. Give each child a jersey gameboard. In turn, have each player draw a card from the stack. Instruct him to say the picture on the helmet and then place it in the square next to the rhyming jersey. If a child draws a duplicate card, he places it at the bottom of the stack and loses a turn. The first player to collect all five helmets and correctly place them wins the game.

Touchdown!

A coin toss starts this fun rhyming football game! To prepare, make two copies of the picture cards on page 211 and one copy of the football field pattern on page 213. Color the cards and pattern as desired. Use one set of picture cards and ten index cards to make ten rhyming cards, as shown, and use the other set of picture cards and ten more index cards to make playing cards that do not rhyme. Place the cards, two pennies (game markers), and the field pattern at a center.

To play, have each child place her penny on the 50-yard line. As in an actual game of football, let a coin toss determine which player goes first. The winner of the toss draws a card and names the two pictures on it. If the pictures rhyme, she moves her penny to the 40-yard line. If her pictures do not rhyme, she stays in the same position. Play alternates between each player. The first child to reach the goal and say "Touchdown!" wins the game.

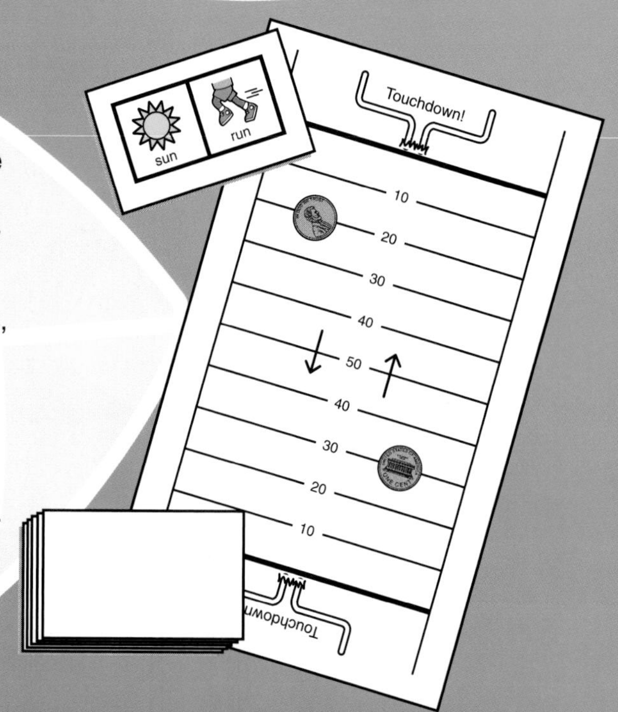

Cheerleader and Pom-Pom Patterns

Use with "Let's Cheer" on page 209.

Picture Cards

Use with "Let's Cheer" on page 209 and "Touchdown!" on page 210.

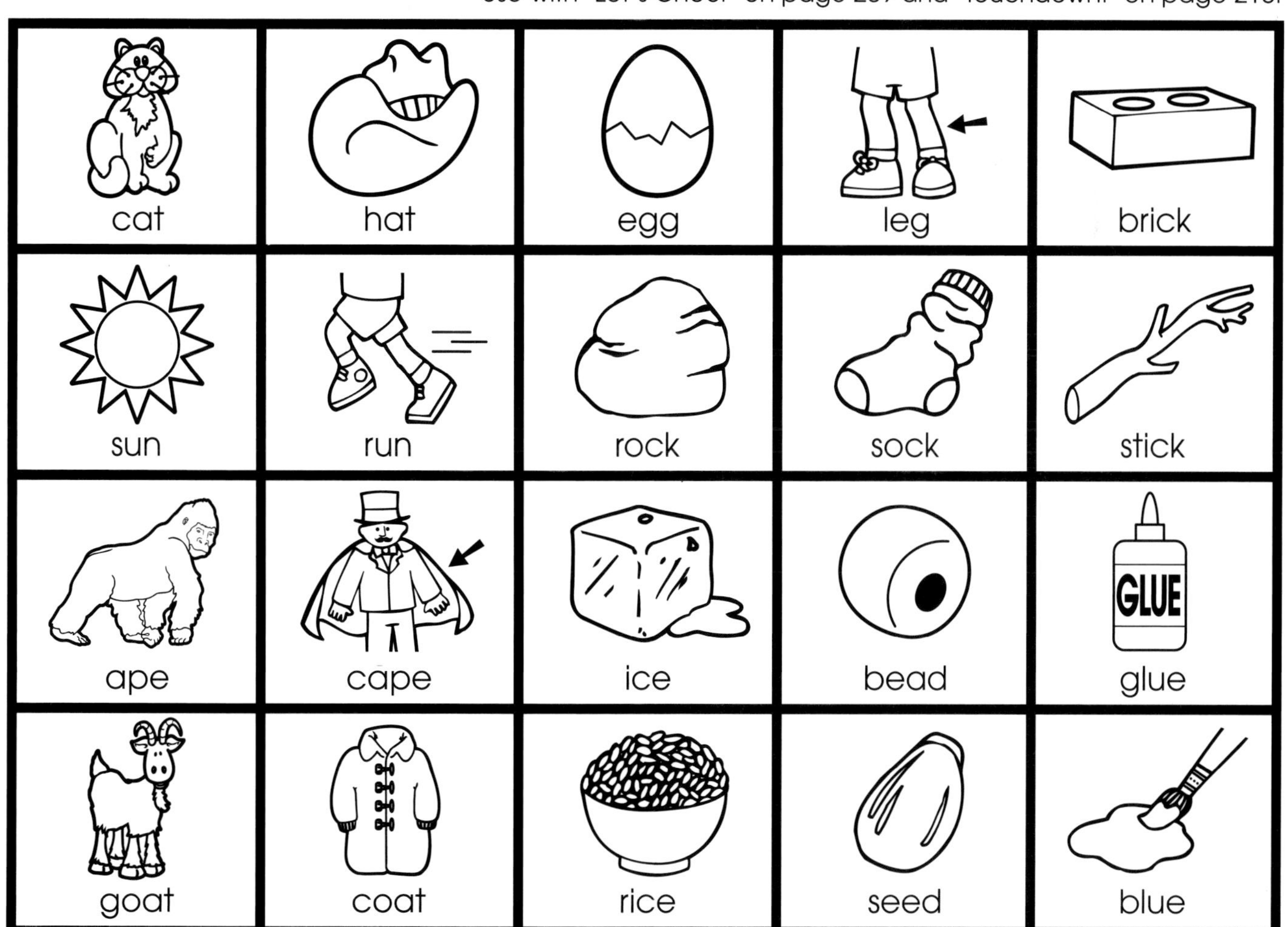

Rhyming Uniforms

 Note to the teacher: Use with "Rhyming Uniforms" on page 210.

Gameboard

Use with "Touchdown!"
on page 210.

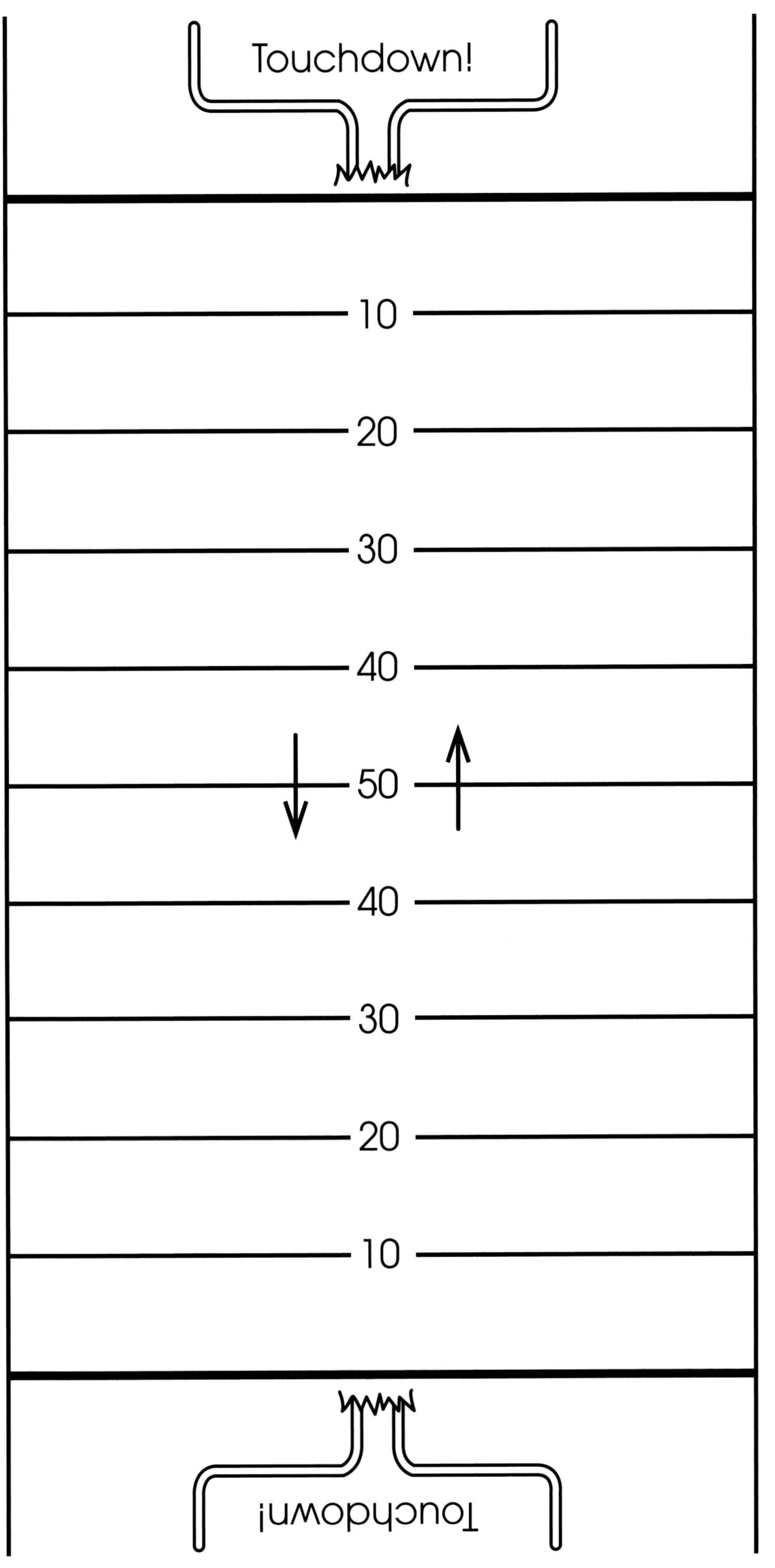

Space, Here We Come!

Get ready to blast off with this unit that will have your little astronauts learning about the planets and beyond!

by Angela Van Beveren

Sky Gazing

Start your space unit by purchasing plastic glow-in-the-dark stars (found at discount or party stores) and attaching them to your classroom ceiling. Invite youngsters to lie on the floor as you turn out the lights. Ask students to think about the things that are found in the sky. After a moment, turn on the lights and make a list of students' thoughts *(planes, stars, clouds, rainbows, the moon, planets, etc.).* Talk about the list and explain to students that some things, like planes and clouds, are found within our atmosphere and that stars and planets are found in space. Then use the chart at right to tell students a few facts about the planets of our solar system.

Planet Facts

Mercury	• This planet is closest to the sun. It is the second smallest planet.
Venus	• This planet is very hot and bright.
Earth	• This is the planet we call home. It is covered by lots of water and various land masses.
Mars	• This planet is called the red planet.
Jupiter	• This planet is the largest of all nine planets. It is famous for its great red spot.
Saturn	• This planet has over a thousand rings around it.
Uranus	• This planet is blue-green with at least 11 rings. It is tilted on its side.
Neptune	• This blue-green planet is very cold and very windy.
Pluto	• This planet is the smallest. It is called the ice planet.

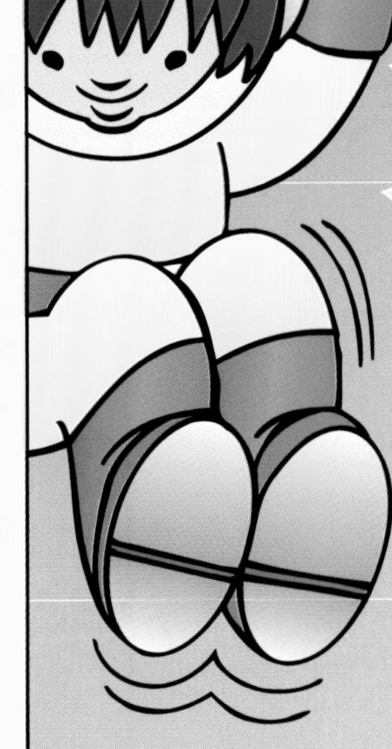

The Solar System Song

Teach your youngsters this catchy song, and they will be able to list all nine planets in order in no time!

(sung to the tune of "A Tisket, a Tasket")

The planets, the planets, I can name the planets.
This brain of mine, it knows all nine.
Listen while I name them.

Mercury, Venus, Earth, and Mars and Jupiter,
Saturn and Uranus,
Neptune and then Pluto.

The planets, the planets, I just named the planets.
This brain of mine, it knows all nine,
All in the right order!

Student Spaceship

Your students' imaginations will soar with this center activity that combines cooperation and lots of fun! Turn your dramatic-play area into a space adventure. In advance, obtain a large appliance box. Cut a doorway on one side of the box and then cut circular windows on the other sides of the box. Have students assist in painting the outside of the spaceship, adding decorative touches such as a U.S. flag. Tape a scrap of laminating film to the inside of the box over each window opening. Top the spaceship with a radar, fashioned by covering a Styrofoam fruit tray with aluminum foil. Then hot-glue the radar to the top of the box.

To decorate the inside of the spaceship, draw instrument panels, attach knobs or buttons, and add elements such as an old computer keyboard and a small radio.

Finally, outfit your astronauts with space suits: large white shirts, moon shoes (large sponges attached with rubber bands), gloves, and helmets (see "Paper Bag Space Helmets" below). You can also make air tanks by inverting two two-liter bottles, taping them together, and adding yarn loops to each side to create a backpack-style apparatus. We're ready for liftoff!

Paper Bag Space Helmets

No astronaut is prepared to blast off into space without a helmet. Make these simple helmets with youngsters to ensure they are ready for flight. To prepare, collect a class supply of standard paper grocery bags. Cut six inches from the open end of each bag. Then cut a face opening on one side of each bag. To cut a face opening, begin approximately 2 1/2 inches from the closed end of the bag and cut a 5 1/2" x 6" rectangle, rounding the corners as you cut. Then have each youngster use markers, crayons, or paints to decorate his helmet. Invite students to suit up and take a voyage into space!

Astronaut Training

Do your students have the right stuff? These astronaut-training activities will certainly get them in shape for space travel! Explain to students that in order to become astronauts, candidates must meet educational and physical requirements. Then challenge youngsters with the following exercises that practice skills such as counting, letter recognition, and skip-counting.

Countdown Exercises

To begin, have students stand. Instruct youngsters to count backward from ten, gradually bending their knees into a squatting position. When it's time to blast off, have each child jump into the air. Vary the activity by beginning at different numbers appropriate to your students' skill level.

Moon Walk

Have students walk around the room in very large, exaggerated, slow steps. While walking, instruct them to say the alphabet or count.

Swim

Have your junior astronauts take the swim test. Instruct each child to skip-count to 100 as he walks around the room, moving his arms in a regular swimming stroke. Then have him skip-count backward from 100 doing the backstroke.

Solar System Swat

Have students practice eye-hand coordination with this exercise. Suspend several planets (foam balls) from the ceiling. Vary the position of each ball, but make all of them slightly higher than the students' arms can reach. In turn, have each child jump and try to swat a planet.

Eye Exam

Have each student cover one eye with her hand and then read flash cards.

Space Snack

Your youngsters will experience the challenge of eating in space with this creative snack. Prepare two or three batches of instant pudding according to package directions. Then put a small serving of pudding in a snack-size resealable plastic bag for each child. Cut a supply of straws in half so that each child will have one half. Give each student a straw and a bag of pudding. Have her open her bag just enough to insert her straw. Then instruct each child to sip her pudding through her straw!

Spaceship Shapes

Students will have a blast with this puzzle, which offers practice in "space-tial" relationships, counting, and numeral writing. In advance, make several copies of the spaceship pattern on page 219. Laminate them for durability. Make a class set of the recording sheet on the bottom of page 220. Place the spaceship patterns, recording sheets, and a supply of pattern blocks at a center. Challenge students to fill in the spaceship using pattern blocks and following the gray outlines or by creating their own patterns. Instruct students to have the blocks stay within the bold lines and leave no empty spaces. When the pattern is covered, have him record the number of each block he used to make the spaceship. After each child has completed the activity, encourage him to use the pattern blocks to create a spaceship of his own!

Kindergartners on the Moon

Your youngsters will picture themselves walking on the moon with this clever bulletin board. In advance, photograph each child. Make a class set of the astronaut patterns on the top of page 220. Have each student color and cut out an astronaut. Then help each child cut out the face portion. Tape each youngster's photo onto the back of the pattern so that her face shows through the opening. Next, have students sponge-paint a large semicircle of bulletin board paper to resemble the moon. Attach the moon and astronauts to a bulletin board as shown. Then add the title "Our Class Is out of This World!"

The Shuttle Game

Here's an activity that provides practice in counting and number recognition. Make a game strip similar to the one shown. Photocopy the strip to make a class set. Program ten clean milk jug lids with a different number from 1 to 10; then place the lids in a bag. Put the bag, strips, a supply of Unifix cubes, and several pencils at a center. Invite a small group of students to visit the center. In turn, each player closes his eyes and draws a lid from the bag. The player circles the corresponding number on his game strip and places a cube on his launch pad. He then returns the lid to the bag. If a player draws a number he's already circled, the game continues with the next player. The winner is the first player to circle all ten numbers and build his space shuttle ten cubes high. Have students count backward from ten before launching a new game. 5, 4, 3, 2, 1, blastoff!

Constellation Exploration

Your little learners will be reaching for the stars with this activity. Enlarge the constellation patterns on page 221. Make a paper copy and a transparency copy of each pattern. Cut apart the patterns. Use a hole puncher to punch out each star on the paper copies. Explain that groups of stars form patterns, or pictures in the sky. These pictures are called constellations. Then place one of the paper constellations on an overhead projector. Have students look at the projected stars and guess the picture they show. After a discussion, remove the paper pattern from the projector and replace it with the corresponding transparency to reveal the constellation's picture. Continue the same process with the other constellation patterns. Way to reach for the stars!

Leo the Lion

Constructing Constellations

After your youngsters have had some practice interpreting the stars, it's time to let their creative minds construct their own configurations! Provide each child with a supply of miniature marshmallows and one or two pieces of uncooked spaghetti. Instruct each child to break her spaghetti into pieces and then use the pieces to connect her marshmallow stars, creating a unique constellation pattern. Next, have her name and illustrate her constellation. Invite each youngster to share her constellation with the group; then provide some extra stars for snacking!

Meteorite Masterpieces

Aspiring artists will enjoy the creativity that this craft allows. Explain to students that meteorites are pieces of matter from the solar system that are found on Earth. Gather the supplies listed below and then guide each child to complete her meteorite. After each project is complete, hang the meteorites from the ceiling using fishing line to create a display that's out of this world!

Materials for each child:

Styrofoam ball
pencil
paintbrush
paint in various colors
glitter glue

Directions:

1. Press a pencil tip into the ball to make small craters.
2. Paint the ball with different colors, swirling the paint as you go. Allow the paint to dry.
3. Brush on glitter glue to add sparkle.

Pattern-Block Puzzle

Use with "Spaceship Shapes" on page 217.

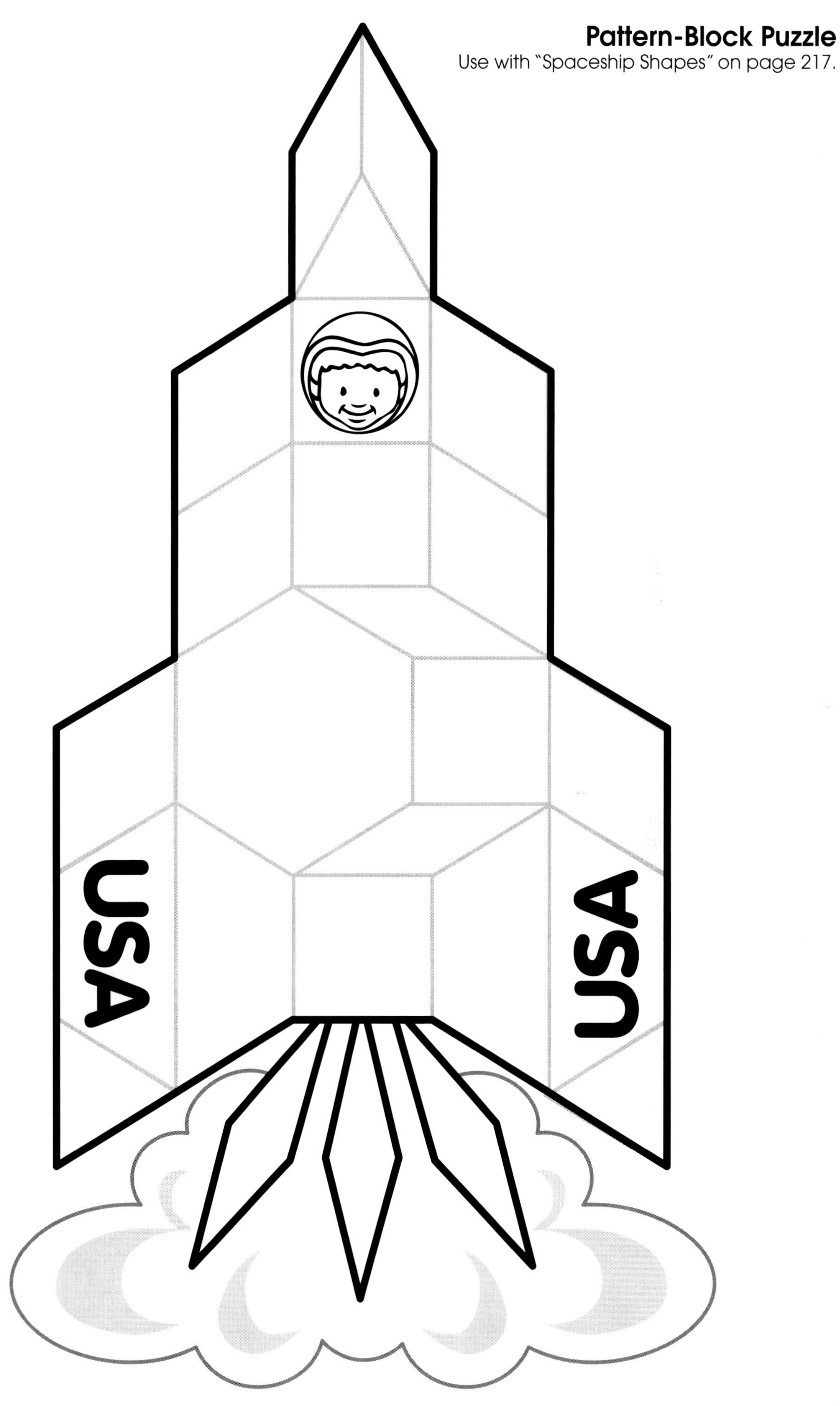

Astronaut Pattern

Use with "Kindergartners on the Moon" on page 217.

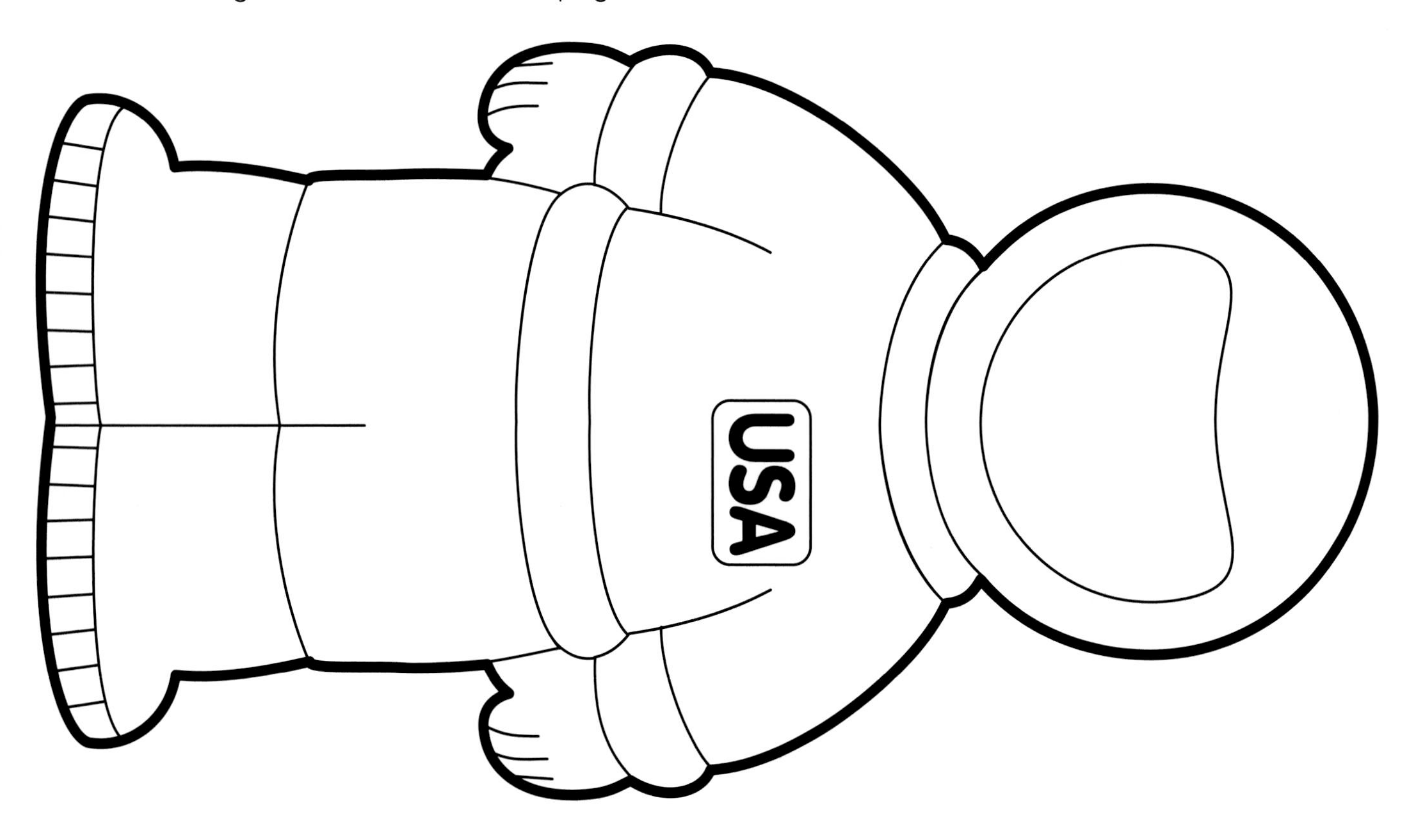

Name____ Recording sheet

Spaceship Shapes

Write how many blocks were used.

_______ _______ _______

_______ _______ _______

 Note to the teacher: Use with "Spaceship Shapes" on page 217.

Constellation Patterns

Use with "Constellation Exploration" on page 218.

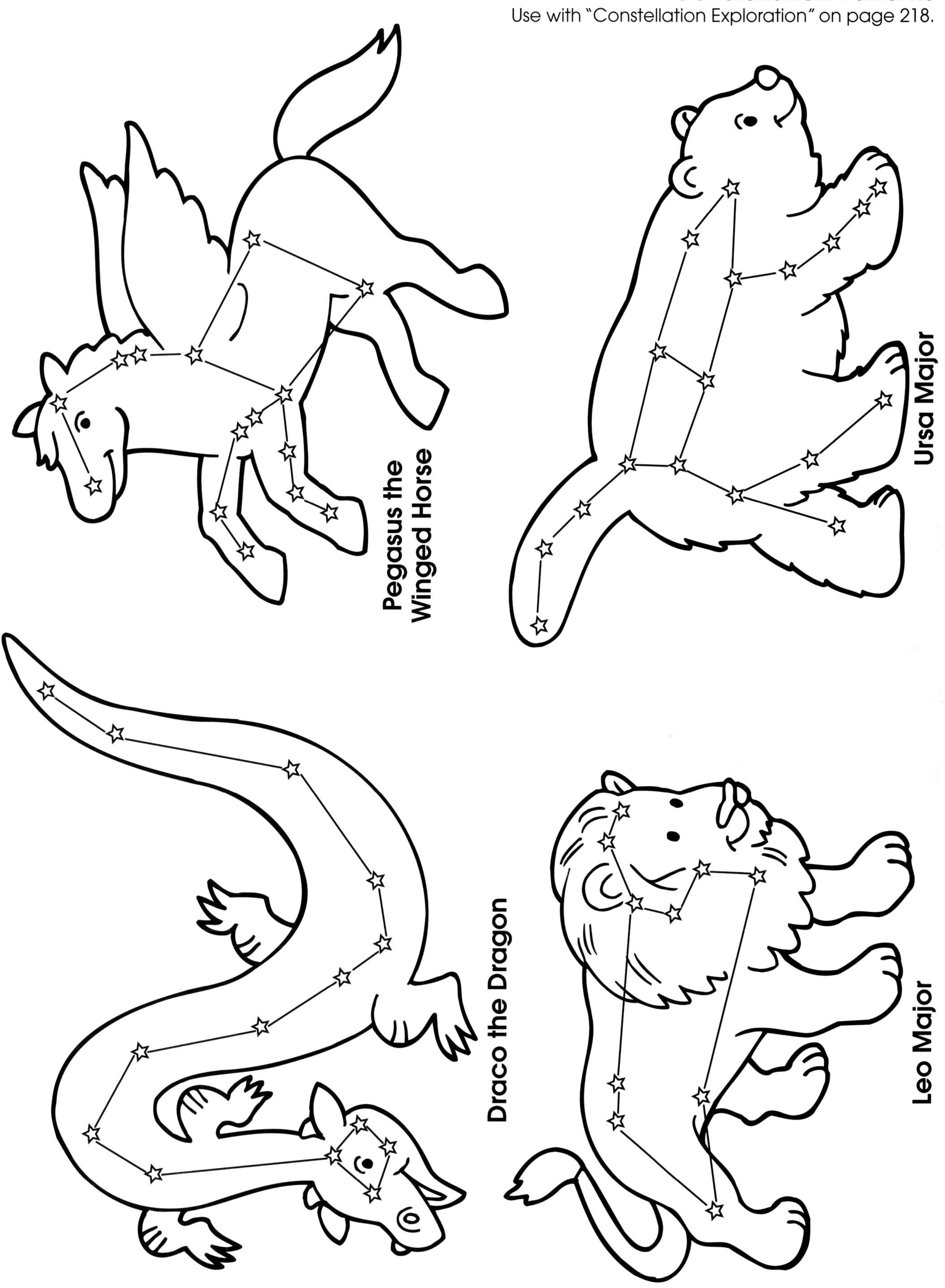

The Inside Scoop on SKELETONS

Scary skeletons? Not in this unit! Help your little ones bone up on science skills with this informative selection of skeleton-related ideas.

by Lucia Kemp Henry

Bag o' Bones

Even though our bodies look different on the outside, inside we're much the same because of our bones! Begin your skeleton study with a riddle activity that gets students thinking about what's inside them. To prepare, enlarge the skeleton patterns on page 225 by 40 percent and then photocopy them on an 11" x 17" piece of paper. Laminate the page and cut out each pattern piece. Place the pieces in a paper bag labeled with a question mark. Read the riddle below, pausing periodically to allow students to guess the identity of the items in the bag. This bag o' bones won't be a mystery for long!

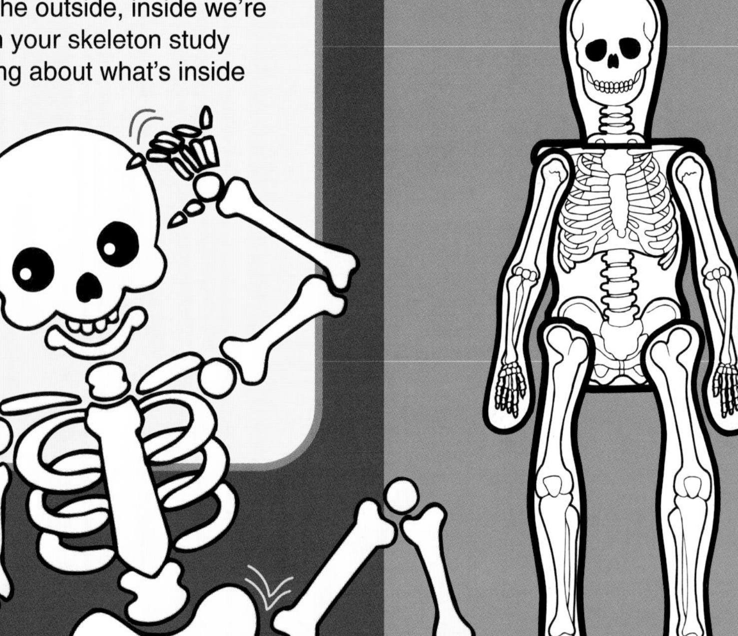

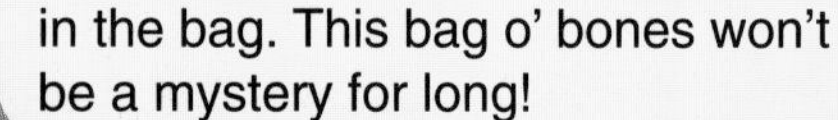

There are some things inside this bag.
They help in all we do.
These things are **white.**
These things are **hard.**
These things can **grow** *with you.*
Though they are **strong,**
These things can **break,**
But can be **mended** *too.*
Do you know what's inside this bag?
They're **bones** *like the ones inside of you!*

The Bones in Our Bodies

Do our bodies hold just a bunch of jumbled bones? Your little ones can piece together an answer to this question with an easy puzzle activity. Prepare the skeleton pattern pieces from "Bag o' Bones" on this page for flannelboard use. Next, display the patterns randomly on your flannelboard. Invite volunteers to help you arrange the jumble of bones on the board to make a skeleton. Then explain that every person has a skeleton, along with muscles and organs. Complete the activity by singing a verse or two of "Dem Bones." The head bone's connected to the neck bone!

My X Ray

This X-ray activity is a great way to let your little ones take a peek at the bones inside a body. Photocopy the body and skeleton cards on page 226 on white paper for each child. Give each youngster a copy of the patterns and have her personalize her body by drawing hair and features on the head to represent her face and by coloring the clothes and body with light-colored crayons. Next, direct the child to cut out the two halves of her X-ray card. Help each child position the two halves back-to-back so that the skeleton illustration is centered behind the body outline. Then staple the halves together along the top, bottom, and sides. To use the X-ray card, each child holds it perpendicular to the floor with the body side facing her. Then have the child hold her X ray up so that the skeleton side is facing a sunny window or a bright light. What will each little scientist discover? Her very own X ray!

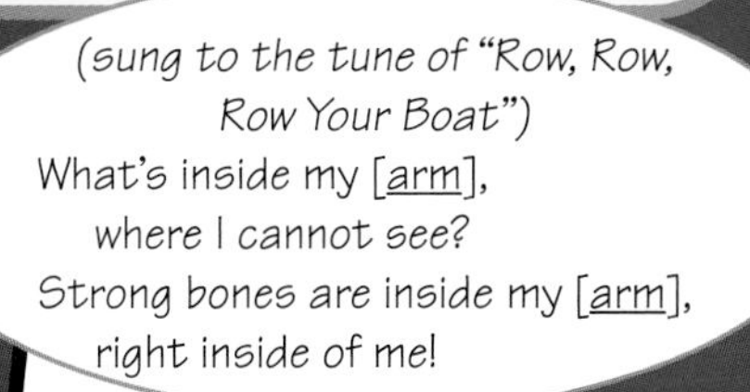

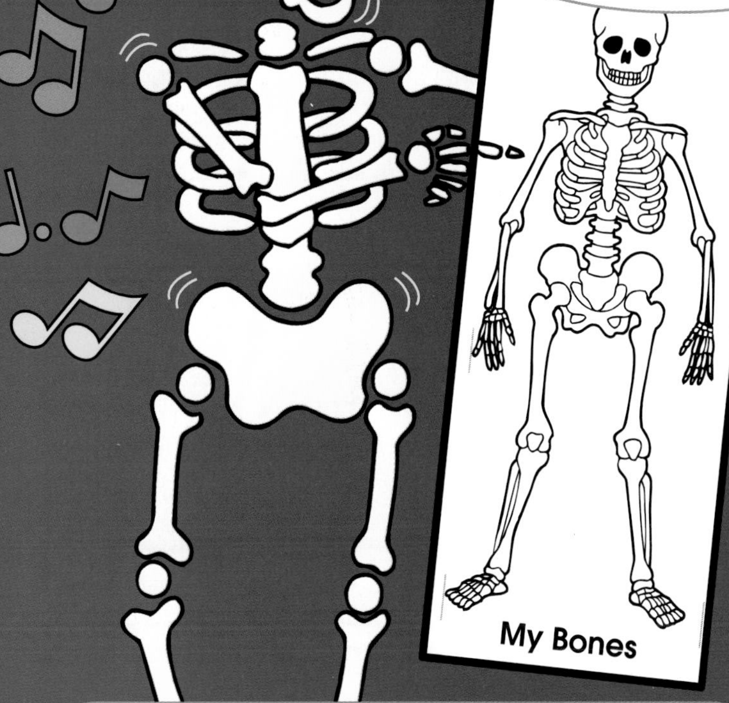

Now put those skeleton cards from "My X Ray" on this page to good use with this little ditty, which has youngsters relating bones to body parts! As each child sings the first line of the song to the left, have him point to an arm on the body side of his X-ray card. Then have him point to one set of arm bones on the skeleton side as he sings the second line. Sing the song seven more times, replacing the word *arm* with *hand, leg, foot, hip, chest, neck,* and *head.*

Inside Animals

People aren't the only creatures with bones—animals have skeletons too! In advance, if possible, ask a veterinarian to loan an X-ray film that shows the bones of a dog. Or enlarge the dog skeleton card on page 227 and use it in place of an actual X ray. Share the X ray with students and discuss the bones that are visible and how they are similar to human bones. Reproduce the skeleton cards on page 227 on white paper and the body cards on page 228 on a clear transparency sheet. Cut all of the cards apart. Have students lay each body card on top of its matching skeleton card for a nifty X-ray effect. Cool!

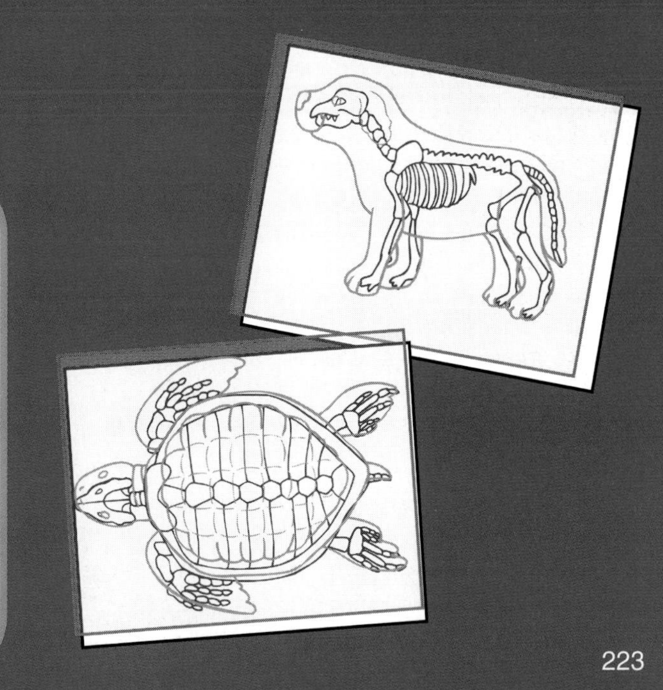

What Do Bones Do?

Now that your little ones know that bones are a part of the body, use this demonstration to show them what bones do! Obtain a child's thin winter glove or a garden glove. Cut five plastic drinking straws into lengths to fit inside the fingers and thumb of the glove. Staple the straws to a small piece of cardboard, as shown, to create a simplified set of hand bones. Begin the demonstration by showing the glove to students. Ask them to imagine that the glove represents a hand; then hold the glove up so that the fingers flop over. Direct each child to compare his own hand to the glove; ask volunteers to explain why the human hand is not floppy like the glove. Next, show students the drinking straw "bones." Then insert the bones and hold the glove up to show how the bones help keep the glove from flopping over. Explain to youngsters that bones give our bodies shape and support. To extend the activity, place the child's glove and matching "bones" at a center. Add a few more sets of gloves and bones of different sizes for students to match. What a handy way to show why our bodies need bones!

Skeletons in Motion

Here's a movement activity that will extend your skeleton study to include wrists, elbows, and knees. Discuss with students how our bodies can bend at their joints. Explain that these joints allow us to move in different ways. Prompt each child to suggest an activity or sport involving movement. Then have youngsters slowly go through the motions to perform an action. After each movement, talk about which joints made it possible for their bodies to move as they did. Bend, bend, bend that skeleton!

Dancing Skeleton Puppet

Our strong bones keep our bodies from flopping over. But if our bones are so rigid, how are we able to move? Make this skeleton puppet to help youngsters see how the connections between bones enable us to move. Give each child a white construction paper copy of the skeleton patterns on page 225. Have her cut out the skeleton pieces along the bold lines. Instruct each child to glue a craft stick to the bottom of her torso pattern. Help each child attach the arms, legs, and head to the torso with small brads. Then invite each youngster to move her puppet as she sings the song below to the tune of "Buffalo Gals."

Repeat the song two more times, replacing the word *head* with *legs* and *arms*.

Mr. Skeleton can you show us a dance,
Show us a dance, show us a dance?
Mr. Skeleton can you move your head,
And dance by the light of the moon?

Knowledge-Building Bone Books

Bones (Body Books) by Anna Sandeman
Dem Bones by Bob Barner
Skeleton (Eyewitness Books) by Steve Parker
The Skeleton Inside You (Let's-Read-and-Find-Out Science) by Philip Balestrino
You and Your Body (It's Science!) by Sally Hewitt

Skeleton Patterns

Use with "Bag o' Bones" and "The Bones in Our Bodies" on page 222 and "Dancing Skeleton Puppet" on page 224.

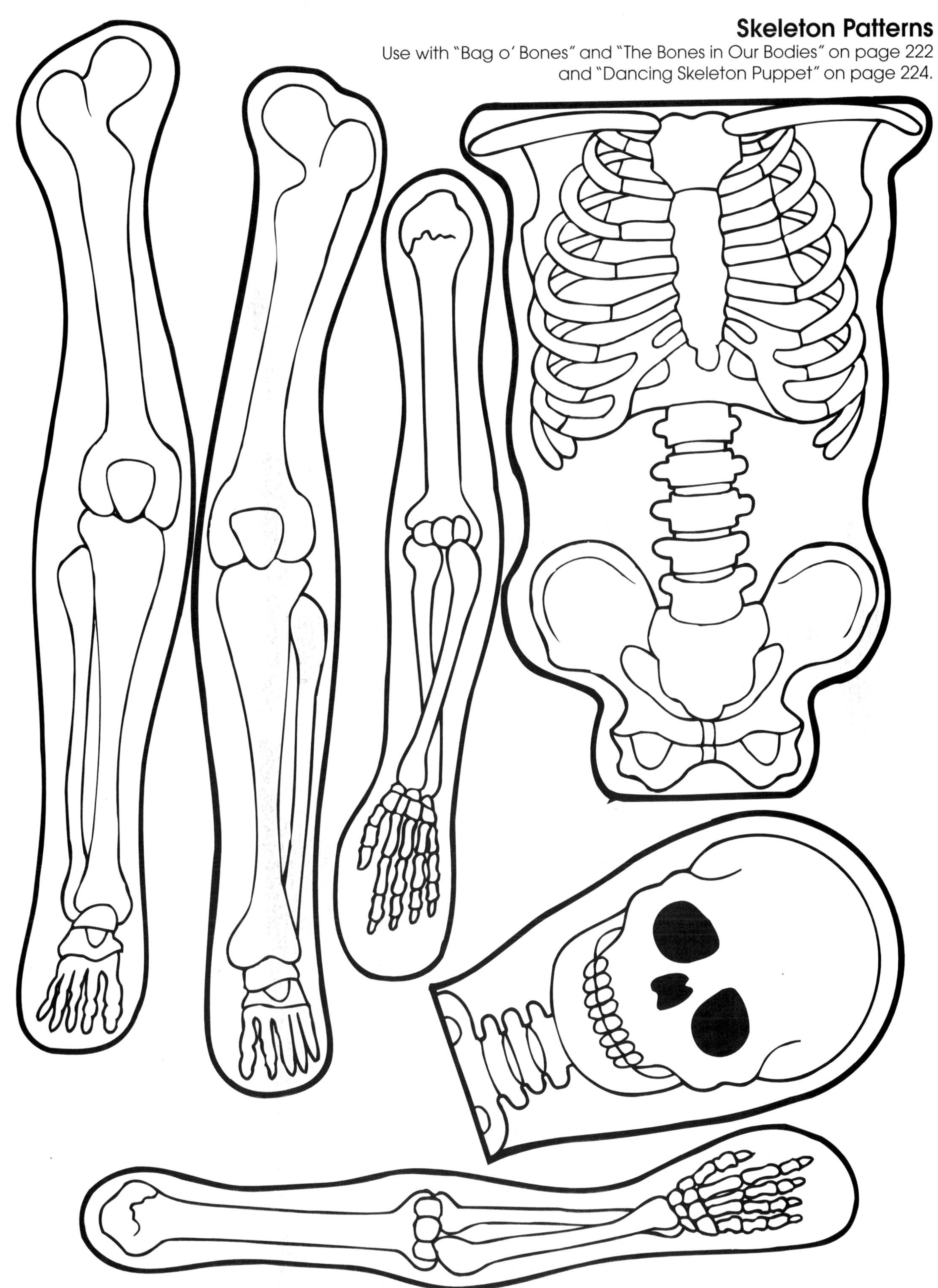

Body and Skeleton Cards

Use with "My X Ray" on page 223.

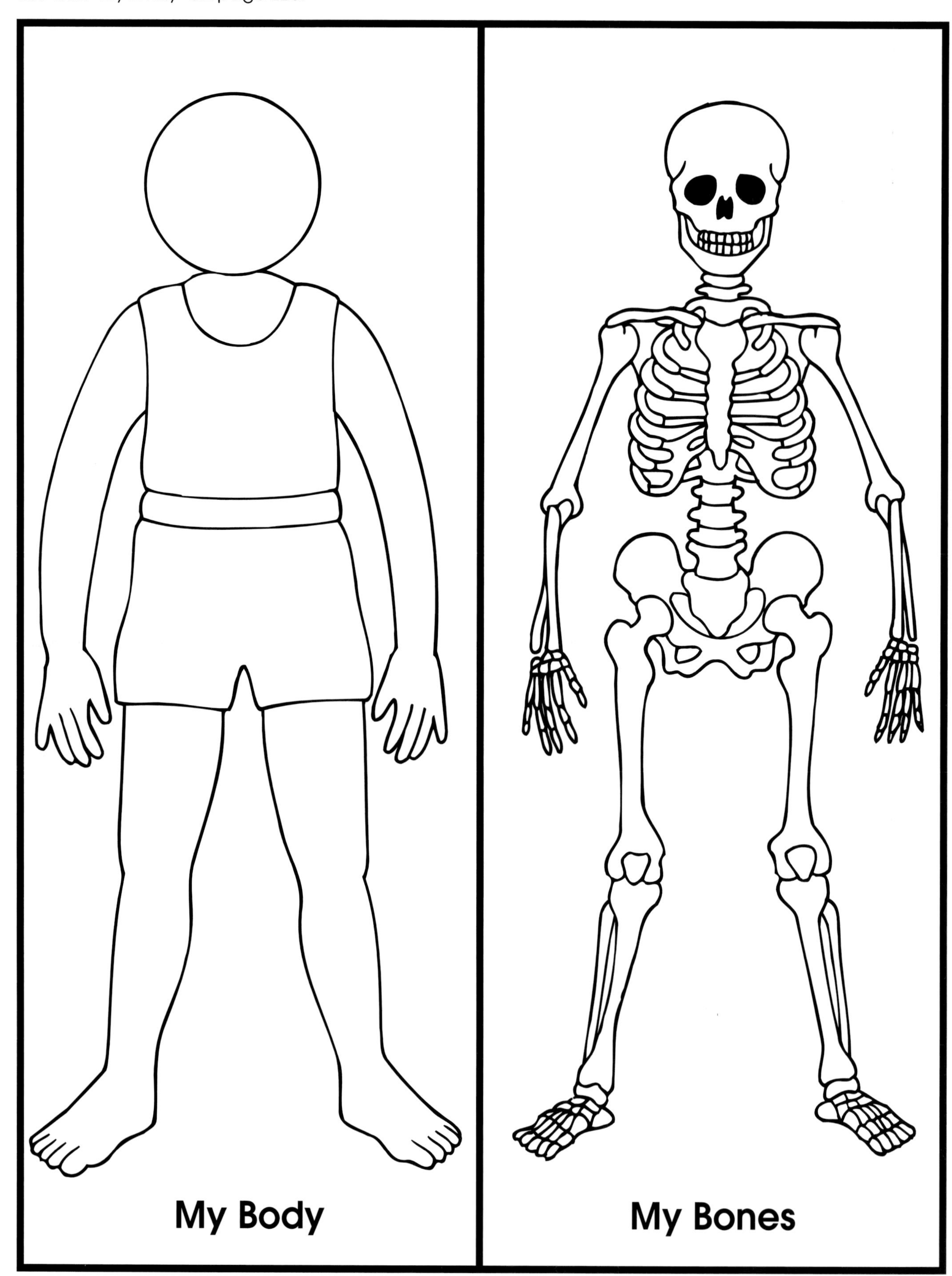

Use with "Inside Animals" on page 223.

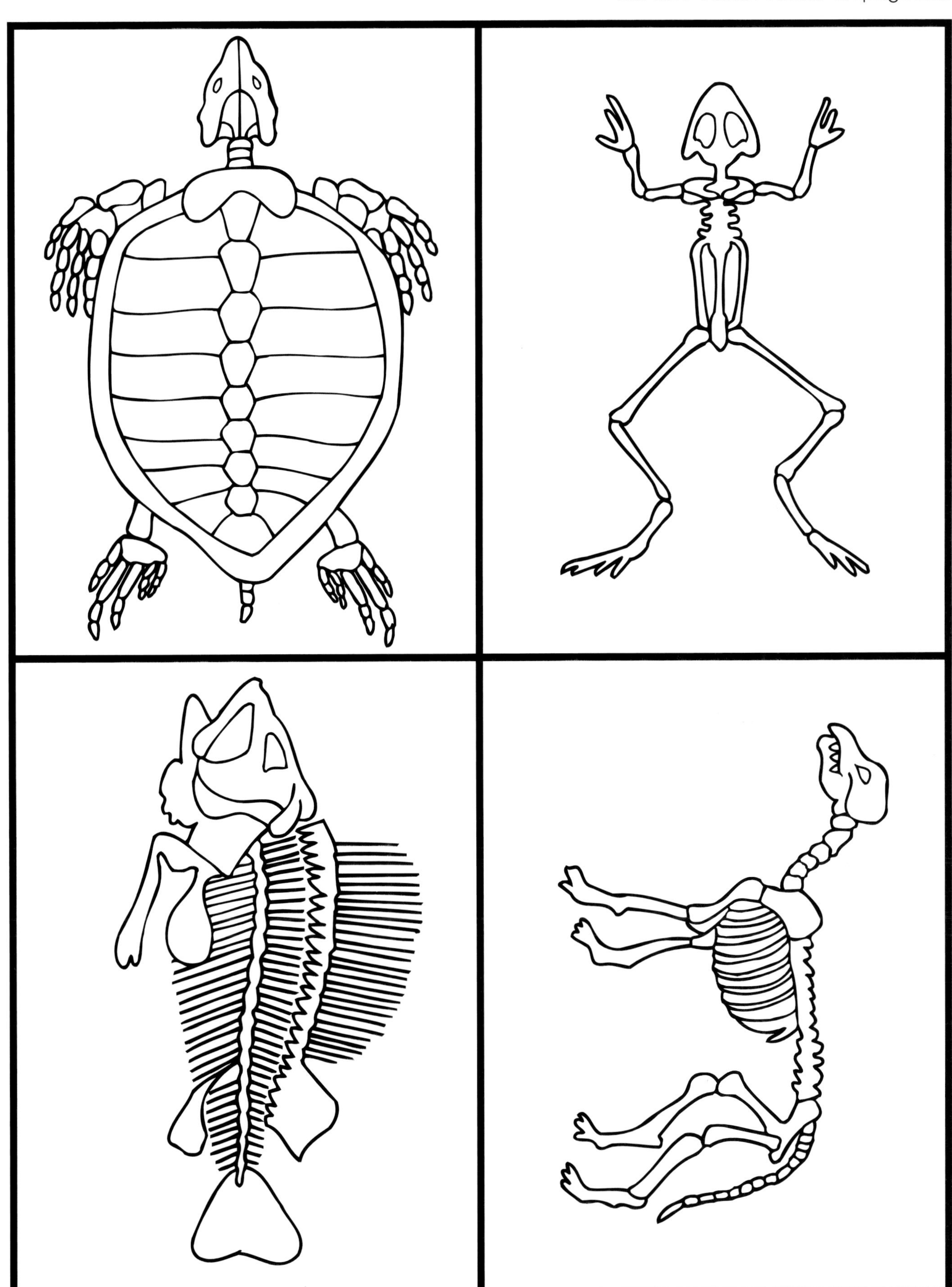

Animal Cards

Use with "Inside Animals" on page 223.

Tasty Sounds at the Bakery

Let cookies, muffins, pies, and other bakery sweets help make learning about onsets a real treat!

by Lucia Kemp Henry, Fallon, NV

What's Cookin' at the Bakery?

Tasty treats of all kinds are found at a bakery, promoting lots of initial sound identification! Invite your youngsters to help you highlight the names of baked goods with this brainstorming activity. First, cut a large sheet of chart paper into the shape of a bread loaf. Title the chart "What's Cookin' at the Bakery?" Then prompt students to generate a list of baked goods they've eaten or seen at a bakery. Use a black marker to write the names on the chart. Next, have volunteers use a red marker to circle the onset of each word. Complete the activity by leading the group in an oral review of each word and its onset. Sounds yummy, doesn't it?

Our Big Bakery Book

This class-made big book will surely be a hit with your kindergartners! Give each child a sheet of white construction paper that has been trimmed to fit inside a large cardboard sheet cake box donated by a neighborhood bakery. Have each child revisit the chart from "What's Cookin' at the Bakery?" on this page and pick a delicious item she would like to bake! Instruct the child to draw and color a picture of her item on the paper. Then have her write the name of the item on the paper, highlighting the onset with a yellow marker. Have each child dictate a sentence about her item. Stack students' papers between construction paper covers and staple them together. Put the bakery book inside the cake box and display it in your housekeeping center along with a variety of aprons, bowls, spoons, and other baking tools. Encourage each child to read the book to find baking inspiration that's just right for dramatic play. What a tasty reading treat!

Sorting Baked Goods

This sorting activity will have youngsters grouping baked goods according to their onsets. Mix up a large batch of your favorite salt dough and invite each of your budding bakers to model a breadstick, cookie, bagel, or pie slice. Have each child brush his dough creation with water and then sprinkle it with sesame seeds, kosher salt, or cookie sprinkles. Bake the mock bakery items until golden brown. When cool, direct each child to glue his faux baked good on a paper plate. Display the plates of pretend goods on a table. Then have students sort the treats according to their onsets. Display a sign nearby that says “Sounds Good Enough to Eat!”

Cookie Sound Sort

What’s one of the most popular treats made at a bakery? Cookies, of course! Follow these directions to prepare a batch of pretend cookies for use with this initial-sound-sorting activity. Use the round cookie pattern on page 232 to make a tracer. Trace the circle on colored paper to make a large supply of cookie shapes. Cut out each cookie and glue clear glitter sprinkles along the edge of each one. Reproduce the onset picture cards on pages 233 and 234. To complete each cookie, cut out an onset picture and glue it to the center of the cookie. Then glue a piece of felt to the back of each one to prepare it for flannelboard use. Begin the activity by inviting your group to join you at the flannelboard. Display several cookies on the board. Next, say a word, emphasizing the beginning sound. Direct students to find the cookie with a picture of an item that begins with the same sound; then have the class isolate and recite the onset for the word. Continue the activity for the onsets of your choice.

Cookie Sorting Center

Cook up independent sound-sorting success with this center idea. First, label each of two cookie sheets with a different letter. Select a pair of letters, such as *C* and *G.* Place the cookie sheets at a center along with a spatula and a cookie tin. Also place at the center a selection of cookies used in “Cookie Sound Sort” on this page, including cookies with onset pictures for *C* and *G* and a few cookies that do not represent either onset. Have each child sort the *C* and *G* cookies into two piles and then have her use the spatula to place each cookie on the appropriate cookie sheet. Have the child put the cookies that don’t belong on either sheet in the cookie tin. To extend the center, change the cookies and cookie sheet labels to feature different pairs of onsets. Ding! These cookies are done!

Sound Bites

Have your youngsters mix onsets with rimes to bake up plates of words with this matching activity. To prepare, use the cookie pattern on page 232 to make cookie shapes and then cut them out. Then use a pencil to lightly trace a curved line near one side of each cookie. Cut along the line with scalloped decorative scissors to take a bite-shaped piece out of each cookie. Use a marker to program each "bite" with an onset and each cookie with a rime so that when put together the two pieces make a word. Store the cookies and bite pieces in a cookie tin. Place a supply of small paper plates and the cookie tin at a center. To use the center, have each child put each cookie word puzzle together on a plate to make a word. To the right is a list of simple rimes on which you may wish to focus.

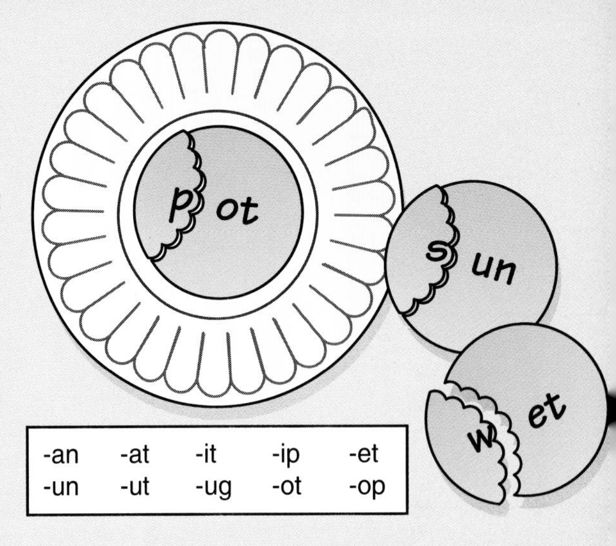

-an	-at	-it	-ip	-et
-un	-ut	-ug	-ot	-op

Muffin Match

More muffins mean more matching opportunities for your sound-savvy students! Trace or photocopy the muffin pattern on page 231 on tan construction paper to make a supply. Cut out each muffin. Glue an onset picture card from pages 233 and 234 to each muffin bottom. Program the top of each muffin with the onset of the item in the picture. Then cut each muffin along the line that separates the muffin top and bottom. Have each student match each muffin top with the appropriate muffin bottom. Later, have each child make her own set of muffin-matching materials to take home. Muffin /m/!

Muffin-Making Basics

Mix up this muffin game to have youngsters sorting pictures by onset! Use the muffin pattern on page 231 to make a tracer. Trace 12 muffin shapes on tan construction paper or card stock and cut them out. Glue a different onset picture card from pages 233 and 234 to each muffin. Next, put paper muffin cup liners in a muffin pan, and use a marker to program the bottom of each cup with a letter to match each onset picture you have chosen. To use the center, a youngster places each muffin cutout in the appropriate cup in the pan. Muffins, anyone?

Slices of Pie

Finish this onset unit with an activity that features another classic bakery favorite—pie! Make one copy of the pie pattern on page 232 and cut it out. Write four words that begin with the same onset each on a separate section of the pie pattern and cut the four sections apart. Next, tape a matching onset picture card from pages 233 and 234 to the bottom of a disposable eight-inch aluminum pie pan. Make several sets of pie puzzles, each featuring a different onset. Then mix the pie slices and put them at a center along with the pie pans. Have student bakers sort the slices and place them in the proper pans. Wow, this phonics fun was as easy as pie!

Cookie Pattern

Use with "Cookie Sound Sort" on page 230 and "Sound Bites" on page 231.

Muffin Pattern

Use with "Muffin Match" and "Muffin-Making Basics" on page 231.

Pie Pattern

Use with "Slices of Pie" on page 231.

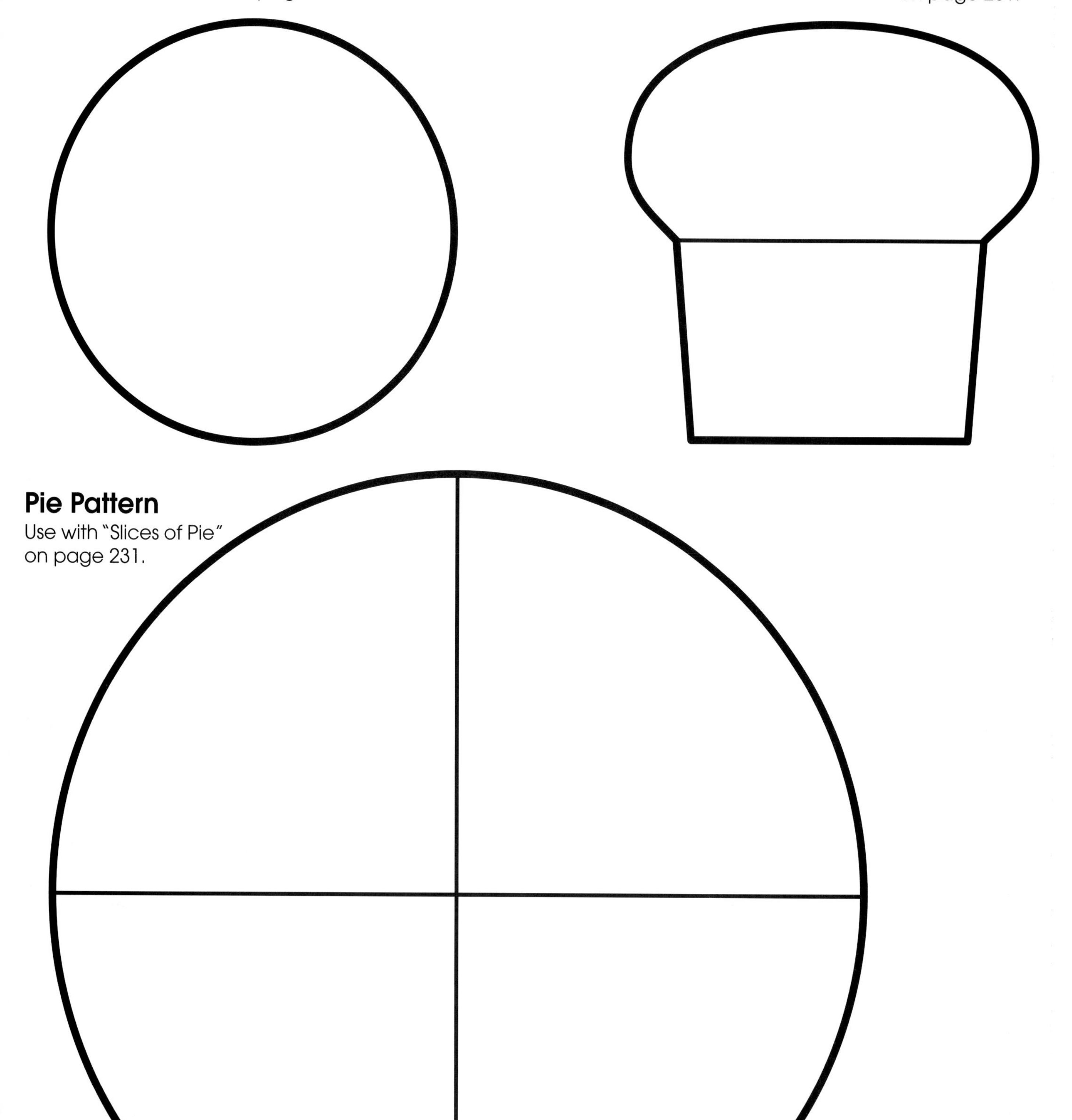

Onset Picture Cards

Use with "Cookie Sound Sort" on page 230 and "Muffin Match," "Muffin-Making Basics," and "Slices of Pie" on page 231.

Onset Picture Cards

Use with "Cookie Sound Sort" on page 230 and "Muffin Match," "Muffin-Making Basics," and "Slices of Pie" on page 231.

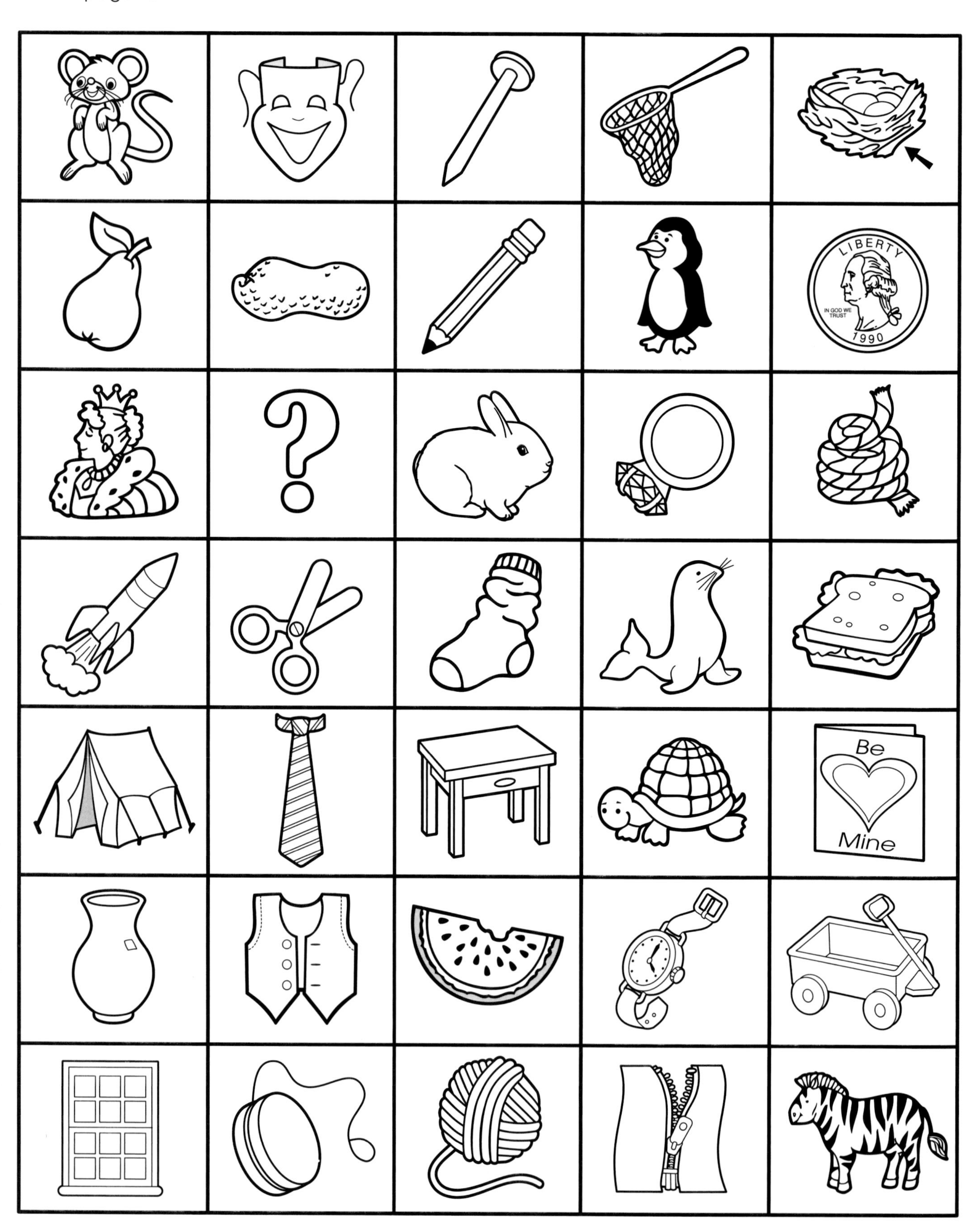

A GATHERING OF GUINEA PIGS

Count on this set of guinea pig–themed math activities to boost your pet-loving youngsters' knowledge of number concepts!

by Lucia Kemp Henry, Fallon, NV

Counting objects up to ten

Counting Guinea Pigs

Kick off your numeration unit with a flannelboard activity featuring ten appealing guinea pigs. Prior to the activity, make five copies of the guinea pig patterns on page 238 on brown, tan, and white construction paper. Cut out the guinea pigs and prepare them for flannelboard use. Make a set of numeral cards, each labeled with a different number from 1 to 10. To begin, put two guinea pigs on the flannelboard. Cover them with a large piece of fabric so that only the noses of the guinea pigs are showing. Then invite your group to gather near the board by saying, "How many guinea pigs can there be? Let's count the guinea pigs and we'll see!"

Have youngsters guess how many critters are hiding; then remove the fabric. Instruct students to count the guinea pigs. Have a volunteer select the numeral card that matches the set of guinea pigs. Have youngsters repeat the activity with different sets of guinea pigs.

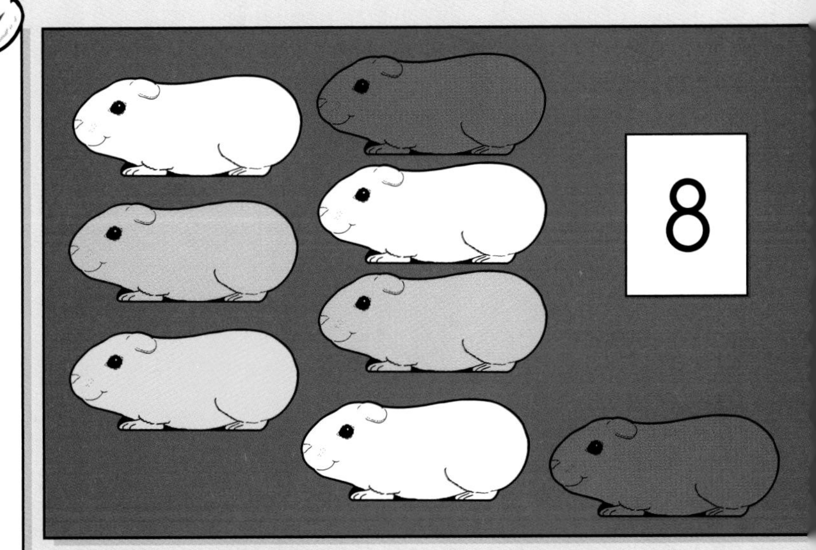

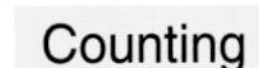

Counting

Potato-Print Pets

Making sets of perky guinea pig pets will keep your youngsters counting! Set out pans of black, tan, and gray paint, along with a supply of potatoes cut in half lengthwise. Place flash cards for the numerals 1 through 5 in a bag. Have each child draw a card from the bag and then use a potato half to print a matching number of guinea pig bodies on a 9" x 12" sheet of white construction paper. When the prints are dry, have each student use a black marker to add eyes, feet, a mouth, and a nose to each guinea pig. Then instruct her to glue a construction paper ear to each guinea pig. Next, encourage youngsters to place paintings with the same number of guinea pigs together in a stack. Later, display each group of pictures on a wall or bulletin board and label each group with a large numeral card. Then use the abundant number of guinea pigs for counting practice and to inspire a discussion of *alike* and *different.*

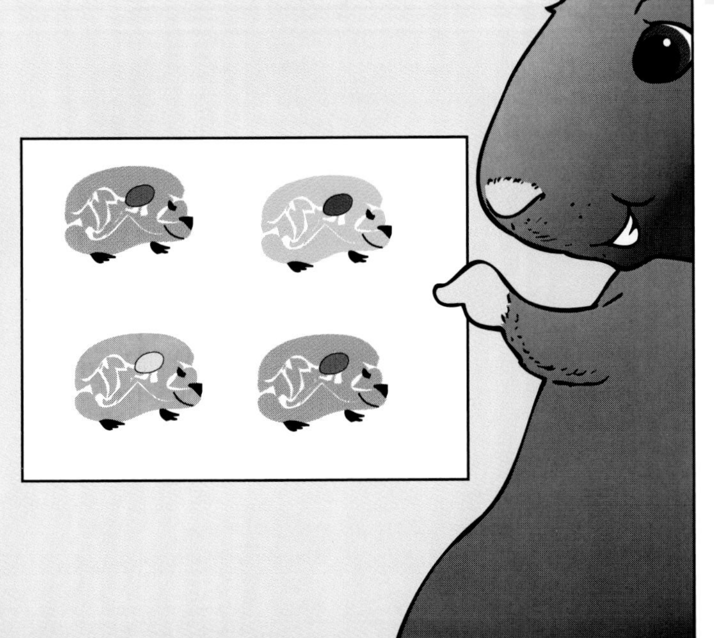

Counting
Graphing

Graphing Guinea Pigs

More counting opportunities occur when your little ones graph the kinds of guinea pigs they like the best. Make a long horizontal graph on white bulletin board paper. Divide the graph into five sections as shown. Use a crayon to draw and label each section with a swatch of guinea pig fur in black, tan, white, black-and-white, and tan-and-white. Photocopy page 238 so that each child will have one guinea pig pattern. Have each child use crayons to color her pattern with one of the five fur colors or color combinations. Next, have youngsters predict which color of guinea pig will be the most popular. Then invite each child to graph her guinea pig according to color. Top off the activity by having students use the data on the graph for counting and comparison tasks. Way to graph guinea pigs!

Counting
Comparing sets

Guinea Pig Grub

Guinea pigs like to eat crunchy, colorful foods like carrot sticks and apple slices. Use this information and the food card patterns on page 239 to have youngsters count and compare sets. To prepare, make ten white copies of page 239. Color, laminate, and then cut out the cards. Place the food cards in an empty, plastic, guinea pig food container. Place a set of number cards and the food container in the center of a table. Invite a pair of youngsters to join you. In turn, have each child draw a number card from the deck. Prompt each child to read the numeral and place a matching number of food cards on the table. Have youngsters compare their sets using the terms *more than* and *less than.* Mmmm, great guinea pig grub!

Counting to ten
Recognizing numerals from 1 to 10

Carrot Count

Reinforce numeral recognition and counting skills with this center idea. Cut 55 small carrot sticks from orange craft foam; then place them in a clean plastic carrot bag. Make ten construction paper copies of the food dish pattern on page 240. (Save the cage-base patterns for "Mini Guinea Pig Counting" on page 237.) Color and cut out the dishes. Label each dish with a different number from 1 to 10. Put the bag of carrots and the food dishes at a center. Then direct each child who uses the center to fill each food dish with the appropriate number of carrot sticks. Yummy mealtime math!

Problem solving

Pet Food Problems

Why do little ones enjoy having guinea pigs in the classroom? It's fun to feed them! Invite students to give faux food to pretend guinea pigs and practice one-to-one correspondence at the same time. Make two to three copies of the guinea pig food cards on page 239. Color and cut out the cards or use the food cards from "Guinea Pig Grub" on page 236. Make five copies of the large guinea pig patterns on page 238. Color the patterns, as desired and cut them out. Then invite a small group of students to use the patterns to solve math problems similar to those below. It's dinnertime!

- There are 8 guinea pigs. One guinea pig wants a carrot and the rest of them want apple slices. How many apple slices do you need?
- There are 2 guinea pigs. They both want a carrot and an apple slice. How many pieces of food do you need all together?
- There are 5 guinea pigs. Two of them want a carrot and 2 want an apple slice. One guinea pig wants an apple slice and a carrot. How many carrots and how many apple slices will you need?

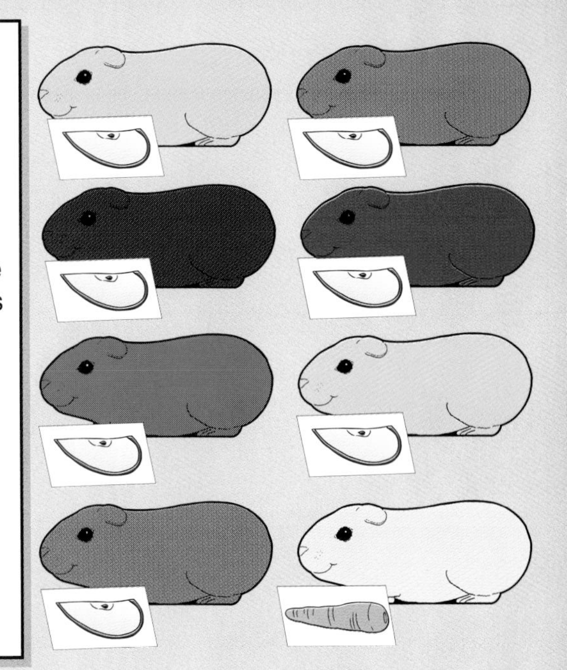

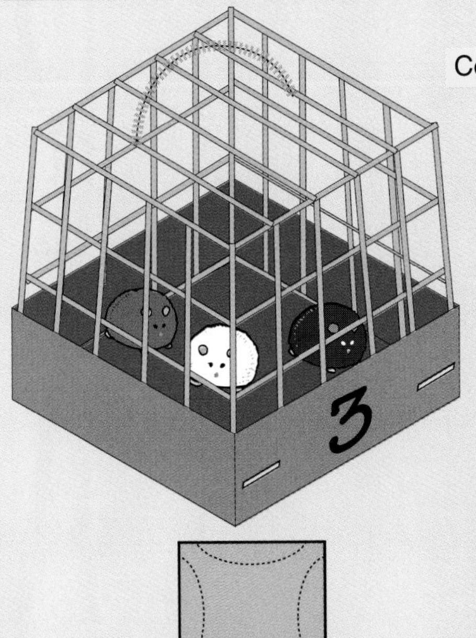

Counting to ten

Mini Guinea Pig Counting

Counting practice is lots of fun when its done with mini guinea pigs and itsy-bitsy critter cages! To make a mini guinea pig, gather a one-inch black, brown, or white pom-pom, or a cotton ball; black, white, and pink dimensional paint; and a 3/4" square of pink craft foam. Cut the foam square to mimic four feet as shown. Glue the foam feet to a pom-pom. Use dimensional paint to give the pom-pom critter two tiny eyes and a small pink nose. Use tacky craft glue to add two round paper-punch ears to the mini guinea pig, if desired. You will need 55 mini guinea pigs for the activity. Next, gather ten plastic mesh berry baskets. Add a pipe cleaner to the bottom of each basket, as shown, to create the handle. Make ten copies of the cage-base pattern on page 240 or use those saved from "Carrot Count" on page 236. Cut out each pattern along the bold outer lines and then along the dashed lines. Fold along each remaining line where indicated to create a tray-style cage base. Staple the corners of the base to secure the flaps. Then label each cage base with a different numeral from 1 to 10. Set a berry-basket cage inside each labeled base. Place the cages and guinea pigs in your math center. To use the center, encourage students to place the corresponding number of mini guinea pigs inside each numbered cage.

Counting to 15
Writing numerals

Guinea Pig Getaway Game

Extend the use of the pom-pom guinea pigs and cages from "Mini Guinea Pig Counting" on this page with this great escape game! You will need 30 mini guinea pigs, two unlabeled cages, a die, paper, and pencils. To set up a game for two players, put 15 mini guinea pigs in each cage. Place the cages and supplies at a center. To play, direct each child, in turn, to roll the die, count the dots, and write the matching numeral on scrap paper. Next, have the child read the number out loud and then count and remove the corresponding number of guinea pigs from his cage and place them next to the number on his paper. Play continues until each player's cage is empty. Instruct youngsters to put the guinea pigs back in their cages for the next round. Your little ones will have tons of fun helping little guinea pigs escape from their cages!

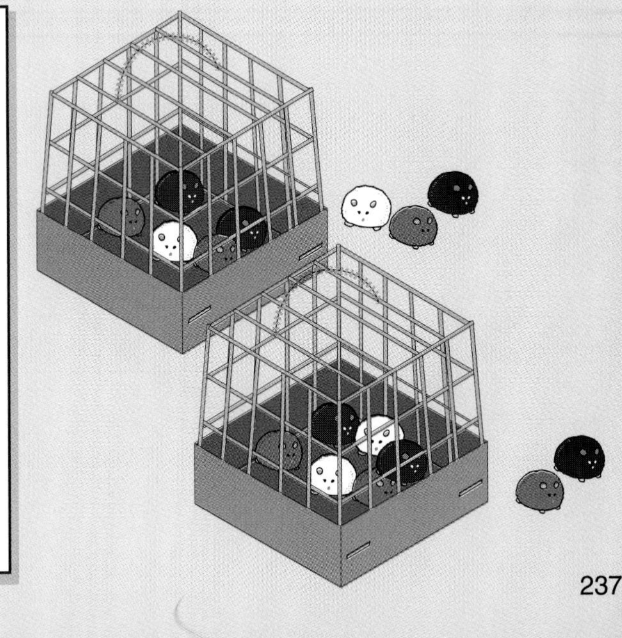

Guinea Pig Patterns

Use with "Counting Guinea Pigs" on page 235, "Graphing Guinea Pigs" on page 236, and "Pet Food Problems" on page 237.

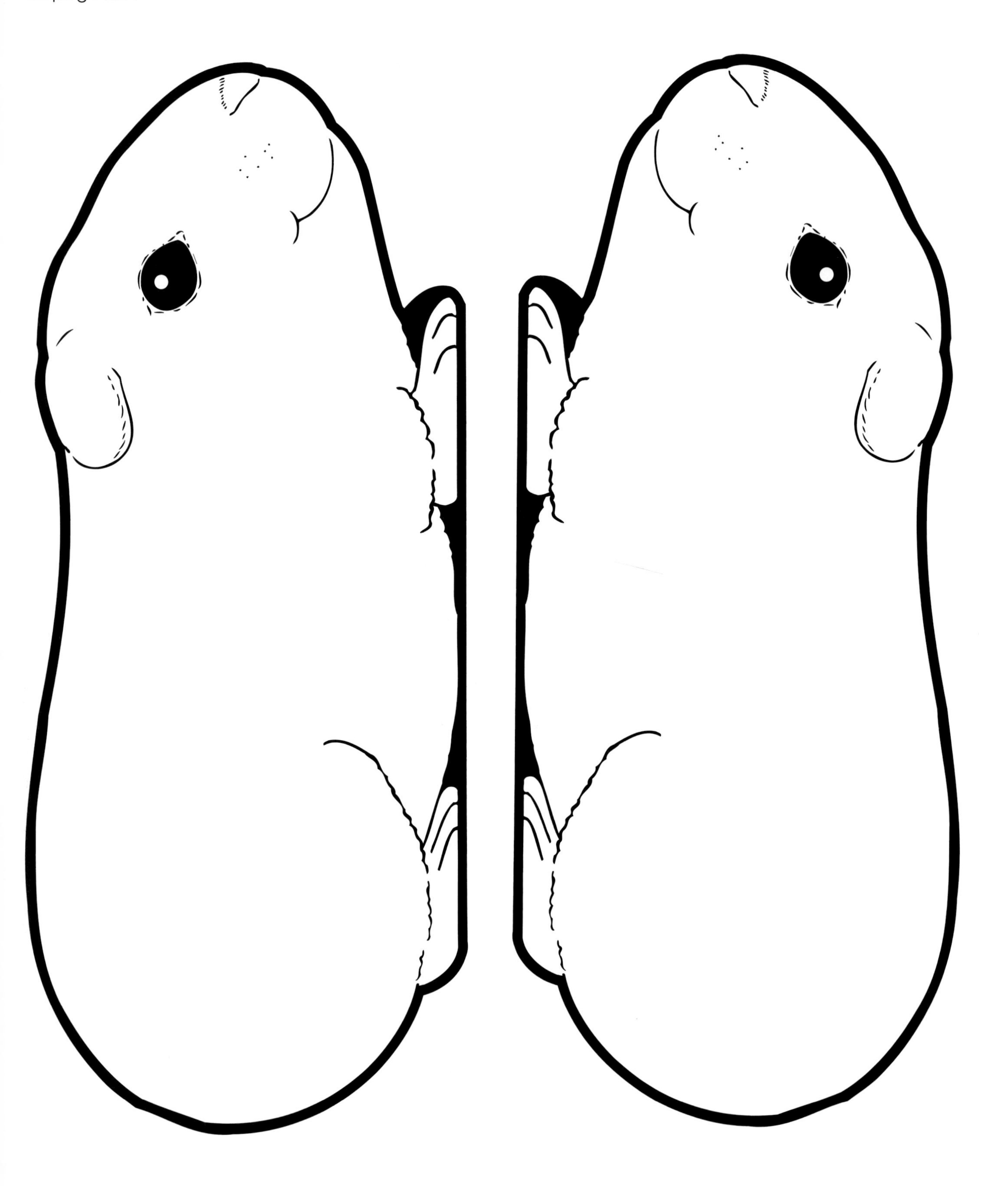

Food Cards

Use with "Guinea Pig Grub" on page 236 and "Pet Food Problems" on page 237.

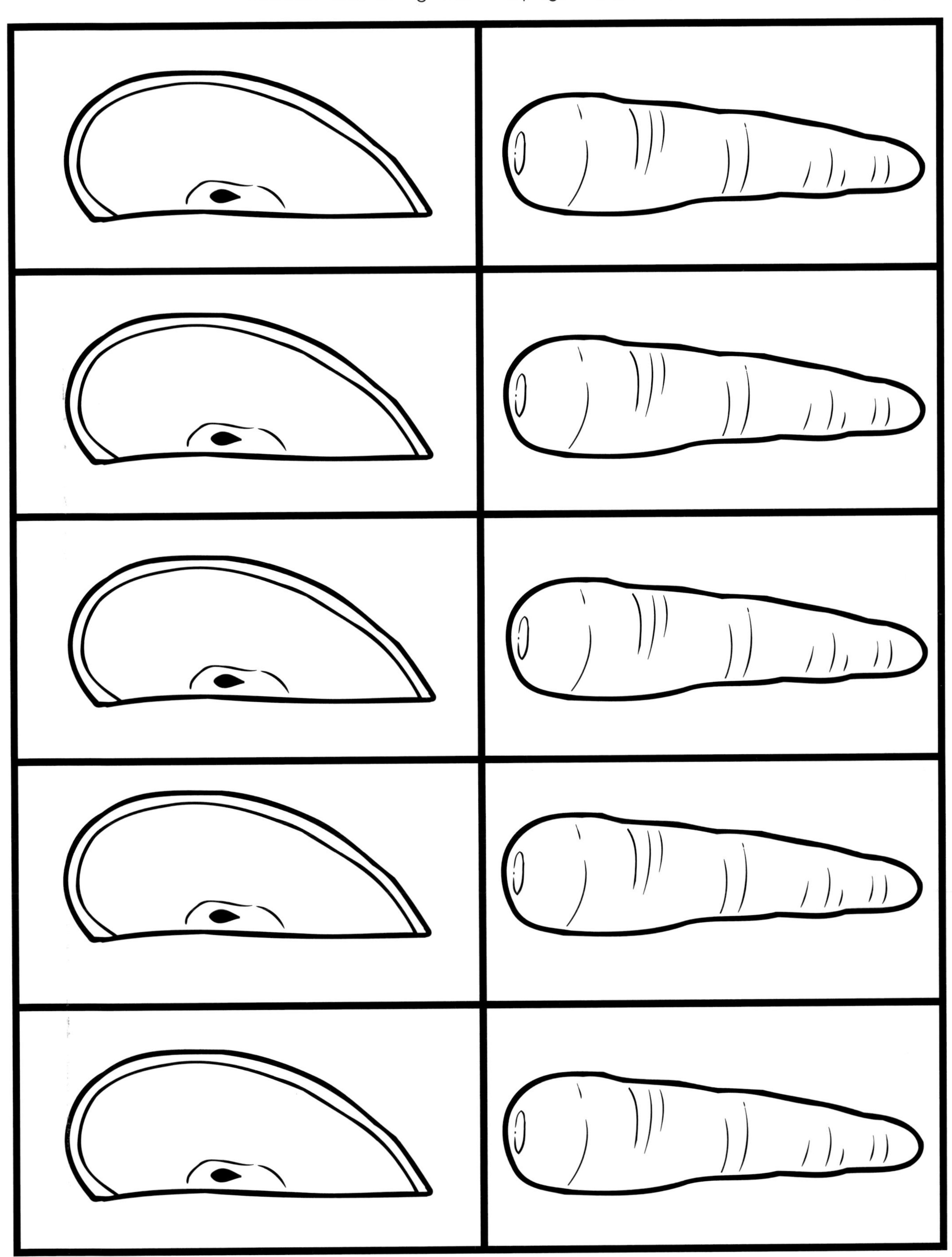

Food Dish Pattern

Use with "Carrot Count" on page 236.

Cage-Base Pattern

Use with "Mini Guinea Pig Counting" and "Guinea Pig Getaway Game" on page 237.

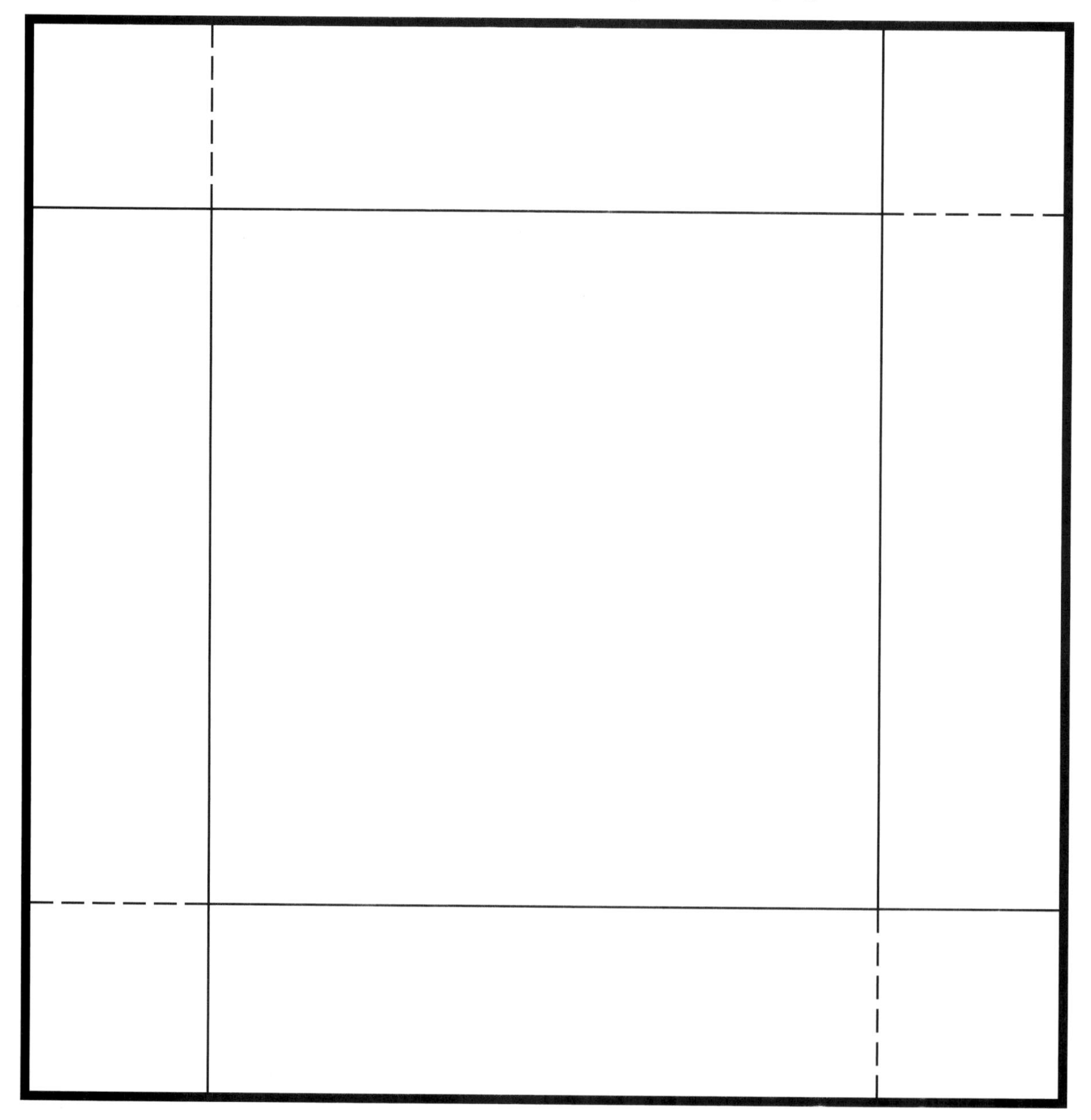

Let's Celebrate!

Happy Hanukkah, Merry Christmas, and Happy Kwanzaa! No matter what holiday your youngsters celebrate, you'll find ideas in this unit to make each holiday special!

Handy Dreidels

This simple art activity will make an attractive bulletin board display and inspire your youngsters to spin, spin, spin a dreidel! To prepare, cut a 6" x 6" piece of white construction paper for each child. Pour a thin layer of blue tempera paint in a shallow pan. Help each child dip his hand into the paint and then make a print on his paper. Then have him dip his index finger into the paint and make a print at the base of his palm print as shown. After the paint has dried, use silver glitter paint to write the Hebrew letter *heh* on each print. Have each youngster cut out his dreidel print. Staple the dreidels to a bulletin board and then draw spinning-motion lines around each one. Title the display "Spin, Spin, Spin the Dreidel!"

Lisa Crystal—Gr. K, Bret Harte Elementary School, Burbank, CA

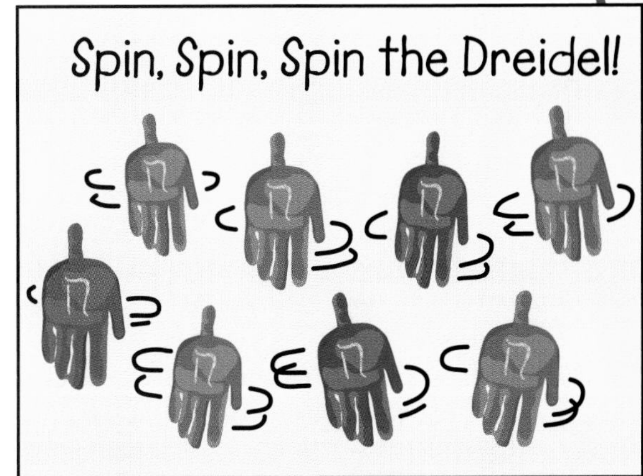

Necktie Menorah

This flannelboard menorah will be just what you need to help celebrate Hanukkah! In advance, request donations of old neckties from parents and friends, or purchase them from a thrift store. To make a *menorah* for your flannelboard, cut a sheet of gray felt as shown. To make the candles, cut the center 12 inches from each of eight neckties. Slide a strip of cardboard into each tie piece to give it shape. Use hot glue to close the ends and then glue a hook-side Velcro piece to the back of each candle so it will cling to your flannelboard. To make the *shammash* (the candle used for lighting the other candles), cut 15 inches from the center of a tie and then finish it as you did the other eight candles. Cut nine flames out of red felt. On each day, pretend to light a candle with the *shammash* by placing a flame atop one of the candles. Happy Hanukkah!

Janice McCarthy—Gr. K, Bicycle Path PreK–K Center, Selden, NY

A Dreidel Snack

This sweet treat will make your youngsters spin! Provide each child with a paper plate, a large marshmallow, a Hershey's Kisses candy, a pretzel stick, and access to blue-tinted vanilla frosting that has been heated slightly to thin it. Have each child push her pretzel into one end of her marshmallow. Then instruct her to hold the pretzel stick handle and dip her marshmallow in frosting. Have her unwrap her Hershey's Kisses candy and place its flat side on the bottom of the marshmallow. Invite her to spin her *dreidel* into her mouth!

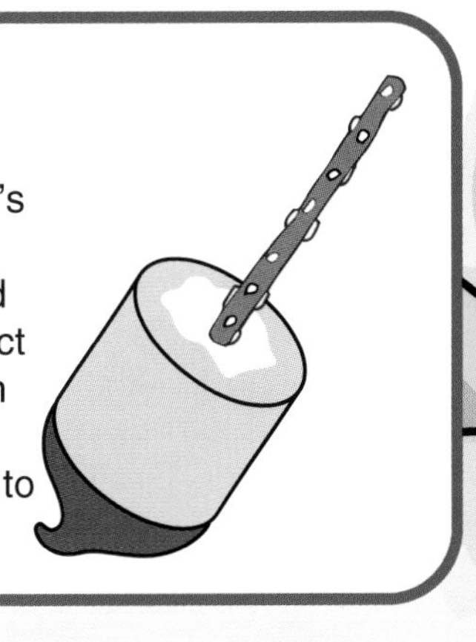

Christmas Tree Costume

This festive tree costume is sure to be a hit at your holiday program! Gather the supplies listed below and then follow the directions to make these simple costumes. Oh Christmas tree!

Materials needed for one costume:

white poster board	circular sponge	scissors
green tempera paint	tinsel	tagboard
red tempera paint	glue	
blue tempera paint	heavy tape	
yellow tempera paint	hole puncher	
triangular sponge	yarn	

Directions:

1. Draw a tree shape on the poster board.
2. Have a child use the triangular sponge and green paint to sponge-paint the tree. Allow the paint to dry.
3. Have the child use the circular sponge and various colors of paint to make ornament prints on the tree.
4. Cut out the tree, dividing it into two pieces.
5. Glue strands of tinsel to the base of the tree as shown.
6. Add a tagboard headband to each tree's top.
7. Add a strip of heavy tape to the top of the tree's bottom; then punch four holes near its top where indicated.
8. Lace yarn through the holes as shown, leaving enough length for tying the ends.

Sheli Gossett—Gr. K, Avon Elementary School, Avon Park, FL

Paper-Chain Tree

This crafty Christmas tree gets your classroom decorated for the holiday and displays the paper ornaments your students make! In advance, cut a large supply of green bulletin board paper strips. Demonstrate for students how to use the strips and glue to make a paper chain. Then have each child make a long chain. (Make sure each chain is the same length and will reach from ceiling to floor.) Attach one end of each chain to a 12-inch embroidery hoop. Then use fishing line to hang the hoop from the ceiling. Attach the opposite end of each chain to a Hula-Hoop toy positioned on the floor. If desired, tape garland to the hoops as shown to disguise them. Attach paper ornaments made by students using tape, glue, or staples. Beautiful!

Rachel R. Pasichow—PreK–1
P. S. 235 Early Childhood Center, Brooklyn, NY

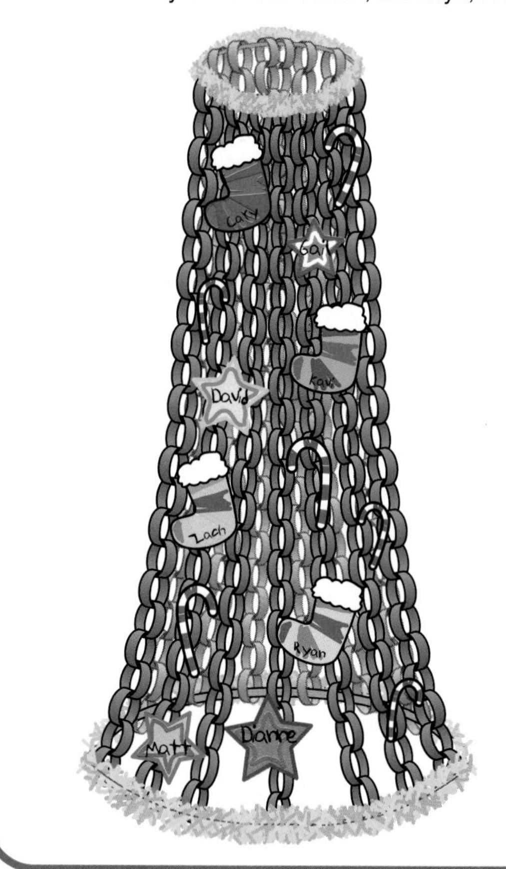

Santa Snack

Four ingredients is all you'll need for this kid-friendly recipe! Purchase Nutter Butter cookies, vanilla frosting, M&M's Minis candies, and mini white chocolate chips. Tint half of the frosting with red food coloring. Gather a paper plate and plastic knife for each child. Arrange the ingredients and supplies for easy student access. Have each youngster spread half his cookie with white frosting and the other half with red frosting. Instruct him to add three M&M's Minis candies for his Santa's eyes and nose. Then have him add a mini white chocolate chip to the red half to represent the pom-pom on Santa's hat. Your youngsters are sure to have a ho-ho-whole lot of fun decorating these cookies!

Handprint Kinara

These *kinaras* will be as unique as your students because they are made with their handprints! To prepare, gather brown, red, black, green, and yellow paint; paint brushes; and a 9" x 12" sheet of white construction paper for each child. Fold each sheet of construction paper in half. Working with one child at a time, paint his left palm and four fingers with a generous amount of brown paint. Help him position his hand on the paper so that his index finger makes a print along the fold. Refold the paper to transfer the print to the other side; then unfold it. Next, paint his finger with a generous amount of red, black, or green paint and help him make prints for candles as shown. Finally, instruct him to dip his finger in yellow paint and make a print at the top of each candle to represent the flame. Wow, these *kinaras* are bright, beautiful, and unique!

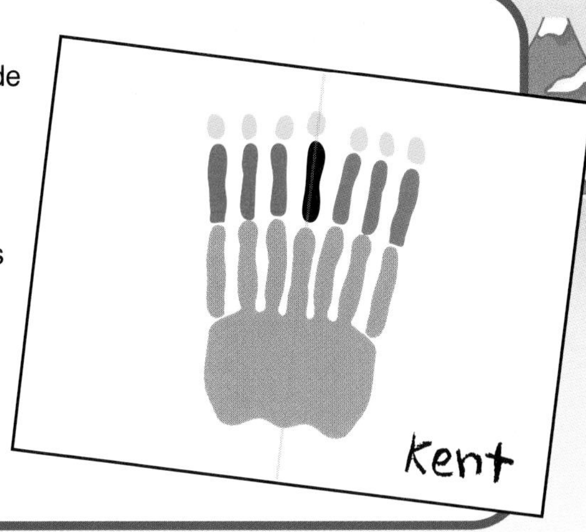

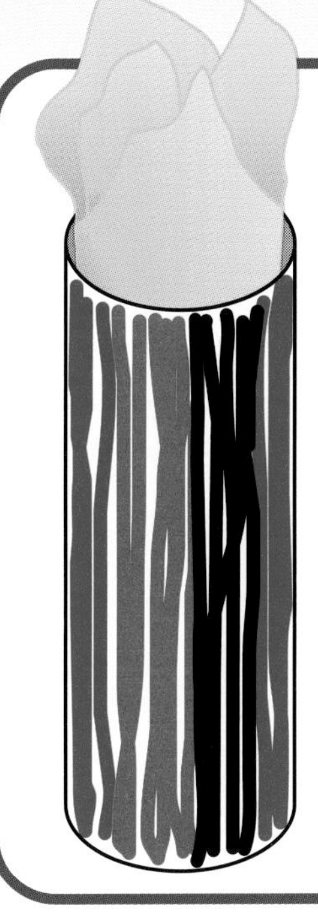

Crafty Candles

Your students will love making these special candle crafts, especially when they learn that a treat for them has been placed inside! In advance, collect a class supply of toilet paper tubes. Provide each child with a $4^{1}/_{2}$" x $6^{1}/_{2}$" piece of paper and red, black, and green markers or crayons. Instruct her to color her entire paper, creating a pattern with the three colors. Tape her patterned paper around a tube. To make the flame, place a small treat in the center of a 12" piece of yellow tissue paper. Gather the corners of the tissue and twist the ends together. Slip the flame into the tube so that the twisted end sticks out of the top. All done!

Harvest Snack

Your little ones will be eager to make one of these sweet corn treats for Kwanzaa! Gather the ingredients, utensils, and supplies listed below. Then help each child follow the directions to make his own harvest snack.

Ingredients needed for one snack:
Nutter Butter cookie
vanilla frosting tinted yellow
2 leaf-shaped pieces of green Fruit Roll-Ups Snacks

Utensils and supplies per child:
paper plate
plastic knife

Directions:

1. Spread a cookie with frosting.
2. Use your knife to score the frosting in a grid pattern to look like corn kernels.
3. Put a piece of Fruit Roll-Up Snack on each side of the cookie to represent the corn husks.

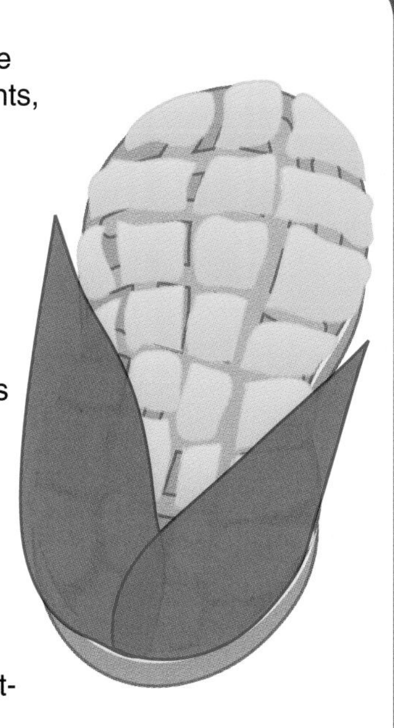

Hats Off to Community Helpers

From firefighters to veterinarians—introduce your kindergartners to community helpers with the activities in this clever unit.

by Rhonda L. Chiles, South Park Elementary, Shawnee Mission, KS

Getting to Know Community Helpers

Promote exploration and dramatic play by creating community-helper boxes. In advance, gather the items listed below to create several community-helper boxes. Then lead students to list community helpers in your area. Talk about each helper's job and items related to the job. Next, divide students into small groups. Give each group a community-helper box. Instruct students to explore the items and decide to which helper they belong. Then invite each group to share the items in its box to highlight the special features of the community helper. After the discussions, place the boxes in your dramatic-play area for role-playing during center time. Toothbrush, dental floss, and an X ray—these things belong to a dentist!

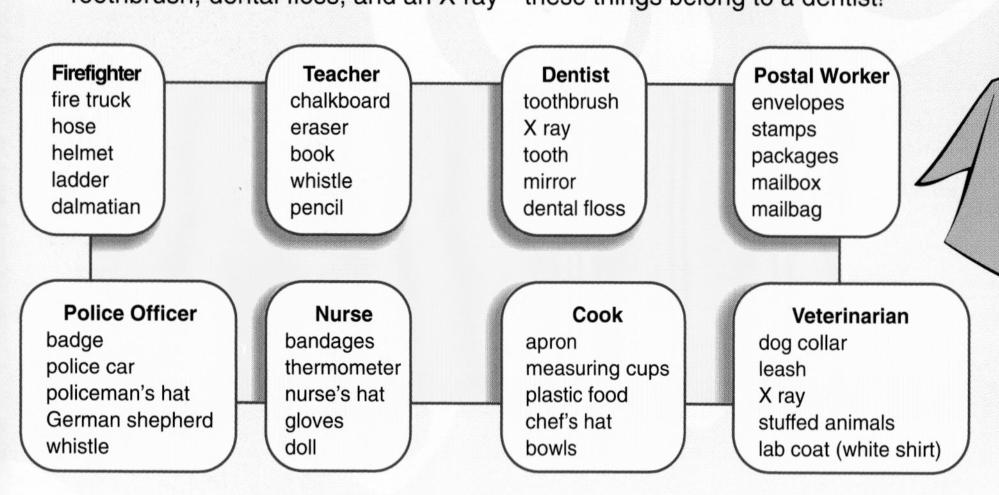

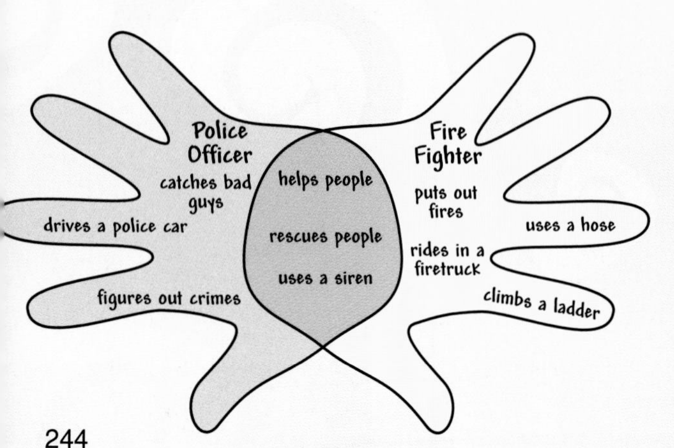

Helping Hands Venn Diagram

Help youngsters learn the similarities and differences of various community helpers with this unique Venn diagram. Begin by tracing your hands on a sheet of transparency film so they overlap as shown. Project the image onto a screen. Label each hand with a different community helper. Have students discuss the similarities and differences between the professions and record responses on the diagram. Repeat the activity to compare more community helpers' jobs. Hands down, this is a great activity!

Tool Matchup

This matching game will have youngsters pairing community helpers with the tools they use on the job! In advance, cut out pictures of community helpers from discarded magazines and then glue each one to a separate index card. Then collect an item that each helper could use on the job, such as a book for a librarian, a toothbrush for a dentist, a tool belt for a builder, a stethoscope for a doctor, a letter for a mail carrier, or a stop sign for a crossing guard. Divide the class in half and give each youngster on one team a helper's picture and each child on the other team a helper's tool. On your cue, have students search for the child holding the matching helper card or tool. After all pairs have been made, invite youngsters to share their community-helper pictures and tools with the class. It's a match!

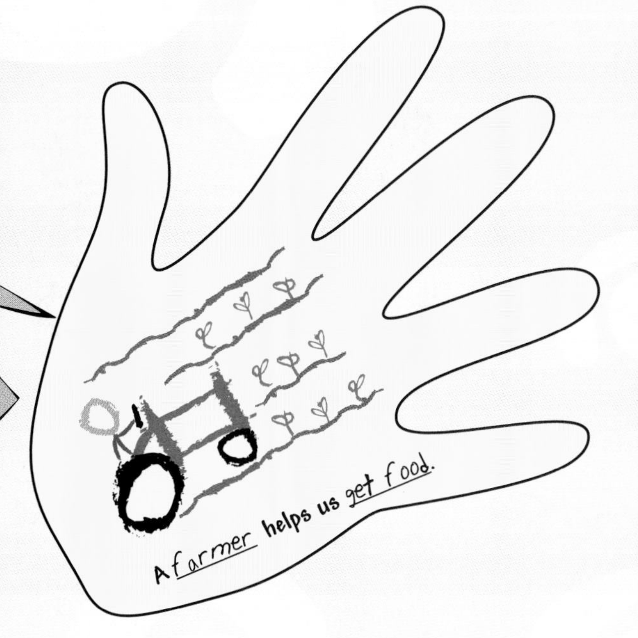

Helping Hands in Our Community

You can count on it—your students will certainly reach for this hand-shaped class book in your reading center! To prepare, trace your right hand in the center of a sheet of paper and then program it as shown. Increase it by 15 percent and make a class set. Distribute the copies and have each child choose a helper he would like to feature. Then help each child complete the sentence. Have him illustrate his page and then cut it out. Bind the completed pages between construction paper covers and title the book "Helping Hands in Our Community."

Community-Helpers Game

Your little ones will practice using descriptive language by playing this simple game. Make a copy of the gameboard on page 247 and color it as desired. Then laminate the gameboard for durability. Place the gameboard, two markers, and a die at a center. To play, have a pair of students take turns rolling the die and then moving their markers. When a youngster lands on a hand symbol, have her describe characteristics of the pictured profession next to the symbol and then tell how the person helps others in the community. Have youngsters continue to play until they each reach the end of the game. This game deserves a high five!

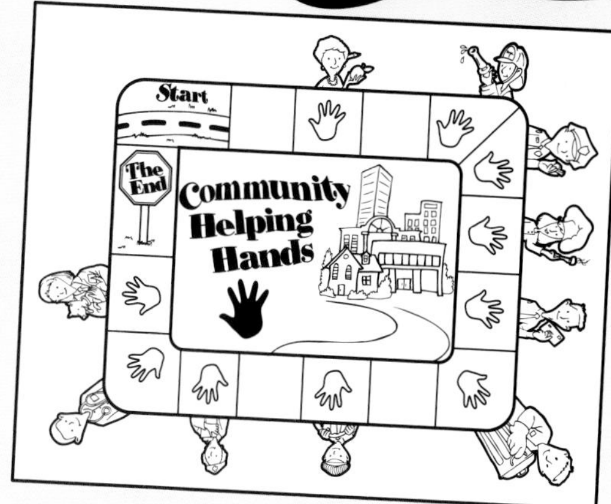

Community-Helpers Song

Teach youngsters this catchy song and then encourage them to help you think of other verses featuring different community helpers.

(sung to the tune of "Skip to My Lou")

Firefighters help in many ways,
Putting out fires every day,
To keep us safe throughout the day.
Firefighters help us every day!

Mail carriers help in many ways,
Picking up our mail every day,
Sending our letters on their way.
Mail carriers help us every day!

Teachers help in many ways,
Reading with children every day,
Teaching students throughout each day.
Teachers help us every day!

Policemen help in many ways,
Patrolling the streets every day,
To protect us as we work and play.
Policemen help us every day!

Helpers' Hat Graph

Work in some graphing practice with this idea for choosing a favorite community helper. Photocopy the hat patterns on pages 248 and 249 several times to make a supply that will allow youngsters to have the choice of a favorite community helper. Cut a $2\frac{3}{4}$ inch circle from flesh-toned construction paper for each child. Draw a graph on a length of bulletin board paper, as shown, and glue one hat pattern to each row. Review the duties of each community helper and then allow each student to choose a hat pattern that represents a career she would like to have as an adult. Give each child a circle and have her draw her face on it. Next, instruct her to color and cut out her hat pattern. Have her glue her hat to her self-portrait. Finally, in turn, invite each child to glue her portrait onto the graph, and then discuss the results.

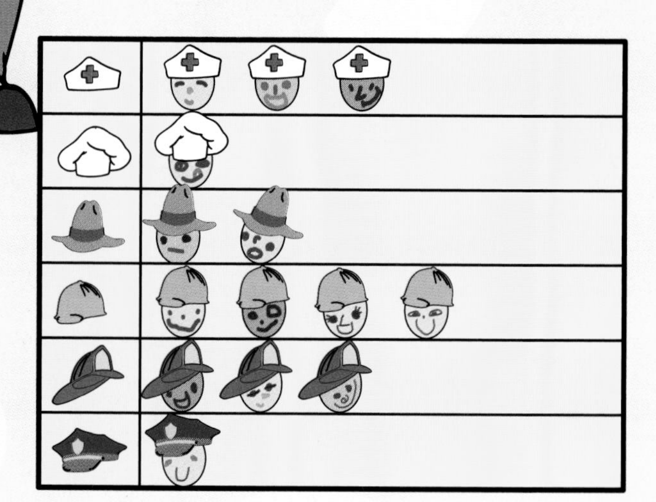

Helping-Hands Assessment

A flash of these puppets will let you know which students have learned facts about community helpers. Give each child a 9" x 12" sheet of construction paper. Have him trace his hands and then write "yes" on one shape and "no" on the other one. Instruct him to cut out the resulting shapes. Then help each youngster tape each hand shape to a craft stick. Next, say statements similar to those below. Instruct students to hold up the "yes" puppet if the statement is true and hold up the "no" puppet if the statement is false.

A community helper helps others.
A nurse drives a mail truck.
A teacher helps by teaching children to read.
A police officer can help a lost child.
A firefighter can use a ladder.
A cook wears a special badge.
A mail carrier delivers pizza.
A dentist shows us how to brush our teeth.
A plumber fixes cars.
Community helpers are an important part of our community.

Note to the teacher: Use with “Community Helpers’ Game” on page 245.

Hat Patterns

Use with "Helpers' Hat Graph" on page 246.

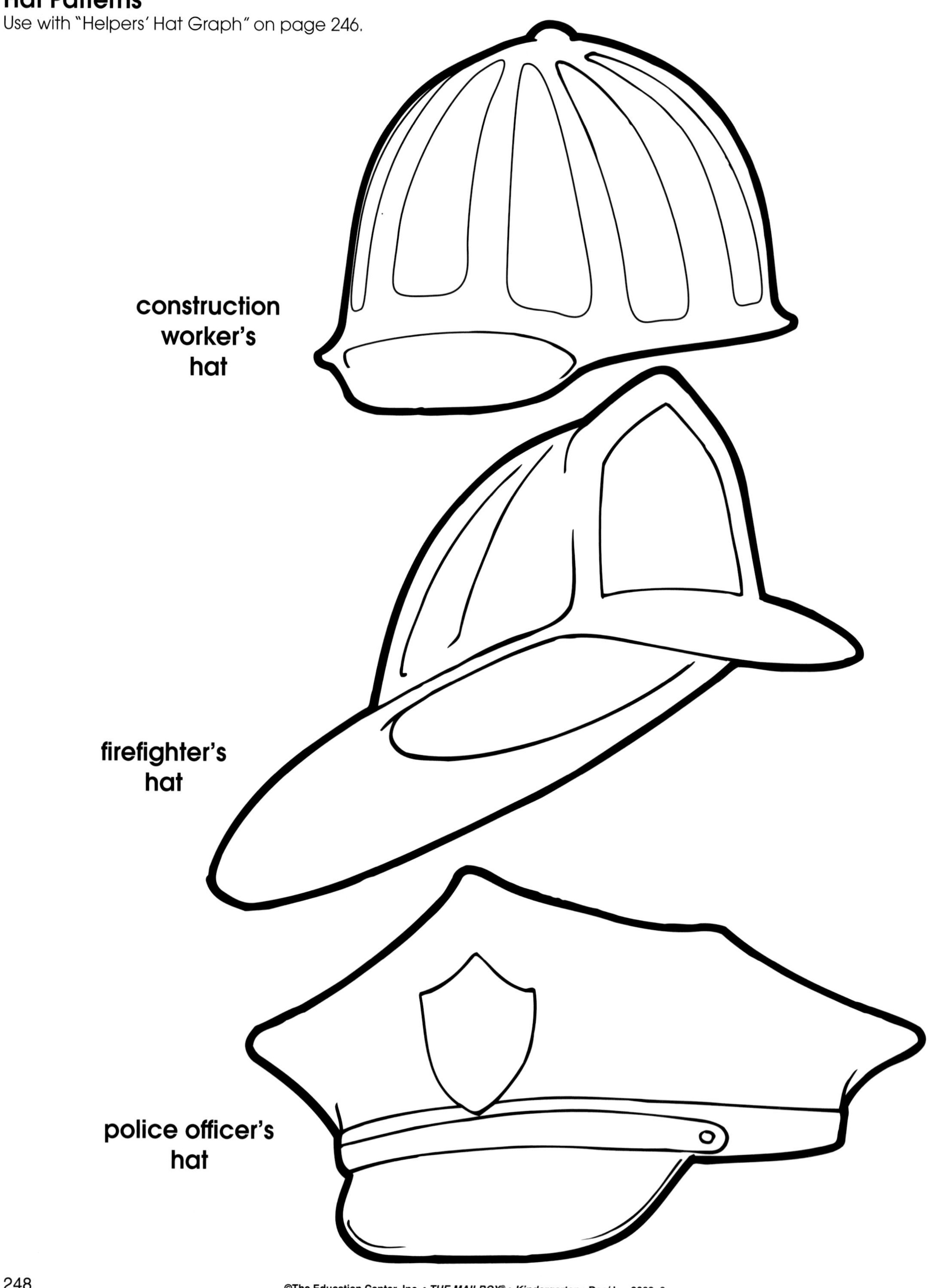

Hat Patterns

Use with "Helpers' Hat Graph" on page 246.

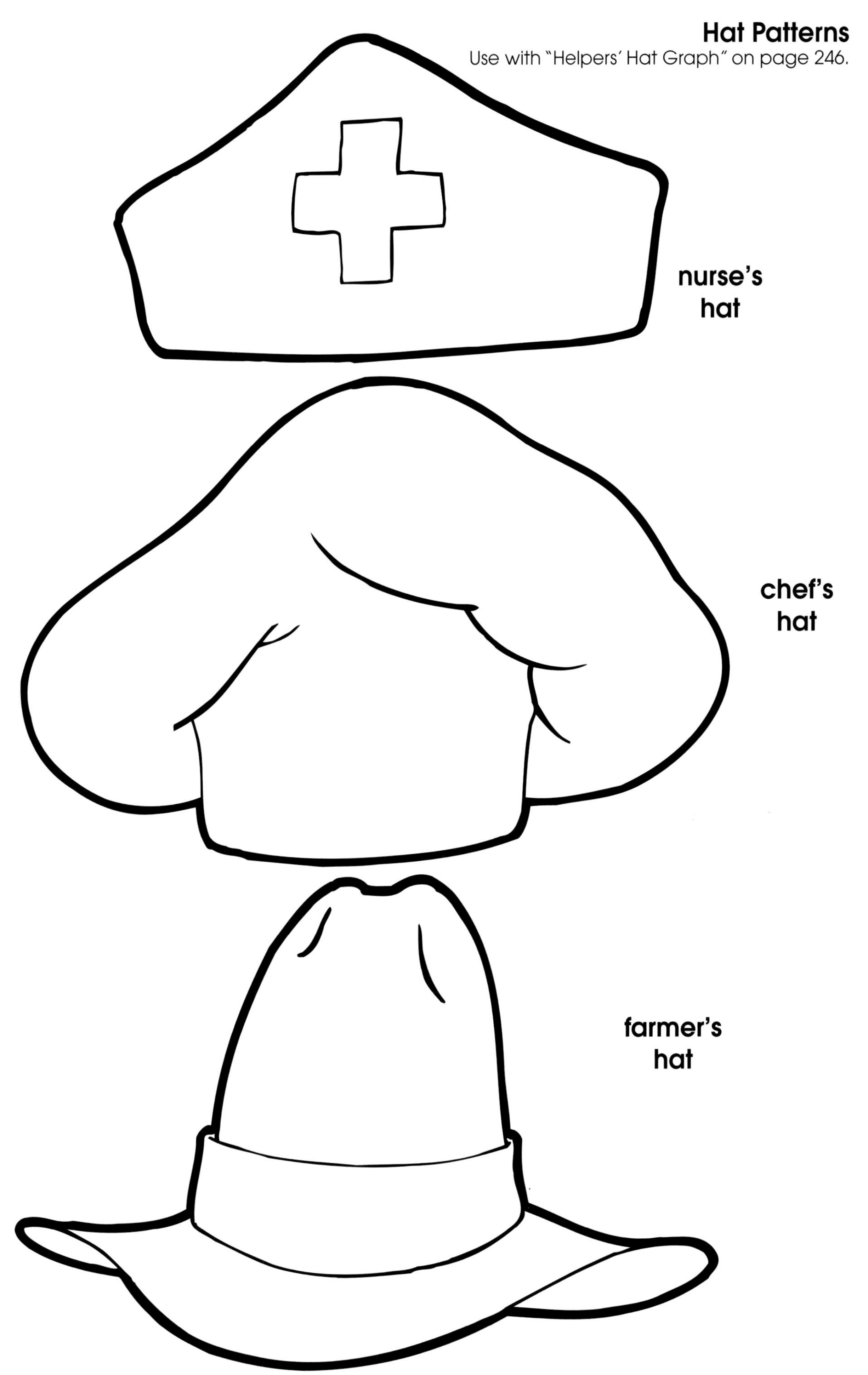

IT'S TOOTH TIME!

Your youngsters' toothy (or toothless) grins are sure to shine with the ideas in this dental health unit!

TOOTHY SMILES

This two-day activity will have your little ones learning the importance of brushing their teeth. On day one, have each child cut out two red construction paper lips, similar to those shown, and lots of white construction paper teeth. Have each youngster glue the lips and teeth to a sheet of blue construction paper as shown. Discuss the importance of brushing teeth each night before going to bed. Explain to students that when we don't brush before going to bed, *plaque* forms on our teeth, which can cause *cavities,* or areas of decay.

After students leave for the day, use a yellow marker to color the teeth on each child's project. The next day, explain to youngsters that the teeth in their projects didn't get brushed and plaque has formed. Have each child brush away the plaque with a toothbrush and toothpaste (white paint). What pretty smiles!

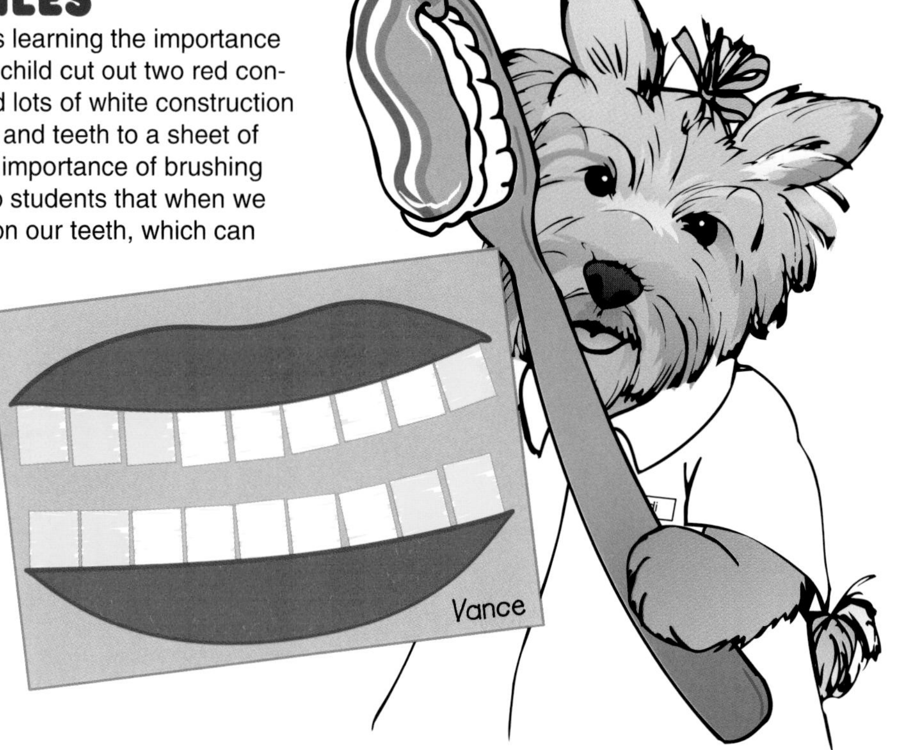

Erin Wernimont—Four-Year-Olds
OEG Early Learning Center
Platteville, WI

TOOTH PARTS

Your little ones will learn the parts of a tooth in a snap with this simple idea! Have one child stand in front of the class. Explain that the part of a tooth we see above the gum line is called the crown. Place a crown on top of the child's head. Tell youngsters that each tooth has a root and that some have two roots. Explain that the student volunteer's legs represent the roots of a tooth. Finally, wrap a piece of pink fabric around her midriff and tell students that it represents the gums around the tooth. Repeat this activity each day of your tooth study.

Millie Morris—Gr. K
Berkmar United Methodist Church
Lilburn, GA

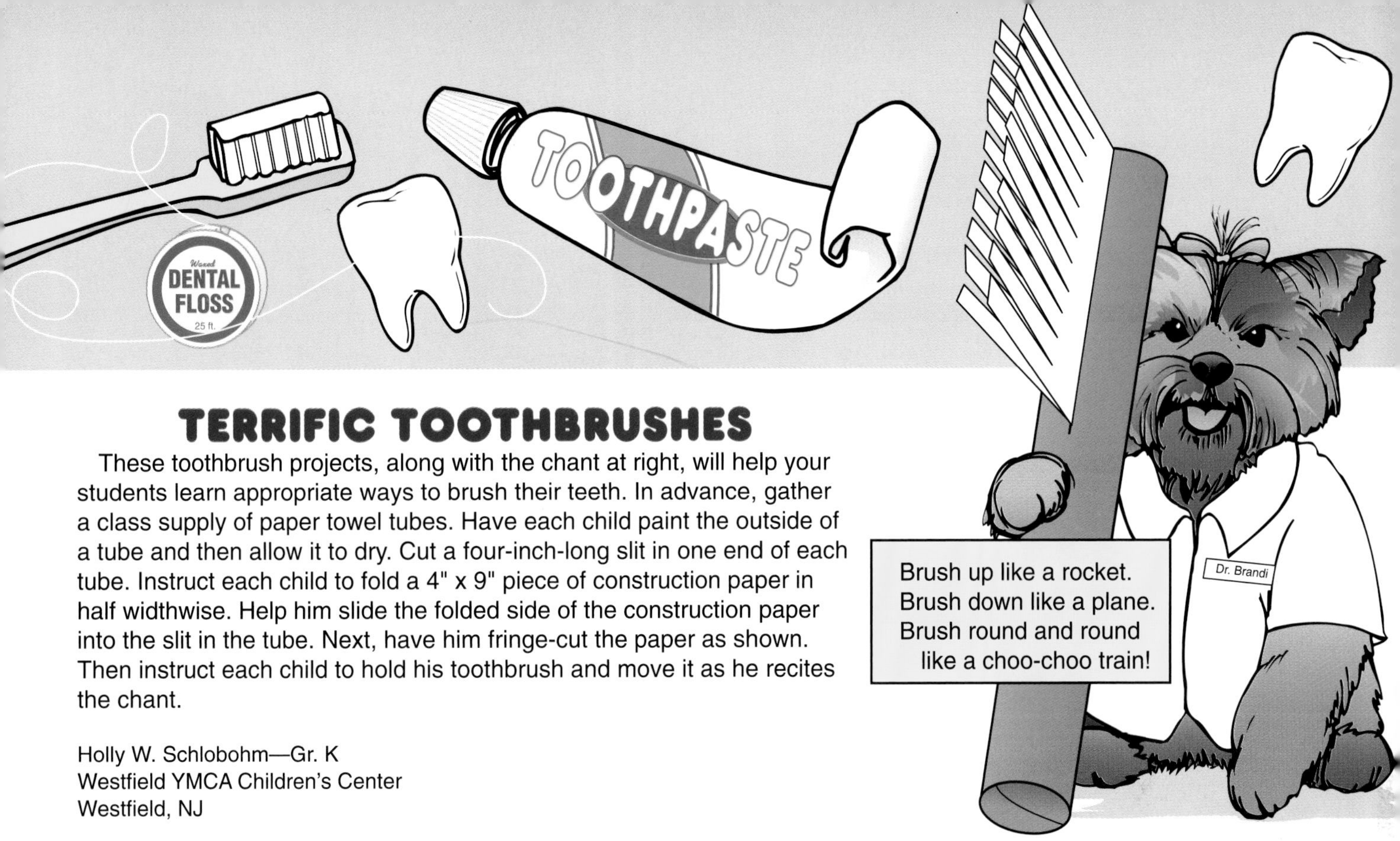

TERRIFIC TOOTHBRUSHES

These toothbrush projects, along with the chant at right, will help your students learn appropriate ways to brush their teeth. In advance, gather a class supply of paper towel tubes. Have each child paint the outside of a tube and then allow it to dry. Cut a four-inch-long slit in one end of each tube. Instruct each child to fold a 4" x 9" piece of construction paper in half widthwise. Help him slide the folded side of the construction paper into the slit in the tube. Next, have him fringe-cut the paper as shown. Then instruct each child to hold his toothbrush and move it as he recites the chant.

Holly W. Schlobohm—Gr. K
Westfield YMCA Children's Center
Westfield, NJ

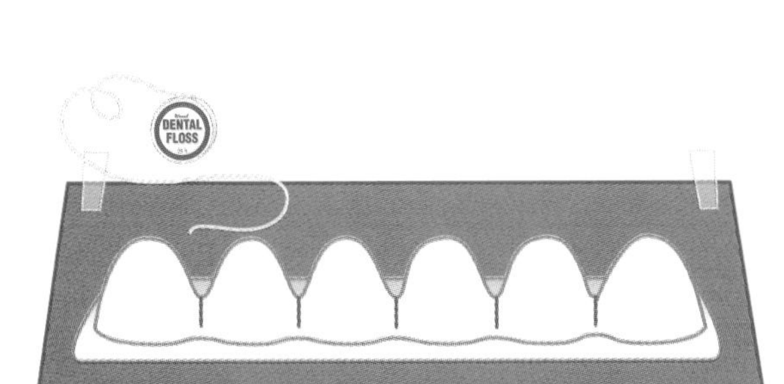

EGG CARTON FLOSSING

Your youngsters' flossing techniques will improve with this fun activity. Cut several white egg cartons into strips as shown. Glue each strip to a sheet of construction paper and tape it to a table at a center. Use a knife to carefully cut half-inch slits between each egg cup as shown. Then invite each youngster to visit the center. Give her a length of dental floss and have her practice flossing between each tooth.

Erin Wernimont—Four-Year-Olds, OEG Early Learning Center, Platteville, WI

HEALTHY TEETH GAME

Get ready to see plenty of happy smiles when you play this dental health game with students. To prepare, label approximately 30 index cards with healthy and unhealthy dental practices, such as drinking sugary soda, flossing teeth, brushing teeth, or chewing sugarless gum. Also make five "great checkup" cards and shuffle them in with the other cards.

To play, give each child in a small group ten white Unifix cubes and a golf ball–sized ball of red clay. Have each youngster form the clay into a U shape and then place the cubes on it to resemble teeth and gums. Place a supply of black Unifix cubes in the center of the table along with the cards. In turn, instruct each child to draw a card from the stack. Read the card to the group. If an unhealthy practice card is drawn, the child exchanges a white tooth for one with a cavity (a black cube). If a great checkup card is drawn, all teeth with cavities are replaced with white teeth. Play continues until all cards have been drawn. Students with cavities can trade them in for healthy teeth by telling you one healthy dental practice for each cavity. All students are winners with this game!

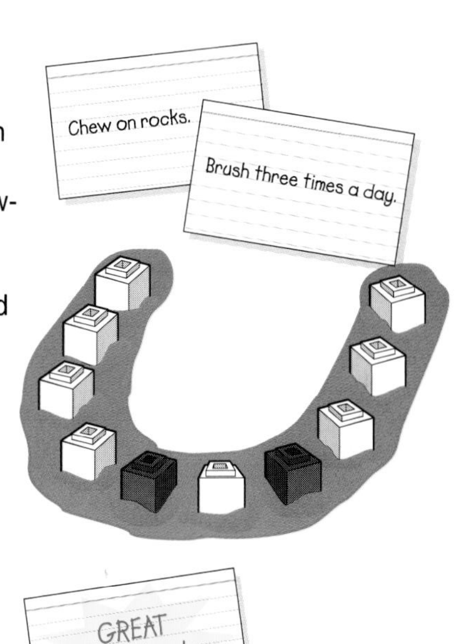

Debra L. Erickson and Katy Avery—Grs. K–1, Edward Fenn Elementary, Gorham, NH

HAVE YOU SEEN MY MISSING TOOTH?

Sing this little lost tooth song with your students to get them thinking about the teeth that used to occupy the spaces in their mouths! Repeat the song several times, inviting each student to suggest places where his missing tooth might be found.

(sung to the tune of "The Muffin Man")

Have you seen my missing tooth?
I lost my tooth. It is the truth.
Have you seen my missing tooth?
It disappeared like that!

Yes, we found your missing tooth.
We found your tooth. It is the truth.
Yes, we found your missing tooth.
We found it [in the sink]!

Betty Silkunas—Gr. K
Lower Gwynedd Elementary
Ambler, PA

TOOTH FAIRY PILLOWS

These handmade pillows make waiting for a visit from the Tooth Fairy extra special! Cut an 8" x 10" tooth-shaped template from tagboard. Use the template to trace and cut out two white felt teeth for each child. Hole-punch the edges of each pair of teeth at one-inch intervals. Have each child sew a pair of teeth together using white yarn and a plastic needle, leaving a three-inch opening for stuffing. Instruct her to stuff the pillow with fiberfill and then sew the opening closed. Cut a red felt heart for each child. Hot-glue a heart on each pillow, leaving an opening at the top to form a pocket. Use fabric paint to label each youngster's pillow as shown. Encourage each student to store any lost teeth in the pocket of her pillow for the Tooth Fairy to find!

Jamie Nolan—Gr. K, P. S. 229, Woodside, NY

PENNIES FROM THE TOOTH FAIRY

After the first child in your class loses a tooth, use this idea to build on the excitement! That day after students go home, toss a few pennies on the playground. When students find them the next day, explain that the Tooth Fairy flew over the playground during the night and the pennies must have fallen out of her pocket! The child who lost his tooth the day before will probably announce, "She was flying to my house!"

Robin Harrington—Grs. K–1
The Harrington School
Farmers Branch, TX

Bread-Slice Pattern

Use with "Bread-Slice Match" on page 255.

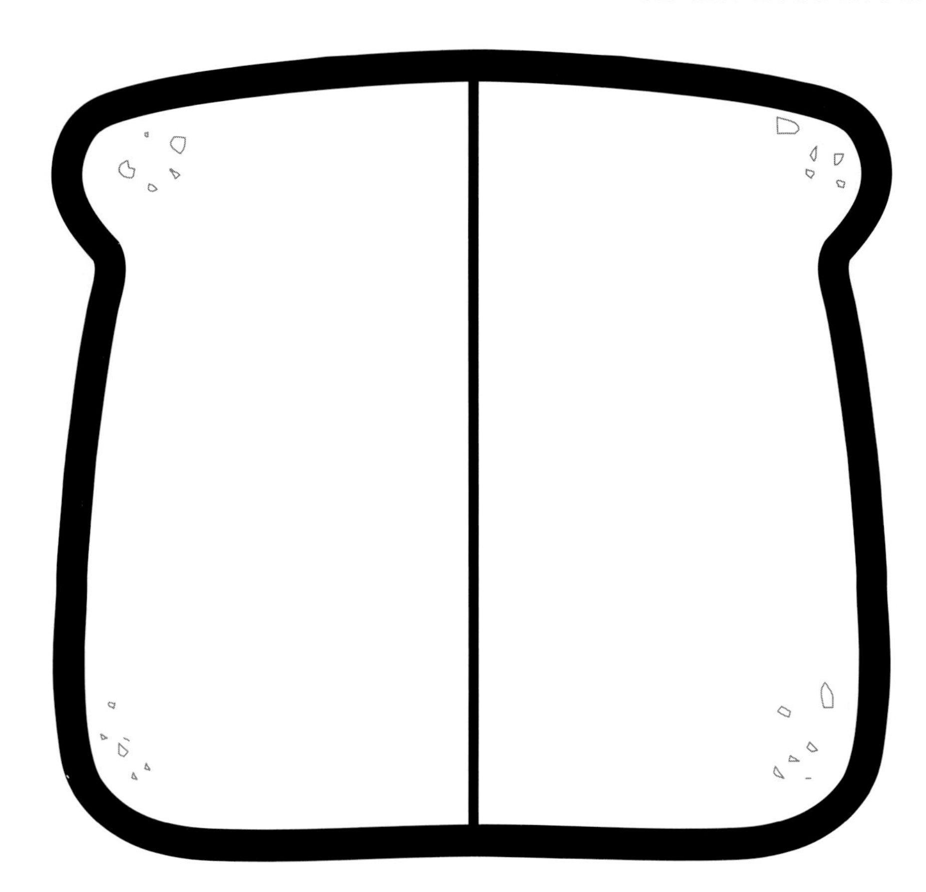

Parent Letter

Use with "Bag It!" on page 255.

Dear Family,

We need your help in gathering an assortment of nonperishable food items. We will use the items for sorting activities that focus on each item's initial letter or blend. Later we will donate the food items to a local food bank. Please send one nonperishable food item to school with your child by ________________.

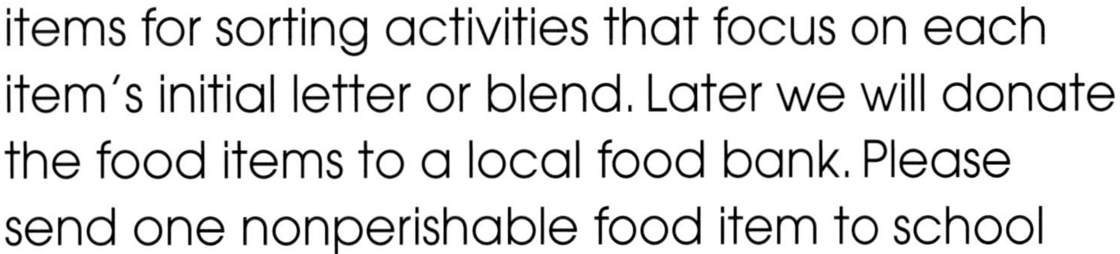

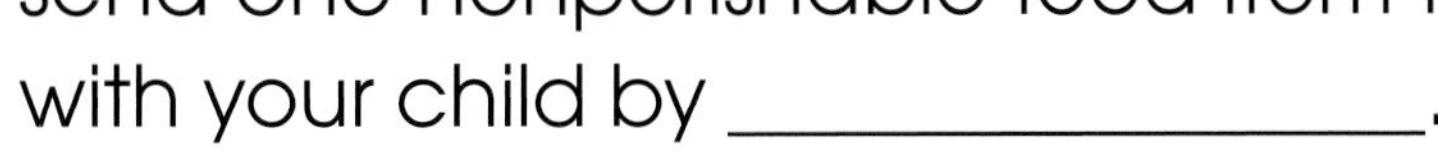

Thank you,

____

Beginning Sounds SUPERMARKET

Fill up your cart with ideas for teaching onsets and blends with a thematic unit that focuses on a trip to the grocery store!

by Suzanne Moore, Irving, TX

What Do We See?

What's one thing usually taken to the grocery store? A grocery list, of course! In advance, make four charts from the panels of large paper grocery bags. Label each chart with a different section of the grocery store: "Dairy," "Produce," "Meat," or "Deli." Invite your young shoppers to brainstorm a grocery list by singing the song below.

(sung to the tune of "Six Little Ducks")

What do we see at the grocery store?
Fruits and vegetables, meat and more.
Get your cart and come with me;
Let's make a list of things that we can see,
We can see, we can see!
Let's make a list of things that we can see!

As students brainstorm items, help them categorize their responses; then jot their ideas on the appropriate chart. Emphasize the initial sound of each word as you read the lists.

Dairy
milk
cheese
yogurt
butter

Produce
apples
lettuce
carrots
oranges
grapes

Meat
turkey
hamburger
steak
chicken

Deli
potato salad
fried chicken
sandwiches
pickles

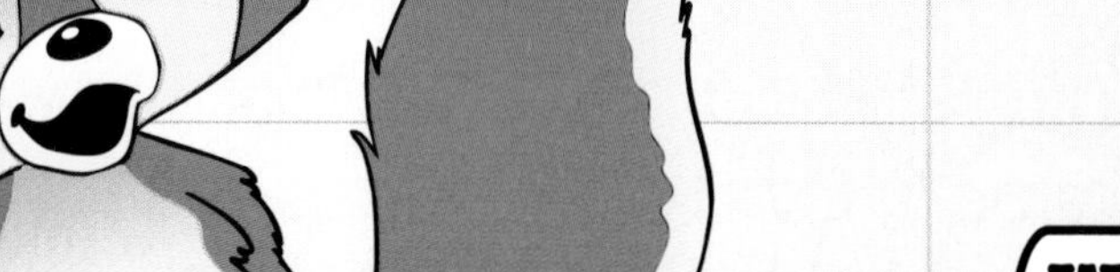

What Will You Buy?

The student-generated charts from "What Do We See?" on this page come in handy when your little grocery experts work together to make this class book. In advance, cut out a class supply of grocery bag panels. Have each child choose an item from one of the charts that begins with the same letter as the beginning letter of his name. Then encourage him to draw a self-portrait on a grocery bag panel holding his chosen item. As each artist shares his illustration with the class, write his dictation, such as "Tom will buy a tomato" or "Chris will buy a carrot," on his panel. Then bind the pages to make a class book and title it "Shop 'til You Drop in [your name]'s Class."

It's in the Bag

Here's a simple circle-time activity that will reinforce beginning sounds. In advance, fill a paper grocery bag with empty plastic containers, empty cereal boxes, and plastic foods from your dramatic-play center. Invite youngsters to pass the bag around the circle while reciting the rhyme below. At the end of the rhyme, the child holding the bag will take out an item, say its name, and then say its beginning sound or blend. Encourage the rest of the class to repeat the initial sound. Have students repeat the activity until the bag is empty. Learning while unloading!

Grocery shopping sure is fine;
Fill your cart and get in line.
Pay your bill and load your sack.
Then next week—you'll be right back!

Bread-Slice Match

Butter up letter sound-association with this fun center idea. To prepare, make 16 light brown construction paper copies of the bread-slice pattern on page 253; then cut out the patterns. Photocopy, color, and cut out the food cards on the bottom of page 258. Glue a card on the right side of each bread-slice pattern. Program the left side of the pattern with the picture's beginning letter or blend. Cut each bread slice in half. Mix the slices and place them in an empty plastic bread sleeve. To play the game, students match a letter slice of bread with a corresponding picture slice. Any way you slice it, this idea's terrific!

Bag It!

Need a motivating language arts center that will get your students thinking and moving, too? Look no further! In advance, photocopy and send home with each child the parent letter on page 253 asking for nonperishable food donations. Then label a supply of paper grocery bags with different letters. Collect the food donations in a large basket. Stock a center with the basket of food and the labeled bags. Have youngsters look at each label or box and then sort the items into the corresponding bags. Later, donate the food to your local food bank. Aha! Beans go in the *B* bag!

Blend Basket Shopping

Your students will shop 'til they drop with this blend activity! Program "shopping" baskets (any baskets will do) with blends like those below. Stock a nearby shelf with pretend food, kitchen utensils, and empty food containers, most beginning with your chosen blends. Have each youngster take a shopping basket and shop for items that begin with his blend.

cr- crackers, crab, cranberries, cream cheese
br- broccoli, bread, brussels sprouts, bran flakes
sp- spaghetti, spatula, spoon, spices, spinach
gr- grapes, graham crackers, grapefruit, grits

It's a Snap!

Your little ones will flip their lids when they visit this manipulative center! To prepare for this activity, collect 16 clean yogurt containers. Make one copy of the food cards on page 258. Glue one picture card to the side of each container. Program the matching lid with the corresponding beginning letter. Place the lids and containers in separate baskets. During center time, encourage students to look at each picture and then find the matching lid for each container. It's a snap!

What Is in My Basket?

Here's a cute booklet about blends that will be fun for your little grocery shoppers to make and read. In advance, make a copy of pages 257 and 258 for each student. Have each child color and cut out the booklet pages. Then have her write her name on the cover where indicated. Next, instruct each child to color and cut out the food pictures on the bottom of page 258 and then glue them to the appropriate page of her booklet. (Not all the cards will be used.) Have her stack her booklet pages in order. Staple the pages along the left edge to bind the booklet. Encourage pairs of youngsters to read their blend booklets to each other. What's in your basket?

Use with "What Is in My Basket?" on page 256.

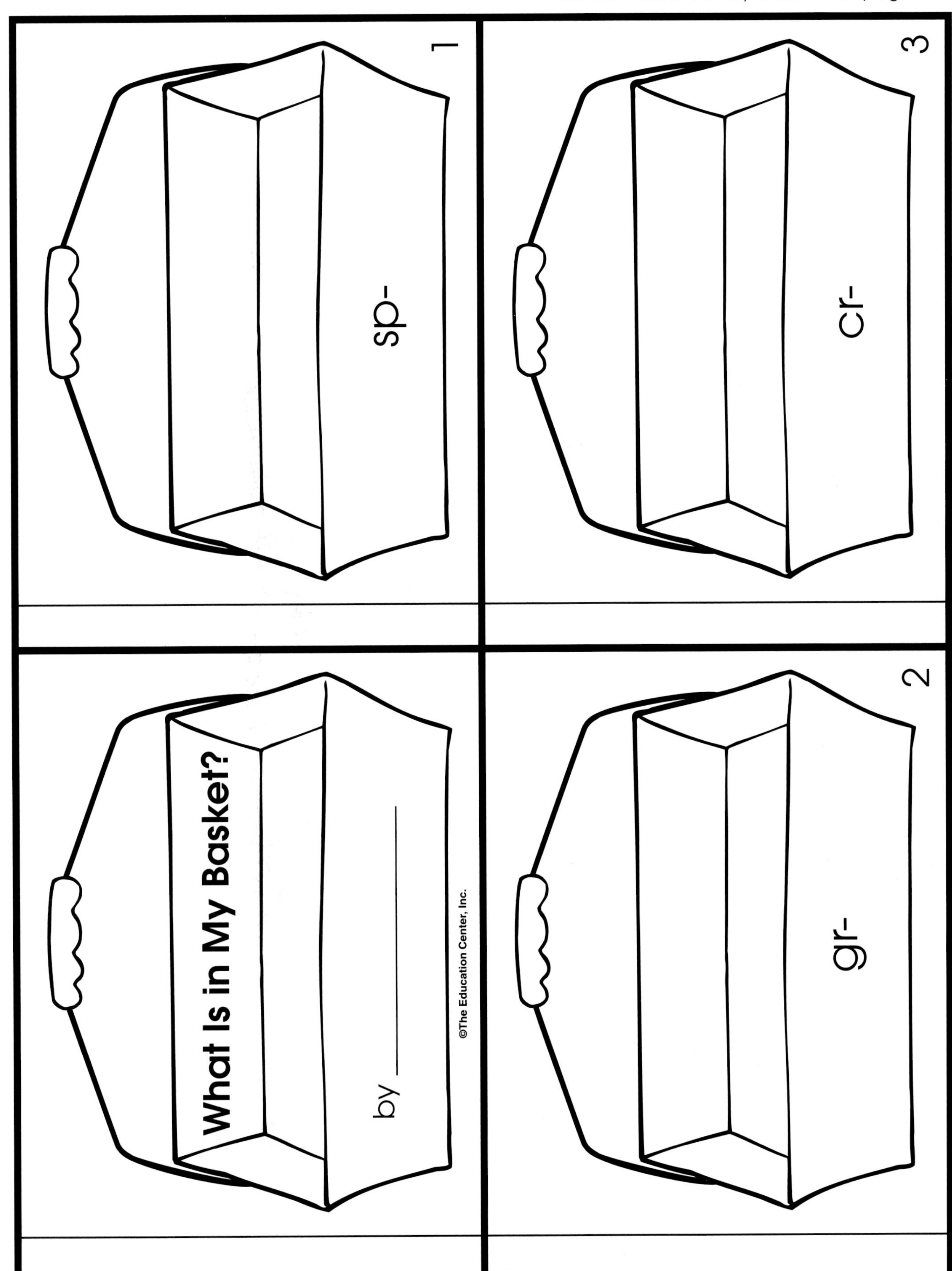

Booklet Page

Use with "What Is in My Basket?" on page 256.

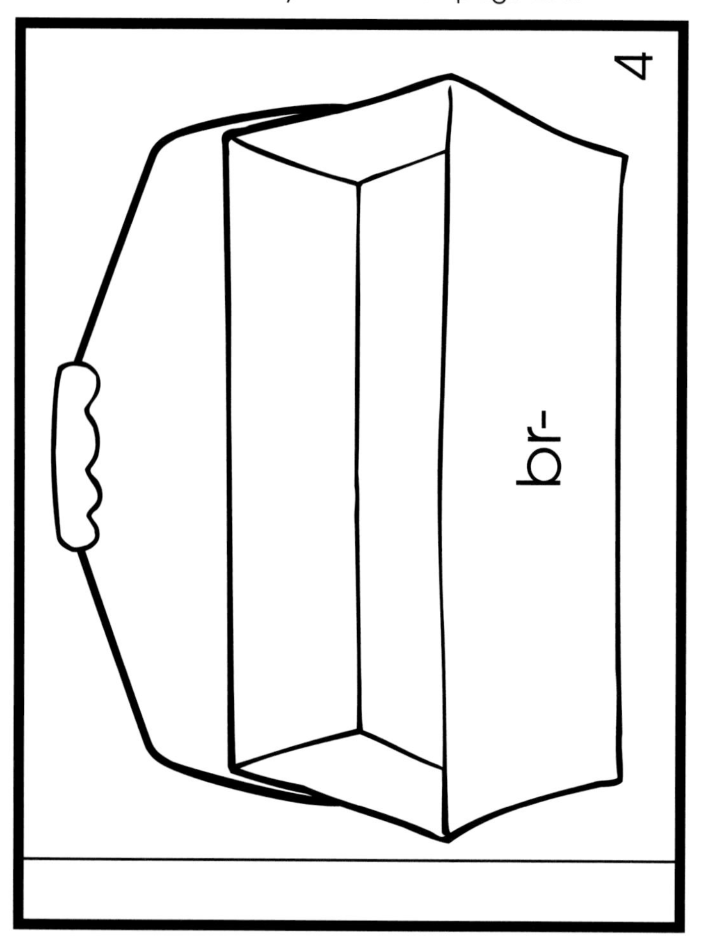

Food Cards

Use with "Bread-Slice Match" on page 255 and "It's a Snap!" and "What Is in My Basket?" on page 256.

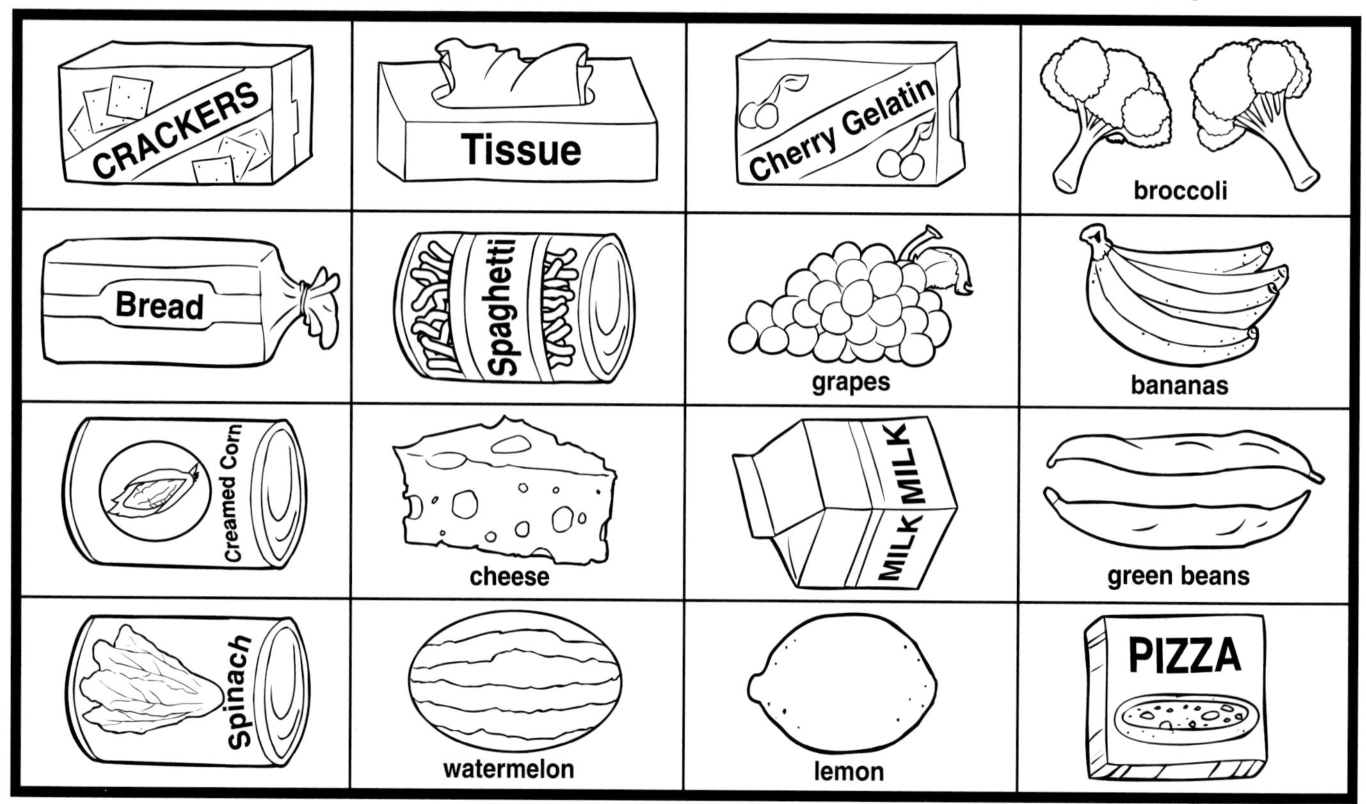

Weighing In at the Produce Stand

Use fresh fruits and veggies to cultivate your youngsters' knowledge of basic weight concepts and skills with a scale. Enlist the help of parents to donate a supply of vegetables and fruits for this study. Then display this collection of garden goodies to use as math manipulatives that any greengrocer would envy!

by Lucia Kemp Henry, Fallon, NV

The Basics of Weight

Invite students to explore the contrast between light and heavy with this easy introductory activity. Set out a cantaloupe, a pineapple, a head of red cabbage, a strawberry, an apricot, and a stalk of celery. Have your group stand in a circle around the display of fruits and veggies. Prompt students to name each item. Have a volunteer hold his hands out, and place a cantaloupe in them. Have him think about the weight of the melon as you sing the first verse of the song below. Then instruct him to pass the cantaloupe around the circle so others can feel its weight. Next, invite another student to hold the strawberry as you sing the second verse of the song. Instruct him to pass the strawberry around the circle so that each child can feel its weight also. Continue to sing the song for the remaining produce. After students have explored all the items, explain that when we say something feels heavy or light we are referring to its weight. Wrap up the activity by prompting youngsters to discuss how they know whether something feels light or heavy.

(sung to the tune of "Did You Ever See a Lassie?")

Does a [cantaloupe] feel heavy, feel heavy, feel heavy?
Does a [cantaloupe] feel heavy? Just hold it and see.
Oh yes, it feels heavy. It feels very heavy.
A [cantaloupe] feels heavy. Just hold it and see!

Does a [strawberry] feel light, feel light, feel light?
Does a [strawberry] feel light? Just hold it and see.
Oh yes, it feels light. It feels very light.
A [strawberry] feels light. Just hold it and see!

Fruits and Vegetables

Heavy or Light?

Now that your little ones have "weighed in" with an understanding of heavy produce versus light produce, encourage them to estimate the weight of more veggies and fruits. Place the suggested fruits and vegetables in a large basket. Direct each child in a small group to pick up each item and estimate its weight, using the terms *light* or *heavy.* Then ask students to sort the produce into two groups: one group for light items and another for heavy ones. Heavy or light?

Lighter Produce	Heavier Produce
carrot	cantaloupe
radish	large baking potato
lemon	pineapple
tangerine	head of cabbage
celery stalk	grapefruit
green onion	honeydew melon

Comparing Produce

A potato is heavy, but a pineapple is heavier! Introduce students to weight comparisons with this activity. Put the heavy produce items from "Heavy or Light?" on this page in a child's plastic shopping cart. Remind students that the items in the cart are heavy. Have a child select two items from the cart, such as a potato and a pineapple. Place each item in a separate plastic shopping bag, using bags of different colors, if possible. Place a shopping bag in each hand of the child. Have her think about the weight of each bag and then lean or tilt, as a balance scale would, toward the heavier bag. Instruct her to compare the weight of the bags by saying, "The potato is heavy, but the pineapple is heavier." Continue the activity until each child has had a turn comparing two pieces of heavy produce. Way to be a human balance scale!

More Estimation

Increase your youngsters' comparison skills with a different kind of produce problem. Display the shopping cart of heavy produce as before. Ask each child in a small group to select three items and then arrange them on a table in order using the words *heavy, heavier,* and *heaviest.* Extend the activity by replacing the heavy items with light items and use them to explore the terms *light, lighter,* and *lightest.* Now that's a great way to get produce in order!

More, Less, or Equal?

Making complex comparisons is fun and easy when students do it with fruits and veggies! Use the produce and plastic shopping bags from “Comparing Produce” on page 260 to focus on the concepts of more than, less than, and equal to. Put a one-pound weight in one of the bags and a potato in the other one. Have a child stand with his arms raised to shoulder height. Place the handle of the shopping bag containing the weight over one hand. Instruct him to notice the weight of the bag. Next, loop the handle of the bag with the potato over his other hand. Then prompt him to compare the weights of the two bags using the term *more than, less than,* or *equal to*. After each child has had a turn, place the one-pound weight, the plastic bags, and the produce at a center for independent exploration.

Making Weights Match

Introduce your youngsters to a balance scale with this weighty activity. Display produce on a table along with crayons, paper, and a balance scale. Invite each child in a small group to put a piece of produce on one side of the scale. Then have her put smaller pieces of produce on the other side of the scale until it is balanced. Explain that there is an equal amount of weight placed on each side of the scale. Have each child draw to record the results of her weight exploration on a sheet of paper. Post youngsters' completed drawings on a bulletin board titled “They Weigh the Same!”

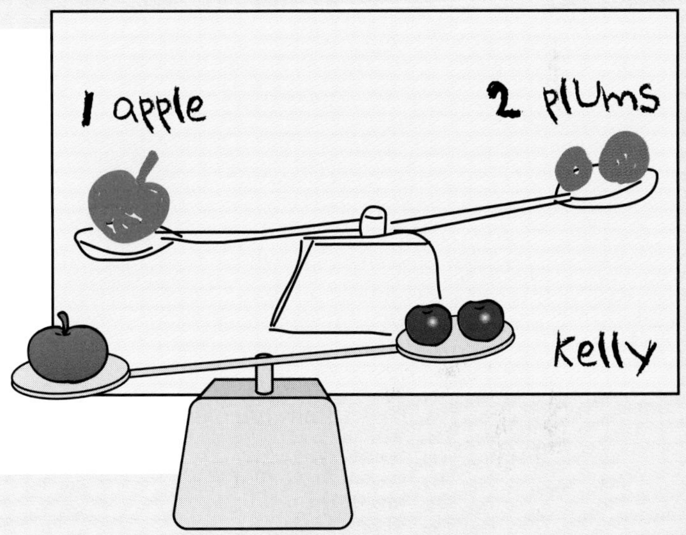

Name Kent Critical thinking

What's in the Bag?

Bag Number	? Guess. Draw.	✓ Check. Draw.
1		grapefruit
2		lemon
3		orange

In the Bag

Wrap up your exploration of weight with this guessing game. To prepare, make a copy of the recording sheet on page 262 for each child. Set out two grapefruit that weigh the same, two lemons that weigh the same, and two oranges that weigh the same. Place one grapefruit, one lemon, and one orange in separate brown paper lunch bags. Fold down the top of each bag and secure it with a paper clip to prevent peeking. Label each bag with a different number from 1 to 3. Place the bags in a center along with a scale and the remaining unbagged fruits. Help each child weigh each bag on the scale and then have him guess which item is inside. Instruct him to record his guess on his paper. Next, have him weigh the corresponding loose piece of fruit to compare its weight with the mystery bag's. After each piece of produce has been matched to a mystery bag, have the child open the bags, look inside to check for accuracy, and then record the actual results on his paper!

Name ____________________ Critical thinking

What's in the Bag?

Bag Number	? Guess. Draw.	✓ Check. Draw. Label.
1		____________
2		____________
3		____________

 Note to the teacher: Use with "In the Bag" on page 261.

A Mapping Module

Learning about maps is a snap with the clever ideas in this unit. Use these ideas to teach youngsters about their neighborhood, their country, and the world!

by Jana Sanderson, Rainbow School, Stockton, CA

Any Town, USA

This map doesn't lead to buried treasure, but to engaging mapping activities centered around a neighborhood or town. Use duct tape to create city blocks on a long length of white bulletin board paper. Lead students to discuss the types of businesses that can be found in a neighborhood, such as a school, a hospital, an airport, a grocery store, a library, a police station, a fire station, and a movie theater. Then give each youngster a blank index card and a sheet of paper. Have him draw a picture of his home on his card and a picture of a business on this paper. After the pictures are complete, have students place their cards and papers on the map and then glue them in place. Next, instruct students to use crayons or markers to add trees, grass, bodies of water, stoplights, a park, and railroad tracks to the map. Label the map with cardinal directions. Finally, have students name the town and streets; then label the streets.

Taking Care of Business

Completing tasks will be fun when your little ones participate in this activity. To prepare, gather a supply of small vehicles, such as cars, trucks, a school bus, a police car, a fire truck, an ambulance, a train, and an airplane. In turn, give each child a scenario, such as "Tricia needs milk from the grocery store" or "Kevin, a firefighter, puts out a fire at the pizza parlor." Have her select the appropriate vehicle and drive it on the map to complete her task. Encourage each youngster to talk about the path she took by using the street names and directional words, such as left, right, north, south, east, and west.

I Spy a Map

"I spy with my eye" a fun activity to introduce children to real maps. Gather a magnifying glass and a map. Display the map on a wall at student eye level. On index cards, make a supply of "I Spy" cards appropriate for your map, including symbols for cities, camping locations, lakes, national parks, museums, and highways. To play, a child draws a card and then uses the magnifying glass to locate the place on the map. Play continues until each child has had a chance to participate. Invite youngsters to revisit the game during center time.

The Key on the Map

Sing this catchy song with students to get them thinking about what the symbols on a map represent. Each time the song is sung, substitute a different key description from the list below.

(sung to the tune of "The Wheels on the Bus")

The [key on the map] show(s)
[Where things are],
[Where things are],
[Where things are].
The [key on the map] show(s)
[Where things are]
All around our state!

Additional key descriptions:
little black dots, cities and towns
star in a circle, the capital
long, colored lines; all roadways
little green tents, all campsites
little green trees, all state parks

Pam Crane

Stitching Across the States

Students will love an activity that has them using cardinal directions as they stitch their way across the United States. In advance, photocopy page 267 and cut out the pattern. Photocopy the spinner on page 266 on tagboard. Add a brad and paper clip to the center as shown. To make a gameboard, trace the pattern onto a sheet of plastic canvas and then cut out the resulting shape. Use a paint pen to label each gameboard with cardinal directions as shown. Tie a large bead to the center of each board with 18-inch lengths of red and blue yarn. Thread each loose end of the yarn pieces through the eye of a different plastic needle.

To play, invite each student in a pair to choose a color, red or blue. In turn, have each child spin the spinner to determine in which direction she will stitch. Instruct her to count over three holes in the canvas toward the direction she spun and make a stitch. Then have her pass the spinner and gameboard to her opponent. Play continues until one player's road leads off the map!

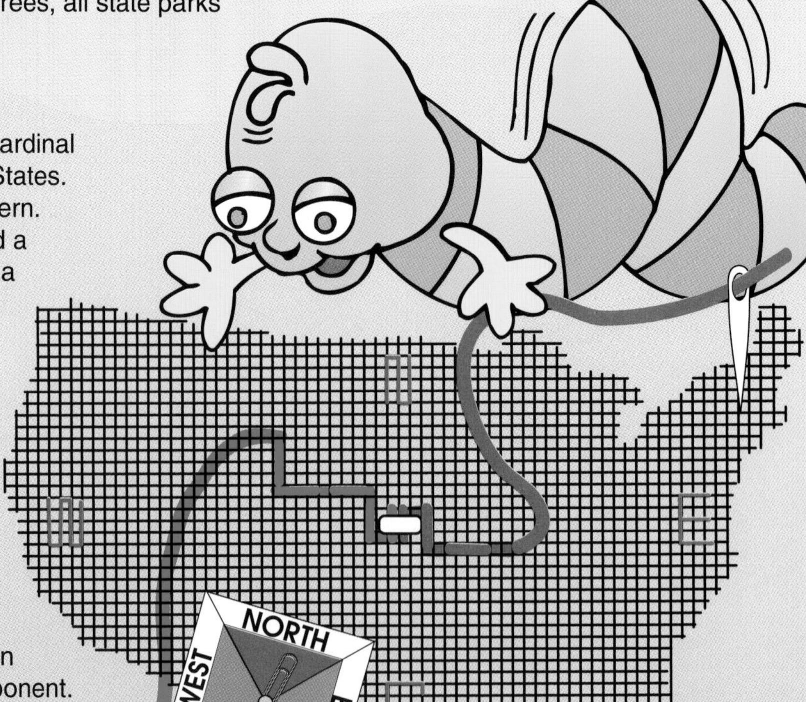

Cool Maps

Hang these windsocks outside for children to observe the wind and the direction from which it blows. Make a copy of page 267 and cut out the pattern. Cut a 12" x 18" piece of Con-Tact covering for each child. Fold each piece of covering in half and then use a permanent marker to trace the pattern from page 267 on one side of the covering (not the paper backing). Hole-punch black construction paper to make a large supply of dots. Cut red and blue yarn into varying lengths. Cut a clear shower curtain into 1" x 18" strips so that each child will have five strips.

Give each child a programmed piece of Con-Tact covering and a supply of dots (cities) and yarn lengths (highways and interstates). Help him remove the paper backing from his piece of covering. Instruct each child to place cities, highways, and interstates on the adhesive side of his map outline. When he is finished, fold the covering to seal the project. Help each child cut out his map as needed. Have him tape five plastic strips to the bottom of his project as shown. Hole-punch each map and add a yarn hanger as shown. Hang the windsocks outside. On a breezy day, have youngsters determine from which direction the wind is blowing by observing their maps.

Earth Model

These models of the earth teach students that globes show blue water, green land, and brown mountains. In advance, purchase enough Chinet paper bowls so that each child will have two. Cut the rims off the bowls. Explain to students what the colors blue, green, and brown represent on a globe. Then have each child paint the bottoms of his bowls blue. After the paint has dried, mix brown powdered tempera paint with liquid starch to make extra thick brown paint. Repeat this step to make extra thick green paint. Have each child spoon the paint onto his bowls to make landmasses and mountain regions. Make a class supply of yarn loops for hanging. When the paint is dry, hot-glue each child's bowls together, trapping the knotted ends of a loop in between. Then hang the globes from the ceiling. What good-looking Earth models!

A Worldly Workout

Reinforce cardinal directions by singing this action song. Label your classroom with the cardinal directions and discuss them with students. Then sing the song below. Yay!

(sung to the tune of "The Hokey-Pokey")

You bend your body north.
You bend your body south.
You bend your body east.
Then you bend your body west.
You do the worldly workout,
And you spin yourself like Earth.
Now give a great big shout—yay!

A Global Treat

Here's a mouthful of mapping fun! Mix two white cake mixes in separate bowls according to package directions. Tint one bowl of batter with blue food coloring and the other bowl with green food coloring. Have each youngster add spoonfuls of each color of batter to a paper muffin cup until it is two-thirds full. Bake the cupcakes according to package directions. After cooling, invite each child to bite into her cupcake and identify the blue water and green land of her global treat!

Spinner

Use with "Stitching Across the States" on page 264.

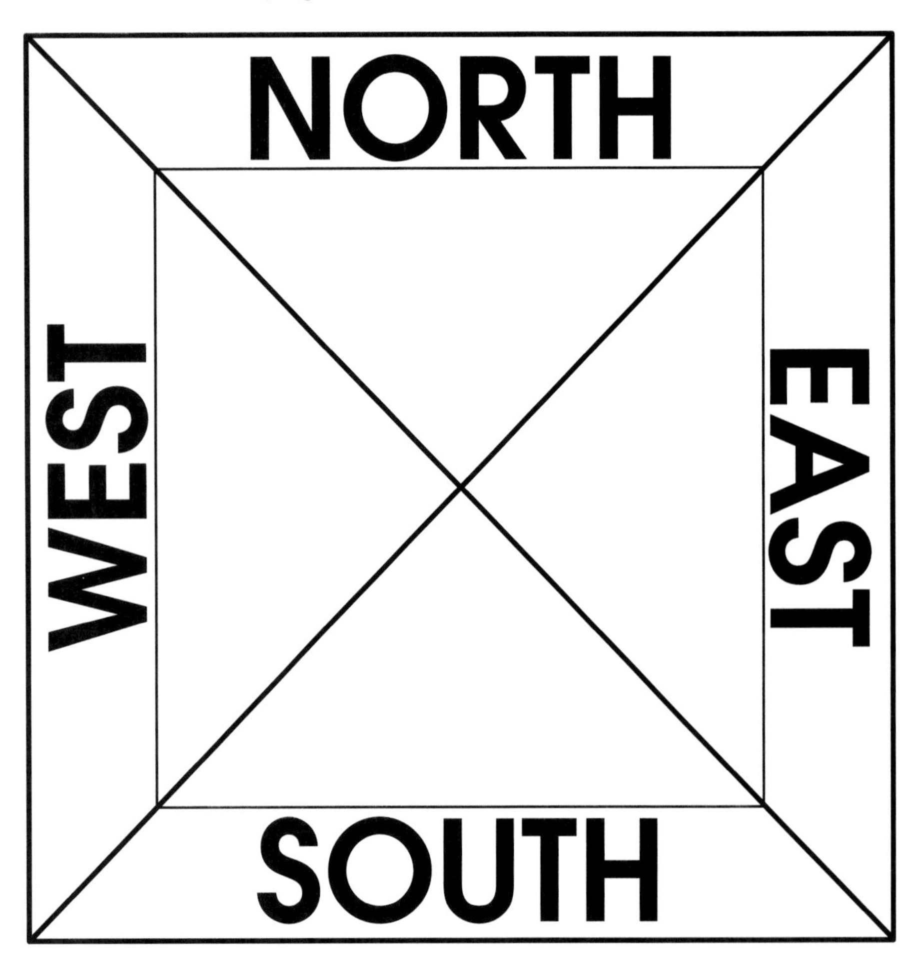

Map Pattern

Use with "Stitching Across the States" on page 264 and "Cool Maps" on page 265.

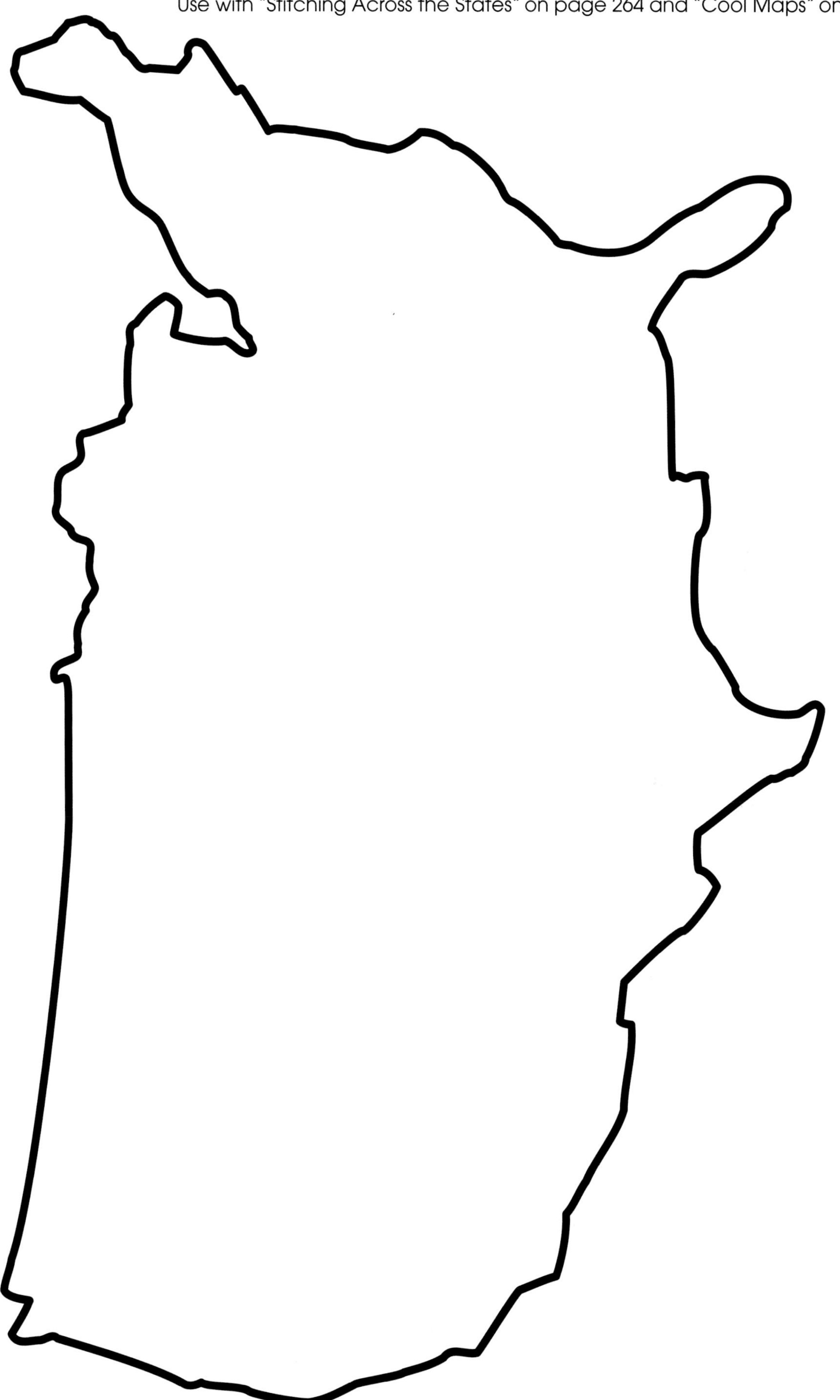

Place your order for cross-curricular learning fun with these delicious delicatessen lessons!

by Lucia Kemp Henry, Fallon, NV, and Suzanne Moore, Irving, TX

Deli Descriptions

What do sandwiches, pickles, bagels, and chips have in common? They can all be found at the deli, of course! Get your youngsters thinking about deli items with this listing activity. To prepare, cut a sheet of chart paper into a slice-of-bread shape and outline the edges with a tan marker to resemble crust. Then dish up a deli discussion with students, encouraging them to describe any deli dining experiences they have had. List all of the deli foods mentioned on the chart. During the remainder of your deli unit, add to the list as needed.

Deli Delights

sandwiches
chips
pickles
bagels
cookies
subs
salads
soda
juice
soup

Down at the Deli

Sing this catchy song with your youngsters to encourage them to think about food choices at the deli. Repeat the song for each child in your class, substituting her name in Line 4 and her food choice in Line 6. I'll have a sandwich, wrapped to go!

(sung to the tune of "Down by the Station")

Everyone: Down at the deli,
Lining up at lunchtime,
See the hungry customers all in a row.
Teacher: [Child's name], now it's your turn,
Time to place your order.
Child: I'll have [name of food], wrapped to go!

A Pickle on the Side

A lunch from the deli wouldn't be complete without a pickle on the side! Discover which pickles your little ones prefer with this tasty graphing activity. Provide a sample of sweet pickle, dill pickle, and spicy garlic pickle for each child. Place the pickle types in labeled bowls. Make a graph, as shown, and attach it to a wall within students' reach. Invite each child to taste the pickle types and then write his name in the column on the graph that identifies his favorite type. After the graph is complete, discuss the results and determine the class's pickle favorite.

Sweet Pickle	Garlic Pickle	Dill Pickle
Jake		
Mia		
Gavin		Simone
Pauli	Garrett	Lorna
Anna	Ava	Brad

Take a Number, Please!

Use this activity to have your youngsters lining up deli-style—in sequential order. In advance, gather one paint chip (available from your home improvement store) for each child. Number the chips in sequence, beginning with one. Place the chips in a white deli bag and then shake the bag to mix them. Have each youngster remove a chip from the bag. Instruct the group to line up so their numbered chips are in sequence. After students are in line, call each number and have youngsters place a pretend order. Now serving number one!

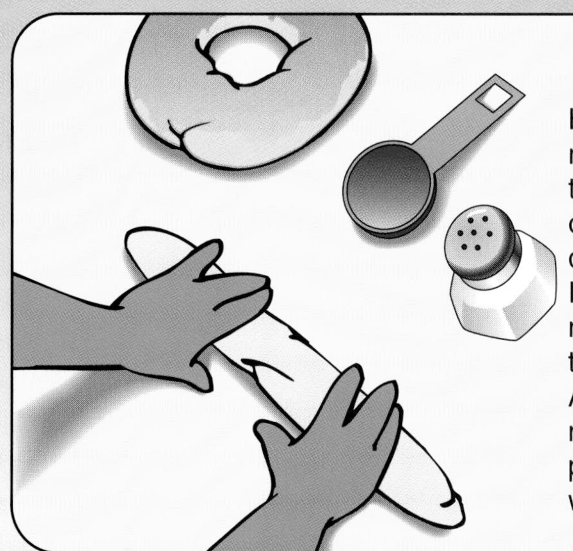

Bagel Time

Bagels are a typical choice when visiting a deli for breakfast. Have youngsters follow directions to make these salt dough bagel manipulatives. To make a bagel, have each child mix together four tablespoons of flour, two tablespoons of salt, and four tablespoons of water. Then instruct him to knead the dough. Have him roll his dough into a snake and then form the snake into a bagel shape. Instruct him to place his bagel on a personalized piece of aluminum foil on a cookie sheet. Have each youngster brush the top of the dough with beaten egg. Bake the bagels for $1\frac{1}{2}$ hours at 350°. After the bagels have cooled and hardened, use a permanent marker to write each child's name on the bottom of one. If desired, provide each child with a real minibagel to snack on while his pretend one bakes!

Bagging Bagels

Your students will have fun bagging bagels and practicing counting skills with this easy activity. In advance, program a supply of white lunch bags with a different number from 1 to 12. Place the student-made bagels from "Bagel Time" on page 269 in a basket. Stock a center with the programmed bags, the basket of bagels, and some tongs. Have each student select a bag and read the number on the front of it. Next, have him use the tongs to place the appropriate number of bagels in the bag. Instruct a second student to remove the bagels from the bag, counting as he goes to check for accuracy. I'll have four bagels, please!

Deli Tray Relay

Serve up lots of gross-motor fun when your students play this deli relay game! In advance, gather two plastic trays, two plastic forks, two plastic spoons, and two clean Styrofoam take-out containers. Fill each take-out container with dry pasta and then tape it closed. Place each container on a tray along with a spoon and a fork. Divide your class in half and have each group form a line. Give a tray to the first child in each line. To start the relay, say, "Order up!" Instruct the first child in each line to pass the tray to the youngster behind her. The relay continues in this manner until the tray reaches the end of the line and then returns to the front of the line. Along the way, if items fall off the tray, they must be returned to the tray before it is passed to the next child. Wow, this order was ready in record time!

Deli Dramatics

Turn your kindergartners into deli workers and hungry customers by transforming your dramatic-play center into a delicatessen. In advance, trace the patterns on pages 272 and 273 onto appropriate colors of craft foam to make a supply of deli fixin's. Then cut out the shapes. Use permanent markers to add details to each piece as desired. At the center, cover a table with a checkered tablecloth. Place the foam food, the number chips from "Take a Number, Please!" on page 269, aprons, trays, plastic utensils, plates, order pads, pencils, play money, and a pretend cash register at the center. Invite small groups of students to the center to role-play customers and deli workers. A ham sandwich with extra pickles—coming right up!

My Sandwich

This sandwich booklet will have your youngsters hungry for reading time! Make a white construction paper copy of the food patterns on pages 272 and 273 for each child. Instruct each youngster to color and cut out the patterns. Then have her write her name on the slice-of-bread cover. Next, instruct her to stack her sandwich parts. Then help each student hole-punch the sandwich and attach it to a six-inch paper plate with a brass fastener as shown. Encourage each child to read her booklet to the class. No matter how you stack it, this deli sandwich makes delicious reading!

Deli Day

End your deli unit by serving up a selection of deli treats! In advance, write a letter to parents requesting sandwich items for your deli day. On the designated day, arrange the ingredients, utensils, and supplies for easy student access. Invite each youngster to prepare a sandwich to his liking using the ingredients of his choice. "Deli-licious!"

Food Patterns

Use with "Deli Dramatics" on page 270 and "My Sandwich" on page 271.

Use with "Deli Dramatics" on page 270 and "My Sandwich" on page 271.

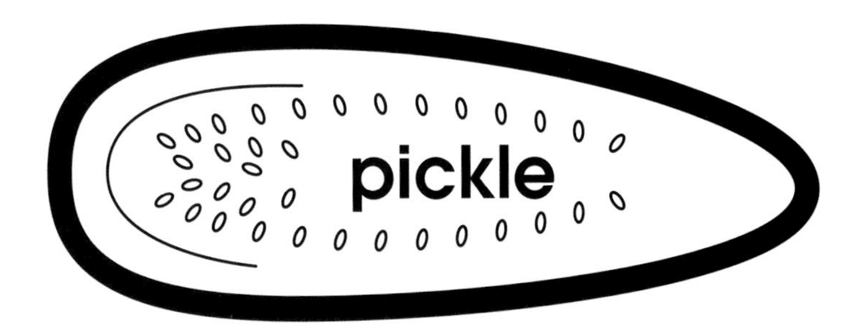

All Aflutter Over Rimes

Your youngsters will take flight while learning about rimes with the ideas in this butterfly-themed unit.

Sorting rimes

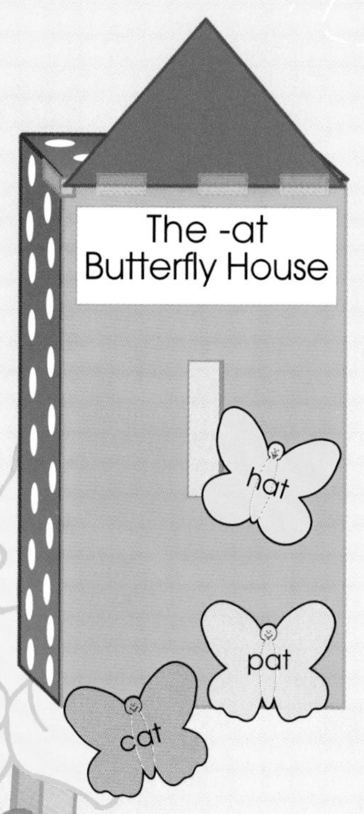

Butterfly Houses

Students gain rime-sorting practice when they help little butterflies fly to the right houses! In advance, duplicate the butterfly patterns on page 276 to make a large supply. Then make a butterfly house for each rime you want students to practice. To make a butterfly house, cover the outside bottom of a shoebox with construction paper. Cut a 1" x 4" rectangle in the bottom of the box as shown. Tape a triangular cardboard roof to the box as shown. Add decorations as desired. Label each house with a different rime. Color and cut out the butterfly patterns. For each house, program several cutouts with words ending with its rime. To make the center self-checking, also write the words on the inside of the box. To play, a child sorts the butterflies by rime and then flies them into the appropriate houses. After all of the butterflies have been sorted, have him look inside the box to check his work.

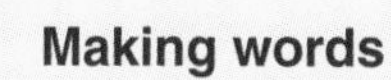

Making words

Building a Butterfly

This butterfly-building activity will have your little ones reading word families! To prepare, make one copy of page 277 for each rime and then color the copies as desired. Label each pattern with a different rime as shown. Program a supply of large craft sticks (butterfly bodies) each with a different consonant. Place the butterflies, the butterfly bodies, paper, and pencils at a center. When a child visits the center, have her choose a butterfly and read its rime. Then instruct her to position a body and read the resulting word. Have her write the words she makes on her paper. Instruct her to circle the real words and underline the nonsense words. Building butterflies—building words!

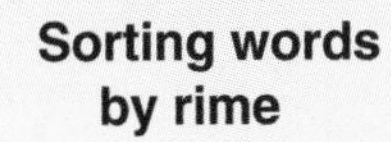

Sorting words by rime

Attractive Flowers

Little ones will stick to this idea that has them sorting words by rimes. Make three copies of page 276. Color the flower and butterfly patterns as desired. Program each flower with a different rime. Write a different word on each pair of butterflies to match one of the rimes. Slip a paper clip onto each butterfly. Glue a magnet to the back of each flower and then stick them to your board within students' reach. (Use tape if your board is not magnetized.) Draw a stem below each flower. Place the butterflies on the board's tray. Have each child read the word on each butterfly and then place it on the correct flower. What an attractive idea!

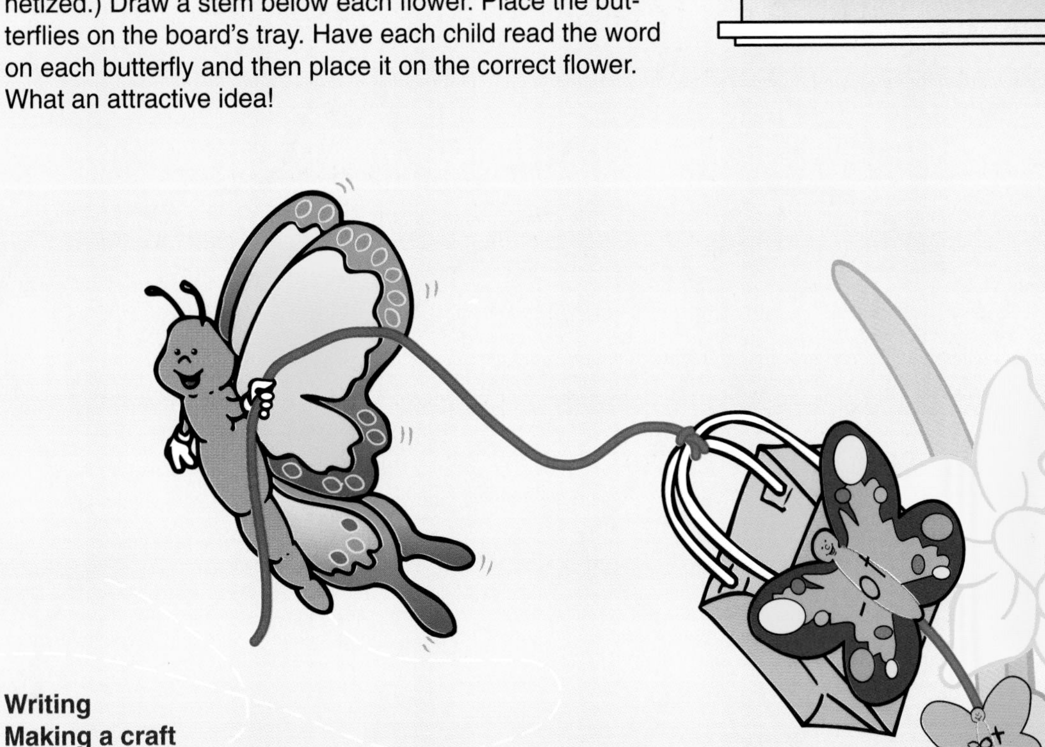

Writing
Making a craft

Butterfly Word Families

You'll see lots of fluttering butterflies after youngsters make these word family kites! To prepare, make a class set of page 277. Duplicate the butterflies on page 276 to make a large supply (at least four per child). Cut the butterflies apart. Program each large butterfly pattern with a rime. Give each child a programmed copy of page 277, at least four small butterfly patterns, two three-foot lengths of yarn, and a gift bag. Instruct him to read the rime on his large butterfly and then write one word on each of his small butterflies that includes that rime. Have him color his butterflies as desired and then cut them out. Instruct him to glue his large butterfly to the side of the bag, catching one end of a length of yarn between the bag and the butterfly. Have him tape or glue his small butterflies to the attached yarn length. Then help each child tie his remaining yarn length to the handles as shown. Allow the glue to dry. Then invite each youngster to share his word family butterflies with the class. Finally, take students outside and encourage them to run with the wind to make their butterflies flutter!

Butterfly Patterns

Use with "Butterfly Houses" on page 274 and "Attractive Flowers" and "Butterfly Word Families" on page 275.

Flower Patterns

Use with "Attractive Flowers" on page 275.

Butterfly Pattern

Use with "Building a Butterfly" on page 274 and "Butterfly Word Families" on page 275.

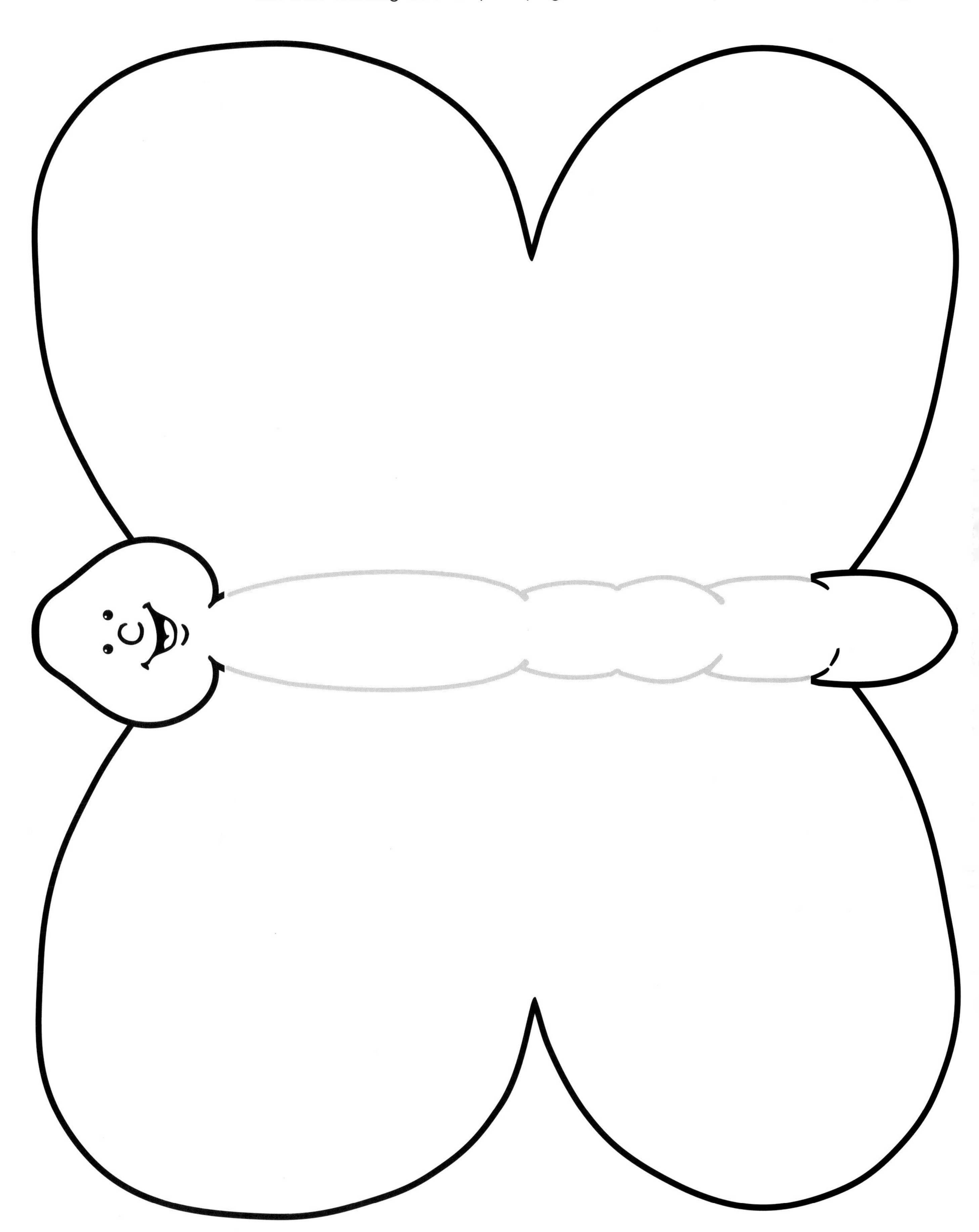

Welcome to the MATH RODEO

Round up your kindergartners to develop number comparison skills with the rootin'-tootin' ideas in this unit!

by Rhonda L. Chiles, South Park Elementary, Shawnee Mission, KS

The Rodeo Song

Singing a song

Get your students thinking about the rodeo with a reading of *Armadillo Rodeo* by Jan Brett. Then teach youngsters the rodeo song below. Yippee-yi-yo!

(sung to the tune of "This Old Man")

This cowboy,
He sees one,
One bareback rider having fun.
With a hat on his head
And a yippee-yi-yo!
This cowboy's at the rodeo.

This cowgirl,
She sees two,
Two bronc-riding buckaroos.
With a hat on her head
And a yippee-yi-yo!
This cowgirl's at the rodeo.

This cowboy,
He sees three,
Three calf ropers on bended knee.
With a hat on his head
And a yippee-yi-yo!
This cowboy's at the rodeo.

This cowgirl,
She sees four,
Four steer wrestlers keeping score.
With a hat on her head
And a yippee-yi-yo!
This cowgirl's at the rodeo.

This cowboy,
He sees five,
Five bull riders ready to ride.
With a hat on his head
And a yippee-yi-yo!
This cowboy's at the rodeo.

Rodeo Riders

Comparing two numbers

Have your little cowpokes wear identifying numbers on their backs—just like real rodeo contestants—for this number comparison activity. Program enough sheets of paper each with a different number to make a class set. Tape a number to each student's back and pair students. In turn, have each pair sit on chairs, straddle-style, so that their numbers can be seen by the rest of the class. Instruct students to think about the numbers worn by their classmates and decide which number is larger and which one is smaller. Then ask the group comparison questions such as "Is 13 less than 20?" or "Is two greater than or less than six?" Continue until all students have been riders. Yee-haw!

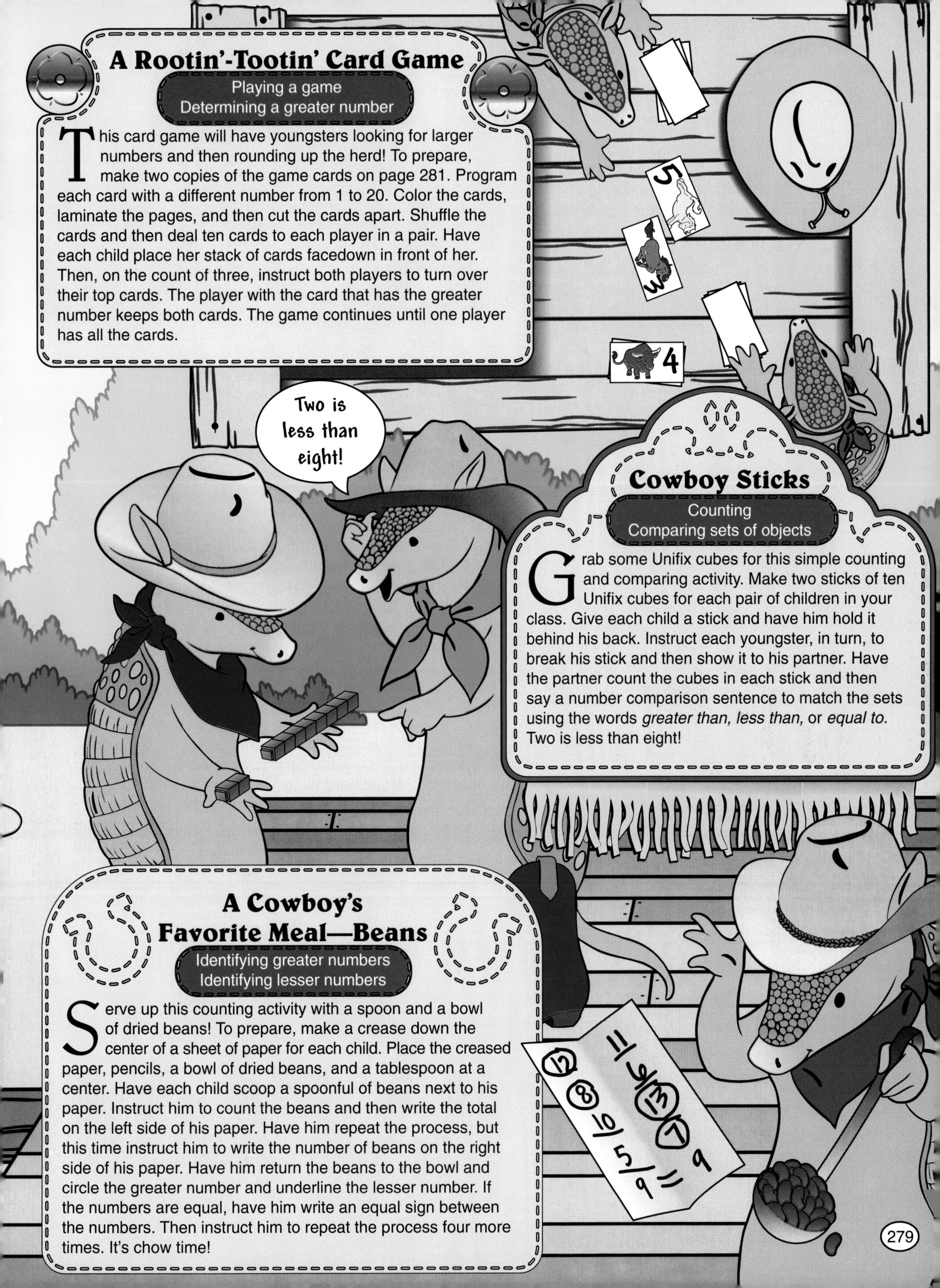

A Rootin'-Tootin' Card Game

Playing a game
Determining a greater number

This card game will have youngsters looking for larger numbers and then rounding up the herd! To prepare, make two copies of the game cards on page 281. Program each card with a different number from 1 to 20. Color the cards, laminate the pages, and then cut the cards apart. Shuffle the cards and then deal ten cards to each player in a pair. Have each child place her stack of cards facedown in front of her. Then, on the count of three, instruct both players to turn over their top cards. The player with the card that has the greater number keeps both cards. The game continues until one player has all the cards.

Cowboy Sticks

Counting
Comparing sets of objects

Grab some Unifix cubes for this simple counting and comparing activity. Make two sticks of ten Unifix cubes for each pair of children in your class. Give each child a stick and have him hold it behind his back. Instruct each youngster, in turn, to break his stick and then show it to his partner. Have the partner count the cubes in each stick and then say a number comparison sentence to match the sets using the words *greater than, less than,* or *equal to.* Two is less than eight!

A Cowboy's Favorite Meal—Beans

Identifying greater numbers
Identifying lesser numbers

Serve up this counting activity with a spoon and a bowl of dried beans! To prepare, make a crease down the center of a sheet of paper for each child. Place the creased paper, pencils, a bowl of dried beans, and a tablespoon at a center. Have each child scoop a spoonful of beans next to his paper. Instruct him to count the beans and then write the total on the left side of his paper. Have him repeat the process, but this time instruct him to write the number of beans on the right side of his paper. Have him return the beans to the bowl and circle the greater number and underline the lesser number. If the numbers are equal, have him write an equal sign between the numbers. Then instruct him to repeat the process four more times. It's chow time!

The Barrel Run

Comparing recorded times

A few orange cones (barrels) and two stopwatches are all you need for this time comparison event. Position two sets of three cones outdoors in the formation shown at left, making sure that the cones are at least ten feet apart. Divide students into two teams. Have another adult stand on the opposite side of the finish line and time one team while you time the other team. On your signal, have one child from each team run around each barrel and then across the finish line. Call out each team's time. Instruct the team with the faster (lesser) time to say, "Yee-haw!" After each child has run the race, treat the class to tasty root beer barrel candies!

Crunchy Corrals

Following directions

After all of this number comparison practice, your little buckaroos will be hungry for this snack. Gather the ingredients, utensils, and supplies listed below and then guide each child to make her own crunchy corral snack.

Ingredients for one:
slice of bread
peanut butter (for students with peanut allergies, substitute almond butter)
8 pretzel sticks
2 animal crackers

Utensils and supplies:
paper plate for each child
plastic knife for each child

Directions:
1. Spread peanut butter on a slice of bread.
2. Place pretzels around the edges of the bread as shown.
3. Add two animals to your corral.
4. Enjoy!

Game Cards

Use with "A Rootin'-Tootin' Card Game" on page 279.

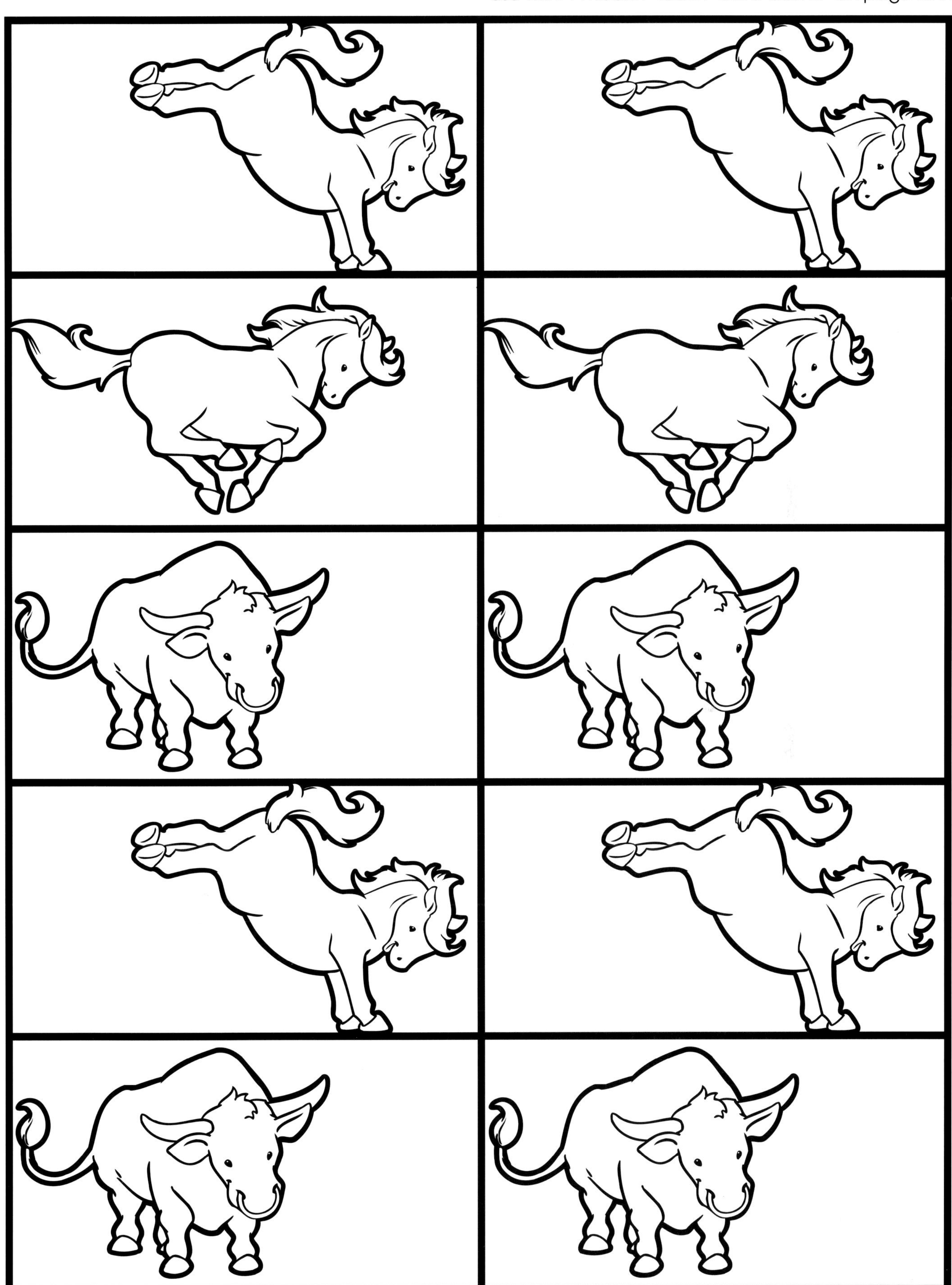

Kindergarten Kingdom

Hear ye! Hear ye!
Provide your youngsters with royal treatment using this collection of curriculum-related activities that are fit for a king or queen!

by Jana Sanderson, Rainbow School, Stockton, CA

Counting
Building with blocks

Castle-Building Blocks

Help little ones work as a team with this group castle-construction activity. To prepare, gather a supply of blocks and a die. Place the blocks in a pillowcase. Choose a child to roll the die and count the dots shown on top of it. Then have her select the appropriate number of blocks from the pillowcase. Instruct her to place her blocks on the floor to begin building the castle. Allow each child to take a turn and then add her blocks to the growing castle. When finished, take a photograph of the castle to display in the classroom.

Dictating information

Knights of the Classroom

Prepare yourself for a classroom filled with delighted knights when your youngsters create helmets and a kindergarten coat of arms. Using the dimensions below, make headband and visor tracers from tagboard. Trace the helmet parts on gray construction paper for each child. Have each student cut out the helmet pieces. Staple his headband to fit his head; then use brads to attach the visor as shown above.

Explain to the class that knights held a shield decorated with a coat of arms. The coat of arms helped identify the knight as belonging to a particular family. Create a classroom coat of arms to show the students that they belong to your kindergarten class. Cut a large shield out of white bulletin board paper. Invite students to supply information about the class, such as the school name, your name, the room number, topics studied, and classroom pets. Label the shield with students' responses. Then have each student sign the shield. Display the coat of arms and then have each youngster wear his helmet while you declare him a knight of your classroom!

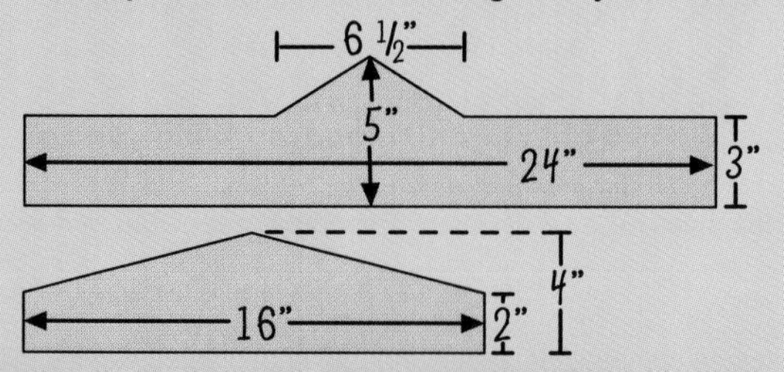

Matching uppercase and lowercase letters

Crown of Jewels

Matching uppercase letters with lowercase letters is a royal treasure when children use this letter-recognition activity to create a crown of jewels! In advance, cut out several crowns from construction paper. Make a blank game spinner. Laminate the crowns and spinner for durability. Use a dry-erase marker to label each section of the game spinner with a lowercase letter. Then write the corresponding capital letters on the points of each crown. Gather a supply of colorful bingo chips to use as jewels. To play, have each child spin the spinner, read the lowercase letter, and then place a jewel on the corresponding capital letter on her crown. If desired, reprogram the crowns to review a different set of letters. That's a gem of an idea!

Singing a song

A Medieval Melody

Everyone lives happily ever after when your youngsters sing this song about a knight, a princess, and a dragon! Challenge students to create actions to match each verse.

(sung to the tune of "The Wheels on the Bus")

The wings of the dragon go up and down,
Up and down, up and down.
The wings of the dragon go up and down,
All through the land.

The princess in the tower says, "Please save me,
Please save me, please save me!"
The princess in the tower says, "Please save me!"
All through the land.

The knight scares the dragon far away,
Far away, far away.
The knight scares the dragon far away,
All through the land.

The people in the kingdom dance happily,
Happily, happily.
The people in the kingdom dance happily,
All through the land.

Using descriptive words
Writing

Descriptive Dragons

Descriptive words are hot stuff with this crafty dragon-themed project! To prepare, gather a shallow pan, a class supply of drinking straws and red, orange, and yellow tempera paint. Make a copy of page 287 for each child. Give each child a straw and a 9" x 12" piece of white construction paper. Have each youngster place the paper in a shallow pan. Direct her to put several drops of each color of tempera paint on her paper. Then have her use her straw to blow the paint across her paper. When the paint is dry, show each child how to cut her paper into a flame shape. Next, give each child a copy of page 287 and instruct her to glue her flame near the dragon's mouth. Then have her use crayons to decorate her dragon. Instruct each student to write two words that describe her dragon to complete the sentence. My dragon is blue and scary!

Making a craft

Kindergarten Castles

Students will be the hit of the kingdom when they master plaster with these artful castles! In advance, purchase plaster of paris and a class supply of eight-ounce paper drinking cups, paper plates, and resealable plastic bags. Pour one cup of plaster of paris and one-half cup of water into a plastic bag for each child. Then seal the bag and allow the child to gently squeeze to mix the ingredients. When the plaster begins to thicken, help each youngster snip a corner of his bag and have him squeeze the mixture into his cup. Allow the plaster to set. Then have each child remove the paper cup mold and invert the plaster form on his plate. Provide paints for him to decorate his castle as desired. When the paint is dry, have each student use glue and construction paper scraps to create turrets, flags, and other embellishments. Display the projects on a table labeled "Kindergarten Kingdom!" Ahh! Castle, sweet castle!

Blending sounds to make words

Princess Hat Mix-Up

What word did the princess put under her hat? Your little ones won't have to kiss a frog to find out when they practice blending sounds with this playful activity based on the traditional fairy tale *The Frog Prince.* In advance, purchase three plain cone-shaped party hats. Decorate each hat as desired with stickers and streamers. Make several copies of the frog cards on page 288. Label each card with a different consonant. Use a permanent marker to program each of several yellow tennis balls with a different rime.

Begin by reading *The Frog Prince* by Jacob and Wilhelm Grimm. Working with a small group, have each child, in turn, draw a frog card from the pile. Place a golden ball underneath one of the hats. Shuffle the hats and then have the child guess which hat is hiding the ball. When she finds it, have her read a word by blending the letter on her frog card with the ending provided on the ball. Hats off to reading!

Problem solving

Sensory Mattresses

Fill cloth mattresses with different objects to give your youngsters the chance to prove their nobility, as did the princess in *The Princess and the Pea,* with this fun sensory activity! For each mattress, cut two 6" x 6" pieces of fabric and two 6" x 6" pieces of quilt batting. Place a small item—such as a LEGO block, a die, a clothespin, a small plastic animal, a key, a wooden star, or a coin—between the layers of batting. Then put a piece of fabric on the top and bottom of the batting layers. Staple the layers of fabric and batting together as shown. Put identical items in a tray. Place the mattresses and the tray at a center. Invite each child to feel each mattress and guess what is inside by viewing the items in the tray. I feel a key!

Making a craft

Crayon-Melt Shields

These fancy shields will be the perfect addition to your little knights' attire! Cut a shield and handle from cardboard, as shown, for each child. Warm an electric warming tray on low. Place a large piece of heavy-duty aluminum foil on the griddle for a student. Roll newspaper and place it on the edge of the tray for padding. With adult supervison, have the student use crayons to make a colorful design on the foil. After the crayon wax has dried, fold the foil around a cardboard shield and tape it in place. To finish the shield, staple a handle to the back as shown. Wow! What great shiny shields!

Tactile exploration

Feel-and-Find Saltcellars

In medieval times, kings and nobles had saltcellars, small containers for holding salt. Use this feel-and-find game to have youngsters searching through salt to find objects. To prepare, fill several small shoeboxes two-thirds full with salt. In each box, hide five small objects in the salt, such as a rubber band, a shell, a cotton swab, a large paper clip, and a pom-pom. Make a feel-and-find gameboard for each box by gluing matching objects to a piece of tagboard. To help with cleanup, place each saltcellar box inside a larger shallow container to help catch any salt that overflows.

To use a box, a child puts on a pair of plastic gloves, feels around in the salt to find the objects, and then places them on the gameboard next to the matching objects. After all objects have been found, instruct each child to hide them in the salt again.

Making a craft

Dragon Hats

Your youngsters are going to be oh so cute in these bright green dragon hats! To prepare, increase the hat patterns on page 289 by 50 percent and copy it onto tagboard. Cut out the pattern pieces to make tracers. Trace each pattern piece two times on green construction paper for each child. To prepare flames, cut red, orange, and yellow construction paper into strips. Give each child the patterns and have her cut them out. Instruct each youngster to glue a wing and a horn to each dragon body as shown. Then have her add a sticky dot eye to each dragon. Staple the dragons together, as shown, adjusting as needed to fit the child's head. Staple red, orange, and yellow paper strips at the mouth to represent fire. Have each youngster wear her hat during your "Hot and Spicy Tasting Party" (see below).

Writing

Scribbling Scribes

Your little ones will be eager to try this clever writing and drawing activity. In advance, brew several tea bags in hot water. To make a writing quill for each student, cut a feather quill at an angle. Next, cut a small slit in the point to draw up ink. To make ink, defrost a package of frozen blackberries. Put the berries in a bowl and have students help smash them with the back of a spoon. Give each child a piece of paper and have him crumple it and then smooth it out. Instruct him to rub a cooled tea bag over his paper until it is completely tinted. Then have him turn his paper over and tint the other side. After the papers have dried, invite each student to use a quill and berry-juice ink to write and draw on his paper. Encourage youngsters to write and draw about what they've learned during this thematic study. Write on!

Making a graph

Hot and Spicy Tasting Party

Have youngsters don their hats from "Dragon Hats" on this page and finish up your "Kindergarten Kingdom" unit with this fiery snack-sampling activity. Prepare tasting samples, such as salsa on chips, barbecue sauce on crackers, radish slices, pepper cheese pieces, and spicy pepperoni slices. Create a graph similar to the one shown. Invite each child to taste each spicy food and then determine his favorite. Give each youngster a sticky dot and instruct him to place it in the appropriate column of the graph to show his favorite spicy food. Discuss the graph results with students. Now that's a hot activity!

Name ______________________________

My Dragon

My dragon is ______________ and ______________.

Note to the teacher: Use with "Descriptive Dragons" on page 283.

Frog Cards

Use with "Princess Hat Mix-Up" on page 284.

Dragon Hat Patterns

Use with "Dragon Hats" on page 286.

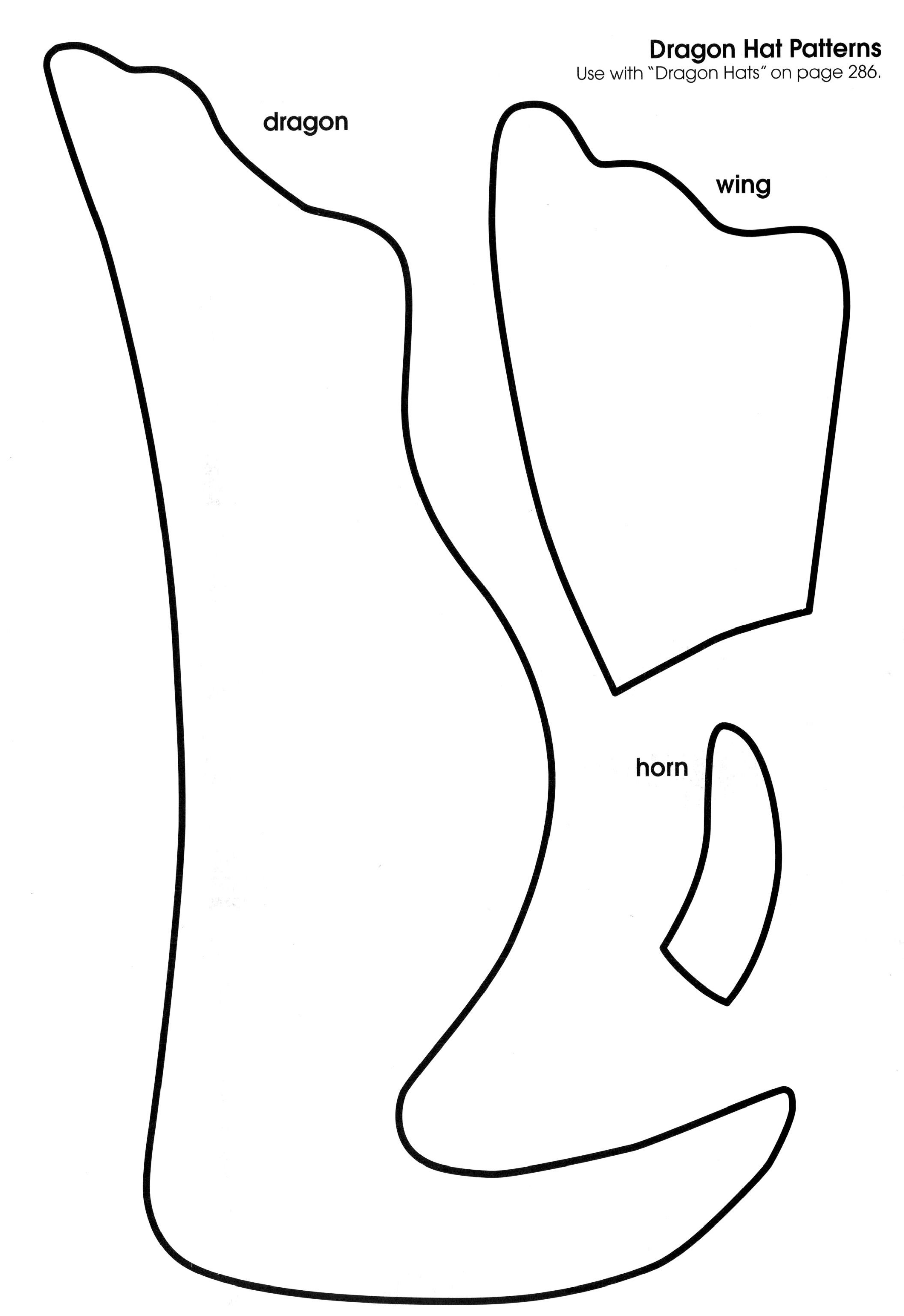

Sand, Sea,

Ahhh...the warmth of the sun, the softness of the sand, the roar of the waves! The beach is the perfect place to...learn about sight words? Sure! Here's an ocean of ideas to help your beginning readers focus on word families and high-frequency words.

by Ada Goren, Winston-Salem, NC

Octopus Words

Help your kindergartners see just how many words they can read with the help of a friendly ocean animal—the Word Octopus! Make a large cutout of an octopus, laminate it, and post it in your group area. Then make small cards with consonants and blends printed on them to keep close by. Each day, label the octopus with a different word ending. Then ask youngsters to think of words in this word family. When a child names a word, give her the letter card for the initial sound and ask her to hold it up in front of the word ending on the octopus. Then have her use a bit of Sticky-Tac to put the card on one of the octopus's arms. Can your students think of initial sounds for the octopus to hold in all eight arms?

Seashell Hunt

Collecting shells is a time-honored tradition at the beach. And when your students collect *these* shells, they'll also be collecting practice with word families! To prepare, duplicate the shell patterns on page 294 to make as many shells as you desire. Choose five or six different word families; then label each shell with a word from one of the families. Cut the shells apart and scatter them in your classroom. Set out plastic sand pails, each labeled with a word family. Then invite students to hunt for shells and deposit each one in the pail with the corresponding word ending.

and Sight Words

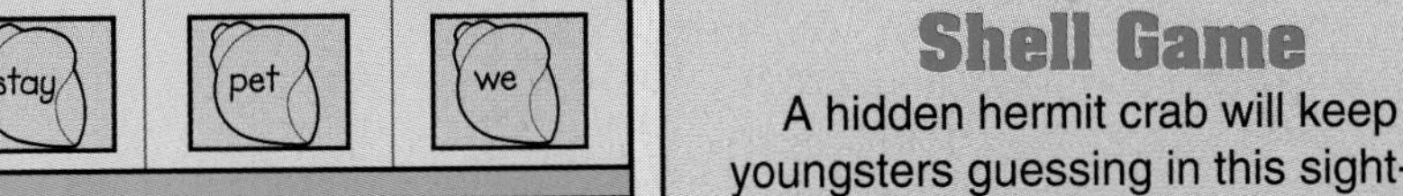

Beach Ball Zigzag

Your young beachcombers will love tossing around this idea! Inflate a large striped beach ball; then use a permanent marker to write four or five sight words on each colored stripe. Have your class form two lines facing one another. Give the ball to the first child in one line and have her toss it to the child across from her. Have students keep tossing the ball back and forth, zigzagging between the lines, until you call out a color word, such as "Yellow!" The child holding the ball must stop and read the sight words on the yellow stripe. Then say, "Zigzag!" and have students pass the ball back and forth until you call out another color.

Sharon Vandike—Gr. K
Visitation Inter Parish School
Vienna, MO

Shell Game

A hidden hermit crab will keep youngsters guessing in this sight-word shell game that's perfect for filling in a few minutes of spare time. To prepare, use the patterns on page 294 to make 12 shells and one copy of the hermit crab. Write a different sight word on each shell; then place the shells in a grid in a pocket chart, three across and four down. Tuck the hermit crab pattern behind one of the shells. To play the game, one child at a time calls out one of the sight words. Lift the corresponding shell to see if the hermit crab is hiding behind that word. The child who finds the hidden hermit crab is the winner! When you're ready to play again, simply change the hermit crab's hiding place.

adapted from an idea by
Diana Phillips—Gr. K
Murrayville-Woodson School
Murrayville, IL

Fishing for Color Words

Reel in some practice with word sorting when you try this idea! In advance, make a magnet fishing pole by attaching yarn or string to one end of a yardstick or dowel. Then tie a magnet to the free end of the string. Cut out a supply of paper fish; then label each one with a sight word, making some of the words color words. Slip a metal paper clip onto each fish.

When the materials are ready, spread the fish word-side-down on a section of blue bulletin board paper. Have a child try to attach the magnet to a paper clip on a fish. When a fish is "caught," have the child read the word on it. If the word is a color word, have him keep it in a plastic sand pail. If the word is not a color word, have him throw the fish back in. Encourage him to keep fishing until he's caught a predetermined number of color words.

Sounds and Sand

You'll see sight words in the sand when you try this small-group activity that focuses on hearing and recording sounds. Give each student a tub of dampened play sand and a small stick. Say a sight word and have each child use her stick to write the word in her sand. (Words with a simple consonant-vowel-consonant pattern work well.)

As a variation, provide letter-shaped cookie cutters. Give each child her own word to write and have her press the appropriate cutters into the sand to spell her word. Have everyone show her finished word to the group. Sand and spelling? Super!

Dig Into Spelling!

Digging in the sand is fun—especially when you unearth a treasure like magnetic letters! To prepare this center, bury a supply of magnetic letters in your sand table. Then label each of several index cards with a sight word you want your kindergartners to spell. Have a student at this center use a plastic shovel or sand scoop to dig up letters. Then have him use the letters to spell a sight word, either from memory or by matching the letters to one of the cards.

Take a Turn on the Towel

Ask youngsters to kick back on a beach towel, pop in a tape, and then read a few sight words at this beach-scene center! To prepare, make a tape recording of yourself reading a list of sight words, leaving plenty of time between each word. Reread the list more quickly at the end of the tape. Then make a set of word cards to match those on the tape. (If desired, use the shell patterns on page 294 as word cards.) To set up the center, lay out a comfy beach towel and place the tape in a tape recorder next to the towel. Stack the word cards nearby. A child at this center sits on the towel, listens to the tape, finds the corresponding word cards, and places them in order. He checks his work by listening as you read through the list at the end of the tape.

Waves of Words

You've heard of a word wall, but how about a word wave? Keep the surf-and-sand spirit going with this wet and wonderful display of familiar words! Simply give each child a wave shape cut from a sheet of blue construction paper. Ask him to write on it as many sight words as he can think of. Display all the wave cutouts end to end on a wall for everyone to "sea"!

Musical Beach Chairs

It's spelling by the sea when your little ones try a game of Musical Beach Chairs! To play this small-group game, bring in a number of beach chairs and set them up in a circle. Beneath each chair, place three magnetic letters that can be used to spell a CVC (consonant, vowel, consonant) word, such as *cat* or *mop*. Play some music and have youngsters walk around the outside of the circle. When you stop the music, have each child find a beach chair in which to sit. Have him use the magnetic letters under his chair to spell a word. Check the words; then have youngsters scramble the letters and put them back under the chairs. Start the music again for another round of play.

Shell Patterns

Use with "Seashell Hunt" on page 290, "Shell Game" on page 291, and "Take a Turn on the Towel" on page 293.

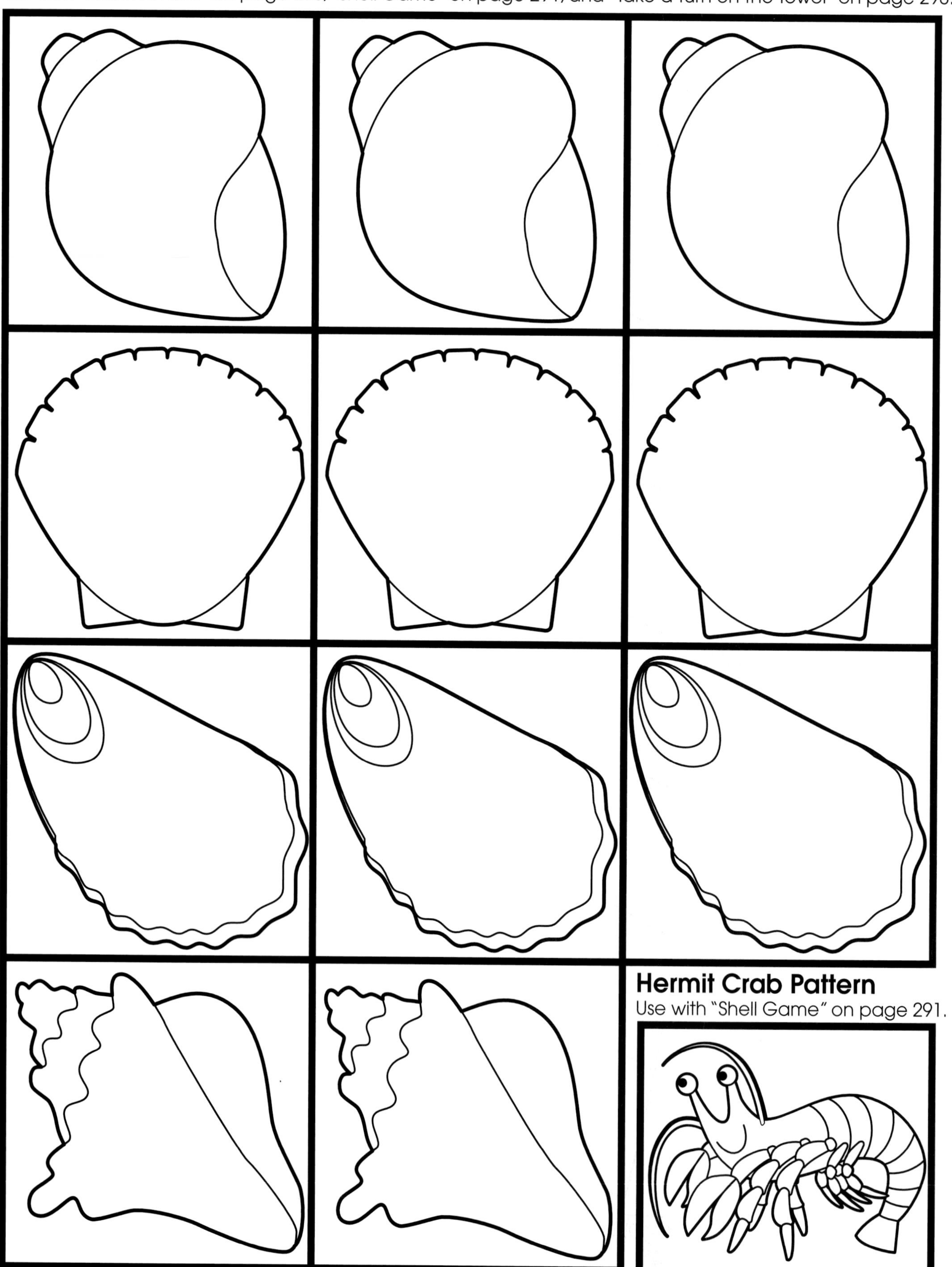

Hermit Crab Pattern

Use with "Shell Game" on page 291.

Name____

Stripes on the Sand

Read.

Color.

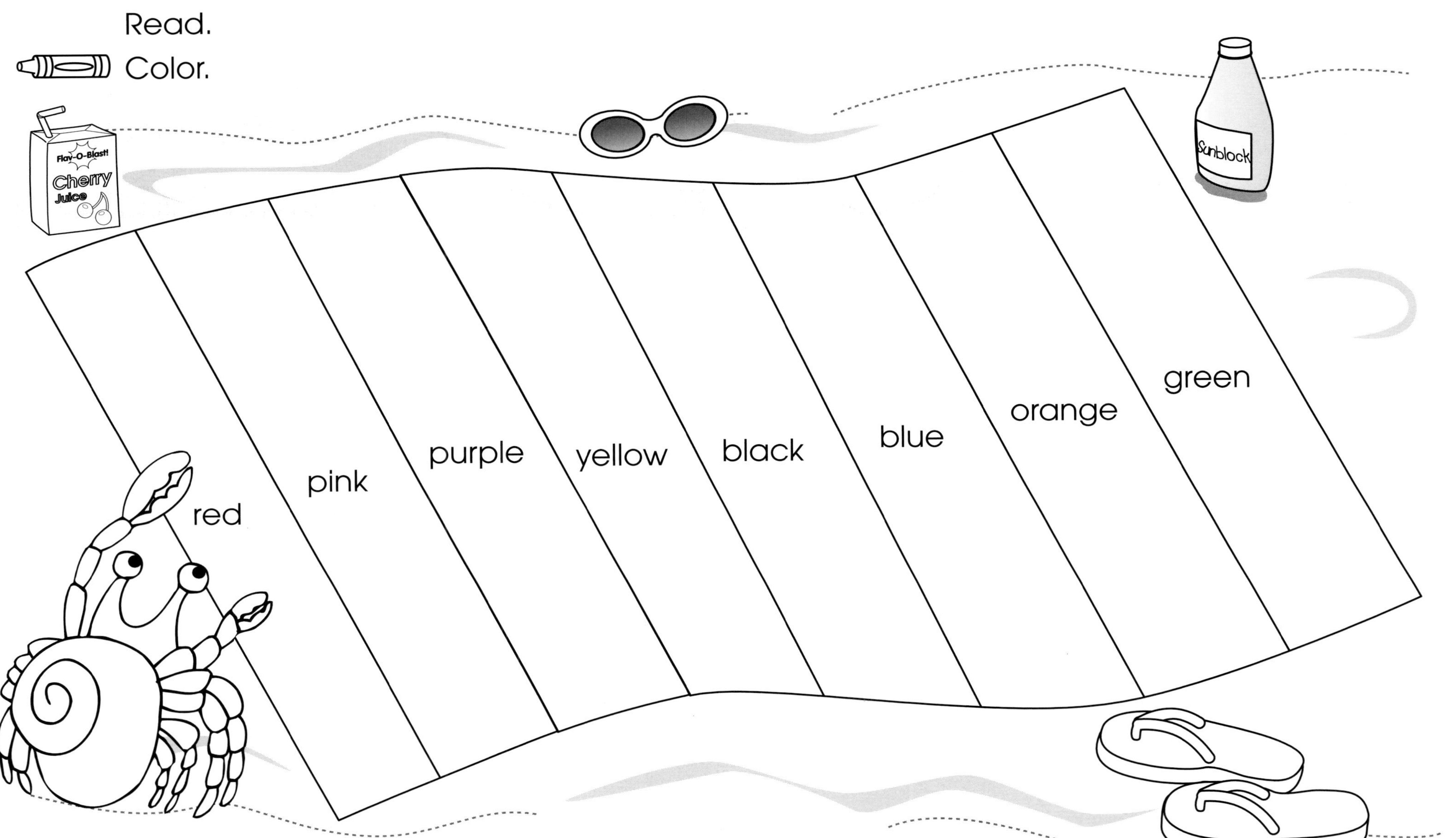

Name____

Pail Pals

Cut.
Match.
Glue.

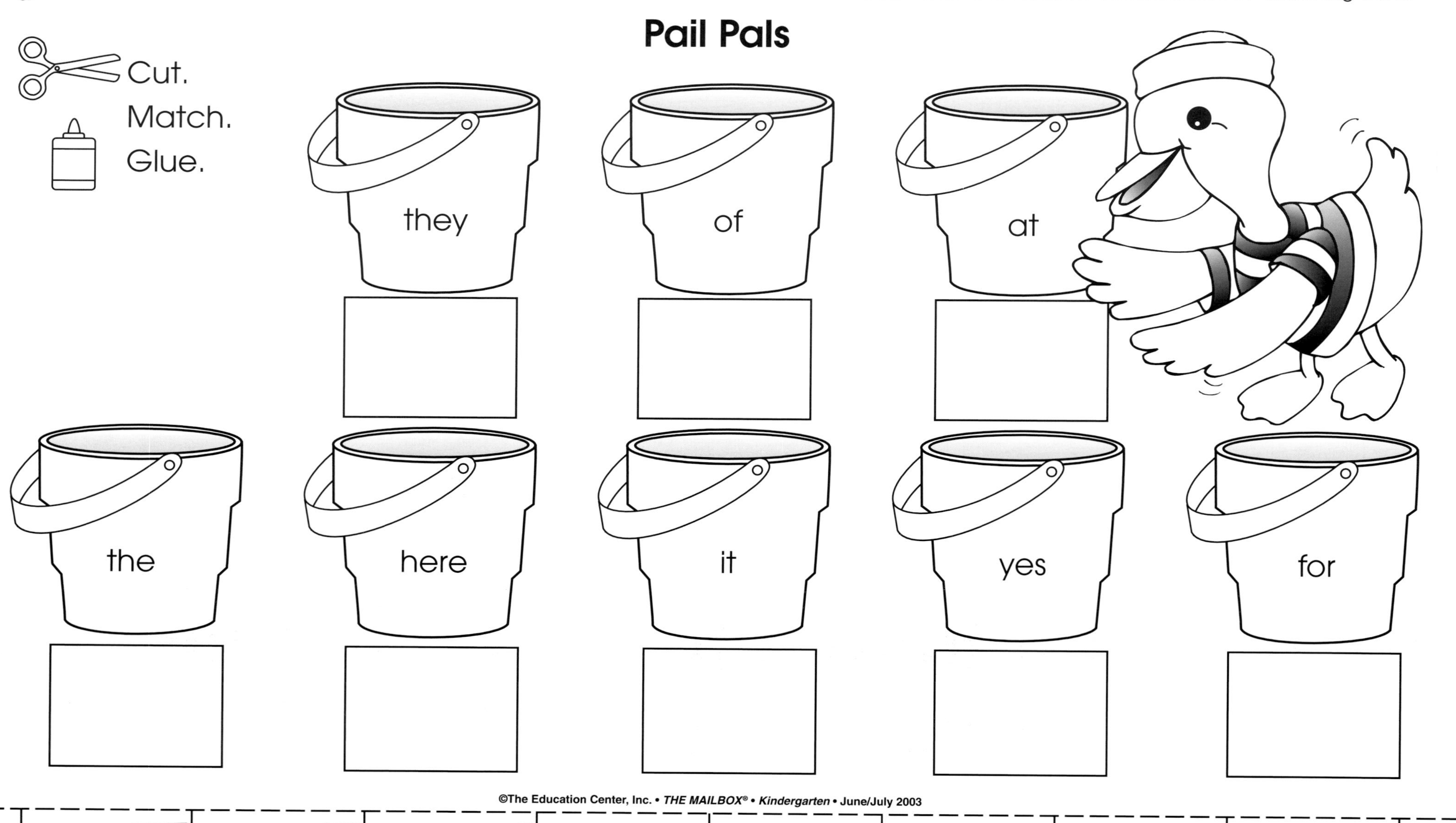

Let FREEDOM Ring!

Celebrate Independence Day with these clever ideas for our symbols of freedom. Happy Birthday, America!

Making a craft

Regal Eagle Hats

Your youngsters' pride will soar when they make and wear these eagle hats! To prepare, make several tagboard copies of the head and wing patterns on page 299. Cut out the patterns to use as tracers. Fold a 9" x 12" sheet of white construction paper in half and trace the wing pattern for each child as directed. Gather the supplies listed below and then guide each student to complete an eagle hat. As youngsters don their hats, explain to them that the bald eagle was adopted as the national bird of the United States on June 20, 1792, because of its strength, long life, and majestic beauty. Have your little patriots proudly wear their eagle hat creations while completing the other ideas in this unit. Let freedom fly!

Materials needed for one hat:
9" x 12" sheet of white construction paper, folded and traced with a wing pattern
4" x 6" piece of blue construction paper (body)
4" x 6" piece of white construction paper (head)
access to a head tracer
scissors
black marker
yellow marker
red paint
paintbrush
glue
silver star stickers
3"-wide strip of paper long enough to fit around a child's head
stapler

Directions:
1. Cut out the wings.
   Cut the wings apart along the fold.
2. Trace the head on white construction paper.
   Cut out the head.
3. Use markers to draw an eye and color the beak on the head.
4. Paint red stripes on the wings.
   Allow the paint to dry.
5. Glue the head to one end of a blue body piece.
   Glue one wing to each side of the body.
6. Attach star stickers to the center of the body.
7. Staple the eagle to a headband strip and then staple the strip to fit the child's head.

dayle timmons—Inclusion Teacher
Chets Creek Elementary
Jacksonville, FL

Creating a bulletin board

I Spy Our Flag

This flag display is sure to get oohs and aahs when you utilize your school's bulletin board showcase. To prepare, sketch the American flag on a large piece of white bulletin board paper sized to fit your display case. Die-cut 50 white paper stars. Gather red, white, and blue Christmas tree garland or shiny, shredded gift bag filler and a large supply of red and white objects, such as crayons, plastic silverware, gift bows, toy cars, small counters, LEGO blocks, colored toothpicks, or milk jug lids. Make a list of the objects to post in the display. To decorate the flag, paint one stripe or section at a time with glue. Have students place the appropriate color of garland or gift bag filler on the glue. Tape or glue the stars to the blue section of the flag. Hang the flag in the display case and then use tape, glue, or pushpins to attach the small items to the flag. I spy a beautiful flag!

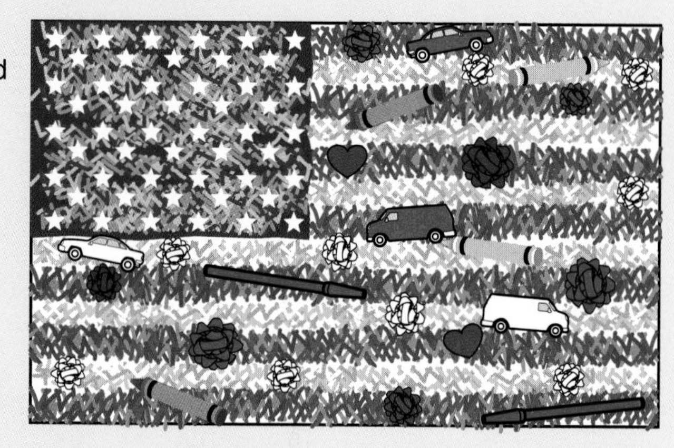

Fran Morcone—Gr. K
Memorial Elementary
Milford, MA

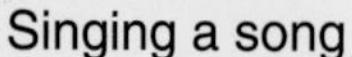

Singing a song

The Liberty Bell

Sing this song with your little ones to remind them of the importance of the Liberty Bell. Before singing, tell students that the Liberty Bell rang on July 8, 1776, to summon the public for the first reading of the Declaration of Independence. The bell rang for many years until a large crack formed. Introduce your youngsters to this icon of history with the song below.

(sung to the tune of "When the Saints Go Marching In")

Oh, when the bell
Rang out for freedom
On that Independence Day,
It was named the Liberty Bell,
And it rang to guide the way.

Oh, then a crack
Silenced the bell.
It now stands in dignity
As a symbol of our freedom.
It proclaims our liberty.

dayle timmons—Inclusion Teacher
Chets Creek Elementary
Jacksonville, FL

Making a snack

A Birthday Cake for America

Students will be eager to help decorate this cake to celebrate Independence Day. In advance, make a cake according to package directions. Photocopy a small map of the United States. Cut out and discard the map, leaving a stencil of it. Gather several different colors of candy sprinkles. Frost the cake with vanilla frosting and very gently lay the map stencil on top. In turn, invite each child to add sprinkles to a section of the cake. After the area has been filled in with sprinkles, gently lift the stencil to reveal the resulting colorful map. Before serving the cake, sing "Happy Birthday to You" to America!

Eagle Head and Wing Patterns

Use with "Regal Eagle Hats" on page 297.

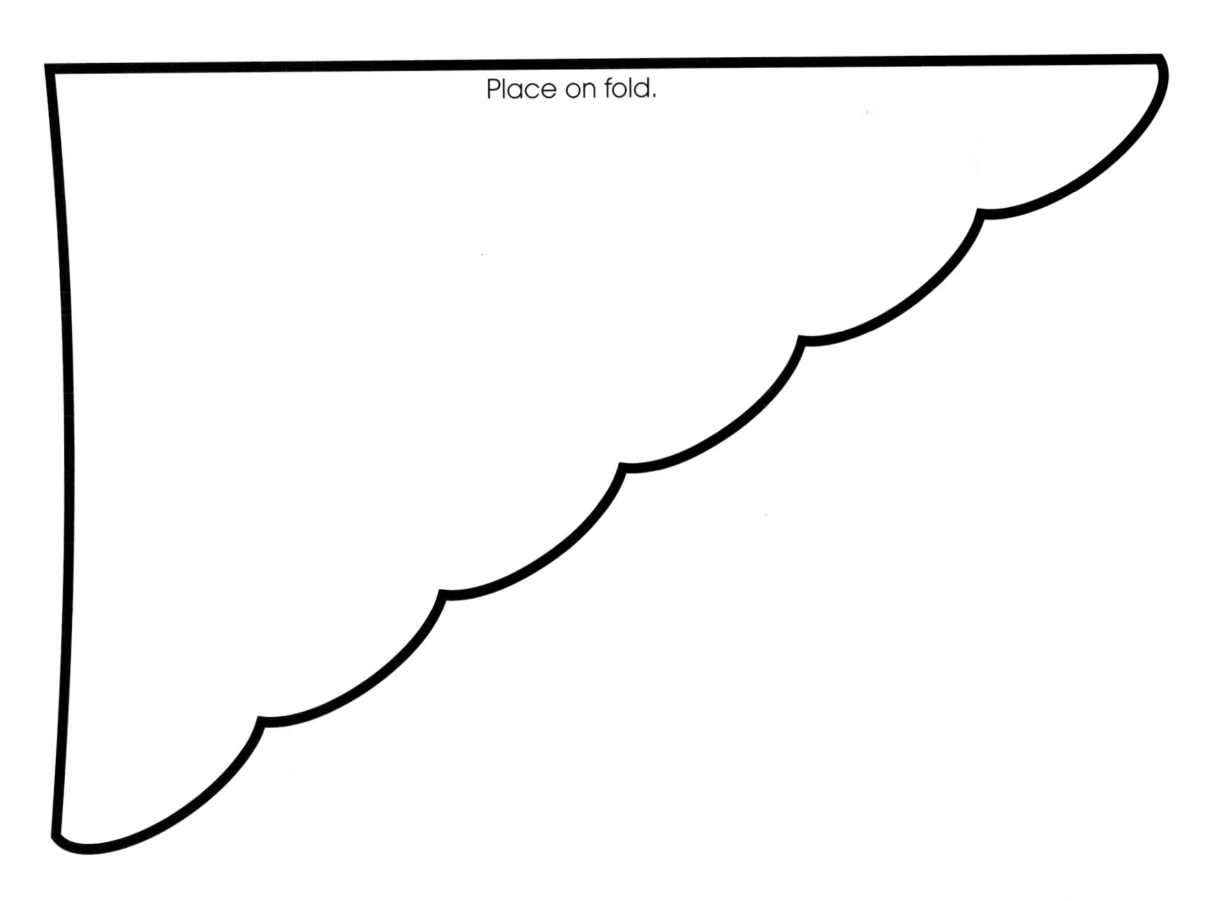

Camp Kindergarten

Pack your bags and load the bus—a trip to Camp Kindergarten is about to begin! Use the ideas in this fun cross-curricular unit to help your little campers learn a few things while having a whole lot of fun! Go, Camp Kindergarten!

by Jana Sanderson, Rainbow School, Stockton, CA

Singing a song

Camping Fun

No camp would be complete without a campfire song. Teach your youngsters this little ditty and camping will be at the top of their summertime activities lists!

(sung to the tune of "Twinkle, Twinkle, Little Star")

Camping, camping, fun galore,
How I love the great outdoors.
Hiking, fishing, watching stars,
Roasting marshmallows in the fire.
Camping, camping, fun galore,
How I love the great outdoors.

Addition

Let's Tackle Math Facts

No bait is necessary to lure little ones to this fun math game! To make a tackle box, paint the outside of a cardboard egg carton; then allow the paint to dry. Glue a strip of felt over the holes in the lid. Make two holes in the felt and then add a pipe cleaner handle. Next, write a different number inside each cup. Place two small fishing bobbers in the box. (Close the lid, turn the tackle box upside down, and shake it. Open the lid and check to see that the bobbers were small enough to move to different cups. If not, choose smaller bobbers.) To play, have each child, in turn, shake the tackle box, open it, and then add the two numbers from the cups that the bobbers landed in. During the last round of play, reward your little fishermen with a Goldfish crackers treat equal to the sums of their equations!

Writing
Making a book

Something Has Been Sleeping in My Tent!

This class book doubles as both a writing and a circle-time activity. To begin, have each child select and cut out a picture of an animal from a discarded magazine. Give each student a 9" x 12" and a 12" x 18" sheet of construction paper. Show youngsters how to cut the smaller sheet of paper into a tent shape as shown. Instruct each student to glue his animal picture to the bottom of his larger sheet of paper. Next, help him glue the top and side edges of his tent to his paper so that the animal can be revealed by lifting the tent flaps. Have each child write clues at the top of his paper describing the animal sleeping inside. Invite each child to read his clues to the class and encourage them to guess what is sleeping in the tent. Then bind the pages along with a cover and title the book "Something Has Been Sleeping in Our Tents!"

Playing a game

Pass-s-s the Snake, Please!

Your youngsters may not be lucky enough to find a snake skin while camping, but this game allows campers to see a snake shed its skin right before their eyes! Wrap a class supply of gummy worms in plastic wrap. Cover the plastic with a layer of tissue paper. Add sticky-dot eyes and a paper tongue. Wrap the snake in several layers of tissue paper, adding eyes and a tongue each time. Play music and have students pass the snake around the circle. Periodically stop the music and tell students that the snake must shed a layer of skin. The child holding the snake must carefully unwrap one layer of tissue. The game continues until the last layer of skin is shed and the slithery sweets are shared!

Playing a game
Addition

Catch of the Day

Once your campers play this fishing game, they'll be hooked on addition! To prepare, cut a large supply of fish from construction paper. Program each fish with a different addition problem. Attach a paper clip to each fish and string the fish on a long length of yarn. Cut a class supply of nine-inch paper plates in half. Place the two halves of each plate together and hole-punch along the curved side. Give each child a pair of plate halves and a long length of yarn and have her lace the two halves together. Tie another long length of yarn to the pouch to make a strap. Have students color their fish bags if desired. Tie the string of fish up just within students' reach. In turn, instruct each child to run up and catch a fish (pull one off the line) and then place it in her fish bag. After all of the fish have been caught, have each child read her problems and answer them for the class. Nice catch!

Estimating

Grizzly Guesstimation Jars

You can count on this activity to get youngsters excited about estimating! Label each of four plastic jars with a different one of the following letters: *B, E, A,* and *R.* Line the jars up in that order; then fill each jar with different objects used or seen while camping—such as small pine cones, rocks, marshmallows, and leaves—so that the *B* jar contains the least number of objects and each of the others contains more than the previous one. Display the jars so that the letters are out of order. Give each child a piece of paper and a pencil and have her write an estimation of the number of objects in each jar. As a group, count the objects in each jar and then order them from least to greatest. Your campers will be surprised to learn that, when placed in the correct order, the letters on the jars spell the word *bear!*

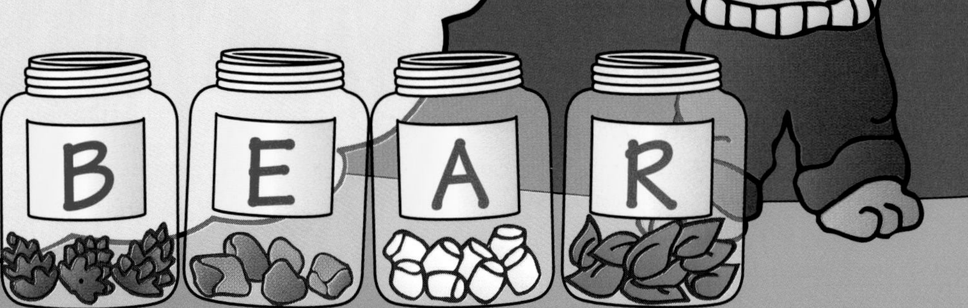

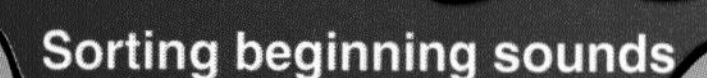

Here's a hot idea for sorting beginning blends! To prepare, fold several 12" x 18" sheets of black construction paper in half. On one side of each folded sheet, glue red, orange, and yellow tissue paper flames as shown. Using a white crayon, label each fire with a blend. Write words beginning with your selected blends on toilet paper tube logs. To play, have each child match the correct logs to the appropriate fire.

Suggested blends and camping-related words:

br:	**br**anch	**sl:**	**sl**eeping bag
	brush		**sl**eep
	bread		**sl**ither
	breeze		**sl**ug
st:	**st**ars	**sm:**	**sm**older
	stew		**sm**ell
	stick		**sm**ile
	storm		**sm**oke
tr:	**tr**acks	**sn:**	**sn**ake
	trout		**sn**eak
	trail		**sn**arl
	trees		**sn**ack

Storytelling

A Campfire Story

Set the scene for a great storytelling experience. In advance, explain to students that a story needs a beginning, middle, and end. Encourage them to keep this in mind when they create this group story. Build a campfire ring by crumpling newspaper into balls and then placing them in a circle. Put a few logs (paper towel tubes) in the center and then add a few tissue paper flames. Then invite students to sit around the fire. Dim the lights; then turn on a flashlight and hand it to a student. Explain to youngsters that they will be adding a sentence or two to a story as the flashlight is passed around the circle. Begin the story by saying, "One day we went on a camping trip." Then have the child holding the flashlight add the next part to the story. As the story is told, write it down on chart paper, using a different color of marker for each child. After the story is finished, retell it by reading the chart. What wonderful adventures will your little campers experience?

> One day we went on a camping trip. We set up our tents and then started fishing. There were so many fish. They were jumping in our canoe. The canoe got full. We started to sink. The fish swam away. We swam to shore. There wasn't any real fish for dinner, so we ate fish sticks!

Reciting a poem
Dramatizing a poem

Five Happy Campers

This poem will put smiles on the faces of all your students! Invite five children to act out the roles of the campers as the rest of the class recites the poem. Repeat the activity until each child has had a turn to participate in the dramatization.

Five happy campers were paddling a canoe. *(All pretend to paddle.)*
The first one said, "The water looks so blue." *(Shield eyes and look to the ground.)*
The second one said, "That fish just did a flip!" *(Stand and twirl a finger in the air.)*
The third one said, "Sit down before we tip." *(Pretend to steady the canoe.)*
The fourth one said, "Let's row. Let's row." *(Pretend to row.)*
The fifth one said, "Feel the wind blow." *(Brush hair away from face.)*
Then zip went the canoe back to the shore,
And five happy campers paddled out once more! *(All pretend to paddle.)*

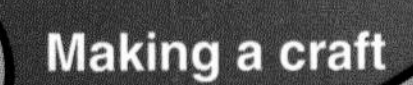

Paper Bag Backpacks

A few simple supplies are all your youngsters need to make these cute backpacks! In advance, gather a class supply of medium-size brown paper bags. Trim the top two inches of each bag as shown. Place two strips of packing tape on the back of each bag to reinforce the strap area. Cut two slits four inches apart on each strip of tape as shown. Cut two three-foot lengths of heavy yarn for each child. Give each youngster a bag and have him decorate it using crayons. Help him thread two lengths of yarn through the slits in the back of his bag and then tie the ends in a knot. To close the backpack, have him attach the hook side of a self-adhesive Velcro fastener to the flap and the loop side to the bag. Have youngsters wear their backpacks while collecting items on a nature walk. After you've returned to the classroom, invite each child to empty his pack and share his nature walk finds!

Making a snack

Campfire Snack

Here's a sizzling snack that will have your students gathering round to make it. Gather the ingredients, utensils, and supplies; then guide each child to complete her tasty campfire snack.

Ingredients for one snack:
rice cake
peanut butter (or almond butter for those students with peanut allergies)
popcorn (rocks for fire ring)
six pretzel stick halves (logs)
small spoonful of strawberry jam (flames)

Utensils and supplies for each child:
paper plate
plastic knife
plastic spoon

Directions:
1. Spread peanut butter on a rice cake.
2. Add rocks around the edge to make a fire ring.
3. Add logs.
4. Add fire.

Five Senses Centers

Five Senses of Camping

Get your youngsters thinking about camping by reading *When We Go Camping* by Margriet Ruurs. Then have students think of things they might see, hear, smell, taste, and touch while camping. Record their ideas on a chart. Review the chart and then place it in your writing center. Encourage youngsters to refer to the list when writing about their camping experiences.

see—birds, leaves, logs
hear—rain, wind, birds
smell—campfire, flowers, pine sap
taste—marshmallows, water, hot dogs
touch—bark, rocks, fishing pole

Feely-Bag Puzzle

This simple center has students using their keen sense of touch. Place in a pillowcase several nature items, such as a rock, a stick, a feather, a piece of bark, and a small pine cone. Draw a picture of each object on a strip of paper and tape it to a table at a center. Have each child place her hand in the case and feel the objects. Instruct her to look at the pictures on the strip and move the items in the bag so that they are in the same order. After she is satisfied with their positions, have her peek in the bag to check her work. Then instruct her to mix the items for the next student.

Sensory Graph

Set up this graphing activity and have students thinking about whether things can be sensed by more than one of our five senses. Make several copies of pages 305 and 306. Color the cards and then cut them apart. Glue each set of cards to a different piece of poster board as shown. Then use a marker to create a grid. Laminate the mats for durability. Place the mats and a supply of Unifix cubes at the center. Have each child look at each picture and then place cubes on the mat to show which senses are used when observing each object.

Five Senses Picture Cards

Use with "Sensory Graph" on page 304.

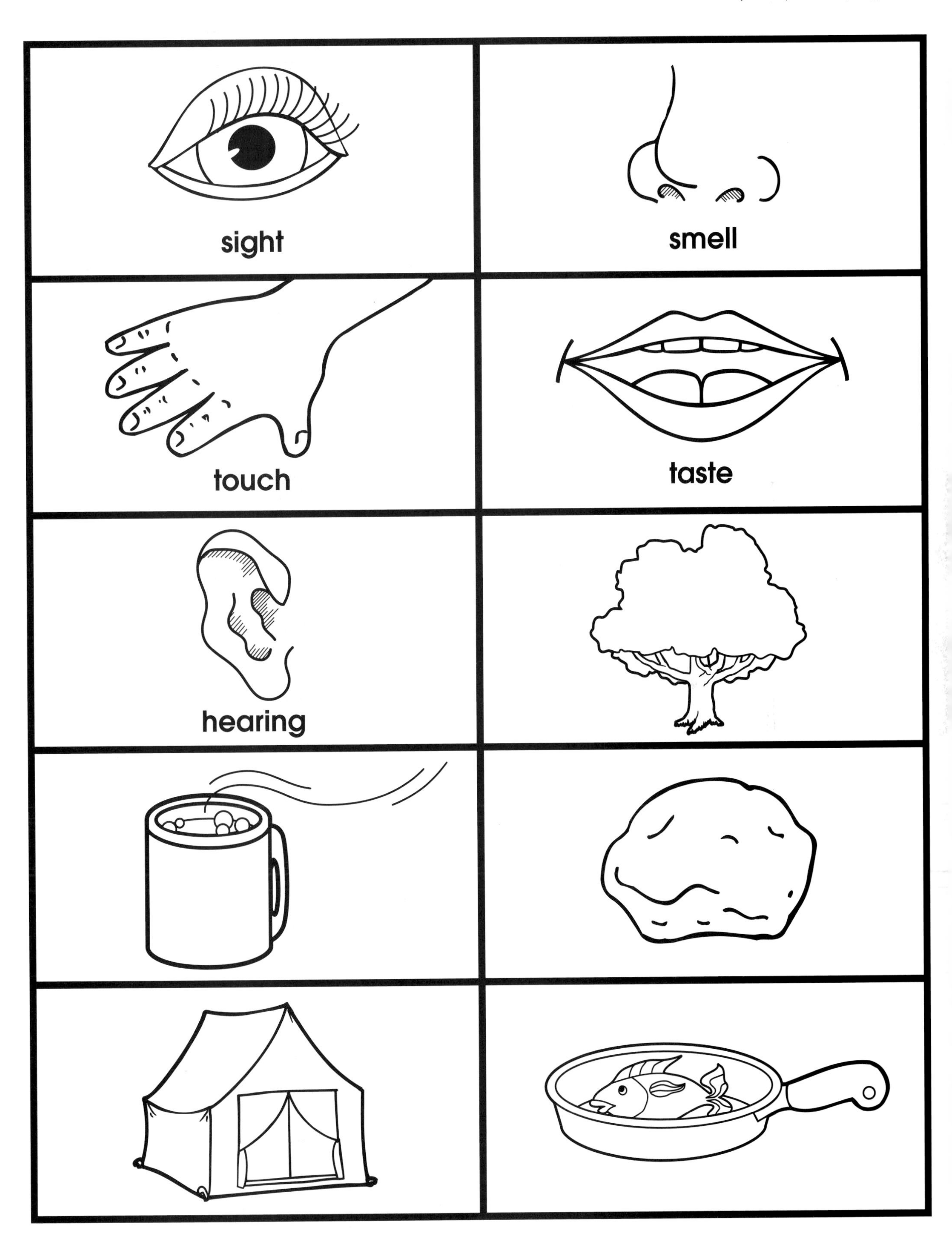

Five Senses Picture Cards

Use with "Sensory Graph" on page 304.

Adding and Subtracting at the Picnic

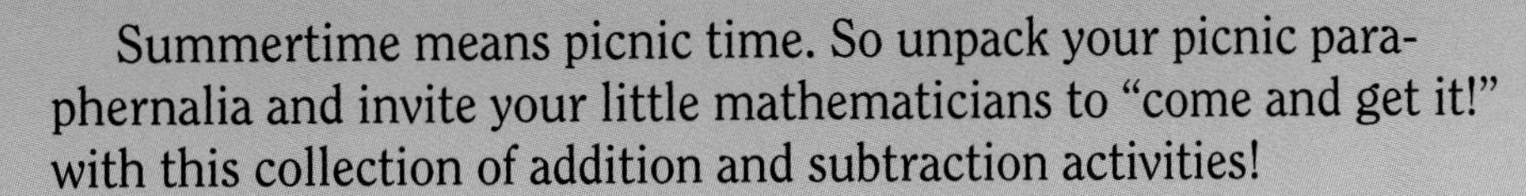

Summertime means picnic time. So unpack your picnic paraphernalia and invite your little mathematicians to "come and get it!" with this collection of addition and subtraction activities!

by Lucia Kemp Henry, Fallon, NV

Friends Have Fun at a Picnic!

What is the most important ingredient at a picnic? People! Invite youngsters to come to the picnic with this active addition exercise. To prepare, purchase a supply of red paper plates and blue paper plates. Cut two two-yard lengths each of red and blue bulletin board paper. Tape the paper, as shown, to create two picnic cloths; then lay them on the floor. Place the paper plates in a picnic basket nearby. Choose up to 12 volunteers to take a plate from the basket. Then direct each child to sit at the cloth that matches the color of his plate. Next, ask volunteers to count the people sitting at each cloth. Then add the numbers together as a class by counting the total number of people. Finally, have the students sing the song below, prompting them to insert the appropriate numbers in Lines 5, 6, and 7. Continue playing the activity until all students have had a chance to choose a plate. Great!

(sung to the tune of "Take Me Out to the Ballgame")

Friends have fun at a picnic.
Friends all sit on the ground.
They smell the hot dogs and hamburgers.
They can't wait 'til the food's passed around!
I see [number] friends there at the red cloth,
And [number] right there at the blue.
I see [total number] friends waiting to eat.
Wow! I'm hungry too!

Ant Addition

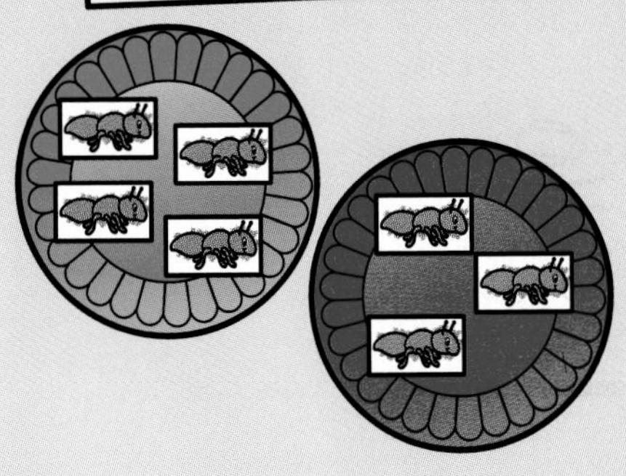

Use colorful plates and a few unwelcome picnic guests to have youngsters practice addition facts! In advance, copy the ant cards on page 310 to make a class supply and gather the paper plates used in "Friends Have Fun at a Picnic!" on this page. Also program several sentence strips with addition number sentences, as shown, making the two addends reflect the two colors of the plates. To begin the activity, give each child one plate of each color and a page of ant cards. Have the student color the ant cards and then cut them out. Next, present one of the programmed sentence strips. Explain that the colored numbers in the addition problem match the colored plates. Direct each child to place the correct number of ants on each plate to represent the number sentence. Then instruct him to add the numbers together by counting the total number of ants. Extend the activity by challenging students to use the ants to think of their own addition facts. Have each child write his number sentence on a sentence strip using the appropriate colors. That's a fact!

Packing for a Picnic!

Have students pack picnic supplies for addition and subtraction success! Prior to the activity, make copies of the addition and subtraction cards on pages 311-312; then fill in the blanks in Lines 1 and 2 of each card with desired numerals. Collect a supply of paper plates, cups, and plastic forks; then place them next to a picnic basket. Begin the activity by presenting one card to students. Assist a child in following the addition or subtraction problem to appropriately pack the basket. When finished, instruct the youngster to answer the question in Line 3 and then write the number problem on the card. Picnic's packed!

Flip a Fact!

Cook up some addition facts with this hamburger-flipping activity. Decorate a large sheet of white poster board to look like a grill; then program it as shown. Laminate the poster board for use with dry-erase markers. Cut 12 small circles from a piece of cardboard to represent hamburgers. Provide a spatula for the children to use. (If desired, also provide a chef's hat for the activity.)

Begin the activity by instructing a child to join you at a table. Invite her to put on the chef's hat. Then direct her to use the spatula to place several hamburgers on each side of the grill. Have her count the hamburgers on either side and then use a dry-erase marker to write each number in the appropriate blank as shown. Next, direct the child to count the total number of hamburgers. Instruct her to write the answer in the final blank. Then have the child recite the rhyme at right, filling in the appropriate numbers in Lines 1 and 2. Finally, have her answer the question in Line 4. Wipe off the numbers and you're ready for another clever cook!

[Number] hamburgers are on the grill.
Add [Number] more burgers, oh what a thrill!
Everyone's waiting to eat their fill.
How many burgers are on the grill?

Watermelon Math

Add Some Watermelon to My Plate!

2 + 2 = 4
2 + 3 = 5
1 + 3 = 4
4 - 3 = 1
5 - 3 = 2

What food is sweet, juicy, and a favorite at picnics? Watermelon, of course! Guide your little ones through this watermelon seed subtraction and addition activity. In advance, gather a supply of small black pom-poms and white paper plates. Instruct each child to color a paper plate, as shown, to look like a watermelon slice. Then give each child 12 pom-poms to represent watermelon seeds. Present oral addition or subtraction problems. Have each child use her seeds to reproduce each problem on her watermelon slice. To extend the activity, give each child a subtraction or addition problem written on a sentence strip. Have her reproduce the problem with her seeds and then glue the pom-poms to her watermelon slice to represent the answer. Display the sentence strips and watermelon slices on a bulletin board with the title "Add Some Watermelon to My Plate!"

Those Uninvited Ants!

Use this flannelboard activity and a swarm of picnic pests to enhance students' subtraction skills! Make one construction paper copy of the ant cards on page 310. Color the ants; then cut out the cards and prepare them for flannelboard use. Cut an anthill shape from brown felt and cut a red felt square to represent a picnic blanket. Then display the anthill and blanket on a flannelboard. Next, have a child choose several ant cards and place them on the blanket. Then instruct the children to recite the first two lines of the rhyme below, describing the number of ants on the blanket in Line 1. Have a second volunteer remove a smaller set of the ants from the blanket and place them on the anthill. Then have the children recite the remaining lines of the rhyme, describing the number of ants moved to the anthill in Line 3. Finally, have a child answer the question in Line 4 of the rhyme. Five ants are left!

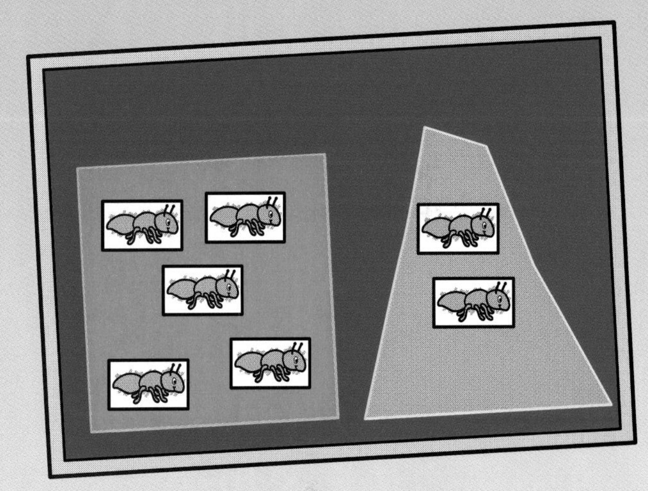

[Number] little ants came out to chew.
Shoo, ants! This food's not for you!
[Number] little ants are running away.
How many ants are left to play?

Speedy Spatula Subtraction

You're sure to see smiles when youngsters subtract hamburgers with this speedy spatula race. Gather the spatula, cardboard hamburgers, and grill used in "Flip a Fact!" on page 308. Place 12 hamburgers on the grill; then line up 12 volunteers on the side of the room opposite the grill. Place a paper plate on a table near the volunteers. To begin the activity, have the first child in line take the spatula, walk to the grill, and scoop up a hamburger. Then have her walk back and place the hamburger on the paper plate. Instruct her to give the spatula to the next child before taking a seat with the rest of the class. Repeat the procedure with each child. Several times throughout the activity, stop the children and direct their attention to a chalkboard. Have students assist you in writing a subtraction problem showing the number of hamburgers on the plate subtracted from 12. Direct a volunteer to count the hamburgers left on the grill and then write the answer on the board. Continue the activity until all children have had a chance to join the race!

Ant Cards

Use with "Ant Addition" on page 307 and "Those Uninvited Ants!" on page 309.

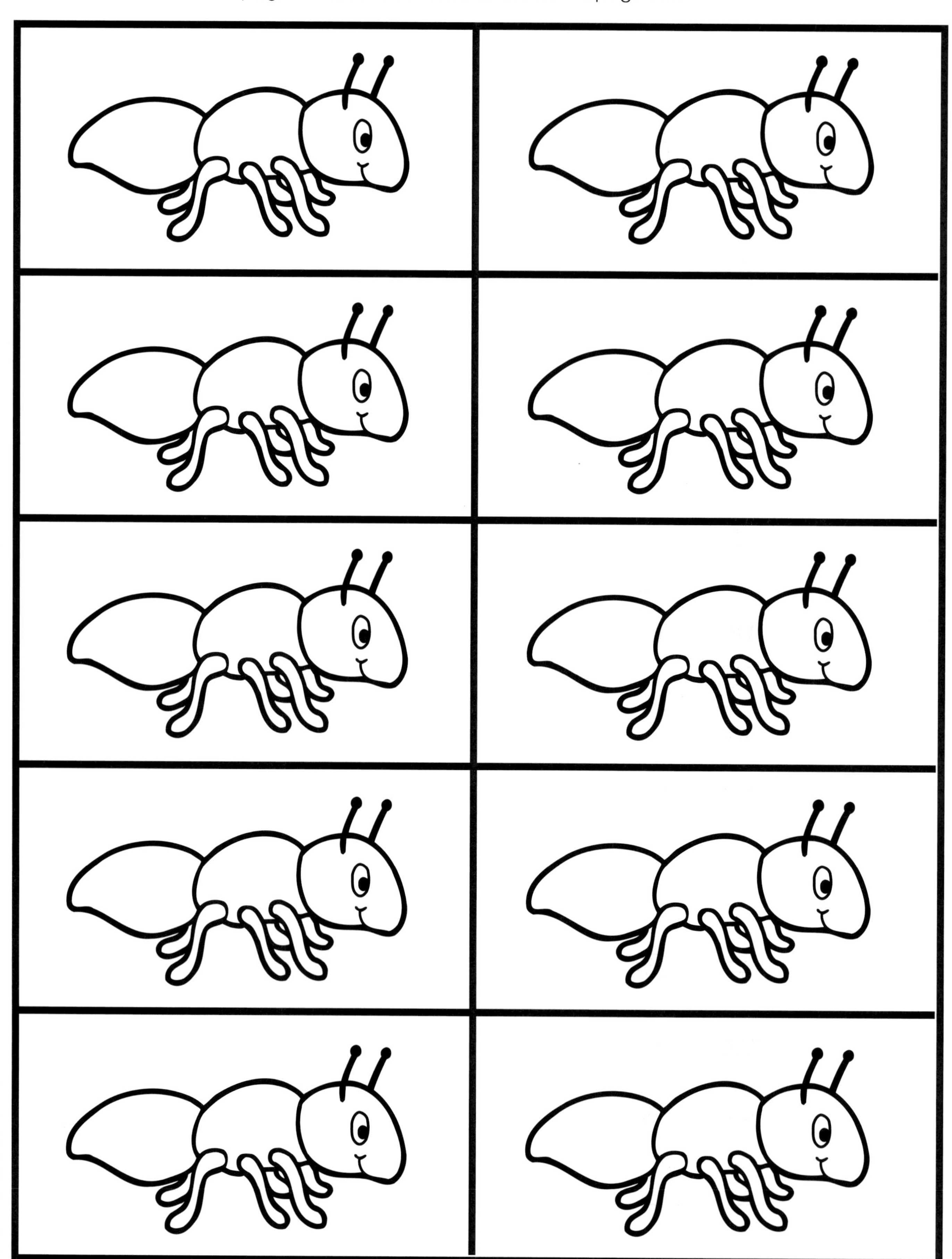

Use with "Packing for a Picnic!" on page 308.

Put _______ 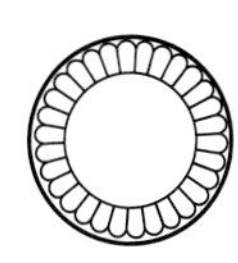 in the basket.

Put _______ more 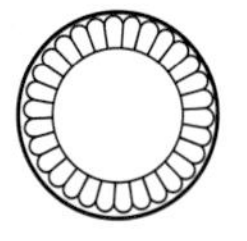 in the basket.

How many 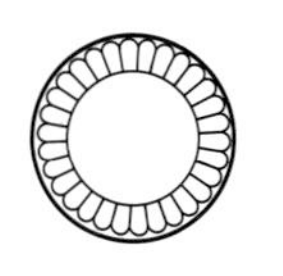 are there in all? _______

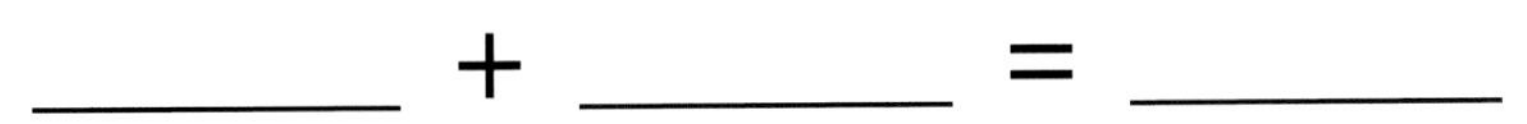

_______ + _______ = _______

Put _______  in the basket.

Put _______ more  in the basket.

How many  are there in all? _______

_______ + _______ = _______

Put _______ in the basket.

Put _______ more  in the basket.

How many  are there in all? _______

_______ + _______ = _______

Subtraction Cards

Use with "Packing for a Picnic!" on page 308.

Put ______ in the basket.

Take ______ out of the basket.

How many are left in the basket? ______

______ – ______ = ______

Put ____ in the basket.

Take ____  out of the basket.

How many  are left in the basket? ______

______ – ______ = ______

Put ______ in the basket.

Take ______ out of the basket.

How many are left in the basket? ______

______ – ______ = ______

Index

7 21202 04529 2